GARY MOORE

THE OFFICIAL BIOGRAPHY

HARRY SHAPIRO

GARY MOORE
THE OFFICIAL BIOGRAPHY
HARRY SHAPIRO

For Kay—for everything
For Bobby and Winnie Moore

Published by arrangement with Hannibal Verlag,
an imprint of Koch International GmbH, A-6604 Höfen
www.hannibal-verlag.de.

This edition published in the UK and the USA by
Jawbone Press
Office G1
141–157 Acre Lane
London SW2 5UA
England

ISBN 978-1-911036-97-5

Printed by Short Run Press, Exeter, Devon

1 2 3 4 5 26 25 24 23 22

CONTENTS

I've been searchin' for somethin' I might never find
I've been looking for something I have left behind
I've been searchin' every day ok in the risin' sun
I've been trying to find my way till the day is done
I've been searchin'

I've been reachin' for something I might never touch
And I've been dreamin'
Of something that I want so much
I've been counting all the tears in the falling rain
I've been trying to hide my fears but it's all the same
And I don't know if I'll ever pass this way again

I can't wait until tomorrow
It's somethin' I might never see
I can't wait until tomorrow
For tomorrow never waits for me

PREFACE

Ian Hunter, a friend of Gary's in his teenage years, caught up with him many
years later at a concert. Gary came off stage, sweat pouring down his face,
the packed, heaving crowd baying 'We want Moore ... we want Moore ...'
'Gary, how on earth do you relax after that?' asked Ian.
Quick as a flash came the reply: 'I play guitar.'

*'The thing that makes you exceptional ... is inevitably
the thing which must also make you lonely.'*
LORRAINE HANSBERRY

Q MAGAZINE What do you never leave home without?
GARY My reputation.

RECORD COLLECTOR Who would you do for *Stars In Their Eyes?*
GARY Eartha Kitt!

After I finished writing my last music book in 2010, the biography of the late and
greatly missed Jack Bruce, thoughts inevitably turned to 'What next?' The months
went by and nothing caught my imagination. And then in February 2011, Gary
Moore tragically passed away. I was obviously aware of Gary, had a few of his
albums and had seen him in various bands, but what took me by surprise were
the glowing tributes paid to him by the likes of Joe Bonamassa, Joe Elliot, Brian
May, Bob Geldof, Slash, Paul Rodgers, Kirk Hammett, the members of Saxon and
Europe, and many others, citing how much of an inspiration and influence Gary
had been in the world of guitarists.

Over the following weeks, I looked online and found the same outpourings
from ordinary fans across the world. His guitar playing was favourably compared
to the very best guitarists ever. Gary's music and his songs had clearly touched
the hearts of millions. Yet, there was a puzzle. Reader polls on 'greatest musicians'
are of little value. Music is not like boxing, where you might be able to say who
the greatest is on the basis of the number of fights won. Current popularity
and commercial success also play their part in determining poll positions. Still,

magazines like to run reader polls and they are popular. So, checking through recent reader polls of 'greatest guitar players', I found they rarely if ever mentioned Gary, whether it was a Top 50 or even Top 100. Why not? It seemed like a story waiting to be told.

This was confirmed once the book was under way and people subsequently asked what my next book would be. When I said 'Gary Moore', brows were furrowed until I filled the silence with 'He was in Thin Lizzy'. I soon realised that I was dealing with a musician—like Jack, in fact—who was hidden in plain sight, known for high-profile but brief moments in a career that spanned five decades. It became even more interesting because reading magazine interviews told me little or nothing about Gary Moore the person. While always erudite and intelligent, with plenty to say, Gary kept his comments confined to the business of being a musician and band leader—latest albums and line-ups, favourite guitars and amps—and I learned that personal questions were quickly deflected or laughed off. Who was Gary Moore, this stellar guitarist who was so revered by musicians and fans alike, yet not really in the public eye?

Almost the very first thing Gary's wife Jo said to me was, 'You will come across people who will say Gary was the biggest arsehole in the world, but when you were hugged by Gary Moore, you stayed hugged.' And how right she was—she had captured the paradox of Gary in a sentence. Here was a guitarist of quite exceptional talent, driven to great artistic heights both by his natural abilities and by his insecurities, fathoms-deep canyons of doubt that could cripple him, who could be extremely difficult and arrogant, often letting his mouth rule his head with untethered comments that, over the years, won him few friends in the industry. Yet he was an absolute perfectionist and a serious self-critic who set the bar incredibly high for himself and expected the same of all those around him. Once he was offstage and out of the studio, and when, crucially, the guitar came off—a guitar that was for Gary as much a shield as it was an axe—a different person was revealed. Here was an extremely shy, sensitive, warm, funny and generous individual who never took his abilities for granted and was forever learning, searching and looking around the next corner. I too went searching for the real Gary Moore, hoping in the process to bring more of his music out into the light. How successful that journey has been, of course, is for others to judge.

With few points of published reference, such a quest very much relied on the people who knew and worked with Gary. I extend my thanks to Gary's family for their endorsement of the project and particularly to Gary's wife Jo for all her help and support. A huge debt of gratitude also goes to Graham Lilley, who started out with Gary as his guitar technician way back in 1988 and is quite literally the fount of wisdom on all things Gary. Thanks also to Darren Main, Gary's personal assistant for many years, for his insights, help and encouragement. And much appreciation to Gary's business manager, Colin Newman, who made the whole project happen.

It seemed like every time I interviewed somebody, I would come away with another clutch of names of people 'you really need to speak to'—people who were not on my already extensive list. There was also a gratifying by-product of the interview process: putting people in touch who had been out of contact, in some cases since school days, half a century ago. Unless a published source is mentioned, all the interviews were conducted by me while writing the book. I conducted one interview with Gary for my biography of Jack. All other direct quotes from Gary are from published sources.

Sadly, since the book was completed, eight of those interviewed have passed away: Noel Bridgeman, Jack Bruce, Jon Hiseman, Greg Lake, Craig Gruber, Frank Murray, Chris Tsangarides and Steve York, as have Gary's father and mother. So, thanks to them and all the others for sharing their memories of Gary:

Don Airey, Bill Allen, Prue Almond, Stuart Bailie, Gerry Raymond-Barker, Steve Barnett, James Barton, Eric Bell, Smiley Bolger, Kerry Booth, Tim Booth, Andy Bradfield, Rob Braniff, Ceri Campbell, Donna Campbell, Jeannie Campbell, Ted Carroll, Neil Carter, Clem Clempson, Peter Collins, Chris Cordington, Andy Crookston, Brian Crothers, Steve Croxford, Pete Cummins, John Curtis, Bob Daisley, Ed Deane, Barry Dickins, Steve Dixon, Harry Doherty, Bill Downey, Brian Downey, Johnny Duhan, Hans Engel, Gary Ferguson, Magnus Fiennes, Steven Fletcher, Mo Foster, Melissa Fountain, Lisa Franklin, Jeff Glixman, Scott Gorham, Tim Goulding, Rob Green, Richard Griffiths, John Henry, Nik Henville, Bill Hindmarsh, George Hoffman, Tim Hole, Glenn Hughes, Billy Hunter, Graham Hunter, Ian Hunter, Gary Husband, Andy Irvine, George Jones, Pearse Kelly, Roger Kelly, Sylvia Keogh, William Lamour, Austen Lennon, Dave Lennox, Cass Lewis, Dave Lewis, Ivan Little, Bernie Marsden, Neville Marten, Colin Martin, John Martin, Vic Martin, Paul McAuley, Pete McLelland, Dick Meredith, James Meredith, Malcolm Mill, Alan Moffatt, Darrin Mooney, Charlie Morgan, Neil Murray, Mark Nauseef, Tony Newton, Geoff Nicholson, Jon Noyce, Chris O'Donnell, Terry O'Neill, Sharon Osbourne, Ian Paice, Jim Palmer, Teddie Palmer, Willie Palmer, Ivan Pawle, Simon Phillips, Tony Platt, Guy Pratt, Peter

Price, Andy Pyle, Pete Rees, Ian Robertson, Jan Schelhaas, Paul Scully, Brush Shiels, Eric Singer, Nigel Smith, Dirk Sommer, Mike Starrs, Joe Staunton, Ian Taylor, Otis Taylor, Tony Tierney, Graham Walker, Jon Webster, Stuart Weston, Terry Woods and John Wooler.

Special thanks to Zoli Csillag, curator of the Gary Moore fan site, Lord of the Strings, for all kinds of help and assistance, especially with the discography. I am also grateful to O.J. Backman, John Berg, Carl Culpepper, Colin Harper, Lola Martin, Peter Neilsen, Adam Parsons, Mary Pawle, Ton Pickard, Mark Powell, Carl Swann, David Talkin and Rhys Williams.

I never knew Gary, never met him. My only contact was a telephone interview about BBM for my book on Jack. Although this is an official biography, I made it clear at the outset that I would not be writing a very long press release on behalf of Gary Moore, that this would be no simpering hagiography, but as far as possible an honest account of Gary's life and music.

I hope I have kept to that aspiration, and yet, probably because of all the candid cooperation I have received from so many people, I have felt much closer to Gary than I would have thought possible at the start. With such proximity has come the conclusion that his career was 'chequered'; that Gary never received the acclaim and success his talent deserved; and that perhaps too many of the reasons for this could be laid at his own feet. Even so, I do believe that I have been in the presence of a very special musician, somebody with a musicality that stretched way beyond the easy tag of 'guitar hero'.

If I had to pick one moment in the life of this book that did it for me, this would be it. I was listening to a bootleg recording of Thin Lizzy during their 1977 US tour with Queen—their February 6 gig at the Nassau Coliseum on Long Island, New York. It came to Gary's solo on 'Still In Love With You' and before I knew it—and I don't mind admitting this—I had a golf-ball size lump in my throat and tears were just rolling down my face. I have been listening to rock music for half a century and writing about it for decades—no musician has ever managed to do that to me. 'Nuff said.

HARRY SHAPIRO

PROLOGUE

Phil Lynott was never far from Gary's mind. Outside his family, Gary's relationship with Phil was one of the most intensely personal of his life, both artistically and emotionally. They loved and fought like brothers and wanted to be each other: Phil wished he had Gary's exquisite talent; Gary wished he had Phil's good looks, charisma and leadership qualities. When Gary first came to Dublin in the summer of 1968 aged only sixteen, Phil (nearly four years older) took the young whizz-kid from Belfast under his wing and, as he later said with a cheeky grin and a twinkle in his eye, 'showed him the sights of Dublin'. Gary often told the story of when Phil took him to a Chinese restaurant and suggested he ordered sweet and sour pork. 'I'd never tried it before and I absolutely hated it. Phil ate mine and that,' he said, laughing, 'established the precedent for our relationship, really, whether it was girlfriends, royalties, anything.'

Some of Gary's greatest commercial successes came through working with Phil and if they had found a way to accommodate each other (as many creative but volatile rock partnerships have managed to do), who knows what more they might have achieved? But it wasn't to be. In January 1986, medical complications arising from years of drug and alcohol abuse claimed Phil's life, but for Gary, the memory of the wild Irish rover never dimmed.

Flash forward to the spring of 2005. Gary was wondering where to take his career next; he had been a very successful rock act in the 1980s, reinvented himself as a best-selling blues guitarist in the 1990s, but now he was restless and bored. The twentieth anniversary of Phil's death was only a few months away. Gary began to think that he might revisit the power and dynamism of the Celtic rock that drove Thin Lizzy and had influenced his last work with Phil, the *Run For Cover* album with its hit single 'Out In The Fields' and its follow-up, Gary's biggest-selling album of the 80s, *Wild Frontier*. He wrote three new songs: 'Where Are You Now?', 'Days Of Heroes' (first recorded as 'Now Is The Time') and 'Wild One', all with strong links to his Irish roots and past glories with Phil. Gary's bass player at the time, former Jethro Tull sideman Jonathan Noyce, recalls, 'We got together for a play in April, for a little jam down in Brighton where Gary lived. He had a few ideas around the Celtic rock themes and as I had been in Tull, he reckoned I knew a little bit about folk music.' Gary and Jon, along with Gary's drummer Darrin Mooney (also resident with Primal Scream) and keyboard player Vic Martin, went into Trevor Horne's residential studio at Hook End Manor in Oxfordshire with producer and long-time friend Chris Tsangarides to record some demos. However, the time wasn't right; record companies showed little interest and the idea was shelved.

Shortly afterwards, Gary read that Dublin City Council was unveiling a statue of Phil in the city centre on August 19, which would have been Phil's fifty-sixth birthday. Worldwide, there are only a few statues honouring musicians, among them Elvis Presley, John Lennon, Buddy Holly, Freddie Mercury, Otis Redding, Jimi Hendrix, B.B. King, Rory Gallagher and Stevie Ray Vaughan, so Phil was in hallowed company. But in a sense, Ireland was honouring more than just a musician; Phil helped put Irish rock on the map and he had a strong sense of what it meant to be Irish (and black Irish at that), draped like a flag over his shoulders. His importance as a national cultural figure was maybe even more significant than that of his illustrious peers. Gary phoned former Thin Lizzy drummer Brian Downey with the idea they should gather all the ex-Lizzy guitarists back together. Brian mentioned some promoters were planning to put on a low-key event, but Gary, now well fired up, said they should book the Point, Dublin's largest venue, and put on a proper show befitting Ireland's most iconic rock star. 'Sure,' said Brian, the perfect storm of bullshit and intrigue surrounding events like these looming in his imagination, 'so long as you organise it.' 'Deal,' said Gary.

Jon Noyce winces at the memory: 'My goodness, there was loads of politics, loads of politics, between the musicians and behind the scenes.' Nothing involving Thin Lizzy was ever straightforward; guitarist Scott Gorham has said, 'We were the most unprofessional professional band ever.' During their time together, they rode the high seas of rock, Pirates of the Caribbean, led by their loveable rogue captain, full of swagger and mischief, and composer of some of rock's most timeless, fist-pounding anthems. But the good ship Lizzy was forever lurching from one titanic catastrophe to the next. And they fought like cats in a sack—Gary left halfway through the 1979 US tour and didn't speak to Phil for four years. The band never really recovered and, once it all ended, Phil never recovered. Gary and Scott had never spoken since; Scott and Brian Robertson weren't really on speaking terms. There were also ongoing issues between managements about royalties owed to Gary during his last stint in the band.

But Gary made separate calls to Scott, Brian and the founder Lizzy guitarist

Eric Bell, who himself had stormed offstage in the middle of a gig—and began the healing process. Says Scott, 'When Gary phoned, I could hear it in his voice, he was sincere about the whole thing about him leaving, there was no brashness, he was almost sheepish. We had never talked out the whole Lizzy thing properly and I think he wanted to get this all out. So, we did and I agreed that it was all water under the bridge. So, let's get out there and make a great show.'

Even so, Graham Lilley, Gary's head of operations, still felt a firm hand would be needed once everybody came together. He called ex-Royal Marine Ian 'Robbo' Robertson who had been Gary's tour manager back in the 1990s. 'I got a call from Graham,' says Robbo, 'he told me who was playing, and it obviously had potential to be a nightmare and they needed somebody with some balls to make sure it all hung together.'

Gary had a very clear idea what this show would be, or rather what it would not be; this was not going to be a Thin Lizzy reunion gig—it would be Gary Moore and Very Special Guests. The main band would be Gary, Jon Noyce and Brian Downey with each of the Lizzy guitarists coming on in turn—and there would be no big encore jam at the end. This, says Scott, was fair enough: 'It would have been pretty shambolic to have us all on together because everybody wants to solo and it was being filmed and recorded, so Gary wanted to play it safe and bring the guys on one at a time.' To do otherwise would have been reminiscent of the chaotic farewell Lizzy gig back in 1983.

Rehearsals began at Music Bank rehearsal studios over in east London. Jon Noyce went down with Brian Downey and Gary, the idea being to rehearse with the Lizzy guys one at a time. Inevitably, there was a fair bit of mane tossing and pawing the ground as Gary came face to face with his former band mates. 'It was hilarious,' recalls Jon. 'Scott hadn't seen Gary for about twenty years; he walked in the room and they just starting ripping shreds out of each other—funny and jokey but with an edge.' They had one musical problem to sort out: when it came to playing 'Black Rose', Gary found Scott playing the parts he used to play, but he went along with it and learned Scott's original parts instead.

Gary was very conscious of the rock hierarchy and while he wasn't dictatorial around the guys, everybody was acutely aware of where Gary's career trajectory was compared to the others. He determined the nature of the show and they all acquiesced because they were getting paid (it wasn't a charity show) and there was such a good feel around the event that nobody was going to throw their guitar out the pram.

In his own gentle way, though, Eric Bell wasn't going to quite play the game. When he came in to rehearse 'Whiskey In The Jar', it wasn't right to Eric's way of thinking. 'No, no, no, Gary, fuckin' listen …' Gary laughed when Eric put him down and took control because Gary recognised and respected the musician in Eric, a very understated and underrated player. When Eric was living in London in 2007, they became close friends; he would go down to Brighton to hang out at Gary's house and play. There were plenty of guitars to choose from; Gary had one in every room.

There were also some issues between Gary and his former Skid Row leader, bassist Brush Shiels. Brush says that Gary had asked for them to play together. But Brush wouldn't do it without the Skid Row drummer, Noel Bridgeman, so eventually Brush just did a solo spot.

If sorting out the musicians was a logistical challenge—'it was like a bunch of divorced couples getting back together,' reckons Graham Lilley—dealing with the backroom shenanigans was no easier. Gary's organisation was trying to work with the promoters who were originally planning the small, low-key event that Brian Downey had mentioned.

Once it became clear that this would be a major Dublin music event, Robbo says, 'We had to ask ourselves if we trusted the promoter, because he was way out of his depth. None of the signals were right, none of the language was right, none of the money was forthcoming. As far as I was concerned, if it walks like a duck and sounds like a duck, it's probably a duck.'

The promoter suggested he could get Sony to support the show, do the recording and so on, but in the end, Gary's management took over and brought in Eagle Rock to do the filming and recording of Gary's section, because there was a whole roster of acts to come on before Gary, which the promoter took care of. Poor promotion led to concerns about ticket sales but the walk-up sales on the night ensured that the 6,500-capacity venue was rammed to the rafters.

Once everybody was in Ireland, Gary and the band went off to Grouse Lodge, a residential studio outside Dublin, about a ten-minute drive away from the Hill of Uisneach, a former residence of the High Kings of Ireland and a location for the pagan festival of Beltane. Nearby was the mythical resting place of the goddess Érui who gave her name to Éire.

In this romantic, mystical place, Gary began to focus his mind on the gig. He knew only too well what he had taken on, what was riding on this being a success, and they rehearsed hard for five days to get it right. It was a concert to honour Phil, but it was Gary's name in lights, his band, his organisation, him at the front all night and singing the songs most closely associated with his friend. The country wanted in. Jon Noyce says that Brian Downey was put under a huge amount of pressure: 'He told me the whole world was on his back, everybody wanted a piece of it. He was getting calls from all kinds of people wanting to get on the bill or get tickets. Phil was national property.'

The day before the show, in the afternoon, they moved into Dublin for a cloak-and-dagger production rehearsal when everybody came in. The core band was tight and solid, the vibe was very positive. Everybody wanted to do right by Phil. Later in the day came the unveiling of the statue in Harry Street, just off Grafton Street. Complete pandemonium. There was supposed to be a roped-off area for the Mayor and other dignitaries, but that disappeared under the weight and push of a crushing throng. Before Phil's mother, Philomena, was due to pull the cord on the statue, Jon, Darren Main (Gary's personal assistant), Brian Downey and his wife, Gary and Jo and Eric Bell were in a little pub on Grafton Street where kids were throwing themselves through the window to get items signed. Then the moment came and, from the footage, Gary can be seen at the back, with his little daughter Lily tightly hugging his neck, while her dad looked quietly on.

Once Gary hit the stage, all the tensions, the problems, the politics just melted away. He took stick in some quarters for starting with 'Walkin' By Myself' rather than a Lizzy song, but it was Gary's way of laying down the marker that this was not a Lizzy gig and it served as a good warm-up for the band. The audience could care less; they sang along, happy just to be there. And then straight into 'Jailbreak' and the crowd went nuts. Throughout the evening, Jon Noyce was rock solid and Brian's drumming was a masterclass in power, precision and poise, making it look so easy, hardly breaking sweat. Phil once said, 'if you write a slow song, speed it up'—and he did with the two versions of 'Don't Believe A Word', with Gary wrenching every ounce of soul from the song, head cocked, listening to the notes and playing each one as if it would be his last.

Brian Robertson was first up and, like Gary, was still gunslinging a Les Paul, but he seemed very subdued on 'Emerald' and 'Still In Love With You'. By contrast, Scott came onstage, bounding with energy, and absolutely went for it. Gary seemed to muff a vocal on 'Cowboy Song' but laughed it off and instead shouted, 'C'mon Strat', to acknowledge Scott's desertion of the classic Lizzy sound featuring twin Gibson Les Pauls. But their unison playing was pin-sharp, accompanied by grins and onstage banter. They blasted their way through 'Black

Rose' and when they whacked into 'The Boys Are Back In Town', some audience members looked like they had died and gone to heaven. Finally, Eric Bell delivered 'Whiskey In The Jar' as only he can on his beautiful vintage Strat.

At the end, Gary bracketed the concert again not with another Thin Lizzy favourite, but with his own signature song, a true tribute to Phil, 'Parisienne Walkways'. He introduced the song with a snapshot of Phil's 'Old Town' and the refrain 'won't be the same, now you're not around', and then launched into one of the most blistering versions of the hit song ever heard. He changed the opening lyric to 'I remember Paris in '69'—a homage to his time with Phil in Dublin (Parris being Phil's middle name). As usual, he found that sweet spot on the stage where he knew the dynamics would be right to get that long sustain note, holding the tension with his powerful left-hand vibrato, to breaking point, the audience similarly holding a collective breath, and then releasing it, descending into a torrent of notes.

Gary stood on that stage and just let all the emotion pour out of him through the guitar, sweat as tears, feelings of love, rage, and frustration that he could never have verbalised, the conversation with Phil that could never happen. The song went on and on, and just like he could never really let go of Phil, so, drained as he was, he held on to the last possible moment to leave the audience with 'Happy Birthday' to send them on their way.

Backstage, there was a swirling stir-fry of hangers-on, family, friends and musicians. A surging melee of humanity always put Gary ill at ease, but after the overwhelming emotion of a successful show, he really did want time alone in his locked dressing room. There was nothing he felt he could say, the guitar had said it all—and it took some coaxing from his wife, Jo, to get him out of there. Once the door was opened, a whole throng of people pushed in and Gary went nuts ordering Darren to get rid of them. According to Eric Bell, even Brian Robertson was given short shrift. Then, the whole throng moved off to the Gresham Hotel, for more rock politics, VIP area, VVIP area with Darren barring the way—simply because so many people wanted to bathe in the reflected glory of a remarkable evening. That night they drank the hotel bar dry.

Next morning, Robbo was trying to get everybody together: 'Darren phoned Eric Bell to say that he was needed down in the lobby. To which Eric replied, "Which way is down?" Everybody was in absolute tatters.'

But at 4am, while most people were sleeping it off, a small group of people headed off towards Harry Street. Darren takes up the story: 'There was me, Jo,

Gary, Gary's sister Maggie and Robbo. We were off to look at the statue; because of the chaos of the unveiling, we had no time to stand there. Ahead of us was a young lad with a guitar case on his back and he was talking to the statue, quite openly and freely as if he was talking to Phil. He was quite angry and upset, asking Phil why he had left him, how much he missed him, how he was playing the music now, getting more and more emotional. And he started talking about Gary, without realising we were standing there listening. "You know, you had Gary ..."'

Gary was really quite upset by now and he had a private moment with Phil, his arm around Jo; there were tears, prayers and a flood of memories back to the carefree acid-drenched days of late-60s Dublin, nearly forty years ago. But first there was Belfast.

Back in 1984, Virgin Records (Gary's label at that time) commissioned the American National Football League (NFL) film company to shoot a documentary about Gary's first gigs in Ireland for a decade. Starting in Northern Ireland, Gary took the film crew along the coast to Dunluce Castle, saying he had forgotten how beautiful the countryside was. It was a different story in Belfast, where Gary tramped the wounded landscape of a war-torn city and boarded-up houses remarking how well he remembered these streets, pointing out where relatives used to live. He said that being brought up in Belfast, surviving as a kid, even before hostilities broke out, was no easy ride—and that it instilled a toughness, an edginess in him that he took into his adult life and helped sculpt the musician he became. There were at least two reasons for the long absence. Firstly, there was the incendiary political situation; in the film, he said it had been impossible to persuade previous band members to go with him to his home town. But the second reason was that Gary's memories of his childhood were not good. Even before the Troubles, there were troubles.

01

AGAINST
THE ODDS

Opinions about Belfast have been as divided as the political and religious tensions that have split the city for generations. As far back as 1649, John Milton called it 'a barbarous nook of Ireland', when Belfast amounted to little more than half a dozen streets. The nineteenth-century poet Sam Lyons, however, wrote in 1822, 'How shall I style thee famed Belfast? (On whom let none aspersions cast.)' But even leaving aside the notoriety of recent years, to outsiders, Belfast has presented a backward, grim and cold face to the world, crushed by the weight of religious repressions from both Protestant and Catholic communities. As Patricia Craig wrote in the introduction to her *Belfast Anthology*, 'Growing up in Belfast, if it does nothing else, gives you something to react against.'

Robert William Gary Moore was born on April 4, 1952 into a Protestant family living in the staunchly loyalist area of East Belfast. His mother Winnie was one of five children born to Robert and Margaret Gallagher, with sisters Phylis (the youngest), Ruby, Ellen and brother William. Although the Troubles didn't start until 1969, there had been sectarian violence in the city going back to the early nineteenth century and the communities have barely tolerated each other. So, there was a big fuss in the family when William later married a Catholic girl; Phylis was to marry a Catholic too, with tragic consequences.

East Belfast was dominated by the sights and sounds of the shipbuilding industry, Harland & Wolff and its much smaller rival Workman Clark, established on opposite banks of the River Lagan. Workman Clark did not survive the shipbuilding slump of the 1920s; Harland & Wolff, although very badly damaged in the Second World War, carries on to this day. Winnie's grandfather, an insulation engineer, was one of the many workers who built *The Titanic* in the Harland & Wolff yard. Sadly though, he would eventually die of asbestos poisoning.

Gary's father was Robert 'Bobby' Moore, whose parents were also called Robert and Margaret. Bobby had two sisters, Kathleen and Nancy, and a brother, Phillip. By all accounts Robert Moore senior saw himself as something of a wide-boy entrepreneur; his main income was bookmaking, first on the racecourses and then he owned some shops. But at one time, he had apparently sold bleach from a cart and later ran a stable of street-corner newspaper salesmen. Bobby Moore worked alongside his father in the betting business, but also promoted weekend popular music concerts at the Queen's Hall in Holywood, a couple of miles east of Belfast. Winnie would do the books for these various enterprises and took the cash at the door of the Queen's Hall. Unlike many of their neighbours, the Moores were relatively well off; money was never really a problem.

But Gary's life did not start out well. Bobby and Winnie were married in December 1951, by which time Winnie was five months pregnant with Gary. Given the moral and social outlook of the times, they had no option but to get married. Initially, Bobby and Winnie moved in with Bobby's parents in East Bread Street (named for its proximity to a flour mill, but no longer there), but according to Gary's aunt Phylis (Winnie's sister), Mrs Moore disapproved of the marriage and once Gary was born, threw Winnie out. Winnie and her new-born son went to live with Phylis, Ruby and their parents at 9 Frome Street for the best part of the next four years. There was no money at the Gallaghers for a cot, so Gary's first bed was a cupboard drawer and when he outgrew that, he slept in Ruby's bed with his arms round her neck.

In those early years, Phylis says, 'There was so much love for Gary in our family. My father had a lot to do with Gary. He taught him to walk and used to take Gary to football matches at Glentoran. They went to one match and suddenly this whistle blew and the whole match stopped. Everybody looked around to see what had happened, my Daddy looked down and wee Gary had this gigantic whistle. He would only have been about three. We were quite a musical family; Mummy and Daddy were both amateur singers who would perform publicly. Ruby and Winnie sang and I played the piano and sang. Daddy taught Gary to play the mouth organ.'

Eventually, Bobby's parents vacated East Bread Street and moved further out of the centre to Summerhill Avenue, allowing Winnie and Gary to move back in with Bobby. But Gary still wanted to go to the football with Phylis's dad: 'He used to rush down to our house and, especially if it was an away game, shout, "Is ma grand away, is ma grand away, has he gone, has he gone?" And on the bus, Gary would sing to all the men. He was never shy.'

From East Bread Street, Bobby Moore moved the family to a more upmarket semi-detached house, 44 Castleview Road, around the corner from his parents and close to Stormont Estate and Stormont Castle, now the headquarters of the Northern Ireland government. Gary went to Strandtown Primary School where one of his close friends was Roger Kelly, who also lived in Summerhill Avenue. In later years, Gary would often remark that he was 'useless at everything. If I joined the Boy Scouts, I'd be the one dumped in the river ... I'd be the one the other kids picked on.' He never actually said he *was* bullied, but the suggestion is certainly hinted at. There is some dispute about this from Gary's school friends, but Roger is adamant that this certainly happened at primary school, although perhaps less so when Gary moved to secondary school at 11, met a new group of boys and began to gain his reputation as a guitarist.

'In primary school, we used to look after Gary,' says Roger. 'He was overweight and wasn't the most attractive kid. He was bullied by the other kids.' Gary in turn could dish it out; his friend William Larmour says that Gary got into big trouble from his teacher, Mr McKnight, for telling a girl to 'shut her bracket', 'which was an outrageous thing to say to a girl in those days'.

It was tough for Gary. Roger recalls that 'right from primary school, his attendance record would have been one of the worst. I remember his mother saying to me that they were visited by the school board. I used to call round and say to Gary, "Come on, you are going today." He told me that he was often quite frightened to go to school.'

Life at home wasn't much easier. Gary's friends were quite scared of Bobby; if they were round at Gary's after school, they would have to leave before Bobby came in from work. He was a good-looking man with thick, wavy black hair and always dressed very well: 'We used to call him Buddy,' recalls William, 'because he had that Las Vegas feel about him.' But just like own father, Bobby was a forceful and domineering character, and the marriage was not a happy one. Gary gave some insight into life behind the net curtains in his song 'Business As Usual' (from the *Dark Days In Paradise* album) when he wrote, 'Trembling at night from the violence I heard from my bedroom.'

Gary's relationship with his father was bittersweet. They were at loggerheads right up until Gary left Belfast, and Winnie was powerless to intervene. But it was Bobby who encouraged Gary to perform in public. Gary often told the story that he was with his family at the Queen's Hall one night and either the opening act never showed up or Bobby just thought 'Tonight's the night' and he put Gary on a chair so he could reach the microphone to sing a song called 'Sugar Time'. He could have been as young as six. Gary later told another school mate, Tony Tierney, that it was the scariest moment of his life, although Bobby says he has no recollection of this happening.

Gary always wondered if his dad was a frustrated musician because he said that he saw bits of drum kit lying around the house. But one day, completely unbidden, Bobby came home and asked Gary if he wanted to learn guitar. Gary said yes and shortly afterwards, Bobby produced a large cello-body Framus acoustic guitar almost as big as Gary himself, which came from an uncle's friend. In fact, the very first guitar Gary ever had was a plastic one, which broke when Phylis smashed it over his head during a play fight when Gary was still very young.

Exactly when Gary got this guitar is debatable. There is a photo of him supposedly taken in 1960 when he would have been seven or eight, holding what looks like the very guitar he subsequently described on many occasions. Yet in 1986, he told rock journalist Chris Welch that he got the guitar in 1963, so he could have been ten or eleven. He went on to tell Chris that it wasn't just the size of the guitar that was daunting: 'I was learning the hard way. The action was *that* high off the guitar and I had fitted normal gauge strings so there was no chance of pulling the strings.' He also talked about having a few desultory lessons: 'I went to a tutor, but he only taught the chord of A with three fingers. I didn't even know how to tune the guitar. But I went back to the tutor the next week and I'd learnt how to play "Wonderful Land" by The Shadows. It was the first song I learnt and I played it on the top two strings. The tutor said, "Oh no, that's all WRONG." So, I never went back and just taught myself to play.' It's worth noting here that 'Wonderful Land' wasn't released until February 1962, so if it was the first song that Gary could play, it suggests a later date for acquiring that first guitar. His aunt Phylis says on the day he got the guitar he went round to her house to show her: 'Bobby brought him round and I have a recording of him playing with me singing [Joe Brown's] "Picture Of You".' Gary later said about those two songs, 'I got melody from Hank [Marvin] and rhythm from Joe Brown. And right there you have the basis for any guitarist to learn from.'

Once he had grasped the basics, progress was uncannily swift. For Gary, it was as if a light had suddenly been switched on in his head, a profound awakening. After all the teasing and name-calling, at last here was something he felt he could do. In *The Power And The Glory*, Graham Greene wrote that 'there is always one moment in childhood when the door opens and lets the future in'—and so it was for Gary. Building on his willingness to perform in public, he played Elvis songs in the school playground, gathering a crowd around him, and onstage at the Queen's Hall on the night that Phylis got up and sang with the Pacific Showband. Gary would hang around the bands; one time, he approached a guitarist asking the musician to show him some chords. The guy told Gary to go away, but the upright bass player, David Fletcher, sat Gary down and patiently helped him out.

It became obvious that Gary had supreme natural ability. He was rarely seen without that acoustic guitar round his neck. Jim Palmer and his brother Wilbert belonged to group of older boys who also lived in Summerhill Avenue. 'We'd be sitting outside our house and Gary would appear with his guitar. "Give us a song,

Gary." "What do you want? Everly Brothers? Elvis?" He didn't need to be asked twice and he was away.'

Although Gary's family was not political, the July 11 bonfires gave Gary another chance to play in public. In Protestant/loyalist areas, the big day of the year is July 12, the day in 1690 on which William of Orange, Protestant claimant to the English throne, defeated the Catholic King James II at the Battle of the Boyne and celebrated ever since by Orange Order marches. The night before is marked by the lighting of huge bonfires. Journalist Ivan Little was another of the lads living in the shadow of Stormont Castle: 'In the area where we lived it was mostly middle-class kids and our bonfires weren't quite in the same league as the ones in working-class areas. We'd build them on this bit of waste ground near my home at the bottom of Abbey Gardens near where Gary lived. And after burning our little bonfire, we'd sit around singing and playing and I clearly recall Gary sitting with us playing a tune called "The Sash", which is "The Sash My Father Wore"—a reference to the collarette worn by members of the Orange Order. He wouldn't do this every year, though; he was more into the blues than the orange.'

Finding he could play guitar had huge significance for Gary: 'The thing with the guitar is that attracts a lot of social rejects like me who don't do well at school or people who are not popular. The more you talk to musicians, the more you realise that a lot of them were attracted to playing out of some kind of need to improve themselves.'

In 1964, Gary moved from primary to secondary school, to Ashfield Boys' High School, a tough establishment liberally populated with kids from the rougher end of town. Interviewed by *Mojo* many years later, Gary tried to pretend he had gone to a better school and was teased about this by his old school friend Roger Kelly: 'I think he was embarrassed that he had failed the eleven plus and said he had gone to a school which is now Wellington College. I wound him up about it when we met up, and he tried denying it, but he definitely said it. But actually, we all ended up doing very well. We were all in the A-stream at Ashfield, which was the grammar school stream. Gary was in that top stream with Peter Guinness, who became a top architect, Alastair Heron, who became a senior lecturer in film studies, and I became a principal social worker. And later Gary was used as an example by the teachers to say to the kids, "You can come to this school and do well."'

Which was something of a joke because once he discovered the guitar, Gary's attendance at school became even worse. Roger says, 'the only subject Gary liked was English; he was an avid reader. But he hated all the other subjects and loathed maths. And he hated music because it was so boring.'

Although views of fellow students about Gary were starting to change because of the guitar, the bullying problem hadn't gone away entirely. Roger was his main protection. 'A lot of the toughies from the nearby estate used to pick on him, but because I was good at sport, I used to tell them to leave him alone. I was captain of the football team and the basketball team and ended up playing basketball for Northern Ireland Schools. I used to joke with Gary that there was more chance of me playing for Manchester United than him becoming a rock star. Which came back to bite me big time!'

There was a teacher who once shouted at Gary for staring out the window and not paying attention: 'What are you dreaming about? Being a pop star swinging a big red guitar?' Although he didn't dare answer the teacher back, Gary could have honestly said, 'Well, actually, yes.'

Apart from being chubby and small for his age, Gary was also marked out as 'weird' because he didn't do sports and would never be seen kicking a ball around like all the other boys in the area. And when he started learning guitar, he pretty much disappeared off the streets altogether, preferring instead to be at home. If Gary had been born in Mississippi, the rumours would have been flying that he had sold his soul to the devil as the only way to explain how he got so good so soon. Roger Kelly recalls one time when he went round to Gary's house: 'There was something on the radio. I think it was Segovia, a Spanish guitar thing. Gary couldn't have been more than twelve or thirteen, but just by ear, he was picking this up and playing it. He had a total ear for playing.' But the real devilry was in the detail; Gary simply put in the hours, day in, day out, for weeks, months and years. It was sheer hard work, obsessive dedication and an unrelenting will to succeed. Gary loved Winnie's dad who took him to football, but he was also devoted to his other grandfather, Robert, Bobby's dad. While he might have been a bit of a Jack the Lad, Robert Moore was a dyed-in-the-wool stern Protestant workaholic for whom laziness was complete anathema—and much of this ethic rubbed off on Gary.

Around the age of eleven or twelve, Gary advanced from his jumbo Framus acoustic to his first electric guitar, also bought by Bobby, a Lucky Seven Fender Squire with strings like cables and another guitar with an impossible action rising to about an inch at the twelfth fret, so nobody could understand how on earth Gary could play it. Although he was left-handed, 'through sheer ignorance' (as he said) he just played the guitar as if he was right-handed, 'and it felt alright so that's how I played it'. This meant all the power for bending strings would come from his naturally more powerful left hand. Coupled with all the early playing on heavy gauge strings (again because he didn't know any different), this accounts for his ability to bend and control his signature vibrato to such stunning effect. But for now, in 1964, Gary was ready for his first band—The Beat Boys.

The Irish music scene in the early 1960s was dominated by the showbands. They had started out as big band orchestras in the 1950s, ten or more musicians all sitting down, wearing tuxedos and bow ties with their music on stands in front of them. By the early 1960s, aware of the changing tide of popular music, bands were trimmed down to about seven or eight musicians, they switched to wearing garish suits and started jumping round the stage putting on a 'show'. They played a mixture of pop covers and country music and were phenomenally successful. It was all about the live show, especially where there was little else by way of entertainment apart from the pub. Radio play wasn't important and the recording industry hardly existed because few families could afford the equipment.

Showbands would have dominated the bill that Bobby Moore booked at the Queen's Hall. According to Vince Power in his comprehensive history of the showbands, those in the North found it hard to break through to the lucrative circuit in the South because they wanted to play pop covers rather than country and western. But Northern Ireland was still awash with these showbands; as the *Belfast Telegraph* reported in 1965, 'All over Ulster, ballrooms have been built at a fantastic rate. There is not a single town of any size in the province which does not have a hall of its own.' At the time, it was calculated there were 80 established venues in Northern Ireland and 60 bands to play in them. Local musician Rob Braniff played in The Aztecs Showband: 'They used to call it safety in numbers. With up to ten people in the band, somebody was bound to get it right.'

Belfast, though, was slightly different from the rest of Northern Ireland. The kids growing up there, with a more direct link to the UK, wanted a music scene of their own, resembling Liverpool, and latched on to the likes of Buddy Holly, Gene Vincent and then The Shadows. By the time The Beatles made an impact, the professional and semi-professional group scene rivalled that of the showbands. There was another problem in establishing showbands in the city; George Jones, mid-60s bass player for the Dave Glover Showband, quoted in Power's book, said, 'there was a lack of brass players; sax and trumpet players were difficult to find. But there were plenty of guitarists searching for outlets. The easiest way out for them was to play instrumentals. Hence guitar instrumental groups based themselves on Johnny and the Hurricanes, The Ventures and The Shadows. Their material was easy to pick up and copy. At the outbreak of Beatlemania, the tunes were again easier to play, as distinct from having to play material that required a full (brass) line-up.'

Starting a band became all the rage in the city. And Beatlemania also revealed something else to the hormone-driven youth of Belfast (and everywhere else); form a band—get the girls.

Gary was friendly with another local boy, Bill Downey, who was two years older. Bill was also at Ashfield and at Winnie's pleading, used to come by most mornings to pick Gary up and make sure he got to school. They both had bikes: 'Gary's bike was a pile of shit, with absolutely no brakes, so I had to put my hand under his saddle in order to stop him. It must have looked like I had my hand up his arse.'

Bill was another aspiring guitarist. 'I ordered a £6 wooden guitar from a Sunday newspaper. They also sent me a pickup, which I hadn't ordered, so we plugged it into an old radio and used it as an amplifier. Gary by then had worked out the chords to "Wonderful Land" (I never saw him with a chord book) and he showed me.'

Bill persuaded his parents to buy him an electric guitar too, a £19 Hofner shaped like Paul McCartney's violin bass, and they were good to go. 'We started playing together after school and at weekends. I practised like hell and we did a garden gig in an old scout tent in my back garden, brought all the chairs out from the house and charged the kids threepence to get in. We had a few numbers off by then—mostly Beatles—and that was a sensation for those kids. We made three shillings and nine pence, which was good money for that time.'

Bill knew a boy from primary school, Bertie Thompson, who was reputed to have a bass guitar, so Bill asked him to join, 'the main criterion being that he had a guitar, not that he could necessarily play it. I also knew Robert Wilkinson, the brother of my girlfriend's friend. His dad worked as Chief Engineer on a super tanker, so they had lots of money and lived in a posh house. His dad had bought him a drum kit and he had a dedicated parlour to play in. I asked Robbo if he wanted to mess around with us and could we use his room to practice in?'

Bill says that Gary produced a Vox AC30 (presumably acquired by Bobby) and everybody plugged into it. They toyed around with several names including The Dead Beats, 'where we imagined that at the first fantastic blast of music, the contradiction in the name would be obvious to the audience. That didn't work because there was no real blast yet.' Eventually, they settled on The Beat Boys. 'We heard new Beatles songs on the radio, before they were officially released, and Gary quickly and effortlessly worked out the chords and the lead. He never took any notes, just remembered all the lyrics and the music and some of those songs were in odd keys. He showed us all how to do it, even some of the drumming. We didn't really learn from each other; at twelve years old, Gary was master for all of us.'

But Gary was on a learning curve of his own and would question any guitarist he could find about playing technique and equipment. There were very few guitar effects available in the early 1960s; guitarist Eric Bell had one of the very first treble boosters, just a very simple small white plastic box called a Rangemaster. He'd just finished a gig with a pop covers band, The Deltones, when this young kid came up and asked him about the box. 'The gig was over, but all the gear was on the stage and he asked me if he could try it out and that's how we became friends. One of the songs The Beat Boys played was "She Loves You". There was a little riff in that which I was still trying work out (Eric was nearly five years older than Gary), but he had it off to a tee.'

With either Bobby Moore or Robert Wilkinson's parents providing transport, the band progressed to performing a three-song set at the Queen's Hall while the main band took a break, 'which was a bonus for us,' says Bill, 'because we got to use all their expensive gear'. They chose their repertoire mainly from The Beatles, but also The Swinging Blue Jeans, The Kinks, The Rolling Stones and The Ivy League. Rob Braniff recalls seeing Gary in the band: 'Even back then, Gary didn't just settle for the solos on the record, he'd put his own bit in and later on he'd extend songs with long intros and endings.'

The Beat Boys played at least once a week, sometimes twice, but of course, they were all still at school. The Queen's Hall was a regular spot and they played the Boom Rooms, a popular showband venue in Belfast's Arthur Square. One night they played a 1,000-seater cinema called the Troxy. Backstage, the singer for the evening asked the band if they would back him as it would sound better than him just singing on his own. They agreed and out he walked in front of what sounded like thousands of screaming girls.

As Bill Downey recalls: 'Gary had this cheeky grin on his face and I knew something terrible was going to happen. We were behind the curtain and the poor guy was out front trying to sing Val Doonican's hit song "Walk Tall". It sort of went okay at the start and then Gary decided to put in some extra notes (a lot of extra notes). The singer was virtually booed off as the audience wanted to get on with the excitement of the Big Band—us—the perpetrators of his downfall. We went on stage but were separated by the whole width of it, which we weren't used to as we normally shared a microphone (like The Beatles did) to hear our harmonies. I couldn't see the audience of knicker-throwing nubiles because of the bright lights. We were playing out of time and the singing was shit! But the screams of the girls drowned everything out and what with the din we made playing "Satisfaction", we got away with it.'

Bobby took on the job of promoter/manager and dressed them in white trousers and orange shirts in keeping with the fashion for bands to wear uniforms. And, says Bill, he also gave them money for chips and supplied them with a half-bottle of English sherry and one can of beer between them, secretly guzzled down a back alley near Queen's Hall. Bill says it was difficult to gauge how good they were compared to the professional bands playing similar material, but they garnered attention simply because they were all so young.

Bill and Gary did some school concerts with another boy, Barney Crothers, and Gary and Barney performed at a couple of church halls as a duo, with Barney greasing his hair back like Elvis and, says Bill, 'with his good voice and provocative gyrations, Barney caused a lot of excitement among the church girls'. Barney, Bill and Gary stayed together as The Beat Boys fizzled out around late 1965/early 1966. Bill says Gary became something of 'recluse' for a while and he didn't see that much of him, but then Bill called on Gary towards the end of the summer of 1966, to help out with a band he was in called The Spartans. They had entered the many beat group talent contests held in and around Belfast. Bill reckoned they stood a better chance of winning if they had Gary. Somehow, during the heats, there was a 'palace revolution' and The Spartans were 'hijacked' to morph into The Barons.

As with all teen bands, players came and went with each new day. Alan Moffatt was briefly the band's first drummer when they were The Spartans, because like Robert Wilkinson, he had a good drum kit bought by his dad, a local butcher. He was replaced by Dennis Bell and then Brian Smith. Brian Crothers was on bass, although another guy who would later play with Gary, Sam Cook, held the bass spot for a while. Briefly too, there was a keyboard player, Brian Scott. One element was missing, though; they needed a frontman. Bill went round to see a good-looking lad with a strong voice, Pete McLelland: 'One night, Bill came to the door and said, "Do you want to be in a band?" and that was it. We thought up the name The Barons down at a local chip shop called The Hot Spot.'

As The Barons were coming together in the winter of 1966, two momentous events happened in Gary's life that dramatically propelled his development. When he wasn't going to school by bike, he would take the bus—and sometimes he wouldn't get off at the school stop, but stayed on, going into town to hang around Crymble's music store in Wellington Place, just about fifty yards from the other most popular music shop at that time, Matchett's Music. It was in Crymble's that he spied a blonde Fender Telecaster and persuaded his father to pay 180 guineas for it—an enormous sum in those days, equivalent now to around £2,000. Gary told a friend he had forged Bobby's signature on the hire purchase agreement, a bit of schoolboy bravado that wouldn't have stood ten seconds worth of scrutiny. More importantly though, it did lay down a marker for the aspirations of both Gary and Bobby that a career as a professional musician was calling. In a world of cheap Hofner guitars, it was rare to see a teenage beat group guitarist with a Fender.

The second life-changer was the release of John Mayall's *Blues Breakers* album, with Eric Clapton, affectionately known as 'the *Beano* album', as Eric is shown on the front cover reading the popular British comic as a mark of cool blues disdain, refusing to look at the camera.

It was a landmark album in many respects; it became the most successful British blues album of all time and launched the 'British blues boom'; it cemented Eric Clapton's status as 'God' and introduced the signature heavy crunch of a Gibson Les Paul overdriven through a Marshall amp to the wide-eyed and slack-jawed disbelief of a young generation of guitarists like Gary Moore.

Eric's main guitar during The Yardbirds years was a red Fender Telecaster played through a Vox amp, producing a sound that *Beano* album producer Mike Vernon politely described as 'pissy'. Jeff Beck initially played Eric's Telecaster when he took over in The Yardbirds ('a terrible guitar,' he said later), but Eric retrieved it for his early gigs with Mayall.

Then he spotted a magnificent flame-top maple 1958–60 Les Paul in Lew Davis' music store in London's West End and snapped it up for around £120, which was relatively cheap, because the heavy Les Pauls had fallen out of favour in the face of the challenge from the Gibson ES335 and models from Fender, Rickenbacker, Gretsch and Guild. He now had a guitar whose sound was very far from pissy; its construction and powerful 'humbucking' pickups could drive an amp well past the ten scale into uncharted realms of distortion and sustain.

What about the amp? Eric's own hero, Freddie King, used a meaty Fender Bassman, rare and expensive in the UK, while Eric's limp Vox amp couldn't handle the demands Eric wanted to make of it. The answer came from a small music shop in west London. Jim Marshall was the boss, Ken Bran his repairman. Requests from musicians for more powerful amps led Ken to build a UK version of the Bassman. The results when guys plugged in their new shiny Fenders were impressive. When Eric plugged his Les Paul into the Marshall 45-watt 2x12 combo, the sound was astonishing—a thick, creamy, gut wrencher, out-gunning anything heard in the States. The man was melded with his machine: the key element in the making of the *Beano* album was now in place.

The guitar Eric played on the album encapsulated everything about his development as a musician: his disrupted childhood, his disrupted adolescence and the discovery of an art form, a mode of expression into which he could sublimate all his anger, his sense of isolation, creating notes that expressed more than words ever could. Gary couldn't possibly have known the passion behind the power, but he felt and heard the intensity, the aggression and sheer beauty of what Eric had created and would soon be developing his own cry—ultimately, the hallmark of all great guitarists.

The album was released in July 1966. 'Eric turned more people of my generation on to the blues than anyone else,' said Gary. 'That fantastic intro [i.e., the opening notes of the first track, Otis Rush's "All Your Love"]. I was round this guy's house, I was fourteen and I couldn't afford to buy the album. He lent it to me and obviously he never got it back. I wore that record out. I didn't go out after that; that was basically the end of my childhood.' The very copy Gary borrowed is now at the Oh Yeah Music Centre in Gordon Street, Belfast, housing a small exhibition dedicated to Gary.

Ironically, by the time Gary was wood-shedding over the album, with his Telecaster, Eric had left John Mayall to form Cream. Their first album, *Fresh Cream*, was released in December 1966 and now as the *de facto* band leader—even though everybody else was older than he was, a big deal at that age—Gary was determined that the repertoire of The Barons would be oriented away from pop standards towards the blues. The Barons pretty much followed in the footsteps of The Beat Boys, playing support to showbands, who, with their older audience, would come on much later in the evening. The Palmer boys from Summerhill Avenue became part of the setup; Wilbert was the manager now, brother Jim the roadie using his tiny Austin A35. The band rehearsed above a pub in Holywood. Jim recalls one of their biggest gigs at the King George VI Hall in Belfast where people queued to get in and major groups played there. One night, The Barons were the support act. 'The curtain was closed and from out front all you could hear was "NSU" being played. The curtain opened and there was Gary with the guitar behind his head playing brilliantly. The audience couldn't believe this, they wouldn't let him off the stage and they were shouting for more. The main band was waiting to come on and didn't like it at all.' The story goes that Wilbert used to pay girls to stand at the front of the stage and mob 'Big' Pete McLelland in the hope of whipping up the rest of the audience. But Gary could do it by himself, people pushing down the front to watch Gary as he soloed.

One another occasion, they were playing in one of the ubiquitous talent competitions, this one at the Queen's Court Hotel on the seafront at Bangor. It was the semi-finals, and they were up against the local heroes, a pretty nifty outfit called The Carpetbaggers. Jim Palmer says that, once again, 'Gary blew the audience away.'

So, when owner Dermot O'Donnell got onstage to tell the packed house that The Carpetbaggers had won, there was almost a riot. Dermot had to get back on stage fast to say there had been a mistake and both groups were going through to the final. They didn't win it. I think the winners were a band called [The] High Wall whose keyboard player [Ali Mackenzie] went on to play with Suzi Quatro.'

As all the band members were older, they were fast approaching the time to leave school or they had already gone and were now finding their way in the world, signalling the end of The Barons. The summer of 1967 saw Gary, now fifteen, down at the seaside resort of Millisle staying with Bobby's parents who had a second home there.

The town is located on the Ards Peninsula in North Down, essentially one street with a few shops, including a chip shop, cafés and two pubs—one of several little towns dotted along the coastline such as Donaghadee, Groomsport and Ballywalter, and the larger Bangor (promoted to city status in 2022). These small resorts played host not only to Belfast's working-class Protestants looking for some respite from the grey city, but also the local beat bands who would play in community and Masonic halls.

To earn himself some money over the summer, Gary went to look for work at the fairground on the beach. He presented himself to Paul McAuley who, with his father, owned the fairground and Millisle's Ashley Ballroom. 'It was a boiling hot day,' remembers Paul, 'and Gary turned up in a three-piece suit, long hair and an earring asking for a job. So, we set him to work on the darts stall at ten shillings, which was quite a lot of money back then.'

And it was down at the fair that Gary had his first contact with a family who signalled the next phase in his playing career. Ian Hunter played guitar and cousin Billy was a bassist in a band called The Suburbans. Billy's brother Graham ran into Gary hanging round the jukebox on another scorching day: 'Even though it was hot, Gary had on a black PVC mac. Del Shannon's "Runaway" was playing, and we started talking about music. I showed him around Millisle and he said his father was bringing his guitar down that night. Just after tea-time there was a knock on the door and Gary said his guitar was at his gran's house—coincidentally, they had bought the house that I was born into. He opened the case and there was a blonde Telecaster with a maple neck and my eyes popped out of my head.'

'My brother Billy's band were practising that night, so I took him up there and watched the rehearsal. They were basically a weddings and funerals band. Gary had a bit of a jam with them, didn't show off or anything, playing a few tunes and we left. We were walking back down the street and he said, "Do you think they would let me join?" "Probably, yes," I said.'

Billy Hunter recalls that initially Gary would come on stage and just play a few numbers with them. 'These were the days of flower power; we used to pinch these flowers out of people's gardens so we could throw them out to the crowd.' The band—Reggie Carson (vocals), Graham Drennan (guitar), Robert Apps (drums) and Billy—played pop covers, anything from Elvis to country & western. Once, they were going to play 'Stepping Stone' by The Monkees. Gary's response was 'I can't play that shit', so the compromise was to do the version by The Flies, which had a lead intro. However, Gary had a game plan and it didn't include Scott McKenzie or The Monkees.

The singer and the guitarist would leave the stage when Gary came on and it was obvious to everybody that this was the best part of the show. 'As soon as he picked up that guitar,' says Graham, 'I knew how special he was. It was a privilege to be in his presence. He was doing things years ahead of anybody else at that time.'

They were playing the Donaghadee Masonic Hall. The main band was Ralph's Relations (a very experienced and much older outfit). They played for an hour, then on came The Suburbans to play the half-hour break. Ian Hunter recalls, 'Gary took the roof off the place, he went down a storm. Ralph's Relations came back on to finish the night but were met with boos and hisses and shouts of "Get off." The crowd wanted Gary on, but he'd broken his E string and didn't have a spare. The other guitarist, Billy Harvey, had one, but wouldn't hand it over. Word went round and by some miracle, a string was produced, and Gary was back on stage. Next day, they were rehearsing at the Millisle Orange Hall when the police turned up making enquiries about Ralph's Relations getting roughed up as they were loading up their van after the gig.'

Gary used to practice in Billy's bedroom: 'He looked like a pop star even in those days. He used to come to the house in his big black trench coat, long hair and sandals—weird. We had a piano, so we would tune to concert pitch, and I had a big 50-watt bass amp and we'd practice on that. And we would practice for hours and hours at a time. He'd teach me the songs he wanted to play—Cream, Hendrix, John Mayall and The Who. He said to me, "Let's you, me and Robert get together, just the three of us."'

It seems like he had a similar conversation with Billy's brother Graham. 'Gary said there can't be two guitarists in the band. He was pretty single-minded about it, no sentiment. If I'm to join the band, the other guitarist has to go.'

It fell to Graham to negotiate the politics, essentially engineer the end of The Suburbans, which one local paper had called 'one of the fastest rising groups in the North'. Trouble was, The Suburbans' singer, Reggie Carson, was not only the sole driver, but also the major shareholder of the PA system. 'So, what I had to do,' says Graham, 'was to get Billy and the drummer on board and they would get the singer. To keep Reggie, you needed to keep a few pop songs for him to sing and then Gary would introduce the more rocky stuff. So, the idea was to get the singer a tambourine so he could stand at the side of the stage and bang it. It sounds harsh, but it wasn't really.'

In truth though, both Reggie and the other guitarist, Graham Drennan, quickly saw the direction of travel. They quit the band and The Suburbans became Life. Billy Hunter recalls their first gig at the Donaghadee Youth Club, inside a secondary school. 'We had a big stage; Gary put up some false speakers on the stage and Robert put up a dummy set of drums. At the end of the gig, Gary started trashing the speakers while Robert was kicking this old drum kit around the stage while I carried on playing the bass lines. Gary had this beautiful blonde Telecaster and he used to whack it on the stage and bounce it right into his hands. I asked him where he got all that from. "Pete Townshend," he said.'

At the same venue for an end of term ball, Gary tried his hand at pyrotechnics. He persuaded a member of the audience to light a dustpan full of rubbish behind his amp, so that smoke and flames would rise up behind it. The whole thing got out of hand: somebody had to rush on with a fire extinguisher before the stage burnt down.

Gary was pretty cavalier with his amplification too; he was only playing through a Vox AC30 and he wasn't happy with the sound he was getting. He got hold of an AC50 and made his own twin lead. But he was trying to get two large-diameter cables into one jack plug and so the whole rig was notoriously unreliable, although he seems to have got away with it most of the time.

A typical Life set list with Gary singing looked like this, and it is a source of huge regret that there are no recordings: 'Tallyman', 'Rock My Plimsoul', 'Hi Ho Silver Lining' and 'Beck's Boogie' (Jeff Beck); 'Hey Joe', Red House' and 'Purple Haze' (Jimi Hendrix); 'Hideaway' and 'Crossroads' (Eric Clapton); plus 'You Keep Me Hanging On', 'Midnight Hour' and 'Satisfaction'.

'Red House' was Gary's party piece and he played slide guitar on Vanilla Fudge's 'You Keep Me Hanging On'. He could play 'Strange Brew', but, says Graham, 'he wouldn't play it on stage because he couldn't quite get the ending the way Clapton did it and Gary had said that was the most important bit. One day, he came banging on the door shouting, "I've worked it out, I've worked it out." And he had. And he was the only guitarist I knew who could play Hendrix.' The Life set list shows that Gary was playing some of the most complicated rock music around, but, says Ian Hunter, 'you never saw him sit down and actually work out how to play something like most players would do. It must have all been done in private. As soon as Beck, Hendrix or whoever put something out, he had it off to perfection. He would come to the rehearsal hall, show Billy the bass lines and then play it straight through first time.'

Billy says that Life had no real competition; they attracted a different following from the pop audiences: 'We felt bloody good. The venues were packed; we would hire the hall and call it a social evening to get round some rules and regulations. We used to advertise Gary as "Northern Ireland's Greatest Guitarist", people would come from all over and his name soon got around.'

'There was one gig in Portaferry and we were the warm-up act for a big showband. When we came on, the showband stood there and they were astounded because we were using all their gear. They came over to us at the end and said we were fantastic. They couldn't believe what three people could do.'

For a boy of fifteen, his vision of where he wanted to go was remarkable; he often sat on the beach at Millisle with Ian Hunter to chew the fat about life: 'He told me that he didn't want to be a sideman, he only ever wanted to be the frontman.' He told Graham that 'he wanted to invent a fretless lead guitar so that nobody else could play it'. Gary did exercises deliberately designed to stretch his left hand before he stopped growing to extend his reach on the neck. Graham says that Gary would put his palms together and the fingers on his left hand would be half an inch longer than the right.

Away from the pressures of home and school, Gary began to come out of his shell in Millisle; Ian Hunter saw a very different side to him: 'He was always well mannered, but I wouldn't have described him as quiet. He was very much a fun guy, always telling jokes, having a laugh. He was a showman, but never a show-off. Gary would walk into a coffee bar and if the scene was drab or boring, he'd put on a record and start dancing and clapping and everybody would join in. He did the same one night at a caravan park dance in Ballyferris near Millisle. A band was playing, but nobody was dancing. Gary started dancing and clapping at the other end of the hall, so the audience all went down that end to join him. Mr Fulton, the owner, didn't like what was going on and had Gary evicted. But when he found out what Gary could do musically, he was clamouring to get the band to play there.

'I remember one Saturday afternoon we were in the car park in Millisle and there was a chip van there. "Anybody hungry?" he says. "Yeah," we all said, "but we've no money." So, Gary shouts out, "When I eat, everybody eats!" So, we all went over to the chip van, got ourselves fish and chips and started eating. Only then Gary pipes up, "When I pay, everybody pays." But he never joked at anybody's expense and he was a loyal friend.'

Gary was spending more and more time in Millisle, not just summer holidays, but weekends as well playing with Life, who never played Belfast. He would enjoy sitting around with Ian and his other friends, especially in the summer on the beach, swopping jokes and stories, drinking QC wine. Although he had friends in Belfast, he never really hung out with them as they were usually too busy with football or other sports.

Because of his home life, though, he could still be very sensitive to any form of adult disapproval. Ian recounts the first time he brought Gary into his house: 'I introduced Gary to my mum and he was sitting there wearing odd clothes with long hair, playing guitar and serenading her. My dad was a bit of a boozer and came home with a few drinks in him. Dad looked at Gary and said, "What is it?" Gary got up immediately and left the house and never came back near the door. He used to stand outside, wave at me, try and get my attention, but he would never knock on that door.'

His time away from Belfast was causing some tensions with Bobby, who thought (probably rightly) that Gary was missing out on opportunities to progress his career in the city. Ian says that Gary ran away from home once (this actually happened more than once): 'He came to us and we harboured him. We got a tent off somebody and he said he wasn't going home.' Bobby came looking for him, but his friends didn't give him up. Gary would on occasion willingly stand in for a guitarist who might have gone AWOL from a showband playing at Bobby's venue in Holywood. Once, The Barons were due to play a gig in Greyabbey, but Gary said he was too ill to play. Yet, Bobby got him to the gig, sat him on the amp and no argument—the show must go on. But as he grew older, Gary was more likely to stand up to Bobby if he didn't want to play. They got into a huge argument one day when Bobby came down to the practice hall in Millisle telling Gary that he was needed for a gig. On another occasion, Ian Hunter remembers going with Billy to call for Gary at Castleview Road: 'Gary came out in a foul temper, jumped over the hedge and started kicking the wing mirrors on his father's car. But he would never say what had happened. He always kept it to himself.'

Even Millisle went sour for Gary in the end. Graham Hunter recounts a particular incident at the Masonic Hall: 'We were playing a gig there and a girl came through the door who we knew and Gary went and grabbed her to give her a hug. What he didn't know was her boyfriend was coming up behind and took a swing at Gary. Two big policemen and a bouncer crashed through the crowd. I grabbed Gary and got him through an emergency exit at the back of the stage. That was it, we never saw him for a few months after that. That punch shattered his dream of Millisle. But maybe it did him a favour in a way, it got him away, because his life would have stagnated if he's stayed there much longer.'

On one of the last gigs Gary played with Life, he did the auto-destruct act again, only this time there was no fake drum kit and Robert Apps was left holding his drums sticks and looking quite shocked. It didn't go down too well with the audience either and the place started to empty. Time for Gary to move on.

Back in Belfast, Gary was on the look-out for a new band. He spotted a rhythm section, school friends Dave Finlay on drums and bassist Colin Martin, and approached them, 'I remember we didn't need much persuading,' says Colin. 'Gary already had a reputation as something of a prodigy. We started rehearsing in a little hall in Dee Street, off the Newtownards Road, that Gary had organised for us and the set mostly comprised guitar-based blues: Hendrix and Cream. I remember working a lot on a version of Dionne Warwick's "Walk On By", but I don't think we ever got round to playing it in public.' Bizarrely, though, Gary's party piece in this band was The Spotnicks' tricky pop instrumental hit 'Orange Blossom Special'. Except, at just fifteen years old, Gary played this song behind his head.

They settled on the name Platform Three (they were a trio and the blues has always been associated with railways) and started the round of venues in and around Belfast. They won a talent contest at the Fiesta Ballroom in Hamilton Street, winning £50 and blowing the lot in the pub after the gig—and were noticed by Bill Allen: 'I was knocked out by Gary's playing, but the other two guys were top class as well. Colin Martin caught up with me as I was leaving and we were shortly joined by Gary and Dave, so I became their manager at the front door of that hall.'

They played some of the old familiar places like Bobby's hall in Holywood, but the band were a step up from Gary's previous line-up and they got to play some of the more prestigious venues like Sammy Houston's Jazz Club and the top club spot in Belfast, the Maritime Hotel.

Originally a police station, the British Sailors' Society Seaman's Residential Club, known as the Maritime Hotel, had long been a dance and variety show venue. Then in 1964, Three Js Enterprises (Gerry McKervey, Jerry McKervey and Jimmy Colson) took over a large room on the first floor to open an R&B club. The inspired choice to kickstart the venture was Van Morrison's Them.

By 1964, Van Morrison was an experienced musician having toured Europe with a showband, but back in Belfast, prospects looked none too rosy. He responded to an ad from a new R&B club looking for a band for its opening night. However, his band at the time, The Golden Eagles had just split up, so he created a new band out of an East Belfast band, The Gamblers, led by guitarist Billy Harrison and including future Thin Lizzy founder member Eric Wrixon who suggested the new name taken from the 1950s horror movie Them.

Their powerful, gritty urban blues performances with its arrogant strut and sneer perfectly captured the mood of Belfast's young people looking for something different from showbands and pop covers, a music they could call their own. The Maritime quickly established itself as Belfast's answer to the Cavern or London's Crawdaddy and was packed every weekend way above what any fire regulations might have allowed.

The growing blues scene in Belfast was attracting attention from out of town, in particular from a young guitarist from Cork, Rory Gallagher. Platform Three's manager Bill Allen happened to be in Sammy Houston's Jazz Club on a Friday night when Rory and his band Taste were playing. 'The next night, I was driving Gary to a date and I went out of my way to park outside the Maritime where Rory was playing that night. Gary asked why we were stopping here and I said, "There's someone I'd like you to meet." We made our way in and downstairs to the "café" part of the building. It was quite crowded, but I spotted Rory in his lumberjack shirt. I know this sounds a bit corny, but I introduced them to each other and said, "You're both going to be stars." Gary didn't say anything, but Rory broke the ice by asking Gary what guitar he played. They chatted for about five minutes and then we had to leave.'

Rory and Gary struck up a friendship and Gary often told the story that as neither of them could afford new strings, if Platform Three were supporting Taste, each would leave their guitar on stage for the other in case a string broke. Gary also said they would wire their amps together to boost the power. Amplification was something of a sore point in Platform Three, because both Bill and Colin Martin say that Gary didn't own an amp then, so they had to hire or borrow an amp for every gig. Bill recounts, 'I would often pick Gary up at his home, then drive to Evans Music in Lisburn to hire an amp. Occasionally, I would borrow an amp from a friend, George Cathcart, lead guitarist of The Fugitives, or sometimes Stephen Beckett from Carrickfergus.'

Having been regarded as right off the beaten track, Belfast began to appear on the touring schedules of bands from England. By 1967, the Three Js had sold out to a ballroom dancer named Eddie Kennedy who renamed the venue Club Rado and began bringing over acts like Fleetwood Mac and John Mayall's Bluesbreakers. If Eric Clapton and Jeff Beck had stunned Gary, it was nothing compared to the impact of Peter Green—probably Gary's biggest influence, his key role model, the guitarist who stood on Gary's right shoulder, almost haunted him really, for the rest of his life. Squashed in among the Club Rado crowd, Gary was transfixed as Peter showed him what taste and tone was all about, how playing could be so melodic and soulful without any diminution of power, how less was undoubtedly more.

Gary had taken to wearing some strange outfits; on a trip back to Millisle, he turned up in green baseball boots, green cord trousers, green PVC mac and green John Lennon sunglasses with his hair permed. Another time, he was spotted in Millisle wearing an Egyptian fez. Gear like this would have made him stand out as he left Club Rado at night and so a target of the Market gang who used to wait outside tooled up with bike chains and other weapons. 'You had to run this gauntlet,' recalled Gary grimly. 'They would say, "Have yers any odds?" [meaning small change] They might still beat you up, but they'd nick your bus fare so you had to walk miles home, and then they'd be waiting for you at the other end.'

Apart from unwarranted attention from a group of thugs, Gary's flamboyance was partly a reflection of his new-found confidence, as his reputation as a guitarist blossomed. That confidence didn't extend much to girls. As he was not that good looking growing up, he had never had a steady girlfriend, but with his friends William Larmour and Roger Kelly, he used to hang out at a night club on Saturdays held at the CIYMS sports ground where it was four shillings (20p) to get in. 'We used to go there,' says Roger, 'and go to the off-licence to get bottles of cheap wine and Gary got this love of green chartreuse. Gary always had more money than us; we would go off to this wee wood and drink and then go to the club. All the girls from this posh grammar school—Strathearn Girls' School—used to go there too.'

After a while, William, Roger and another friend, Noel, began seeing some of these girls, and one night the boys hung around the grounds of the school waiting for the girls to come out from a formal dance. Gary didn't have a girlfriend of his own but was besotted by Noel's girl, Philippa. By the time the girls emerged, the boys were a bit tipsy, but as William says, 'That night Gary was way beyond that; he'd put away a whole bottle of QC wine. Gary just went, "Oh, I'm such a mess," and started crying, and he said, "You know, I'm never going to be able to play like Peter Green." We all said, "Don't be daft," and we had to console him. This was obviously preying on his mind and maybe something from home was upsetting him as well.' Very typical of Gary's singlemindedness; he was far more troubled at the thought of not being the best guitarist in the world than of not having a steady girlfriend like his mates.

Gary left school in the spring of 1968 ('he just disappeared on us,' says Roger), got a job as a delivery boy, which lasted about two days when he came off his bike, followed by a brief dalliance with a warehouse job unloading British Rail containers full of lampshades, kitchenware, Tampax and Durex—'"manhole covers", the foreman used to call them,' Gary told a journalist in 1984.

After only about six months, 'Platform Three came to an abrupt end,' says Colin Martin, 'when Gary "forgot" to return a Marshall amp we had hired from Evans Music in Lisburn. I got into some trouble because my name was on the contract and I was well pissed off.' In truth, the amp incident was more of a catalyst than the reason for the split because Colin and Dave were focused on their A-levels and had less time for the band. Bobby had said to Gary that if he wanted to get on, he would have to leave Belfast. Gary took him at his word. One day he was hanging around outside the gates of Stormont when a van pulled up. Out jumped some guys and asked Gary if he fancied coming to Dublin to stand in for their guitarist, Dave Lewis. The band was The Method.

Dave Lewis had started out as a singer, billed aged twelve as 'the Boy with the

Golden Voice', taking part on the competition circuit, playing in pubs and working men's clubs. He moved on to Dave & The Diamonds, but as Dave says, 'they were just a couple of guys backing me. I wasn't really in a band until I joined The Method. I was working in Crymble's music shop and met their manager there.'

The Method began as a blues/soul outfit, 'but it was running out of steam. Hendrix and Cream were happening, Rory Gallagher had come up to Belfast and it was this three-piece set up, the soul thing was fading. I'd been playing guitar since I was eight, but really only rhythm. That changed when the blues thing came along, but I was never as fanatical about the guitar as Gary. I was more interested in writing songs. I started writing songs for the band and getting into John Mayall when the *Blues Breakers* album came out—and then the keyboard player left and it turned into my band. We had Wilgar Campbell on drums before he joined Rory Gallagher and then an English bass player came in, Nigel Smith. It wasn't too long before we were playing gigs in Dublin, Scotland and the Marquee in London. We had a very good thing going.'

Gary and Dave already knew each other: 'I first met him when he won a competition. It looked like he was playing a big fat Guild behind his head and with his teeth. One day, there was a knock on the door and this bass player, Big Sammy (probably Cook), was standing there with Gary. So, we find ourselves in my mother's attic—just started jamming away although we weren't really musically compatible. I was more of a singer, so the idea of us forming band together with him just backing me up was never going to work.'

Then, in the early summer of 1968, Dave Lewis was in a car accident. 'Nigel and I were out with our girlfriends, probably driving too fast down a country road. The car skidded and hit a rock. It was a Mini and just folded up. Nigel was living at my mum's house at the time, so we could rehearse in the attic. He managed to get home, went straight to bed and didn't say anything. Next morning it was, "Oh, by the way, we had an accident and Dave's in hospital."'

'I didn't know Gary,' says Nigel, 'I'd just come over from England. We had to change our set, drop the original stuff and just play blues. We just made it up as we went along and, to be honest, we went down better than we did before. Nothing rehearsed; Gaz knew all the stuff, singing and playing.'

Dave Lewis was out of action for about three weeks. Gary played Dublin and a few other gigs around Ireland, but it was a gig at the Club A Go Go in Sackville Place off Dublin's O'Connell Street, which set him on course for life as a professional musician, swinging that red guitar.

02

OVER THE
HILLS AND
FAR AWAY

By the time Gary arrived in Dublin in the summer of 1968, the city had a healthy alternative music scene far removed from the pop covers/country & western fare dished up by the showbands. As Daragh O'Halloran described it in his Irish rock book *Green Beat*, as well as the pioneering Sound City (renamed Club Arthur in 1966) and '5', 'the main hive of activity was the wide boulevard of O'Connell Street and its adjoining arteries. The Flamingo was upstairs over a café at the corner of Abbey Street ... Later the wandering Apartment Club temporarily set up camp in a basement on the opposite side of the street. Further down the road was the slippery metal staircase leading down to the 72 Club. The Scene Club opened on 14th January 1966 by the in-demand Action ... Club A Go Go situated east of its competitors on Abbey Street, down an alley at Sackville Place, had a reputation for housing some of the harder edged groups.'

DJ Stevie 'Smiler' Bolger reckons that the Club A Go Go was the best club for the longest period, playing blues, soul and rock'n'roll and so was a natural venue for The Method to play in Dublin. In fact, once they started arriving in 1965, the Belfast bands brought a tougher, more uncompromising blues dynamic to the Dublin scene, bands like The Few (to which Colin Martin went after Platform Three split), Sam Mahood & The Soul Foundation and The Method.

Frank Murray, roadie for local band Skid Row, happened to be at the Club A Go Go on the night Gary played: 'I was at the back of the club and I could hear this guitar playing; it sounded brilliant and I thought it was Dave Lewis. And I was thinking that the trip The Method had made to London, well ... Davy's really improved as a guitar player. Then I started to get closer and watch and realised it wasn't Davy on guitar, but this young kid. He spent 90 percent of the show with his back to the audience, standing over close to his amp.'

'Skid Row was playing over at the 72 club and during the break there, I said to Brush and Phil, "There's a kid over at the Go Go and when this is over, we should go over and have a look at him." You could see straight away that he was a great player.'

The other Skid Row roadie who saw Gary early on was Paul Scully: 'The only way I can describe it was seeing Lionel Messi for the first time. Seeing Gary was gobsmacking, absolutely gobsmacking. It was Clapton, B.B. King, the riffs—everything.'

Brendan 'Brush' Shiels, born in Dublin in 1946, was good enough as a teenager to become a professional footballer: 'I signed for Bohemians in 1964, but then I heard an album by Oscar Peterson called *Night Train* and there was a bass solo on it by Ray Brown and that was it.' He spent several months just listening to

Ray Brown and by the time Brush was 19, he stopped playing football altogether and says he never kicked a ball again. And that nickname? Well, he had long sideburns and 'sweeper' is a footballing term for a roving central defender. Then again, during his early bass playing days, Brush sported a long Zapata moustache prompting a roadie to call him Brush. Somewhere in the soup of fact and fiction floats the truth.

Brush concentrated on music, joining country & western outfits Rose Tynan & The Rangers and Brian & The Boys before moving on in 1967 to one of Dublin's first soul outfits, called The Uptown Band. They were managed by Ted Carroll, who, while still working in a bank, had started the very first beat group club in Ireland. He found a small dancehall next to some tea rooms on Killiney Beach on the south coast of County Dublin and opened up as the White Cottage in May 1962. From there, Ted developed a career as an agent, promoter and manager, also starting what became a healthy if short-lived out-of-town tennis club circuit for beat groups by establishing a venue at the Longford Tennis Club, a few miles along the same stretch of coastline.

Not long after Brush joined The Uptown Band, there was a 'coup' and Ted was fired. Ted asked Brush if he wanted to form a band of his own, a different kind of band. 'I knew this guitar player, Bernie Cheevers,' says Brush, 'who I'd played with in Brian Rock & The Boys, but I needed a singer who was good-looking rather than was necessarily a great singer. I knew Dave Robinson [who later founded Stiff Records] who was running a place called Sound City. He mentioned Peter Adler [son of harmonica legend Larry Adler] and then this black guy living in Crumlin [a suburb of Dublin]. "He's the man for you," Dave told me. There was no phone or anything. I found out where he lived and got on the bus. I knocked on the door, said I was forming a band and asked him if he wanted to be in it. The conversation went like this:

'"Tell me what you'll be doing."

'"What do you like?"

'"Simon and Garfunkel, Nico & The Velvet Underground, Jimi Hendrix."'

Philip Parris Lynott was born of mixed parentage in 1949, a short-lived affair between an Irish girl, Philomena Lynott, and a black Guyanese man named Cecil Parris. Philomena left her son in Dublin, in the care of her parents Frank and Sarah, who had other children, while she worked in Manchester. By all accounts, despite being the only black face in school, once the kids and the neighbours got used to seeing him around, Phil did not have the traumatic childhood you might have expected. He grew up a gangly teenager with presence, charm, a sense of style, and a taste in music derived from his half-brother Timothy's record collection, ranging from The Mamas & The Papas to Hendrix and Cream. And he had a voice.

Phil was recruited to sing in The Sundowners, which eventually became The Black Eagles. When the band's drummer went into the army, Phil asked Brian Downey, a drummer he knew from school and the local beat scene, if he wanted to join. The band had plenty of work on the Dublin beat scene, working at least four nights a week. But nobody ever expects a band of teenagers to stay together for long and so, in 1967, predictably, it all fell apart, leaving Phil to ponder 'What next?'

Brush had a place where he would hang out. 'My best pal, Pat Quigley, lived there and he played bass in a band called The Movement. He owned this ferociously loud speaker that blew the plaster off the ceiling, but his ma didn't seem to mind. So, I said to Pat, "Do you mind if I bring this lad over and try him out?"' Having secured the services of Bernie Cheevers, Brush asked Phil to try and get Brian Downey, but he wasn't interested in the repertoire, so Brush turned instead to a talented drummer, Noel Bridgeman, who lived next door to Brush's girlfriend.

'Phil arrived in this long black coat and pair of green sunglasses like Jim McGuinn out of The Byrds,' recalls Brush, 'and started singing "Hey Joe". Afterwards I asked the band what they thought. Bernie said, "I reckon I could sing 'Hey Joe' better than that." My response was "Fuck off!" Phil was in the band.'

They started rehearsing in September 1967 and by the end of October were out on the road. However, when Brush saw the posters advertising a band called 'My Father's Moustache', thought up by Ted Carroll with no consultation, he threw a fit and quickly changed the name to Skid Row, which he says came from seeing saxophonist Alan Skidmore listed on the *Beano* album.

Brush details the repertoire: 'We were playing Jimi Hendrix, "So You Want To Be A Rock 'n' Roll Star", "Eight Miles High", a great version of "Strawberry Fields" with Bernie on wah-wah, "Hey Jude", and "Sky Pilot" by Eric Burdon & The Animals.' Even though they had a lead singer, Skid Row would launch into extended instrumentals, leaving Phil somewhat stranded, so he took to making strange noises into an echo box and trying to get all kinds of weird sounds out of it.

Although he had never seen what was happening on the London psychedelic scene, Brush wanted to develop a show that was more than just standing there playing. 'This friend of mine had a film of Pope Pius XII and we were showing that on the back wall of where we were playing—and it got into the papers. Me mother went mad at me for having a go at the Pope. For the first time in her life, she was nearly hysterical, she could hardly speak.' This was brave stuff in a society that Noel Bridgeman describes as 'dark and priest-ridden'.

By 1968, they were one of Ireland's top bands and in March, Brush won *New Spotlight* magazine's popularity poll. But as the workload increased, so Bernie Cheevers had to drop out. He had a day job as an electrician with Guinness and winning a company award along the lines of 'Electrician of the Year' meant his commitment to Skid Row waned and he left the band. Brush was now more than a little interested to hear the extraordinary guitar playing of this mystery kid standing in for Dave Lewis.

'That first time I saw Gary, I was lost for words. He was doing the whole *Blues Breakers* set—every single track off that album, one after the other. I just couldn't believe it.' Brush went up to Gary afterwards and straight out asked him if he wanted to join Skid Row. Gary asked him if they played blues; Brush said no, so like Brian Downey, another blues fanatic, Gary declined: 'If it wasn't blues, I wasn't interested. I was a real blues snob in those days.' But even so, he went to hear the band and was eventually won over. He could hear they were trying to be different. Besides, Gary knew the gig with The Method was very short-term, and he really didn't want to go back to Belfast. But he was only sixteen and as much as he might be at odds with his father, he knew that he couldn't just run away and say nothing.

The move didn't happen overnight. Platform Three were still officially in existence at the time Gary came home from his stint with The Method. Manager Bill Allen recalls: 'Gary called me and said he needed to talk to me about something. I drove to Castleview Road, where Gary came out of his house and sat with me in the car. He said that Brush Shiels was trying to persuade him to join Skid Row, which would mean a move to Dublin. I asked him what his parents thought. He said it didn't matter what they thought, which slightly shocked me. Gary had always been "a man of few words", but I hadn't, until then, picked up any hints of family tension.' Remarkably, Gary then said to Bill that because the manager had been good to him, he was going to leave the decision to him, as if he was looking for another kind of father-figure approval. 'Gary said to me, "If you want me to stay, I'll stay." I remember saying to him that he was still a bit young for such a move and that he should really consider his family's views. But I also said from the point of view of advancing his career, I was having an uphill battle getting enough dates in Northern Ireland for Platform Three because of the dominance of the showbands, whereas Dublin had a bigger group scene. Joining Skid Row would be the right move.'

The next move, however, would be for Brush to come up and meet Bobby. 'Gary asked me to meet him at Stormont gates. So, I meet him there and he brings me down to the house and his Da is in very bad form—and I thought it was to do with me.' Brush had unwittingly walked into a very tense situation, but eventually Bobby calmed down enough to ask Brush if he could take care of Gary. 'What was I supposed to say to that? Of course, I said yes—when I could barely look after myself.'

Once Gary was signed up, Skid Row progressed rapidly. Brush was the dominant force in the band, responsible for pretty much everything that happened. He had a clear idea that he didn't want Skid Row to be just another Irish beat group doing covers; they had already shown that even when they performed the songs of other artists, they would not be choosing the most obvious repertoire nor would they be performing blind copies. And the 'show' element was ramped up; after about the second gig, Brush had an idea: 'There was this film, *The Defiant Ones*, with Tony Curtis and Sidney Poitier as two convicts on the run, one black, one white. So, Phil and I came out handcuffed together; I'd pull the handcuff apart, get behind Phil, and the bouncers would try and separate us, it looked so real. The show was the most important thing.'

But it wasn't all about the show; the arrival of bands like Cream, John Mayall's Bluesbreakers and the Jimi Hendrix Experience ushered in the cult of virtuoso musicianship, and this is what Brush was striving for coupled with a realisation that for the band to break out of the restrictive Irish circuit, they would need to be writing their own material. Both Noel and Brush were accomplished musicians in their own right; good-looking Phil Lynott fronted the band; Gary squared the circle. 'I didn't think we could fail,' says Brush. There was a slight hiccup in the grand design, however, when Noel suddenly upped sticks and left to go on a tour of German airbases: 'Noel said he was going home to clean his cymbals. Next thing, we get a card from Germany. He'd gone off to play with Colm Wilkinson [the Irish tenor who later found fame as Jean Valjean in *Les Misérables*].' There were other times early in the life of the band when Brian Downey would sit in for Noel, who says there was no big idea behind leaving: 'I didn't give it a second thought. I'd never left Dublin and here was a chance to go to England, Belgium and Germany. It was a big adventure and it was very early on in Skid Row.' In Noel's absence, Robbie Brennan, a regular figure on the beat scene, was drafted in as the day-to-day replacement drummer.

The first song Brush brought forward was 'Photograph Man' recorded at the

OVER THE HILLS AND FAR AWAY **45**

Eamonn Andrews Studio in Dublin, just about the only place you could record. It was an odd setup; the studios were located in a large ballroom called the Television Club on Harcourt Street. The ballroom area itself was used as a live room. Sound booths were constructed as required from large baffles wheeled around the floor. Mics were plugged into a wallboard linked to the control room in a cubicle upstairs. If it was a dance night, the recording act had to vacate and tidy the dance floor by about 7pm.

Ted Carroll took the tapes to Apple Records in London and a few other labels but there was no interest. Inspired by the Beatles' 'Sergeant Pepper's Lonely Hearts Club Band', the song remains unreleased. Brush says they also did some demos in Belfast for Phil and Mervyn Solomon (who managed Them and The Dubliners, respectively), but nothing came of that either.

Their next effort, released in May 1969, found an outlet through the Song label run by Joe Coughlan, a well-known Republican solicitor, and Donal Lunny, a traditional Irish musician. The A-side, 'New Faces, Old Places', played to the Buffalo Springfield tendency in Skid Row, in stark contrast to the more angular and furious set pieces to come. The B-side was 'Misdemeanour Dream Felicity'. Brush says Gary's love of Pentangle was part of the genesis of this song, his first compositional credit: 'Gary loved John Renbourn and Bert Jansch and he could do all the picking.' They were doing a 5/4 thing—Noel was very interested in Dave Brubeck's 'Take Five' and an album called *Time Further Out*. 'That's how we got the idea for all the different time sequences,' says Brush. 'Gary was playing 12-string and singing at the same time. Unbelievable at sixteen; it summed up everything about him. It's difficult to put into words, it was *that* amazing. I was so overwhelmed the way he played it. It summed up everything we were ever going to do, every place we were going to go.'

The single didn't bother the charts, but there was a bigger problem. Brush recalls, 'We did a television show playing "Strawberry Fields Forever" and Philo was badly out of tune. Something wasn't right. I looked down his throat and he had something the size of a golf ball down there. He phoned his mum, who ran this hotel for showbiz people on Moss Side in Manchester and he went over and stayed there while he had a throat operation.'

It had become obvious to Brush that if the band were going to challenge the dominant rock trios like Hendrix and Cream—which he truly believed Skid Row could—then Phil was surplus to requirements. 'He wasn't gone two minutes and we were practising all new numbers,' says Brush. 'I took over the singing, complete egomaniac me, and Gary wasn't far behind. Noel used to say, "I don't have an ego problem. I know I'm great."

'So, Phil came back and I told him we had to let him go and he cried and cried.' This was a big shock for Phil; he had been Brush's best man at his wedding only a few months earlier and arranged his honeymoon over in Manchester. But Brush had some sugar to sweeten the pill. He had another bass guitar bought from Robert Ballagh, the bass player in a showband called The Chessmen. 'I told Philo I would teach him some bass guitar; he already played a bit of rhythm, but I knew he could be a good bassist. He came over to my house every day for six weeks and we practised for hours on end.'

Noel has an interesting take on Phil's departure: 'The Brush was more aware, more astute that people give him credit for. People think he is an eccentric and a comedian. But Brush had good insights, he really knew in his heart that Phil wanted to do his own thing, but didn't have the courage to fly the coop. So, Brush sat him down and said, "You're fuckin' gone, but here's a bass guitar and I'll show you a few things." And he became a really great bass player.'

Phil quickly formed his own band, Orphanage, with Brian Downey, guitarist Joe Staunton and bassist Pat Quigley, in whose house Phil had done his audition for Skid Row—and the rest is a history to which we will return.

When Gary wasn't playing with Skid Row, he immersed himself in a very different scene. If the beat groups offered the modern alternative to the showbands, then the folk scene represented a culture far more ancient. As Mark Prendergast explained in his book *Irish Rock*, 'Irish traditional music has developed in two general directions; the slow air or ballad on the one hand, reflecting the plaintive aspects of life, and the more rumbustious jigs and reels on the other, usually associated with dancing. These have been preserved by musicians and singers down the generations embodying the history of the Irish people in different regions of the country.'

He goes on to signal the huge influence of Bob Dylan in moving some of the younger folk musicians in Ireland and elsewhere to complement or even replace their acoustic instruments with electric guitars and drums updating their sound to create what became known as folk rock. The leading lights of the progressive folk scene in Ireland were Sweeney's Men and Dr Strangely Strange, while a former soul band, Granny's Intentions, waved the freak flag of more progressive rock. Around this hub of Dublin-based musicians was created a whole Bohemian psychedelic scene, a vortex of creativity into which poets, singers and artists were drawn, congregating in a few hip Dublin hangouts and pubs, keeping a weather eye out for the drug squad as they played their music, read their poetry, sang their songs and ruminated on life in a swirling haze of dope and acid.

And it was Phil Lynott, a man with literary and rock star aspirations, who bridged the worlds of the beat and the beatific. He took Gary around, introducing him both to a freedom he could only have dreamt of and a supportive circle of friends, leaving Gary with fond memories of the times and a city he would treasure for the rest of his life.

Although Skid Row was working regularly, the money was hopeless—Gary later said he was promised £15 a week, but he never saw anything like that amount. He often looked quite shabby and lived a peripatetic life, moving from one room in a musician house to another. In exchange, the quiet, shy lad from Belfast stunned his new friends, his new family almost, with his talent.

One of his first stop-overs was with Orphanage guitarist Joe Staunton: 'Brush asked me to put Gary up until he got sorted out. I was just starting out, knew about two chords, but Gary was phenomenal even then. I was trying to learn "Substitute" by The Who and he said, "No, no, play the chords like this," and he was right. He was so ear-trained for somebody so young. He was very quiet and reserved, kept himself to himself. He went for long walks every day and practised a lot by himself.'

Early on too, Gary shared a basement bedsit in Anglesea Road close to Donnybrook Church with Phil and Granny's Intentions' singer Johnny Duhan. Originally a soul band, formed in 1965, Granny's Intentions hooked into the psychedelic revolution and attracted the attention of top London managers like Kit Lambert of The Who as they played with the likes of Jimi Hendrix, Brian Jones, Eric Burdon and Keith Richards in London's fashionable Speakeasy club. But a second version of the band folded and they were now back in Dublin. Phil heard that Johnny's flatmate, Granny's guitarist John Hockedy, had gone back to Limerick and wondered if Johnny needed 'help with the rent'. About a month later, Gary appeared on the doorstep looking for somewhere to stay. 'Dressed in scruffy dark overcoat,' says Johnny, 'with dark, wavy locks spilling over his eyes and shoulders, he looked bedraggled and lost.' Gary had a sob story to tell, of which more later, but in the meantime, he slept on the floor in a sleeping bag. Gary told the *Sunday World* at the time of the Phil Lynott Memorial Concert in 2005 of a very different Phil from the dissolute rock star of later years: 'At the start, Phil was very energetic, very driven, very ambitious sort of guy. I hate to dispel a myth, but he used to wake up in the morning before any of us and he'd make breakfast for us. It was like living with your mother. He was very domesticated at that time.'

Johnny concurs with Gary's memory of Phil; in a brief memoir of that flat-share period, Johnny wrote that Phil 'was always on time with his share of the rent and contributed on a regular basis to our basic weekly groceries of Flahavan's Porridge, Butterkrust Pan and Heinz beans, our staple with the occasional packet of Galtee rashers and Matterson's sausages thrown in when times were rosy.

'Philip and I were early risers. Gary rarely surfaced before midday. None of us owned a watch but Phil was an expert at telling the time by the slant of light on the wall over his bed (a tip he had picked up from some cowboy flick, he told me). If Gary tried to sleep beyond twelve, Philip would invariably shake him into consciousness and insist that he get up so we could tidy up the room. Philip was very domesticated. He kept the kitchen spotless and helped me with the cooking. While Phil and I would be going about the household chores, Gary would crouch over my acoustic Yamaha guitar and play for hours on end, his agile fingers racing up and down the fretboard at astonishing speeds. Whenever Phil had a free moment, he too would practise on his bass or work on his lyrics slouching on his bed. The only place I felt comfortable working on my songs was on long coastal walks from Ballsbridge to Dún Laoghaire. Every afternoon I would set off with a biro and notepad, humming up melodies on the hoof and jotting down verses to go with them. Often when I'd get back to the basement in the evenings with a song in my pocket, I'd find Gary still playing my guitar with his head down, lost in the blues of Elmore James or B.B. King.

'Like myself, Gary wasn't big into socialising in the way Phil was. But occasionally on a Monday night the three of us would doll up and saunter into the Bailey in Duke Lane off Grafton Street for a few beers before heading up to the TV Club on Harcourt Street, where most of the heads from the showband world fraternised. Philip usually had two dress outfits for these occasions. For going to the Bailey—where the artistic set hung out—Phil dressed in casual denims and then, before heading up to the TV club, he would change in the Men's Room into a pair of dark slacks with white shirt and tie, which he carried around in a shoulder bag. Because of the TV Club's strict dress code, Gary and I would also take along neck ties, donned just before entering the venue and quickly removed once inside. On at least one occasion Gary and I were ejected from the hall for being caught with our ties in our pockets.'

During the recording of the Granny's debut album *Honest Injun* at the Decca Studios in West Hampstead, London, John Hockedy suddenly left. Noel Bridgeman was also due to play the whole album, but that didn't work out either and his place was taken by ex-Uptown Band drummer Pat Nash.

'On very short notice,' wrote Johnny, 'Gary was recruited to replace John for the remaining sessions.' According to bassist Pete Cummins (who reappears shortly as a Skid Row roadie), four of the eleven tracks featured John and Noel, the remaining seven tracks were recorded with Gary and Pat. Gary's main contribution was the more melodic and softer American country and traditional folk tracks such as 'We Both Need To Know', 'Susan Of The Country' in waltz time, western swing style, and 'Fourthskin Blues'.

'By this stage in Granny's desultory musical career,' wrote Johnny, 'we were playing a mixture of folk and country rock with a few soulful rockers thrown in to liven up the mix. Though the high energy, riff orientated semi-jazz that Gary was then playing with Skid Row was a million miles removed from our folksy songs, Gary had no problem adapting to our style. In the studio, as on stage, once Gary started playing, all eyes turned to him. He dazzled us with his skill and versatility. Rarely did he need to do a double take and he came up with fresh musical ideas at the drop of a hat. The only thing that puzzled him during the recording sessions was the fact that I had been banned from the studio control room on account of constant musical disagreements between myself and our record producer.'

Gary was also tight with the musicians from Dr Strangely Strange, a band heavily influenced by the eclectic and pioneering acid folk/world music approach of The Incredible String Band. Affectionately known as the Strangelies, the band comprised Tim Booth, Ivan Pawle and Tim Goulding and they made their stage debut in 1968 backing the String Band. As Mark Prendergast observed, 'This music grew out of informal, friendly, sessions where any musician could drop by and add something to the mix. Their records broke new grounds in terms of self-conscious lyricism which was a direct result of psychedelics. More than that, for the first time we had Irish musicians who wrote truly autobiographical lyrics which mirrored their lifestyle, environment and experiences.'

Ivan Pawle explains the environment created for musicians to 'drop by': 'I gave Patricia Mohan the name Orphan Annie when I met her at the Fleadh Cheoil in Mullingar in 1963 and the name stuck. Annie rented a flat in Lower Mount Street [Dublin] and I shared with herself and Christina McKechnie (Licorice). Then Tim Goulding met Annie and I moved on. Licky went back to Scotland with Robin

Williamson (String Band). This was the original Orphanage [the inspiration for Phil's band name and the later Thin Lizzy album, *Shades Of A Blue Orphanage*] and was a popular place for creative folk to drop by, some of whom sometimes smoked a bit of dope, which was just beginning to appear in Dublin. Youngsters like Phil loved to visit, and Gary when he came to Dublin with The Method.

'Annie Christmas and Tim Booth were both working in advertising agencies and rented a house, 26a Newgrove Avenue in Sandymount, and that became the second Orphanage. Gary would frequently visit, stay and play. Annie kindly let me stay there, but then I moved with my wife-to-be to Sydenham Road in Ballsbridge; sometimes Gary stayed with us there too.'

In those playful, innocent times, the Strangelies involved Gary in a home movie directed by Lawrence Bicknell, who went under the nickname of Renchi. Ivan Pawle takes up the story:

'Renchi arrived quite early one morning off the mail boat and we traipsed off to the Botanic Gardens up in Glasnevin to film the first scenes. Annie Goulding was working as a photographer across the road at Creation, the company which published *Spotlight* magazine, and she did some camerawork, so that Renchi could do an Alfred Hitchcock impersonation, pushing Niamh's pram (Ivan and Mary's daughter) ominously and ponderously in front of the large Victorian Glasshouse.'

'After these establishing shots, we travelled down to Bray to a hardware shop to purchase plaster of Paris and then out to Enniskerry, to Dargle Cottage, where Tim Goulding had his painting studio at his parents' place.'

'The story involved a prop which we had brought with us from Sandymount, which was a sculpture of a fairly exotic-looking plant in a pot; it had been made by Mick O'Sullivan, later an artist of some repute.'

The story started with an otherwise innocuous looking flower being injected (an icing gun was used as syringe), which then turned into the Mick O'Sullivan sculpture plant. Gary was the villain, dressed in a long black cloak. He managed to steal the syringe to turn Tim Goulding's character into a golem-like creature. First, he had to corner and catch Tim, involving a chase over the footbridge across the Dargle River. Tim was dressed in a white Pete Townshend-style boiler suit, and after he was injected with the invidious growth promoter, he was swathed in the plaster of Paris, which set rapidly.

'Mary and I were sitting at the table beside the lattice windows in the dining-room, when the photographer Mick Slattery's moustachioed face appeared to warn us of the shenanigans going on without (I think we were possibly the parents of Tim and Slattery the gardener). We all ran out to try and catch Gary before he could make any further mischief. I think there was a struggle, but I can't really remember who prevailed, or was supposed to prevail! We had quite a job getting the plaster of Paris off Tim, and he actually caught pneumonia, which he happily survived.'

Aside from 8mm antics, Ivan recalls some special musical moments with Gary: 'One of the best sessions I saw was when Gary played with Ed Deane at the Pembroke Inn, off Bagshot Street. You went downstairs and there was a photo of a duck and a notice that said, "Duck here." Ed Deane was also left-handed, but he plays upside down. He and Gary were trading blues licks on acoustic guitars— Gary was using a spare one of mine—and it was just the best thing I have ever heard. It went on for about ten minutes and because they were both playing left-handed, the guitar necks were facing each other. One of them would do a few licks and the other would come in and try and outdo him. Ed stood up very well, but nobody could play better than Gary. He had everything.'

It was at the second Orphanage that Tim Booth first met Gary: 'We fancied ourselves as being able to play, but we were in awe of his abilities. Ivan wrote very pretty songs and very good melodies and that really interested Gary, so he loved to come and play with us and he didn't mind that we didn't play very well because when we played with Gary he made us good. He not only played guitar, he could play mandolin and violin. We would be playing some bluegrass and Gary would just pick up any instrument and he'd be right along with you, not a bother on him. And he was pretty proficient on keyboards; we had a harmonium and he'd often be playing things on that.'

Although, as we have heard, Gary was quite shy and quiet, Tim Booth was struck by his sense of humour: 'He was incredibly funny. I can't emphasise this enough. A complete clown. He had this whole Zappa album virtually in his head. And he would just sit down with the guitar and play it to us. And he could do all the voices and all the singing. It was the funniest thing. And for me, Gary's version of Zappa was way better than Zappa.'

Tim recounts the time that he and Gary went to a favoured bar called Slattery's to play a guest spot together: 'I had ingested a healthy whack of lysergic acid and this came upon me as we hit the stage. It made for an interesting set. Gary towed me along in the wake of his guitar and the audience were none of the wiser. Gary, however, sussed me. All it took was for him to look me in the eye. The gig was in the basement of the pub, down a narrow, firetrap stairs, at the bottom of which was a broom cupboard fitted flush with the beauty-boarded wall. When we made our exit, I heard Gary's voice: "Let's take the lift."

'Lift..? Erm … Ga … I don't think there's a … "Come on man, course there is."

'And he ushered me into the cupboard, pulling the door onto interesting lavender fragrant darkness. "Bulb seems to have gone. What floor, man? Going up … Ladies' lingerie … household … haberdashery … and … the roof garden!" Sweeping the door open onto the dingy basement again, where the last stragglers were leaving, I thought it fabulous, in the true sense of the word, that a roof garden could be below ground like this, and so very, very like the basement.

'We were always sitting up late at night playing music, so he got to know our music very well. When we came to record our second album *Heavy Petting* with electric guitar on it, he was the natural choice. We worked out the arrangements with Gary and so it could all be put down fairly quickly in the fabled Eamonn Andrews Studio.'

Island Records producer Joe Boyd sent engineer Roger Mayer (who designed special effects for Jimi Hendrix) to supervise the recording and with him came Fairport Convention drummer Dave Mattacks, who, says Tim, 'kind of bent us into shape with some aiding and abetting from Gary'. Ivan Pawle recounts one memorable moment from the session: 'We were trying to get this track down, one of Tim Booth's—"Gave My Love An Apple"—and I think it was Gary's last day. I was trying to play a bit of bass. At one point, Brush appeared and told Gary they had to get going to a gig. Seeing me struggling, he just grabbed the bass, "Oh, for fuck's sake … right, Gary? … one, two …" and off they both went with Tim on acoustic guitar and Dave. I think we nailed it on the first take. And it was great.' The stand-out track on the album, though, was Ivan's 'Sign On My Mind' with a very mature, lyrical extended solo from Gary.

Most of the guys Gary was hanging out with were anything up to ten years older than he was and they all felt very protective towards him. Ivan did buy Gary his first LSD trip, but in the spirit of the times, also looked after him during the experience: 'We had a great, playful time. We went on the bus to Kilannie Head on the south side of Dublin Bay. We went down to the beach and collected stones.' Gary was right off the leash and so his surrogate parents had to reign him in, as Tim Booth explains: 'We found out he was taking speed and we didn't approve of that. We said to him, "You can take some acid and marijuana, but not speed," and he more or less agreed with that because he'd come back wired to the moon and we'd have to unwire him a bit.' There was an even darker side to the drug scene too; according to Brush, Gary had been hanging with some unsavoury guys who had broken into a chemist and stolen a load of pills. Gary was expected at the studio to do the Strangelies album but was late. Tim and Joe Coughlan went and kicked the door in and found Gary on the floor, completely out of it. They brought him round and got him to the studio.

If drugs turned Gary's head one way, albeit briefly, then moving down to Dublin opened his eyes to a whole other world—women, and one woman in particular—Sylvia Keogh, Gary's first serious girlfriend, who is referenced in Gary's song 'Business As Usual': 'I lost my virginity to a Tipperary woman.'

Sylvia recalls: 'I was a big fan of The Method. I was on my way back home from a gig somewhere with a friend. We went into a Wimpy Bar and a friend of my friend, who I was with, was sitting there with this guy—and that was Gary. We got together pretty fast after he joined Skid Row and were living together.'

Sylvia says this wasn't an easy relationship to maintain, especially if they wanted to share the same bed: 'Sometimes we had trouble with landladies and he'd go and live with Strangelies or Johnny Duhan. We had about nine different flats in Dublin.'

As Noel Bridgeman mentioned earlier, Irish culture was dominated by the Catholic Church, which dictated the social mores of the country. Not only were the couple in trouble with landladies, but Sylvia's Catholic family were not exactly welcoming of a long-haired, Protestant guitar player from Belfast. This did cause tensions, and so Gary's sob story when he rocked up on Johnny Duhan's doorstep was that Sylvia had thrown him out, when more likely there were times when they had to cool things down to keep the peace with family. Gary wouldn't have really understood what was going on and would have regarded anything like that as a rejection. Johnny Duhan does describe their relationship as 'turbulent, but Gary was nuts about her'. Gary had tried to tell Sylvia that he had lost his virginity when he was thirteen in some Belfast park, but in reality Sylvia was his first lover—he was sixteen, she was eighteen—and that made her very special indeed.

It was exciting for Sylvia too: 'Gary was very sweet and different. He didn't look like the civil servants I worked with every day, and he didn't look like the nice boys at home. And there was a little bit of danger in me being a southern Catholic and him being northern Protestant—it gave it a nice little edge.' Sometimes, though, it might get a little too edgy. Gary could become very frustrated very quickly. 'I remember one time in Dublin, one of the Strangelies had given Gary this sitar and he was trying to play it and not doing as well with it as he would have wished. He was getting very impatient with it. A whole bunch of us were in the pub and walked home across the park. When we got to the flat, the first thing he did was smash the sitar to bits.'

Meanwhile, despite being the most popular band in Ireland, Skid Row badly needed a break to take them to the next level. It came in December 1969, when they supported Fleetwood Mac at the National Stadium in Dublin.

Brian Downey saw them that night: 'They were fantastic, really good and that night Gary played spectacularly well.' In a story that Gary told many times, he recounts what happened next, on this occasion to *Beat Instrumental* in 1979: 'Pat Egan compered the show and he came up to me afterwards and said Peter Green would like to meet you—and he was like, my hero; I couldn't believe it, that he'd even talk to me, let alone invite me to jam later on!' Skid Row had another gig to do that night, but on the way back, Gary dropped in at Peter's hotel 'and I sat with him in the hotel jamming all night until about six in the morning. I was walking around six foot off the ground. He was giving interviews saying things like I was the best guitar player he'd ever played with—it was just getting out of hand.'

What Gary couldn't have known was that Peter Green was no ego-driven axe hero, but a deeply troubled and spiritual man who was increasingly unhappy at being involved in the rock business and making what appeared to him as unseemly amounts of money. His experiences with LSD simply served to increase his level of introspection, driving him deeper into his own thoughts. He had been planning to leave the band after the release of 'Oh Well', in October, just a couple of months before the Dublin gig, but manager Clifford Davis (also known as Clifford Adams) persuaded him to stay on. If Peter had left, the story of Skid Row and Gary might have been very different. Knowing that Peter would leave eventually, Davis probably didn't need too much persuading to take on Skid Row at Peter's suggestion—because with Gary, here was clearly an unknown guitar sensation waiting to explode on to the scene.

Davis secured a deal with Fleetwood Mac's label, CBS, and the band recorded some demos in Dublin. CBS sent over Mike Smith to produce the recordings. Smith had had six No.1 records with Brian Poole & The Tremeloes, Georgie Fame, Marmalade, Love Affair and Christie, but he had missed out on the Beatles, turning them down at their audition for Decca Records in 1962. The Skid Row demos appeared in the 80s on vinyl and have been reissued subsequently, for example in 2000 on Castle Music with the title of either *Skid Row* or, from a sign in cover photo, *Dublin Gas Comy. Cooker & Meter Factory* on CD. Once the band moved to London, in Gary's words, 'the album was scrapped and we redid it and managed to make it worse than the first time'.

The move across the water came quickly after the deal was signed. If Gary had to get out of Belfast to progress, then Skid Row needed to leave Ireland altogether. Ted Carroll had only been the manager in the early days of Skid Row. The mantle passed to various others including a firebrand trainee solicitor named Ollie Burn, who would wade in fists flying and emerge without a scratch if anybody threatened the band, like Mickah Wallace, the demented security man who became the drummer in *The Commitments*. Meanwhile, Ted had moved to Bournemouth and drove a bus for two years. Some friends from there had a house in Planchette Grove, east London, where there were two spare rooms. Ted went to Euston, picked Skid Row up off the boat train and whisked them off their new home. The rent and food were covered, so they were given £1 a day to splash out on luxuries. Travelling on the London underground late at night, though, could be a bit tricky; this was the era of the skinheads, many of whom lived out that way. Skid Row, with their long hair, were subject to plenty of menacing glances, but just about avoided getting into fights. They rehearsed at Davis' house in Surrey, played a few opening gigs in the UK, starting at the Roundhouse in London with the Strangelies among others, but most of the time was spent on the album.

From the demos of self-penned numbers recorded in Dublin, five tracks survived: 'Virgo's Daughter', 'Heading Home Again', 'Felicity', 'Unco-op Showband Blues' and 'The Man Who Never Was'. One track that didn't reach the album, 'Sandie's Gone', was released as a single in April 1970, with a country-rock vocal sound not unlike The Band.

The album, *Skid*, included four new tracks, again all written either by Brush or credited to the band. The whole raison d'être of Skid Row was to play fast, intricate music to a new audience of rock intelligentsia who would also be listening to the likes of King Crimson, Colosseum and maybe even the jazz-rock explosions of Tony Williams's Lifetime featuring Jack Bruce and John McLaughlin. And apart from a song like 'Heading Home Again', which would not have been out of place on a Flying Burrito Brothers album, that is pretty much what the album served up—no holds barred, lots of frantic unison playing between vocal, bass and guitar. And what about Gary's assertion that the demos they did were better than the final album? Well, he might have had a point there. Noel believes they were poorly served by people who Skid Row thought knew what they were doing, 'Peter Green was supposed to produce that album, but he wasn't well. So, Clifford Davis took it on and he didn't have a clue, but we didn't know he didn't have a clue—and the sound was really thin. That first album was badly recorded; we needed somebody like Felix Pappalardi who looked after Cream in the studio.' There are no engineer credits on the album, further adding to the impression of an album that suffered from a lack of professional production and post-production input. And the comparison Gary made with the demos recorded in Ireland is best shown by Brush's satirical take on life in a showband, 'Unco-op Showband Blues', which appears on both albums, but which loses a lot of crispness and clarity on *Skid*.

About the speed of his playing, Gary later told *Melody Maker*'s Chris Welch that Brush was just pushing him to play faster and faster: 'I didn't realise how fast I was playing. People think I concentrated on speed, but I didn't know what I was doing. I just thought all the other guitarists were faster than me and I needed to catch up ... then I couldn't slow down after that. It was a problem!'

But the musicianship demonstrated on the album showed the band could hold its own with the best the UK could offer. John Peel was a fan; they did several BBC sessions and when the album was eventually released in October 1970, it made the UK Top 30 and charted in Sweden, the start of a Swedish rock fan love affair with Gary that never ended.

With the album in the can, Skid Row set off for the obligatory UK club and college circuit, but caught a break playing five dates in Denmark, one at K.B. Hallen supporting Canned Heat and a few dates in Aarhus, where roadie Paul Scully recalls that 'I think we got paid in goulash'. But on a more positive note, they played a CBS reception in Copenhagen to celebrate the album's entry into the *Music Week* charts.

The last two gigs on this brief Scandinavian excursion, though, summed up what a shoestring operation CBS were running for the band. There was no hotel, so they had to sleep in the van and, in the middle of the night, it got so cold, they had to leave the van and literally run round it to keep warm.

They had laughs too. 'We had a big box transit,' says Paul Scully. 'Clifford Davis had given us money to buy a PA, so we bought a WEM, which was really hip in those days. One night me and Gary were dropping acid, pulled into this petrol station and just rolled out giggling our heads off. We did a gig that night at Clouds, in Derby, completely stoned, gone.'

Hardly off the boat from the tour, they got the big news—they were going to America. Nobody is quite sure how that happened, but the consensus is that as Davis was the manager of Fleetwood Mac, he had clout with promoters in the

States and may have suggested if they wanted to book Fleetwood Mac, they had to take Skid Row.

At the end of October 1970, off they went, flew to LAX, where their manager and a guy from Epic Records were waiting for them. Brush ran straight into a spot of bother: 'I see these guys looking at me, FBI or whatever. They keep me there for two hours, take me passport, the lads are waiting for me. Turns out I had the same name [as a guy] they were looking for. Checking me for drugs, everything.'

'We were really green kids from Ireland,' says Paul Scully. 'We didn't even have an itinerary. We got the dates, but no idea where we were playing. There was no real support for the band, we just had a good time. We only knew America from the movies. So going to LA and staying on Sunset Strip was a bit of a dream. All very magical.' Although the album did well in the UK, the band were in the States under sufferance as far as CBS were concerned. As Noel observes, 'everything was done hand to mouth. CBS not interested, it was all "Stick them in a gig here, take them out to dinner there, just keep them happy." We were then on $5 a day, and you can have what you want, drugs, booze, women, only don't ask for money.'

After settling matters with America's finest, the band headed off to the Whisky A Go Go for a five-night residency with a soul-funk band called Pollution, whose line-up included singer Dobie Gray. This was followed by a gig at the Fillmore West, fourth on the bill behind Ashton, Gardner & Dyke, Boz Scaggs and the headliners The Mothers Of Invention. There was so much gear on the stage that Skid Row were teetering right on the edge. One of the stage crew came up to Brush and asked him, '"Where do you want the monitors?" I said, "We don't use monitors." He thought we were crazy. We were the loudest band they had ever heard. Gary's echo wasn't working properly, so when he turned it on, it sounded like the sea coming in at 12 knots. And when we were on, all you could hear was this echo. I was furious. Afterwards, I grabbed that guy in the dressing room and pinned him up against the wall.'

Ted Carroll had purchased 'See America' tickets at $299 each, which meant once the band were in LA, they could make as many stops as required along the way back across the States. Gigs were slotted in as they moved eastwards. They played the Spectrum in Chicago with Ten Years After and then hit Detroit to play on the bill with The Allman Brothers and The Stooges. In the best traditions of southern gentlemen, all the band agree that the Allmans were very kind to them; Noel got into conversation with one of the drummers, Butch Trucks: 'He was great. We were chatting away and he gave me his address and invited me to stay.'

They were all in awe of the Brothers and Gary was especially taken with the dual guitar sound, Duane's slide guitar work, the idea of having two drummers—and that overall fusion of blues, jazz and country that gave the band its unique and instantly recognisable sound.

After that, it was Cleveland High School with Jethro Tull and finally they grabbed a slot at the Boston Tea Party at the end of November supporting Mountain. Like the Allmans, the members of Mountain were very gracious to their support band. Felix Pappalardi was getting into Irish music, so Paul Scully gave him a Chieftains record. At the time, Mountain were recording *Nantucket Sleighride*, which features an Irish jig refrain.

Backstage after the gig, Noel recounts an incident that showed a side of Gary's nature he found difficult to control: 'We were jamming in the dressing room, the door opens and in walks Leslie West. He walks over to the amp and starts laying down the most thunderous fuckin' riff. Gary starts playing and within two minutes, Leslie West has unplugged and walked out. The same thing happened with Peter Green. We went round to his house, we had nice cups of tea and the two of them started playing. Eventually, Peter stopped and said, "Listen, let's stop fuckin' each other up and start playing a bit of music."'

It would be easy just to write this off as a bit of adolescent showing off—remember, Gary was still only 18 in 1970—and to some degree it might have been. But Gary found it hard just to jam along with people without this competitive edge, which had more than a hint of seeking approval too. Another great Northern Ireland player, Henry McCullough, once persuaded Paul McCartney to let Gary come up and jam with Wings. Apparently, Paul was on the verge of pulling out Gary's lead himself. This may account for the fact that Gary didn't get invited to some of the big guitar events that, by dint of his talent, he had every right to expect—Eric Clapton's Crossroads Guitar Festival being a case in point. Even when fronting his own band, he could often be caught glancing across the stage during a fiery guitar burst, not so much to say, 'Hey guys, look at me', but more 'Hey guys, is this okay? Is this good enough?'

The other side to this, of course, is that he was a phenomenal talent—the undoubted star of Skid Row. One of his many show-stoppers was Robert Johnson's 'Ramblin' On My Mind'—just Gary on guitar and playing the bass drum like Duster Bennett. But for the most part, the Skid Row show was 100mph take-no-prisoners progressive rock—with added theatricals. One of the crew would hunker down behind the drums, Brush would jump on to his shoulders and jump right over the kit. The band got a mixed response; some of the West Coast hippies much preferred the stoned meanderings of The Grateful Dead, others just lapped it up. In Boston, a staunchly Irish town, the Hell's Angels made Brush an honorary member.

Offstage and between gigs, the band didn't really hang together. In LA, they stayed briefly at a hotel near the infamous Hyatt (Riot) House Hotel. Then they dossed down in an apartment belonging to a friend of Clifford Davis, halfway between LA and Santa Monica. Other than that, it was down to piling into one room at a Holiday Inn.

Roadies Frank Murray and Paul Scully, and Gary, were more of the same age and tended to go around in a group when they weren't making their own 'sleeping' arrangements. For example, Gary went off with a girl and spent Thanksgiving with her family. They also hung out at the home of Byrds manager Jim Dickson, courtesy of a Fleetwood Mac connection. Nineteen seventy saw the start of Mac's transition period, when the survival of the band was by no means assured. Dinky Dawson, one of Fleetwood Mac's main roadies and soundmen, came to LA to work with The Byrds.

Brush, by contrast, was not only abstemious, but very much frowned on the antics of the others, especially the night before a gig. Ted Carroll recounts one furious row with Brush: 'We were all out at Jim's place. They had this large aluminium cooking pot, which held about half a gallon of water. They kept all the grass in there and would boil up all this grass tea. We were invited there for dinner, had a nice time, smoked a joint and had some of this grass tea. Then I get a call from The Brush, "Where's the fuckin' practice amp?" It was in the back of the van having been in for repair.' They had a frank and fearless exchange of views on the matter, 'but he insisted he needed it now, that night—it was about half seven. So, I had to get in the van, stoned out of my mind and drive down the highway doing about 80mph and it felt like slow motion. I managed to get off at the right turn-off. This girlfriend of Clifford had an apartment off Sunset Boulevard. I walked up to the front door, just plonked the amp down. Brush came out. I just walked off and didn't say a word.'

Sylvia reckons that hanging out in LA almost put Gary in limbo because she attributes later panic attacks that Gary suffered to some very heavy grass he consumed out on the West Coast.

Projected gigs at New York's Fillmore East were cancelled, so they just left the gear at Boston airport ('it could still be there,' muses Noel) and flew home. Ted took back with him a large suitcase full of records to bolster his fledging mail-order record business (he went on to start the major reissues label Ace Records in 1978 with Roger Armstrong and Trevor Churchill). Ted decided he would leave but waited until February 1971 when Frank Murray got his driving licence and could take over driving the van. Once back in the UK, they played a dozen more gigs, ending up in Belfast on December 26, where Gary got the shock of his life.

Since his move to Dublin, Gary had hardly been home. Johnny Duhan says that after he had been staying with him for a month in 1968, 'Gary invited me to accompany him to Belfast on a rare home visit. His house, as I remember it, wasn't very homely … soon after we dropped our bags at his house … he dragged me off to meet several of his old friends … In each of the homes we visited, Gary was greeted with open arms not just by his old pals but by their parents also.'

Although Bobby would phone and did make the occasional trip to Dublin to see how Gary was getting on, Sylvia recalls only one trip back to Belfast before Christmas 1970. Gary was now the oldest of a family of five, his siblings being sisters Maggie, Pat and Michelle and brother Cliff. When Gary and Sylvia went to meet Bobby in Belfast, he told them that (just like before) the social services had been round because the children weren't attending school. Sylvia also noticed that Bobby had 'the shakes' and was ordering spirits over a hotel sandwich lunch. As well as all the other problems between Bobby and Winnie, matters got much worse as Bobby slid increasingly into alcoholism. Eventually, he was admitted to a mental hospital now called Knockbracken and from there to a day clinic. To his credit, he beat the drink problem and was sober for the rest of his life. But it was too late to save his marriage. While he was in hospital, Winnie left Castleview Road, taking Gary's siblings, and fled to her sister Ellen in Weston-Super-Mare. So, when Gary came home for Christmas in December 1970, he would have found an empty house, his father in hospital and his mother and family gone.

Although Gary knew only too well the problems at home, Sylvia says, 'it was a very traumatic, emotional time for Gary. He was very confused.' The break-up did have a profound effect on Gary and one he may never have reconciled. Children in that situation often feel irrationally that they were somehow to blame, that somehow they don't deserve to be happy for breaking up the family.

Gary was affected in other ways too; because of his difficult home life, he was always quite wary of people and never felt entirely safe in strange company. The natural maturity of his emotional responses seemed to stall in adolescence as he became profoundly possessive and jealous where women were concerned.

Sylvia recalls an incident in a bar when she was chatting to guitarist Ed Deane, Gary's sparring partner in the blues session so admired by Ivan Pawle. This time, however, Gary just marched up to Ed and tipped a pint of beer over his head. A bemused Ed asked what that was all about, to which Gary replied, 'You were talking to her for too long.'

Although this took some time to blossom, when Gary would stress-test relationships to breaking point almost by way of self-fulfilling prophecy (with men and women), he became a devoted family man, as if determined history was not going to repeat itself. With women, he became an almost desperate romantic, which didn't always serve him well. The way Gary conducted himself in private was also a symptom of his inner core, his driving force, the way he approached his music. For Gary, there were no half measures in anything; he took a binary view of life—on/off, black/white. All or nothing.

Gary was a very private person and rarely discussed his inner feelings with anybody. He had come from a background and an era in which men never revealed themselves for fear of appearing weak, often turning to violence or drink or both as a release from pent-up emotions, low self-esteem, the sense of failure. And Gary was working in the music business, an arena built on ego and self-absorption and therefore profoundly disinterested and unsympathetic concerning the driving force behind your own particular demons.

If the break-up of his family wasn't enough to contend with, by the time Gary went back to Belfast in December 1970, Sylvia was about four months pregnant. 'I wasn't on the pill because of the Catholic background. I got pregnant about six weeks after we moved to London. Up until then, it had just been luck and then the luck ran out.'

In January 1971, Gary and Sylvia moved out of east London and into a shared house in Belsize Avenue in north London with Paul Scully, Frank Murray, Ted Carroll and Eric Bell and his girlfriend Eleanor, who was also pregnant: 'She was from Cork and I'm from Tipperary, two Belfast guitarists, two pregnant southern girls. Eleanor had more family support; her mum and dad came over. It was very tough when Gary was on tour.' A daughter, Saoirse (pronounced 'Sursha'), was born in May 1971; her godfather was Johnny Duhan.

By this time, Skid Row were recording their second album. Clifford Davis still assumed the mantle of producer, but they were in the engineering hands of Martin Birch, who went on to engineer and produce, among others, Deep Purple, Iron Maiden, Black Sabbath, Whitesnake and Rainbow. The sound was richer and denser, especially on the heavier tracks, which were Martin's speciality. It was still a 'time is money' project, though; according to Brush, the whole lot was done in thirty-four hours, giving the album its title.

34 Hours allowed Gary the chance to flex his muscles across rock, country and jazz-rock, blistering wah-wah on one track, a well-controlled extended country solo on another and steel guitar effects on a third. No other band would have given Gary the freedom to take off across the wide sound palette offered by Skid Row. He explored pretty much every genre possible for the electric guitar in the rock idiom because essentially Brush didn't care what people thought about their music. He was determined they would play what they wanted to, how they wanted to and hoped that their unquestionable virtuosity would carry them through to the success he was convinced would be theirs.

However, *34 Hours* demonstrated the same kind of confusing eclecticism that dogged the first album without producing any really strong material. A music press critic at the time commented, in what was a positive review, that 'the music is very far out in any sense and meant to make the listener hear (and feel) the sounds—awkward, uncomfortable, physical, abrasive, vicious, dynamic are words that come to mind'. To which the response has to be, 'How many record buyers crave that experience?' In the case of *34 Hours*, the answer was not many.

With the album done, at the end of July 1971, the band took off for their second tour of North America. Frank Murray had gone off to work with the fledgling Thin Lizzy; his place was taken by former Granny's Intentions band member Pete Cummins, who joined Paul Scully on the road with the band. Pete recalls that the tour actually started in Canada: 'The gigs were Skid Row gigs in Montreal and Ottawa and then some place out east in the mountains, a kind of campsite place. We were due to play there on a Saturday, but on the Friday night, the organisers came up to the cabin to see if we'd come down for a jam. Brush said no, but the others went down and I played bass for about an hour. Brush was not happy about that.'

Entering the States, they went to Cincinnati to play a big festival where Cactus (a precursor band to Beck, Bogert & Appice) were headlining and then over to the West Coast and the Whisky A Go Go for a series of gigs, first playing support to the British afro-rock band Osibisa and then Skid Row headlining in their own right. It was at the Whisky where one of those semi-mythical rock stories unfolded. As Brush remembers it, 'We start playing and somebody shouts out, "Play 'Paddy McGinty's Goat'!" It turns out that Rod Stewart & The Faces are in there with Robert Plant and John Bonham. Next minute, Robert's onstage and playing the drums and John Bonham's singing.' John also jumped on Noel's kit and started hammering out a solo, prompting Pete Cummins to grab the mike and scream 'ego tripper' at full volume—an act of 'disrespect' that wound Brush right up. This went down in the annals as 'Skid Row jamming with Led Zeppelin'. Well, almost.

After the gig, Skid Row realised they hadn't been given any money for a hotel and had nowhere to stay. John Bonham stepped up and paid for the band to stay at his hotel, probably the Hyatt House, where the drummer famously rode a motorbike around one of the floors. Noel was in the lift with John: 'I think the Mothers were in town with Aynsley Dunbar on drums and John said, "What a great drummer. I wish I was half as good as him." To which Noel replied, "What?? You're a brilliant drummer. I wish I was half as good as you!"'

Like Blanche Dubois in *A Streetcar Named Desire*, Skid Row were relying on 'the kindness of strangers' because they were getting precious little support from CBS. There were no records in the shops and nothing playing on the radio. This meant ticket sales were poor and promoters were cancelling gigs. Pete says, 'You'd be in a Holiday Inn and you'd hear that tomorrow night's gig was off. So, you would have to lay over there a few days just kicking your heels.'

This allowed plenty of time for the resentments in the band to fester. Brush was not happy about Pete, Paul and Gary slipping away to smoke dope; they in turn were getting fed up with what they regarded as Brush's dictatorial attitude. Depending on who you talk to, Paul and Pete were either fired in San Diego or walked out. Noel reckons they were stranded somewhere with no driver and were eventually driven back to the airport by a passing fan who'd been at a gig.

Back home, they had a go at recording a third album: seven tracks were laid down, but never released, appearing several years later on the Castle label. History repeated itself—tracks full of excellent playing, but with no coherence, that same frustrating potpourri of influences, nothing that you could latch on to as the Skid Row style, and songs that weren't that memorable.

Brush concedes the mistakes made: 'If we'd stayed with just one thing, the heavy blues, we would have been alright, but we confused too many people. A simple country song, then something in 11/4 time? Nobody would do that, it's bad for business. I take responsibility for everything that went wrong. You couldn't tell me anything. You couldn't advise me in any way. And everybody tried. Nothing to do with Gary or Noel.'

Gary and Brush had a complicated relationship; Brush knew all too well that the success of the band depended on Gary. Noel says, at the start anyway, 'we really liked each other, we felt we were brothers, it was a love and we would have done anything for each other'. He says that Brush did look out for Gary and did warn Gary about who those would try and get close to him by telling him what a great player he was. Others felt that Brush was maybe a bit harsh with Gary and Gary himself eventually rebelled against Brush much as he had against Bobby.

By his own admission, at eighteen, although outwardly this shy, quiet teenager, inside Gary was a firestorm of raging hormones that exploded into sound as soon as he plugged in his guitar. Speaking to Chris Welch, he later admitted that back then, 'I was probably stoned out of my head all of the time. I'd come on stage with my mind occupied with various thoughts and be very vicious. You are deadly serious about life and you just want to kill everybody and blow everybody up. That affects your whole attitude to your playing.'

In December 1971, Gary decided to leave. He told Noel first, 'because I was easier to tell than Brush. He came into the dressing room and told me he was leaving. I was shocked. I didn't know what to say. I think I said something like, "Please don't talk about us when you're gone." He didn't give a reason, but looking back I can see he needed success, he needed fame, he needed to prove he was as good a guitar player as anybody.'

Noel reflects that although the band eventually failed, 'Skid Row was like your first love affair. You never forget it and I loved it for all the right reasons. There was no ulterior motive, for me it wasn't money, it wasn't image or anything like that. We worked fuckin' hard because we loved it. There wasn't a gig where we didn't come off wringing wet and drinking loads to get rehydrated again. Most of the time, we were sent out with nothing, but we thought it was par for the course. This was rock'n'roll. And Gary was a young kid, glowing with this beautiful vibe, a life force, the energy of youth. And because he was inexperienced, the innocence was wonderful.'

Realistically, though, Brush reckons that even if Skid Row had broken through, Gary wouldn't have stayed: 'We were three individuals who played together because it was great. But if any of us could do it on our own, we would have. Everyone one wants to call their own shots. … It wasn't meant to be. It happened the way it happened. For a couple of years, it was the most beautiful and unbelievable playing. Everything you could possibly think of. We were all in it together and we developed a way of playing. You see, the difference between Skid Row and Thin Lizzy was that you could copy them; you could bring somebody in to copy the licks. But you couldn't copy us. We would play the same song completely differently on different nights. We could play without conversation. You didn't have to force it; you didn't have to work out what you were doing. We were completely spontaneous. And Gary was so wonderful. But Gary leaving had to happen.'

Skid Row had come out of nowhere and bravely tried to take on the world with some seriously uncompromising progressive music. They had honed their act, used good equipment, threw twenty sorts of shapes at audiences and, courtesy of some heavyweight agency and management backing, played with the best of the best.

But Gary's departure pretty much killed the band. Eric Bell was drafted in to play some live dates, before Paul Chapman became the band's full-time guitarist as further unsuccessful attempts were made to release a third album. Chapman left in 1972 and later joined UFO. Brush had a number of line-ups flying under the Skid Row banner during the 1970s and then in 2009 released an album entitled *Mad Dog Woman* comprising new recordings and re-workings of Skid Row songs (three further self-released albums since then have ploughed a similar furrow, the most easily accessible being 2021's *The Best Of Brush Shiels Vol.1* on YouTube).

For Gary, the next couple of years took him up a very steep learning curve, not just the byzantine murkiness of the music business, but life itself.

03

GRINDING OUT THE GARY MOORE BAND

As Skid Row slithered to a halt, Brush and Noel found themselves both a victim of their own naivety and let's say the creative accounting that was (and still is) standard operating procedure in the music business. As Noel ruefully reflects, 'We really didn't have a clue. It was the old Dublin attitude, "Oh, everything'll be okay, it'll be grand, let's just do it for the craic." We didn't have bank accounts, all we wanted to do was play. That really costs us. On this island where everybody obeyed the Ten Commandments, we never believed anybody would tell lies, or do anything wrong. But we were torn to pieces; when the band broke up, we owed Clifford Davis money—how did that happen? We had fuck all. No business acumen at all.'

It doesn't appear the band were given any sort of cash-in-hand advance, but they did have equipment, a van, two trips to the States, studio time for recording and (very) basic living expenses—all of which would have been clawed back from quite limited record sales and gig money. If the claim was that they didn't earn back, they would find themselves in debt, without any money to do an independent audit—and very little to show for all their hard work. Worse still, from their point of view, Brush reckons that Gary got a £28,000 advance from Davis to start his own band—money that was very quickly spent on a truck and gear—which, Brush claims, Davis cross-collateralised against what he reckoned he was owed by Skid Row, which pushed them further into debt. Only in 2000 did Brush manage to recoup a meagre £1,200 by hiring somebody to chase the money.

Gary probably set up his deal with Davis before he left Skid Row at the end of 1971, after which Gary went to Dublin to try and recruit new members for his band. He already had one slot filled. So enamoured was he of The Allman Brothers' twin guitar sound that he brought back from the States a guitarist called Chuck Carpenter. In 2013, Chuck Carpenter was involved in a company making an illuminated guitar pick called a Tric Pick. On the site, which now appears defunct, this story appeared:

'Chuck first remembers seeing Gary when he opened the show for the power trio Skid Row, in 1970. Gary had moved to the front of the stage to hear and see Chuck's performance ... Chuck was asked to tour with Skid Row as sound technician and temporary tour manager as Brush had fired the crew in Los Angeles—a role he performed with Skid Row until Gary picked him as his first choice for guitarist with the first GMB (Gary Moore Band). While working together they would play guitars in the hotels, developing a bond that would last for years ... Gary and Chuck would jam on The Allman Brothers' "In Memory Of Elizabeth Reed" and [songs by] Mountain amongst others, finally leaving Skid Row to embark on a career together.' Gary and Chuck were together in Dublin where, according to the Tric Pick website, they 'found themselves mixing it up in the local Wimpy Bar with a couple of taxi drivers! Fighting over women and Wimpy Burgers!'

On Phil Lynott's recommendation, Gary found his drummer in Pearse Kelly, a well-respected player on the Belfast beat scene, who had relocated to Dublin to escape the Troubles. Also recruited from Belfast was bass player Sam Cook, an old friend of Gary's who had introduced him to Dave Lewis. As was fashionable at the time, bands would be sent to the country to 'get it together' (like Traffic). However, if the new band members thought they would be housed in some rural idyll, they were much mistaken. Clifford Davis plonked them in the middle of nowhere in County Mayo, in the far west of Ireland, well away from the pubs of Dublin; in fact, far from anywhere and reminiscent of the remote cottage in *Withnail & I*.

Pearse recalls, 'the van was taken away and we were left stranded, middle of winter and bitterly cold. We used to divide up the chores: who would go and get turf for the fire, who would go to the pub for groceries, which doubled as a trading store. There was a phone outside the post office which you had to wind up so you could talk to the operator. Sam would always have excuses [about] why he couldn't do his chores. When we were in Dublin before we went out the city, the drug squad would frighten the publicans into not serving anybody with long hair. But Sammy always had a showband haircut, so he would say, "Well, I'll see you later." And in he went.'

If Clifford Davis thought he was putting distance between the band and the booze, then he was sorely mistaken. Pearse reckons he put them in a worse position than if they'd stayed in Dublin: 'The only people in the village were the eldest sons of families, fifty-year-old bachelors who'd got lumbered with the farm. But it was four acres of rock, you couldn't do anything with it. So, they were all into making poitín (moonshine) and they'd all been busted for it at one time or another. We'd only been there about ten minutes when one of them came round to see if it would be okay if he set up a still. We were due to go to London in a month, but because the place was so rural, it only had a court every three months. The idea was that even if we got busted, by the time the case came up, we'd be long gone. So, we spent most of our time down there making poitín and testing it out. It was absolutely serious stuff. The first gig we did after our stint in County Mayo was Queen's University Belfast on a Sunday. There was no drinking in Northern Ireland on a Sunday. We had never performed together sober. Gary's father did an emergency run to the golf club to get us some alcohol.'

So not much work was done during the first few weeks of the band. But as soon as they got to London, they were packed off to Germany for a tour, adding a keyboard player, Jan Schelhaas, to the line-up. Jan had been in the National Head Band (also managed by Clifford Davis) with drummer Lee Kerslake (later with Uriah Heep and Ozzy Osbourne). The band folded in November 1971, so Davis suggested Jan might want to meet up with Gary. They met, there was no audition, Jan was in the band and so in early 1972, off they went for a few dates in Germany, including the Zoom Club in Frankfurt.

They had two roadies, a small Irish guy called Davy who, Jan says, 'was four foot nothing but could lift anything' and a gentle giant from Liverpool called Zara, who 'just stood there while people hit him', which came in handy when Davy and Zara got into a fight with the roadies from Chicken Shack. The band had a large Luton van, which took three people up front including the driver, and anybody else had to travel in the back with all the gear. Whenever the back of the van was opened up, huge clouds of dope would come wafting out. This caused a certain amount of concern as they approached borders, but that wasn't all, as Jan recalls: 'We had this situation where Sammy had a driving licence, but he was a terrible driver whereas Davy was a great driver but had no licence. So, we always had Davy driving until we approached the border—when they would swap. The only trouble was that this Luton van had an overhang; Sammy wasn't really aware of this, there was a camber in the road and we were coming up to a Portakabin full of East German border guards. Sammy didn't judge this right and knocked the Portakabin off its blocks.

'There was all sorts of German swearing going on and I was bricking it. Pearse was out cold having got completely stoned and yes, when the back of the van was opened up, there was a massive fog of dope smoke. They got us all in the main building, but I don't think they really wanted all the hassle and just wanted to get rid of us. But Sammy had a bit of a thick skin and instead of quitting while he was ahead, insisted on getting his passport stamped. So, the guard just stamped his hand in frustration.'

Worse was yet to come. All thought Chuck was an excellent player and working well with Gary. The Allman Brothers sound was nailed. But they were dealt a blow when it transpired that Chuck's visa had expired, which they didn't find out until they tried to get back into the country through Heathrow. Chuck was unceremoniously grabbed by immigration officials and deported back to the States. According to Jan, Gary drafted in former John Dummer Blues Band singer and guitarist Nick Pickett to play a few gigs while he planned the next move. By this time, Gary decided that Sammy wasn't really working out ('a square peg in a round hole,' according to Pearse) so Gary needed to find a new bass player as well.

Gary was barely out of his teens in 1972 and attempting to put a band together, which had already got off to a rocky start. He could be forgiven for taking a line of least resistance and just trying to get hold of good musicians, whether or not they were the best fit for music he wanted to play. Philip Donnelly was a fine country-style guitar player who had been out in the States with Donovan but was now back in Dublin. Pearse reckons that Phillip 'talked his way into the band' and brought with him a bass player, Frank Boylan, who was well known on the Irish beat and folk scene having played with The Creatures and Mellow Candle. Both were accomplished musicians, but not the guys you would have immediately thought of to play in an Allmans-style rock band. Briefly, too, Gary experimented with a second drummer, John Donnelly (no relation), but that didn't get out of the rehearsal room.

The line-up of Gary, Phillip, Frank, Pearse and Jan rehearsed to get the CBS deal, resulting in their only recording *Grinding Stone*. Jan recalls, 'we rehearsed in this place in The Mall and the man from CBS came down to okay the deal. I think he just wanted to sign Gary, really; he just heard a couple of numbers and went, "Yeah, that's fine, fine." So, I think the deal was already done.'

Approaching Christmas 1972, the band got their presents early from Sound City courtesy of the advance from CBS. Jan says they were like kids in a sweet shop: 'I got a Hammond organ and a Leslie cabinet and I made sure I got the Green Shield stamps; I had like £600 worth of stamps to stick in the books. My tongue! We didn't really understand our equipment. We got this big JBL system, but without a crossover. So, we had a massive PA and couldn't understand why it wasn't working. We had a Mellotron that broke down after a week and these Acoustic amps—up close you couldn't hear them, but at the back of the hall, they are blowing people's heads off. Gary was okay, all he wanted was a 50-watt top and Marshall cab.'

Gary assumed full-on leadership of the band. 'He was a man with a mission,' says Pearse. 'He never had the guitar out of his hands, and he was a very mature nineteen-year-old, more like twenty-five. He took on the whole responsibility of the band. He knew where he was going, just not sure how to get there. But he was great to work for, never put anybody down, but he was a fuckin' workaholic. We rehearsed at Ginger Johnson's Iroko Club in Hampstead. Lots of musicians used it—Thin Lizzy, Average White Band, Cat Stevens. When we weren't gigging, we'd be rehearsing in there from 10–6 with an hour for lunch. That's the sort of guy he was. And he was harder on himself than those around him.'

The album was recorded late 1972/early 1973 at George Martin's Air Studios, overseen once again by Martin Birch. 'It took far longer than it should have done,' says Pearse, 'because we would have cracked open a few bottles and rolled a few joints to get tuned up.' Jan though thinks it came together pretty quickly: 'Gary had all the basic tunes before we got to the studio.' This makes sense because the band had been road testing the material for months.

Unlike working in the National Head Band, Jan reckons there wasn't much democracy in the band. Despite his age, Gary pretty much called the shots and while Pearse says he was quite happy to follow where Gary led, Philip Donnelly wasn't and tensions built up as Philip was reduced to playing rhythm at Gary's insistence. Frank tended to side with Phil on this and tectonic plates of the band started to rub together as the album—perhaps appropriately titled *Grinding Stone*—progressed. There is a suggestion that resentments grew because Gary would work on the album on his own, even to the point where (according to unsubstantiated rumour) somebody might listen back to a section and say, 'that's nice. I don't remember playing that.' To which the supposed reply was 'Well, that's because you didn't.'

Nobody could deny Gary's ability, but this wasn't The Beat Boys or The Barons, whose members were in awe of him and simply followed where he led. Gary was trying to dominate seasoned musicians with a professional track record—and egos—of their own. Truth to tell, he wasn't a natural leader; he never quite understood that while the leader was in charge and carried the responsibility, nevertheless, in certain situations, tact and diplomacy would get better results than shouting.

When the album was released in March 1973, the band were in for an unwelcome surprise. On the back cover are six bubbles or capsules in which appear the photos of Gary and Pearse, but also a bass player called John Curtis who joined the band shortly after the album was released but didn't play on it. The other three bubbles are blank with Phil, Frank and Jan's work reduced to a brief acknowledgement of 'contributions'. The band launched the album at the Lyceum in a double-header with Argent, so they still existed as a unit at the point of release. But looking at the back cover of the album made it pretty clear, in the most unsubtle way, that the band's days were numbered.

Nobody can offer an explanation as to why this happened or at whose instigation. The most likely scenario was because the band were hardly earning any money, Clifford Davis had insisted they be reduced to a trio—and that he wanted the new line-up to feature on the cover because that would be the line-up touring the album. Gary took the brunt of the blame, but he probably didn't have much say. Davis took a proprietary view of the bands he managed; as far as he was concerned, they were his property, to the extent that in 1974, he toured a 'fake' Fleetwood Mac using the band Stretch.

Grinding Stone made no impression on the charts and was largely confined to a footnote in Gary's history. More recently, though, it has undergone a reappraisal with some Gary Moore fans citing it right up there among their favourites of his albums. While *Grinding Stone* exhibits none of the abrupt shifts of time and pace that were the hallmark of Skid Row recordings, that band did leave its mark on Gary. For one recorded show, Skid Row started with a drum solo while the eponymous opening track of Gary's first solo album starts with a quirky ending sequence before a drum pattern from Pearse introduces the song proper.

Gary was a long way to finding his voice as a composer and musician, so it is hardly surprising that given that he wrote all the songs, they should be redolent of his main influences at the time. These combined not just the Allmans' gutbucket boogie and easy-rolling freedom jazz with clean, biting guitar lines and a tumbling southern-fried rhythm section but also the soaring layered Afro-Cuban rock sound of Santana, as heard on their gorgeous 1972 tone poem *Caravanserai*. The long set pieces on *Grinding Stone* were well constructed, carried off with some aplomb, fire and precision by all the musicians.

The one track that stood out in contrast to the rest was 'Sail Across The Mountain', a template of the haunting 'little boy lost' melancholy of Gary's trademark ballads that would ultimately result in some of his biggest hits and best loved songs. It is a precarious business trying to attribute an artist's songs to real-life events, to assume that songs that sound very personal are indeed autobiographical. Artists will often deny the link—and often they are right, or they will declare that listeners take what they want from the song. In Gary's case, though, and in the light of how his personal and emotional life unfolded, it seems he did give expression to his inner feelings through his songs born from his reticence about confiding in people, having few friends outside the business. Whatever emotional pain he might have been feeling was sublimated in the songs.

'Sail Across The Mountain' reveals the strain he was under with lines like 'I

GRINDING OUT THE GARY MOORE BAND **73**

need someone to come along and take this weight right off my shoulder before I fall' and 'How I got here I can't say / It was my own fault / I admit I should have learned / From watching others I have seen.' Because there was no doubt the band was struggling and there were signs that a shake-up was coming. Jan recalls seeing bassist John Curtis hanging round the rehearsals some time before he was brought in. Even easy-going Pearse was getting fed up: 'The biggest hassle we had was whether or not we were going to get paid on a Monday. I think Gary was in the same boat. I did get pissed off with the whole thing in the end. We had a folk bass player, a country guitar and (with John Donnelly briefly) a Mahavishnu-type drummer. It wasn't where I wanted it to go. I was more into having a Cream/ Mountain three piece. I actually packed my suitcase and was heading towards Finchley Road station, left a note for Gary in my flat. But he never saw it, and I never let on, because as I was walking along, he pulled up in a car with John Curtis and just said, "Everybody is sacked except you."'

John Curtis was a session bass player doing advertising jingles and TV shows like *Whatever Happened To The Likely Lads?* (including backing vocals). He was living in Belsize Park, near where Gary lived, and drank in the same pub as Gary and Phil Lynott—which is where he met Gary. 'He said, "I'm forming a band. Are you interested?" Next thing, we are down a big rehearsal studio in Chalk Farm and all this gear starts coming in, roadies, big truck. I thought, *What have we got here?* I thought it was just some little tinpot band. But it felt like a proper organisation.' John confirms that he did meet the other guys in the band before he officially joined, which is what aroused Jan's suspicions.

John says he had never been in a band before that 'meant business like this one did and it was a steep learning curve. We were rehearsing eight hours a day for about two weeks before we did the first gig. We had the police in a couple of times telling us to turn down, there were people outside with baseball bats waiting to smash all the gear up. The place wasn't properly sound-proofed and we were *loud*. The first night they came in, we stopped. The second time we were doing "Spirit", it was a twenty-minute number and we were really cooking. We were halfway through and weren't going to stop for anybody. The police just stood back and watched, "Oh, that's very good, now would you mind turning it down a bit?" They were very polite.'

On stage, says John, 'We went to war. We were conquering the country bit by bit. We'd go somewhere, nobody would know who the hell we were and then we'd be invited back—only now we are headlining. We needed the album to take off, but it didn't.' Nor was it likely to with, yet again, no effort put into promotion; the album wouldn't necessarily be in the shops where they played and there was little if any airplay. And while they built up a loyal following, which turned up to every gig, it wasn't big enough.

As well as John, another new addition to the crew was Dave 'Mojo' Lennox, who knew Gary from Dublin days when he played keyboards in The Uptown Band. 'I remember watching Skid Row doing a soundcheck with about six other guitarists all hanging around, and I watched them literally wilt when Gary started. He was playing a Les Paul Junior through a Vox AC30 with his back to everyone—and he really was in a different league. Gary was one of the few naturally gifted musicians I have worked with in my life, and I've worked with Herbie Hancock, Al Green and Archie Shepp—and I would put Gary right up there. There was a lot of criticism of Gary for playing too loud, and I would agree, but he had a hell of a lot to say, though. I met up again with Gary again in Belsize Park when I had no job, no gig, no money, nothing. I ended up crashing with Jan Schelhaas in the same house as Gary. At that point, the five piece was still going and I used to watch the band rehearse and you could see there was something going on between Gary and Phil.'

Dave hadn't been in Gary's orbit for long when he became embroiled in what became one of the most talked about episodes in guitar history. By mid-1973, Peter Green had virtually dropped out of public life. He left Fleetwood Mac in May 1970, although helped out briefly in 1971, when Jeremy Spencer left during a US tour. His eccentric behaviour is now the stuff of rock legend—giving away possessions, threatening his accountant with a gun, becoming a Howard Hughes-style recluse with excessively long fingernails and so on. What nobody realised at the time was that Peter had an undiagnosed mental illness (probably exacerbated by LSD) in which thought processes are vague and illogical, the person loses all drive and becomes apathetic and isolated. As the 70s gave way to the 80s, his condition worsened, a tragic outcome for a musician of superlative talents as a songwriter and singer, but above all as a blues guitar player with a touch and tone to die for.

While Peter was going through his phase of possession disposal, he offered his famous Les Paul to Snowy White who declined, instead trying to persuade Peter to hang on to it. Not to be deterred, Peter instead turned to Gary, who was very much his protégé. The guitar was special, ironically, because it was faulty; the exact nature of the fault has been hotly debated for decades, but it seems it was a combination of a factory fault and the incorrectly replaced pickups following a repair job. The net result was a one-off guitar, producing an exquisitely soulful 'far away' sound that was nigh on impossible to emulate on other guitars. Of course, there is no such thing as a magical guitar, only a magical guitarist—and the real value of the guitar was how it sounded in the hands of a master, and that ubiquitous if illogical idea that some of the magic might just rub off.

The shorthand version of the story is that Peter offered to sell the guitar to Gary who replied that he couldn't afford it. Peter then said, 'Sell your guitar and give me what you get for it.' This sounds like a simple face-to-face, done-and-dusted conversation and Gary himself has said that Peter approached him one evening at the Marquee. But according to Dave Lennox, the process was far more protracted. Negotiations were under way, but Gary had no phone, 'so he asked me that if Peter rang, would I take messages and let him know? When Peter did come on the phone at times it was impossible to understand him, he was in such an awful state at the time. You couldn't get a sensible word out of him. I used to say to him, "Can you get your Dad on the phone?" The father was great, you could talk to him, no problem. So, these calls went backwards and forwards for about two or three weeks, possibly longer, where I would be taking a message to Gary and relaying one back to Peter. Eventually, it was established that Peter did want to sell the guitar and the agreed price was whatever Gary could get for his Les Paul Junior. So, I'm in the car like a shot, get to Gary's, tell him what has happened and he says, "Take me down to Denmark Street, now." Off we go, I sat in the car. He walked into the first shop and I had only got about halfway down a cigarette, when he came back out.'

Gary had gone into Guitar Village just round the corner from Denmark Street in Shaftesbury Avenue. By coincidence, guitarist Bernie Marsden was in the shop. About a year older than Gary, Bernie had known him since Skid Row days. In Bernie's diary, there is an entry for October 23, 1970 for a Skid Row gig at the Country Club where Bernie got up and jammed, 'great bunch of lads' he wrote, then at the bottom of the page he'd scribbled, 'Gary Moore brilliant.' That day in the shop Bernie says Gary got £140 for his guitar and that's what he paid Peter. For some reason, Dave didn't go and collect the guitar, that job fell to Philip Donnelly, who brought the guitar back in the case that once belonged to Eric Clapton.

A story has permeated the guitar world that Gary only got the guitar on a promise to Peter that if he ever wanted back, Gary would resell it to him—and that Peter did make that request, which Gary refused. It is a 'code of honour' that such an arrangement exists between guitarists who trade instruments between each other. But Dave Lennox, who was backwards and forwards on the phone for weeks doing the deal, insists that there was no such stipulation at the time—and there is no evidence Peter ever did ask for it back. Peter did appear at the studio where Gary was recording his second solo album (the first solo album under his own name), *Back On The Streets*, in 1979, and apparently walked over to the guitar, stroked it gently as if in remembrance of times past and walked away. He was quoted later as saying one reason he didn't want it back was that it was too heavy. However, there is more to come on the story of Gary and the Peter Green Les Paul.

Dave moved out of the shared house with Gary and into a flat with Pearse in Lythos Road, a few miles away, by which time the band was down to a trio. Initially Dave took on the job of soundman but became more involved in helping Gary run the band, as relations with Clifford Davis soured. He had already prevented Gary playing on Mike Heron's first solo album; Pete Townshend stepped in. Gary asked Dave to come to a meeting, which was really a showdown between Gary and Clifford and his assistant, Bill Gillingham. 'They were being very critical of Gary saying things like, "Oh, you'll never make it. You can't sing. You're an alright guitar player, but there's loads of them out there." They were really putting the guy down. I flipped and kinda went for them. I think the lack of gigs was a problem and some problem with CBS as well. After the split with Davis, the agent John Sherry booked the gigs and I took over as road manager. There was a resurgence of interest and gigs were coming in. We also did three nights at the Zoom Club in Germany.' One of the roadies was Bill Hindmarsh, who shared a flat with Gary at 11 Larch Road, Cricklewood, another part of the north-west London enclave that was home to various members of Skid Row, The Gary Moore Band, Thin Lizzy and their crew, wives and girlfriends in the early 70s.

'After the first night in Frankfurt,' recalls Bill, 'Pearse had this woman in tow and went nightclubbing with her. He had a great time, until he had to pay for the drinks. That night's gig money was forfeited because Pearse had the band money with him.'

Neither was Dave Lennox a stranger to the odd tipple. 'As the road manager, every evening, I met the promoter and the bottle of whiskey would come out. The last night I went in to get the money from the promoter and we put away a bottle of whiskey each.'

During the life of the band, there was heavy drinking and prodigious dope smoking—from poitín to pot. But what about Gary? He always reckoned that the early years were the 'wild years': he did his fair share of dope and acid in

Dublin and was no stranger to a pint. But nobody from that period recollects serious imbibing; he took his responsibilities as a band leader seriously and in Dave Lennox's words, was 'squeaky clean'.

But if Gary had started viewing the world through the bottom of a glass, then few could have blamed him: he was desperately trying to keep his band together. While he might have been off the drugs and booze, Gary did suffer from anxiety attacks, and Bill Hindmarsh says Gary was prescribed tranquilizers, possibly recklessly, by one of the 'Dr Feelgoods' known to musicians. And away from the band, his personal life was no less troubled.

Gary and Sylvia were far too young to be parents; all the childcare fell to Sylvia while Gary was on tour, rehearsing or in the studio—on top of which, Gary was playing away from home right from the time Skid Row came to London. 'Frank Murray, used to let things drop,' says Sylvia. 'There was this Norwegian girl, and when they went to the States, they all screwed around, but that didn't bother me so much because that was there and it didn't come home. But even so, once I was pregnant, I felt very pissed off and insecure. Then these girls turned up with the band, sisters—and they made me feel old and I was only twenty. They caused a lot of problems.' Yet after Saoirse was born, 'he went out and bought himself a white suit and at one point we were going to get married'.

'These girls,' the sisters, were Suzie, Jeannie, Donna, Ceri (also known as Carrie back then) and Cathy Campbell. Jeannie was sixteen in early 1971 (she would be seventeen in August) and living in Exeter while attending Exeter College of Art. In April that year, she went to see Skid Row in Weston-Super-Mare and returned to her flat with Gary. She says Gary subsequently visited her in Exeter and then she moved to London at his behest, and started studying art at Goldsmiths College, moving in with Gary, Bill Hindmarsh and his girlfriend, her sister Ceri.

Over the next two years, the relationship with Gary developed; they attended the wedding of Jeannie's eldest sister Cathy to drummer John Lingwood, who at the time was the drummer with Steamhammer (her sister Donna was seeing Steamhammer's Martin Pugh and apparently band member Martin Quittenton was also involved with one of the Campbell sisters). For Jeannie, though, Gary was the one: 'I was spellbound by Gary. He stood out from the crowd.'

At the same time, Gary and Sylvia's relationship was breaking down. They spent blocks of time apart as Sylvia took their daughter off travelling in Europe, first to France and then Germany—and Sylvia also moved flats around north-west London; sometimes Gary was with her as they tried to make a go of it.

Like Sylvia and the other in women in Gary's life to come, Jeannie saw the intensely romantic side of Gary, bouncing around like an eager puppy: 'He kept asking me to marry him, which made me laugh. We went for picnics in Regent's Park, cooked at home, listened to Hendrix, Incredible String Band and Peter Green records.' Living in the same house as the couple, Ceri says 'they were in awe of each other's creative talents'. While she says they were both passionate and fiery people, Jeannie paints a picture of the kind of quiet domesticity seemingly in contrast to his relationship with Sylvia. She was initially attracted to an edgy, slightly dangerous musician; now, she would have much preferred some stability and security of her own.

Jeannie makes a telling comment when she says Gary was 'in love with love. He enjoyed the journey and I think was trying to find a mother, lover and friend all in the same woman, something that is very hard to find.' This suggests an emotional immaturity, constructing an idealised notion of being in a relationship with a woman, until the prospect of commitment loomed, and then, either metaphorically or actually, he would run away. At the same time, he was hyper-sensitive to anything that felt to him like rejection and needed the undivided attention of whoever he was with.

And this is how eventually it ended with Jeannie; after about eighteen months, she felt that Gary needed to put more into the relationship: 'I told him the magic had gone out of it.' Gary took this to mean it was over. Jeannie and her sister Donna were both at a Marquee gig, sometime late in 1973. It is unclear if this was a Gary Moore Band session or just Gary sitting in, which he did often. At the end of the gig, they all drove off in a taxi, the intention being, assumed Jeannie, to drop Donna off. But when they got to Donna's flat, Gary got out as well, turned to Jeannie and said, 'Sorry, I'm going with Donna.' Just before this fateful day, 'Gary had given me a gold ring he had had for years and bought me a white Moroccan beaded dress. I had thought this was his way of trying to get back together again. Now I thought it was some way of saying goodbye, a parting gift.' But she was more than just confused. She got back to their flat in Larch Road and locked herself in her room. Next day, she went round to Donna's flat to confront them and made what she calls 'a pathetic attempt to cut my wrists in the bathroom'. Gary took her to hospital, where she pleaded with him to reconsider, but to no avail.

Gary didn't move in with Donna straight away but was still at Larch Road. Jeannie eventually moved out to south London to be nearer her college. Her sister

Ceri says that after the split with Gary, Jeannie turned her back on art in favour of dancing, in which sphere she became quite successful.

In November 1973, the band played those dates at the Zoom Club. While he was out there, Gary wrote an overwrought poem or song on the back of a Dunhill cigarette packet dated 13th, concerning his lost love affair with Jeannie. He mentions her paintings and her eyes, something he often marvelled over.

I toy with the idea of self-destruction
Pace the room as a caged animal
On a mountain with no foothold to cling to
Wishing only for your love
The songs are meaningless now
The words are all blackness to me
Wish my next break was my last one
Instant peace, eternity
All your wondrous paintings on the wall
Like teardrops hung to dry in the afternoon sun
That was once ours
I don't care what anyone sees in the world
They are only instruments by which one can
Take feelings through their bodily exit to be
Displayed to the cynical jokers, fools and angels
And you were the angel who
Came to me before
Who shone your lamp of sweet innocences
Upon one so cold and hard, to make him feel for the first time that love had come to stay forever
I was blind to your dissatisfaction hoping it
Would pass and leave you as perfect as always
I am a fool who thrives on self-pitying situations
Instead of respecting your wishes to be free (who is truly free?)
And try to turn your beautiful eyes to my broken heart
If I don't make it, it's only final-proof of my every growing cowardice

Two days later, on November 15, he wrote somewhat less pleading, more bitter words. While there is no direct reference to Jeannie, it is hard to imagine this was some totally unconnected song. The confusions in it are manifest and probably reflect the fact that despite having ended the relationship, Gary really didn't know his own mind at the time. Bill says Gary left the two poems/songs in the flat they shared, saying he'd pick them up if he ever needed them, but he never did. There was a song called 'Jeannie' in the band repertoire, but the sole bootleg recording, from a gig at Bogart's in Birmingham, is of such poor quality that it is impossible to tell if the following were the actual words to the song:

You've taken everything I have to give
Even took my will to live and left me in a world of pain
But still I love to see you, to touch your gentle face
And hold you once again
Every day now is the same to me
Confusion my only friend
And when it's dark, I know you'll come back once more
To open up the wound
The reasons don't mean anything
The truth too hard to face
There's nothing to believe in
The finish of the race
Don't care if I don't breathe again
Don't care if I don't see
Don't care if I can't hear no more
If you don't care about me
And I know I won't go to heaven
Serve me right to burn in the devil's flame
But the hell I'm living in today
It can only be the same
Never been so helpless
Bang my head on the nearest wall
And if I can't make you change your mind
Know I'm surely gonna fall

And what of Sylvia? By December 1973, she'd had enough. 'There were too many women following him around. I went home to Ireland and when I came back, there was evidence that somebody had been sleeping in my bed, one of my purple dyed sheets was missing and I found a photo of one of them [women] lying on the floor. That was the last bloody straw. I couldn't get on with my life and bring up a kid with all that bullshit going on.'

As for The Gary Moore Band, while the gigs were coming in, the band were not really making much headway—and the money was poor; as an example, two gigs in the West Midlands in August only averaged out at £65 a show. When they were living together, Gary was as much dependent on Jeannie's student grant as he was from earnings as a professional musician. And they were hit by bad luck, too. Joe Walsh was due to tour to promote his breakthrough solo album *The Smoker You Drink, The Player You Get,* with the hit single 'Rocky Mountain Way' released in the UK in September 1973. The Gary Moore Band were in line to play support. Then, in October, the price of oil went through the roof as the Arab OPEC oil-producing countries imposed an oil embargo in retaliation for US involvement in the Arab-Israeli Yom Kippur War. The tour was cancelled. The end of the band was in sight.

Bassist John Curtis recalls that 'every time Thin Lizzy played the Marquee, Gary was invited as a guest. And as soon as his name was mentioned, the place would go absolutely mad, mental. He had a strong following at the club and we took the place apart every time we did it.'

So, when Eric Bell walked off stage in Belfast, leaving Thin Lizzy stranded in the middle of an Irish tour, Gary was the obvious first-choice replacement. In the run-up to Christmas 1973, Pearse had been covering for an injured Brian Downey when Eric was still in the band. Quite literally, Brian played with one arm and Pearse played the parts of his other arm. 'I had to be back in London for a gig with Gary at the Marquee,' (probably December 30, 1973) says Pearse. 'I remember standing in the Marquee and my gear hadn't arrived yet and Gary was not fuckin' amused.'

In what some people have described as a very Irish way of doing things, Gary never formally disbanded The Gary Moore Band. He simply told Dave Lennox, Pearse and John that he'd been offered a gig with Thin Lizzy—and that was that. But by way of compensation, John and Pearse were given all their gear, Pearse also gaining the PA and an introduction by Gary to bassist Steve York and Vinegar Joe.

Gary's time in Thin Lizzy was spread over the next five years in circumscribed chunks. In terms of his musical development, however, and following a continuum that starts with Skid Row and goes on to The Gary Moore Band, his major musical development from 1974–1978 was time spent with Jon Hiseman and Colosseum II.

04

GHOST IN
THE MACHINE

Jon Hiseman and Dick Heckstall-Smith profoundly believed, as they rode out the disorganisation of The Graham Bond Organisation, that you could harness all the creativity and excitement within a band while leaving all the nonsense by the roadside. Jon and Dick used to go for what Jon has called 'middle-class meals' to talk through the possibilities. They both went through John Mayall's 'British blues boom rite of passage' band before realising their ambition in Colosseum, one of Britain's best loved and most successful and enduring jazz-rock bands.

Back in 1971, though, it looked anything but enduring. Three years in and the band were running out of steam. To a degree, they were a victim of their own success; the dates sheets were full, gigs packed, leaving little time for writing new songs. Those that did emerge from rehearsals couldn't compete with their signature material like 'Valentyne Suite' and 'Lost Angeles'. They had failed to break in America, leaving Jon to face the perennial problem of trying to get a well-established band to the next level. So, when guitarist Clem Clempson was poached by Humble Pie to replace Peter Frampton, Jon took it as a signal that Colosseum had run its course.

Undaunted, however, Jon tried a different tack; solid rock rhythms, intelligent songs and short solos—still majoring on improvisation, but which would be part of the song and not, as was happening in Colosseum towards the end, almost the other way round.

For this new venture, to be called Tempest, Jon called in former Colosseum bassist Mark Clarke, who was on the run from an exhausting time with Uriah Heep, along with a phenomenal new jazz fusion guitarist on the London scene, Allan Holdsworth, and former Juicy Lucy vocalist Paul Williams, who Jon had tried to recruit for Colosseum. They recorded two albums (*Jon Hiseman's Tempest* and *Living In Fear*), garnered good critical reviews, great crowd reactions, everything you would expect from a Hiseman band. However, first they lost Holdsworth back to jazz, replaced by the highly talented, mercurial Ollie Halsall. Then there were problems with Paul Williams, who was drinking heavily to combat his fear of flying. In any case, though, as the band veered more towards instrumentals, Paul Williams felt increasingly redundant. Another problem was the weakness of the material on the second album and, finally, Ollie Halsall decamped to the Kevin Ayers band saying he wanted to focus more on writing songs and singing. Around May 1974, Tempest blew itself out.

At the same time, Gary had completed his first stand-in stint with Thin Lizzy and although Phil was desperate for Gary to stay, Gary, for his part, needed something more challenging. Back in London, though, he was very much at a loose end with little idea about his next move. He was friendly with Vinegar Joe bassist Steve York and together with Pearse Kelly, they played an unrehearsed gig together at the Marquee. The gig went well, and they started talking about getting a band together. Gary didn't want to sing, so they recruited Graham Bell on vocals, formerly with Skip Bifferty and Every Which Way. Steve says, 'Gary and Graham hit it off almost too well. We did a lot of writing and recorded some long jams with Paul Thompson, the keyboard player from Vinegar Joe, but ultimately there was too much drinking and partying to accomplish anything worthwhile. I recall we had our last band meeting at the bar of the Portobello Hotel. Graham and Gary were always getting into fights in pubs. So Pearse and I called this meeting to express our concerns about getting drunk and fighting. Sure enough, about ten minutes later they started a fight with some of the customers. We looked at each other and walked out.'

Gary's friend Bill Hindmarsh had moved to Bonn and came to London over the summer of '74 with some new German friends including Hans Engel. Bill called in to see Gary who, on the spur of the moment, decided to travel back to Germany with them, loaded his Les Paul and an amp into Hans's large car and off they went. Once out there, Gary played some local gigs in and around Bonn, then they all went off to France and Spain before returning to Germany. 'After we'd been back a few days,' says Hans, 'Gary got a telegram from Jon Hiseman about forming a new band.'

Gary had seen Tempest, possibly at the end of April at the Marquee, almost their last gig, and had gone backstage to meet with Jon, suggesting they should work together. Nothing was settled then, but in August, they met again at the studio where a rock version of Prokofiev's *Peter And The Wolf* was being recorded, organised by saxophonist Jack Lancaster and keyboardist Robin Lumley. Gary and Jon agreed to begin the process of forming a band. But first Jon took Gary back to Germany to play with the United Jazz and Rock Ensemble (UJRE), which produced a defining moment in their relationship.

The UJRE was really a 'band of band leaders', all highly schooled and experienced jazz musicians—some of whom held teaching position in music colleges. The band was formed initially for a TV show on Southern German Broadcasting. Jon and his wife, Barbara Thompson, became regular members alongside others including Charlie Mariano and Albert Mangelsdorff. Gary couldn't read music and became extremely apprehensive about the prospect of playing in such illustrious company.

And when Gary got nervous, he got drunk. Jon was furious, and though he says now he doesn't recall the incident, Gary was adamant Jon grabbed hold of him and said, in effect, 'If you want to play with me, you had better get your act together.' Gary played so loud, says Jon, that 'the TV cameras shook and the crew were going crazy. But he played brilliantly and the band loved him.'

Jon says of Gary, 'I didn't know who he was, never seen him play. But I knew him as one of the new young guys who could do it and wasn't limited in the way I thought Clapton was limited. He was a modern player rather than a blues player, that's what I had heard. And the thing was that Gary couldn't copy anybody. He tried, he might have thought he was copying and, later on, there was a lot of controversy over some of the things he wrote being copies of what other people did. Of course, he was influenced by what he heard and it almost hurt him. He was an egoist and wanted to be the best. I never understood why he felt that need, but he did and he was dogged mentally by people like John McLaughlin and by Eric Clapton, who was much more successful. But I never heard anything that came out of him that felt like a copy. The word was, he was an original player and a very good technician. I wasn't bothered about who was or wasn't famous, just who could play. People like Clem, Allan Holdsworth, Ollie Halsall and Gary—I had four of the most individual guitarists you could wish for.'

As Gary told *Sounds*, 'The first time I played with Jon, I almost fell through the floor. He played everything I've always heard in my head, everything that I thought a drummer should play and a lot more besides. It was just astonishing.'

After Tempest, you might have thought Jon would have baulked at another attempt to fuse strong songs and vocals with technical jazz rock. And it might not have happened, had Gary and Jon not been pondering next steps at the same time. Jon was painfully aware that the boat had probably sailed on the type of music he wanted to play: 'I didn't want to just become a drummer backing singers, working at their whim and being hired and fired at their whim. I'd had a bit of that with Georgie Fame.'

For his part, Gary had been trying for a similar fusion style in his own band, so they were clearly on the same wavelength. As Gary explained to *NME*, 'we wanted to do something that nobody else was doing—find a hot instrumental band with strong vocals. You've got people like the Mahavishnu Orchestra who do great instrumentals and you've got Zeppelin with a good vocalist, but there's no one doing both.'

With a new band they decided to call Ghosts, they set off on the tortuous road of trying to put a band together. There were no advances, no gig money, no manager and no record company backing. Jon took the huge risk of securing a £7,000 bank loan against his house (equivalent to about £50,000 today) and used that to fund the band, paying Gary, for example, just £10 a week.

They started rehearsals in a damp, dark studio underneath some railway arches in east London. Jon asked Mark Clarke again and Graham Bell was brought in, but with no gigs or recording lined up, Mark went off to the States with Uriah Heep's keyboardist Ken Hensley and Graham Bell lost interest too. Former Blodwyn Pig, Juicy Lucy and Savoy Brown bassist Andy Pyle rehearsed for a while. Jon was contacted by a film director to write a film score for a movie he was making—until they went for a meeting with the guy and walked on to a porn film set. Jon didn't have a problem, but neither Andy nor Gary wanted anything to do with it.

But in a letter to Bill Hindmarsh, Gary was clearly committed to the new venture. In it, he speaks of a prospective singer who 'has been going to singing lessons and there just haven't been any improvements. In fact, it's gotten worse if anything. So, it's back to the same old problem of finding the right singer. Never mind, we've got time, no point in dropping our sights that we originally had in mind eh? It'll take time, but it's worth waiting for I reckon. I've gone too far with this to turn back now, so I'm determined to see it through to the end—(and into the valley of death rode the 600 etc to be spoken in your best Vincent Price tongue). Enough of that! Get a grip of yourself man!'

Jon says that Gary would have sung, but like Ollie, he only wanted to do it when he felt like it rather than really working at being the lead vocalist. Another problem, as Gary explained to *NME*, was the way he wrote songs: 'When I write on guitar, I tend to forget people's limitations and the next thing you know is that I've written notes that no one can reach.'

Eventually, though, they found a singer. Mike Starrs had come down from Scotland in the late 60s to seek his fortune in London and had been signed by producer Tony Atkins for Marquee Productions, although the slew of singles that followed failed to make an impact. Mike was also part of a band called Spinning Wheel, which included Geoff Whitehorn on guitar (with whom Gary jammed at one time) and Mike was in the studio when he was overheard by Jon's wife Barbara. She might have got word back to Jon, because the next thing that happened was former businessman Alan Hewitt, who aspired to be the band manager, saw Mike during his residency at the Three Rabbits pub in Manor Park, east London. Mike says when he came down to rehearsal Andy Pyle was there with keyboard player

Duncan Mackay who went on play with Cockney Rebel. Andy hung on for a long as he could, but with pittance wages and a family to support he was forced to bail out, quickly followed by Duncan.

They auditioned several more keyboard players including a guy from Germany. Gary told Hiseman biographer Martyn Hanson that 'he said he was the man for the job and he came in full of confidence. He started playing and it was obvious that he couldn't play at all. We tried not to laugh … it was all so hopeless.'

Despite his upbeat letter to Bill, this was a tricky period for Gary; he had left Lizzy with no plan and was in a situation where, despite working with a musician he deeply respected, there was no end product in sight or even a band to deliver it. And he was in a new relationship with Jeannie's sister Donna.

During 1974, Gary moved in with Donna, who brought out another side of Gary. She maintains they found common cause: 'He had eyes like a child and that's where I saw the child within. I was the same and wanted to play and so did Gary. It was like we needed each other at that time in our lives. He was such a lovely man. He was kind. And I felt some kind of vulnerability, which made him attractive. We didn't want to grow up. He was very protective of me and looked after me. But he also craved love and security. He just wanted somebody to cuddle and protect him. We never really argued, just giggled a lot.'

It wasn't all fun and laughter. Donna confirms Gary did suffer from panic attacks: 'Sometimes they were so bad he couldn't go out. He would start feeling hot, his heart would beat faster. That frightens you and you become anxious. And if you can't control that you start hallucinating. Gary would have to lie down and completely relax until it went away.'

Gary would drink to deal with his fears and anxieties—about the direction of his career, what he felt about his playing, positioning himself in relation to other guitarists. Ghosts had yet to come together. There was concern in the band that Gary was too often in the company of a heavy-drinking crowd and one day the lid on the pressure cooker just blew.

Donna says they were going to see a band and called in at a local pub on the way (possibly the Kensington Park Hotel on Ladbroke Grove). In the bar was a guy we'll call John, an old boyfriend of Donna's who Donna says wouldn't leave her alone: 'I wanted him to back off because I knew Gary would go nuts. This guy kept pushing.' Gary had been at the bar getting some drinks and came back to be faced with a situation similar to the one with Ed Deane and Sylvia back in Dublin. But there was an extra edge here; John was public school with a military background.

Gary was Irish and when he got angry and had been drinking, the accent came through. No matter that he was from Northern Ireland, when tempers are raised and the booze is talking, Irish is Irish—IRA bombs were going off all over London. They continued to wind each other up and finally Gary lost it and poured a pint over John's head. Accounts differ about what happened next. Donna reckons the guy simply meant to do the same, but as he swung his arm, the pint hit a pillar and glass went in Gary's face. Others in the bar reckon Gary was deliberately glassed.

Gary went to hospital where they started to stitch him up, but he refused to let them finish the job and left, saying he just wanted to go home. Both Donna and her sister Ceri talked to him about getting it fixed, but he just wasn't interested. Even much later, when he could easily have afforded plastic surgery, the answer was no. As far as Gary was concerned, it was all his own fault even though it did severely dent his self-confidence. It was almost as if he wanted this mark, this stigmata as a manifestation of some deeply embedded sense of unworthiness, almost like he deserved it at a level beyond simply the events of that night.

Fortunately, musicians and the music business came to the rescue. Around April/May 1975, Jon and Gary found themselves a stellar keyboard player, Don Airey. A classically trained pianist, Don had joined Cozy Powell's Hammer in 1974 and once that folded in 1975, was looking for a new gig. Even better, he brought along Neil Murray, Hammer's last bass player before they broke up. Neil had previously auditioned for Ghosts but reckoned he didn't get the gig because 'at the time I didn't have a very professional bass guitar—it was a short scale Fender Mustang when everyone else was playing a full-size Fender Precision or Jazz. By the time Don was in and suggested they gave me another chance, I had a Fender Precision and got the job.'

Interviewed by *International Musician* in 1982, Gary explained as with the UJRE, he felt daunted at the prospect of playing with Jon and Don: 'They could all read. I found myself in a band who could go out and do gigs that I couldn't. Any one of the group [including Neil's eventual replacement John Mole] could have been called out to do a jazz gig. I felt a bit detached from that. But at the same time, I never wanted to think of myself in terms of little black dots. I worried that if I learnt to read, I'd stop thinking about it and I'd lose my feeling.'

Composition was another matter: even with Don on board, it was still mainly Gary coming up with the material and at the start, as Gary told Martyn Hanson, they didn't necessarily see eye to eye: 'Don and I would clash, because I'd write something on piano and he would say, "You can't do that ... it's not harmonically right."' Don agrees that things could be fraught at times: 'There was some bitter stuff going on. It was hard fought getting things worked out how you wanted them to be—some of the music was so difficult, it was tough going.' He adds diplomatically that 'there was a lot of white heat around especially with Gary', but Don says he did appreciate Gary's input. 'He could always explain to me what he wanted. In the early days he had lots of ideas for keyboard that I was very grateful for. He could listen to something and immediately analyse what was happening in it. It was quite alarming, actually.' They settled into a way of working. Jon says they started writing in the round during rehearsals: 'I would contribute lyrics (which Gary would sometimes dismiss as pretentious rubbish!). Don would come in and play whole blocks of a song and the rhythmical feels would be obvious from the way he was playing. Then he might say, "But I don't know where it goes from here," and then Gary would pick it up and take it on. It was a backwards and forwards, verbal process, all done in the rehearsal room. And then Don might write out all the chord sequences on manuscript paper in letters so we could all read it. Then when we would go out on a gig, we would use the new material on soundchecks, which could last anything up to three hours.'

For Mike Starrs, the music 'was completely alien to me. When I listen back now, I think, *Did I actually do that?*' But in a comment echoing Noel Bridgeman's view of Skid Row, Mike adds, 'But when you're young, you've got no fear and you just get on with it.'

Gary had told *Sounds* they weren't going to be bounced into a record deal: they would want to be on the road for at least three months before they went into the studio. As it turned out, they would be only too pleased to have any record deal at all. Now they had a full band and regular rehearsals, which had to be paid for, the strain on Jon's bank loan was intolerable. Jon turned to former Colosseum manager Gerry Bron, who had bankrolled Tempest. Bron was interested in the band but told Jon that he would have to change the name because he said, 'I can't sell Ghosts.' He had wanted Jon to reprise the name Colosseum for Tempest, something Jon had refused to do, but this time Jon had to relent, although he did ask his former colleagues first if they objected. Nobody did. Ghosts became Colosseum II and they were now in a position, in August 1975, to go into Gerry Bron's Roundhouse Studios to begin recording their first album. Between August and early January, they spent about three weeks recording and about two weeks mixing. Jon later remarked that while they were there, Queen were in one of the smaller rooms trying to sort out a guitar overdub: 'We went in and did the whole of our album and they were still getting that guitar overdub right.'

They tried out some demos first, Graham Bond's 'Walking in the Park' and a song called 'Gary's Lament', which made the second album, and 'Castles', which would eventually appear on their third. During the recording, Bernie Marsden was in the control booth, 'and it was so incredibly good that I actually started laughing. It was just amazing. But when Jon and Gary saw me laughing, they thought I was taking the piss and I got thrown out!'

Gary's influence both terms of writing and playing style meant the debut album had a much lighter, melodic touch than anything produced by Tempest. There seemed to be more space in the music and some passages could have been taken from the later configuration of Colosseum with Chris Farlowe.

Gary's playing style on the opening track, 'Dark Side Of The Moog', certainly nodded towards not only John McLaughlin, but also Bill Connors, Chick Corea's guitarist in Return to Forever; and just as Eric Clapton benefited from access to John Mayall's record collection, so, in Jon's company, Gary was exposed to John Coltrane and Roland Kirk. 'Up until then,' says Jon, 'he never really understood where McLaughlin was coming from—and it was like a revelation, he couldn't believe it. He could never accept what McLaughlin or Larry Coryell were doing unless he understood it. He just felt uncomfortable, even envious, although I have no idea why. But he got into this in a big way and absorbed it like a sponge; rhythmically and harmonically, that was way beyond the simplicity of the blues. Hearing Coltrane play completely opened his head up.'

This song was a good example of the complexities Don referred to. Speaking to Chris Welch to promote the album, Jon said the title was just a laugh at first and then it stuck: 'It's written by Don and the whole track is a keyboard feature using organ, piano and synthesisers. It's in 13/8 all the way … Actually, if you count hard enough, it's 13/4. We used a lot of overdubbing on the album and … used the studio as an environment. There is so much you can do in a studio now, so it's silly to ignore the facilities.'

For Don, 'Gary reached a real peak at this time [1975–1977]—and he kept it up. Over time, he thought more about songwriting, maybe being more radio friendly, but in terms of his technique and feeling, it was at a constant level for a very long time. The only comparison I know about was Oscar Peterson. When he came out of Canada, he was apparently fully-formed and I would pretty much say the same about Gary.'

The most ambitious track on the album was a version of Joni Mitchell's already structurally challenging 'Down To You', which included a reference to 'strange new flesh', and it gave the album its title. Including this song from *Court and Spark* was probably down to a suggestion by Gary, who was a huge Joni Mitchell fan. Jon said to Chris Welch, 'I get shivers listening to this … we took the melody and did it in different ways. From where the piano comes in, it is all arranged by Don and we have used Joni's song as a piece of musical theatre … it develops in an orchestral way and I feel lucky to have the musicians who can play this.'

Strange New Flesh was released on Gerry Bron's Bronze label in April 1976; reviews were generally positive—the ever-loyal Chris Welch called it 'an imaginative and exuberant debut', but the album failed to chart and caused Bron to start rethinking his investment. And privately, neither Gary nor Jon were that enamoured of the album overall. 'It was a serious studio performance,' says Jon, 'but my biggest success had been *Colosseum Live* and this had a big impact on Gary, both its success and the music being played. So, we both felt it was a "dead" record—the stuff got more interesting on the road because there was so much more improvisation and looseness on stage that you don't get in a studio with the struggle to get things right and not make a mistake. With instrumental albums, it is not unusual for live albums to be better than studio ones—whereas with a singer, the singer is the performance and the band are just there because they have to be.'

Gerry Bron was very tied up in America with the success of Uriah Heep, so his wife Lilian came in to oversee the fortunes of the band—and the first thing she demanded was that they get rid of the singer. As Jon recalls, 'Mike Starrs was the only guy who had a strong enough voice to sing the songs we had written ["On Second Thoughts" from the first album being a case in point], but he'd come straight out of pub singing. And the result on stage was instead of being rocky, strong and devil-may-care, it was all a bit too "ladies and gentlemen" and cabaret—Mike had that thing going. Lilian was horrified and said, "He leaves or you leave the Bron agency."' Mike was really on a hiding to nowhere, though, because if you are supposed to be the frontman and the band take off for ten minutes' worth of instrumental, it doesn't matter how charismatic and dynamic you are—as Phil Lynott discovered in Skid Row; what are you supposed to do?

Mike says that rather than being told he was sacked, all he remembers is getting a call to say the band was splitting and only found out later what had actually happened from Neil Murray—who was also heaved out the band around the same time. Their last gig with Colosseum II was June 26, 1976 at Guildford Civic Hall. Both Jon and Gary had a problem with Neil's playing—they thought it was too busy and preferred somebody to be more unobtrusive. Neil saw it differently: 'I wanted the bass to be very up front. A huge influence for me was Jack Bruce—moving around, mid-range, not just plodding away in the background. I was talking to Jon about bass playing and I assumed he would want something pretty adventurous. I wanted to be as expressive as everybody else. But he said, "Oh, I'd rather have somebody right in the pocket."' So, to fill that pocket, they chose John Mole, spotted by Barbara Thompson playing in a club in Southend.

Colosseum II now developed as an instrumental quartet with Gary taking on whatever vocals were required and in theory it meant they could focus on just being one type of band and grow from there. Jon is adamant that 'as soon as we made that change, it worked. No, we weren't going to make any money and yes, effectively it was a jazz group—to build it on a rock model was everybody's stupidity—so it was a jazz group and a very good one, playing music that nobody else was playing.' Cue Gerry Bron to drop them, only for the band to be rescued again, this time by record producer Monty Babson.

Monty was an old-style music producer (everybody from Acker Bilk to Blue Mink) and part-owner of Morgan Studios, which gave the band recording slots during down time. There were four studios, so there was always one they could use. For Jon, 'it was the perfect marriage. He was into our music and the only mistake we made was that he sold the rights to the music to MCA; my deal with him was that he would produce the music but never sell the rights to anybody else. And I didn't find out until our relations with him were over. I thought he would license them for five years; instead, he signed them over in perpetuity.' The band got £60,000 for the each of the next two albums, but that had to pay for studio costs, so Monty Babson took the money and paid the band a wage. But, says Jon, 'if you worked it out over two years, he didn't make that much'.

At the end of 1976, the band went into Morgan Studios to record their second album, *Electric Savage*. Again (and according to the credits), Gary took a leading role in the writing. Much of the album was written in rehearsal, road tested at gigs, then back in the studio to play the songs as live as possible, this time with few overdubs. One track Gary wrote called 'The Scorch' neatly summed up what the band delivered here—a much more coherent album with thrilling, gold-standard playing from everybody from first track to last. And if Gary didn't 'get' John McLaughlin at the outset, he certainly did by the time he came to record 'Desperado'. *Electric Savage* also featured Gary's first vocal outing with the band, a heartfelt song he wrote for Donna called 'Rivers':

Under your wings now, over the worst.
Now that the storm clouds have all blown away.
Now that the spells have been broken.
Feelin' the beauty I am seeing today. It was always there.
Don't let the rivers of our love run dry.
Don't stop the flames we have from burning.
Don't let the rivers of our love run dry. Don't stop our world from turning.
Don't let the rivers of our love run dry.
Don't stop the flames we have from burning.
Yeah, yeah, yeah.
Don't let the rivers of our love run dry.
Don't stop our world, don't stop our world, Don't stop our world from turning.

In January 1977, Gary had an offer to join Thin Lizzy again for a three-month stint to replace Brian Robertson who had been glassed at the Speakeasy trying to save singer Frankie Miller from getting battered. Had *Electric Savage* done the business at the cash tills, Jon might have said no because of the chance to tour a successful album.

That Jon agreed to Gary's sabbatical hinted at the future (or maybe lack of it), even though manager Alan Hewitt was telling anyone who would listen that Gary would be back. And so he was, despite more pressure from Phil to stay. Gary remained loyal to Jon and the project that he had told Bill Hindmarsh he would see right through to the end.

There was no big promotional tour for the album in 1977, but an interesting side project came about when Andrew Lloyd Webber lost a bet to his cellist brother Julian over the outcome of a football match. Julian's reward was for Andrew to compose a work for him, to be called *Variations*, a suite based on an original theme by the violinist Niccolò Paganini. Andrew envisaged some marriage between classical, jazz and rock, but didn't know which musicians he would use. While visiting his record label, MCA, he overheard a test pressing of *Electric Savage* and realised he had found what he was looking for. Webber phoned Jon, they met, discussed the project and the band found itself with ten days' worth of well-paid studio work. Jon was able to row in Barbara too, as the music needed a versatile sax/flautist. What nobody could have imagined was that the album would be such a success. *Variations* went gold and there were live concerts to play, which caused Gary some concerns as once again he would be surrounded by musicians who could read off the charts. However, as he told *Guitar Player* in 1980, 'in many ways it helped. I often had my parts memorised before others had finished reading through theirs. It wasn't all easy though. There were some really hard sections calling for elaborate counterpoint and unison work between bass and guitar.'

Gary needn't have worried about being regarded as inferior; in his autobiography, Julian Lloyd Webber said that he had learnt a lot about phrasing and performance from jazz and rock artists, many of whom were self-taught. He name-checked Stéphane Grappelli and Gary, adding that Gary not only had 'stunning technique, but possesses a musical memory that would be the envy of many a classical musician'. *Variations* had a legacy that far outlived its unexpectedly high ranking on the UK album charts. An edited version became the theme tune to *The South Bank Show*, a landmark television arts programme, for the whole of its 32-year run from 1978–2010.

Despite poor sales of *Electric Savage*, Colosseum II were back in the studio during the summer of 1977 to record their third album, *War Dance*. There was no shortage of material, and the playing was again of exceptional quality, on a par with the best that comparable bands like the Mahavishnu Orchestra or Return to Forever could offer. But there was the rub: those bands were at their height in the early 1970s, this was 1978. The final track of the album was presciently titled 'Last Exit'. Just as Jon had called time on Colosseum when Clem left for Humble Pie, so when Gary got yet a third call from Thin Lizzy during the summer of 1978, Jon called a big meeting at the offices of MCA with the band and the new wave of record executives who were running the company. 'The Managing Director was a personal friend of Monty Babson,' says Jon, 'but now these kids were in charge and to justify themselves they had to have hits. It was obvious that everybody had lost faith in me. I could smell it in the air, but I could see no way ahead.'

So, what went wrong? Why did four of the best musicians in the country playing at the top of their game fail commercially? There is a whole Colosseum II session on YouTube playing a BBC *Sight And Sound In Concert* in 1978 with Gary fronting the band and clearly revelling in the excitement and challenge of having that group of musicians behind him driving him on.

'We played some marvellous gigs and the crowds loved us,' says Jon. 'But we were always fighting the fact that we couldn't fill big halls, we couldn't get beyond 300–400 size club venues. There were lots of gigs, but no big gigs. We had crew, two big trucks, lighting rig. In those days, the average venue did not have a good

PA, so we had to carry it, which was expensive, although we owned the stuff rather than renting. And the booking agents didn't route you properly. If you go from London to Milan and then back to Manchester, you can't make that pay.'

At root was the lack of hit albums and, perhaps even more significantly, even for a band like Colosseum II, no hit singles to grab them some airtime. At least in Europe, especially in Germany and Scandinavia, the audiences were more open-minded about coming out and appreciating more complex music. But in the UK, by the time Colosseum were releasing albums, punk was starting to swamp the scene and the new wave rock critics were giving short shrift to jazz-rock or anything else that wasn't on their playlist.

Even before that, though, Jon looks backs now and admits he was embarking on a doomed project: 'I folded Colosseum because I thought we'd had the best of that style of music back in 1971. Tempest only had one shot at commercial success and that was when we had Paul Williams in the line-up. There was no real reason to form Colosseum II because I thought that style of music was gone, that idea of trying to marry up lyrics and vocals with jazz and rock. The model didn't exist in America; George Duke tried it a few times. The Crusaders had given up what I was trying to do because they knew they couldn't get airplay without the vocal, so you get Randy Crawford and "Street Life".'

Gary had told the press that they wanted to combine the technical prowess of the Mahavishnu Orchestra with the vocal strength of Zeppelin, 'because nobody else was doing it'. And the reason was, it didn't work. The music was great, but the times were seriously not—and they were unlikely to get that elusive hit single with a strong vocal, because they weren't writing like that. Nor was Gary's voice really up to it—he didn't have the range of a Chris Farlowe or Mike Starrs, although MCA heard Gary singing and did say to Jon that they wanted more songs and fewer instrumental work-outs.

Jon always knew he was facing an uphill struggle; as he told Chris Welch, 'It's a bad time to put a band together, I know. The business is in a bad way economically … and this has coincided with a non-creative period in the history of rock music.'

So how does Jon feel now about working with Gary? The argument that Jon had with Gary over drinking wasn't the only one: 'Gary had some serious battles with the manager Alan Hewitt over this, whether or not he was fit to go on stage, or Gary getting very aggressive and taking it out on somebody. All drink-related. But I don't hold grudges against anybody ever. Having worked with Graham

Bond, I came to expect anything from people who have to deliver on stage. And I had nothing but respect for what Gary could do, although I hated all the rest that went with it. I don't understand how Gary could get in such a state; I've only got to look at a glass of wine and I'm feeling tipsy. Gary was inherently a very nice man, an intelligent man, a good man. I also believe there was a side of Gary that didn't want to get involved in the mundane side of life—this, for Gary, was a serious drag. He wanted to be in the band room, waiting to go on stage, be on stage, come off after a successful gig and then do whatever he fancied. I think he liked to feel that normal constraints somehow didn't apply to him, even though for much of his life they did. He felt at odds with the person he was.'

Jon continues: 'The creative moments in life are very short and very small; spending three months making an album is no less donkey work than doing the washing up. But Gary was so full of music and ideas and a talent that fired out in all directions that he found it extremely hard to accept that there might only be 40 seconds of creativity in an hour slog and, ultimately, you might only attain 70 percent of what you were going for—and this was an important source of his anger and frustration coupled with underlying self-doubt. And for somebody as hyper-sensitive as Gary, alcohol could deaden the pain, although of course it never solved anything and as we have seen could cause some very bad moments.'

Jon might have thought he had closed the book on Colosseum II; the Inland Revenue thought otherwise. It took another five years to sort out the tax mess created by the very bad mistake of forming Colosseum II as a partnership as opposed to a limited company or each member being registered as self-employed. The reason you don't do this is because all the members of a partnership are liable for the tax payments of each other. Jon was meticulous about completing tax returns ever year; the others, including Gary, who had no business manager or accountant at the time, were not.

This meant that because Jon filed returns and kept proper records, the Inland Revenue could come to him for the payments they hadn't received from the others—and if he didn't pay, he could lose his house (nobody else owned their own house at the time). Jon realised that from an assessment letter to court proceedings took five months; so, if you made a small payment just before court, the whole process had to start again. In this way, Jon was able to fend off the Revenue for years, until Gary finally acquired a proper accountant and business manager, Colin Newman, who between him and Jon, finally managed to sort it all out.

05

ME AND THE BOYS WERE WONDERING

One evening in 1969, on his Monday night off from playing in a showband called The Dreams, Eric Bell went to see Gary play in Skid Row at the Five Club in Dublin. He hadn't seen Gary for a few years since he left Belfast. The two guitarists had played musical chairs around the city; both had spells in The Deltones and Shades of Blue (although Gary was probably just sitting in with those bands). And when Gary left Platform Three, Eric tried out with them unsuccessfully before the founder members called it a day.

'I was in my showband suit and army haircut in this club with all these hippies who probably thought I was in the drug squad. I heard this incredible music and I made my way to the front of the stage and there was Gary playing his heart out. Things were pretty rough for him in those days; the band weren't making money, while I was doing pretty well in the showband. He was at my flat one night, freezing cold and starving. I had a big roaring fire going and this girl Kathleen cooked him a meal. He was over the moon that night.'

Soon after, Eric had something like an epiphany: 'The showband were rehearsing upstairs at the School of Speech Therapy in Dublin, which had rehearsal rooms. Downstairs, Skid Row were rehearsing. I went down there, opened the door and out came all this music and I started thinking, *What am I doing in a showband?* Here's Gary playing all the Eric Clapton licks and I thought, *Jesus, I've gotta get out of here.* So, in a way, he inspired me to leave The Dreams and start Thin Lizzy.'

In December 1969, Eric got together with his former Them band mate Eric Wrixon and they teamed up with Phil Lynott and Brian Downey, whose own band Orphanage had broken up. By the end of 1970, Eric Wrixon had left and Thin Lizzy had themselves a recording contact with Decca. Two years on from that, Lizzy had a single and two albums under their belt but were still relatively in the shadows. Then, in late November 1972, Decca released a single, 'Whiskey In The Jar', which charted in Ireland, the UK and across Europe. For Eric, this changed everything—and not for the better. He had been in the straitjacket of the uniform and repertoire of a showband; what he had hoped from Thin Lizzy would be much more of a free-form, bluesy improvisational jam band— which it was at the start. But the success of 'Whiskey ...' meant TV appearances, different clothes, interviews and all the hoopla of the pop business, which were miles outside Eric's comfort zone. 'Everybody wanted us to put on a show, no improvising anymore, the same fuckin' songs every night. I might as well have been back in the showband, you know?' Now came the added pressure of a follow-up single, but 'Randolph's Tango' was a flop, so too (outside Ireland) was the next single, 'The Rocker'.

As the pressure built up to cash in on their hit single, Eric hit the bottle and the dope. Then his girlfriend (who had been pregnant at the same time as Sylvia) ran off to Canada with their son. Eric added tranquilizers to his chemical carousel, 'and I was going right off the rails. Basically, I was a fuckin' basket case.'

Thin Lizzy's 1973 Christmas tour of Ireland had not got off to a good start with Pearse Kelly having to play the fills for Brian Downey, whose hand had swollen up from an allergic reaction to the varnish on his drumsticks. They were ten dates into the tour arriving in Belfast on New Year's Eve to play Queen's University's Whitla Hall, the very same venue where Eric had quit Them after a difference of opinion with Van Morrison over guitar volume.

Having spent time drinking with family during the day and drinking again in the dressing room before the gig, by the time he had to face the crowd, Eric was almost hallucinating: 'I heard this voice in my head telling me to quit and I just chucked the guitar in the air, sort of watched it come down almost in slow motion as it hit the stage. Then I kicked over these two 4x12 cabinets, and I just walked off stage, completely off my head.'

Slumped in a heap by the side of the stage, he was threatened by tour manager Frank Murray in no uncertain terms to get back out there and finish the gig. 'Which he did,' says Frank, 'but not before he asked for a couple of pints of Guinness.'

Next day, there was a meeting at the hotel where the band and crew were staying. Eric rolled up with the mother of all hangovers to be met by Phil, Brian and the roadies, who gave him nothing but frosty glares. He took a phone call from manager Chris Morrison who couldn't believe that Eric was walking out half-way through a tour. But Eric remained firm, and although he wasn't officially sacked, Chris simply informed him they would be getting Gary to step in.

Chris Morrison either phoned or went round to Larch Road, Cricklewood to see Gary, whose response to being asked to join Lizzy in Ireland was 'What time's the next flight?' Without admitting The Gary Moore Band was over, Gary put in a quick call to Pearse Kelly and John Curtis to say he was going to finish a tour with Lizzy—and he was gone.

They had to cancel the next two dates on January 1 and 2, to give Gary time to come across, but after only about six hours of rehearsals, Gary was good to go for the first of eleven dates to finish the Irish tour. Brian Downey says that Gary didn't know all the songs in their set at the time, 'but he knew some of the stuff from the first two albums and "Whiskey In The Jar". Whatever he knew would go in or he would just jam along.' This took them to February 1 and the first date of the UK tour at Central London Polytechnic. At that point, Eric was given the chance to re-join the band but declined. Then, says Ted Carroll, 'either me or Phil asked Gary if he wanted to join and at that time he definitely said yes'.

Their encore number was the J Geils Band song 'Hard Drivin' Man'. Listening to this, Chris O'Donnell (then the band's agent, soon to be co-manager) says he turned to Chris Morrison and said, 'You could take on the world with this band': 'That night, Gary was phenomenal. He had no constraints, no thoughts for the future, just a hired gun and he let rip. He jumped on the monitors, was on his back playing guitar. The audience were looking as if to say, "Did I just see that? Was that for real?"'

As good a player as Eric was, no doubt Gary took Lizzy to another level, not just in technical ability, but as a sparring partner for Phil up front. With his all-black clothes, black boots, long swirling hair, cutting and thrusting with the guitar like a scimitar, Gary had the perfect image for the pirate band that was Thin Lizzy.

Phil had also made substantial progress as a frontman. His wake-up call had come in 1972 when Lizzy were on tour with Slade, one of the biggest bands in Britain at the time. Back then, Phil was still quite low key in his presentation, until the towering presence of Chas Chandler, Slade's manager, came storming into the dressing room shouting, 'What the fuck do you call that? You're supposed to warm the Slade crowd up, not put them to sleep. Get it sorted or you're off the tour.' Phil was in shock; here was the former manager of his number one idol, Jimi Hendrix, giving him a total teardown. For the rest of the tour, Phil tried different sorts of poses, throwing different shapes at the audience, projecting himself out into the auditorium. He was expecting to be booed and ridiculed, but instead the audience lapped it up. Philip Parris Lynott was morphing into Phil and together with Gary they were a force of nature, with Brian's double bass drum kit tumbling gloriously behind them.

They stormed through the UK, ending on April 14 at the Bristol Locarno, where the set included a number by Gary called 'Crawling'—John Lee Hooker as whirling dervish. There was a solo guitar interlude in which Gary would mix up classical Spanish, blues and Irish jig riffs alongside hard rocking songs like 'Sitamoia' and 'The Rocker'. 'Slow Blues' from the *Vagabonds* album added contrast to the set, 'Showdown' was road tested for the next album, *Nightlife*, and they threw in a Stevie Wonder song, 'I Love Every Little Thing About You'. In rehearsal, the band would often play around with arrangements of Stevie Wonder material, not something you might expect from their stage persona and standard repertoire.

That night they also played 'Little Darling', their new Decca single and one of the few recordings Gary undertook during that first period. The song had been recorded along with 'Sitamoia' at Decca's Tollington Park Studios, produced by Phil and Nick Tauber. When the single was released, Donna was featured in the promotional material dressed as a schoolgirl.

A more enduring legacy from this period was the recording of 'Still In Love With You' made at Saturn Sound Studio down at Worthing on the south coast. By the time the track was released, Gary was no longer in the band, but neither of the two new guitarists, Scott Gorham and Brian Robertson, thought they could better it and it remains a solo of outstanding beauty and control. Although the song is credited to Phil, he always thought of it as 'Gary's song'. Gary reckoned he deserved more than a 'thought', as he told Lynott biographer Mark Putterford: 'Phil and I had the same chord sequence. My song was called, 'I'll Help You See It Through' and his was called 'Still In Love With You'. We simply put the two songs together, but then after I left the band Phil decided *he'd* written all of it … It didn't seem to matter though—the stakes weren't so high in those days.'

Whatever Gary had said while on tour about joining Lizzy, by May, he had changed his mind. The timing of the offer had been perfect for Gary; his own band was clearly going nowhere and the pressure of trying to hold it all together with no business support was intolerable. With Lizzy, he was a free spirit; the organisation was in place, all he had to do was turn up and play material that, while exciting, presented him with little by way of technical challenges. But if he was throwing caution to the wind onstage, he was being no less cavalier offstage. After nearly two years of keeping in control, he was now drinking far too much, while still taking tranquilizers—a potentially deadly combination that saw Lizzy roadies carrying him out of more than one club and dumping him at home on the doorstep for whoever answered the door. And while this behaviour did carry on for a while in Colosseum II, Gary was sensible enough to realise that he had to rein it all in otherwise his career would have been under serious threat. He readily admitted this to *Melody Maker* in December 1977: 'I was getting out of my brains and playing on automatic pilot all night.' He said he needed Colosseum II 'to keep me away from that sort of thing and which would straighten me out both as a person and a musician'.

Gary had also tired of the trio format; he'd done this in Skid Row and been forced into it for economic reasons with his own band. But as he explained to a guitar magazine in 1978, 'I just found the whole thing [with Lizzy] was becoming too restricting and it wasn't musical because that whole middle range of the music was missing. The rhythm section would be bouncing along and I'd be right over the top of it, but that middle bit was missing the whole time and there was nothing to give the thing any real shape or form to the listener. In a sense you have to play less rather than more because if you are playing anything adventurous, like modally or anything scale-like, over a root bass note, it just wouldn't make any sense. You have to stick real close to what the bass is playing all the time and that's not really music; if you've got to think in the same key as the bass all the time— well it just doesn't work for me, so I got out of the band.'

There were business reasons too. Lizzy's contract with Decca was due to expire at the end of September 1973, the same month as their album *Vagabonds Of The Western World* was due out. For an advance of £10,000 against royalties for 'Whiskey In The Jar', the band's management negotiated an extension to the contract through to the end of May 1974. This would give them a chance to see how Decca would do promoting the album and by the same token give Decca a chance to assess, based on album sales, whether or not they wanted to carry on with the band. Lizzy had gone into the studio to record 'Sitamoia', 'Still In Love With You', 'Showdown' and 'It's Only Money' as demos for the next album. The first song never made the cut, Gary's solo was retained on the second, but he also had significant input into the last two, which also made the next album (*Nightlife*), but those tracks were re-recorded, leaving Gary no credit for his work.

But as the May deadline was approaching, it looked as if Decca were not going renew, as Ted Carroll recalls, 'Island were very keen to sign the band. Richard Williams, who used to work for *Melody Maker*, was their head of A&R and he was knocked out by the band with Gary, but eventually they passed and our options were beginning to run out. Then Gary came to me and said, "I think I should leave now. You're looking for a new deal and you'll sign one soon and I'll be expected to sign as a member of the band, and I don't want to do that."'

Phil and Brian were both very despondent at the news and they could have broken up then as they almost did before 'Whiskey In The Jar' had become a hit. As their agent, Chris O'Donnell had pretty much saved the band in 1973 when work was drying up: 'I phoned Phil and said, "Come on, I didn't book all those gigs for you to give up now." And Phil said, "That's all I wanted to hear. I wanted somebody to tell *me*, rather than *me* tell them what the future could be. I need somebody else with some belief in this.'''

Ex-Atomic Rooster guitarist John Du Cann and Andy Gee, who had played with Peter Bardens, were brought in. Pearse Kelly recalls walking near the Country Club in Hampstead, 'when this car pulls up alongside and stops. Down goes window and it's Phil, "Gary's fookin' left and it's taken two fookin' guitarists to replace him."' Given Lizzy's track record on guitarists, Chris O'Donnell's view was 'if you've got two guitarists and one leaves, you've still got the other one!'

They had to cancel some dates in Germany but managed to set up alternatives and went out there for a tour that nobody recollects with any affection. Brian was so fed up that he had to be coaxed into staying. Finally, and sticking with the two-axe solution, auditions produced Scott Gorham and Brian Robertson.

Still looking for a deal, Ted Carroll and Chris O'Donnell found themselves in the office of Nigel Grange, A&R man for Phonogram. They played him the demos including 'Still In Love With You'. Ted says, 'Nigel just loved the solo and said, "So this is that seventeen-year-old kid from Glasgow?" [meaning Brian Robertson]. I could see Chris was just about to say, "Oh no, that's Gary Moore," so I kicked him under the table just in time and said something like, "Yes it is, and he's only going to get better."'

With the deal in the bag, Ted left because he wanted to pursue his own business interests, but also because 'I told Chris Morrison I thought there would always be problems between Phil and whoever was the lead guitar that would ultimately prevent them from becoming as big as they could be'. History proved him to be right.

As for Gary, he said in 1978, 'I had a real look at myself before calling Jon. I'd got this thing in my head that all I wanted to do was play with the best musicians in England without giving a fuck about what I would actually have to do. I'd decided to raise my own playing standards and the best way to do that would be to play with the very best musos available.'

In 1976, Thin Lizzy broke through in America with the album *Jailbreak* and the single 'The Boys Are Back in Town'. Now, they needed to put in the hard work of consolidating their position in the most important rock market in the world. But their lifestyle was getting in the way; they had a Midwest tour in May, but to cash in on airplay, they were due to support Rainbow on a tour that would herald their New York debut at the Beacon Theater, where all the most influential industry figures and rock critics would show up. Unfortunately, Phil had been drinking heavily and eventually his body turned on him and said 'enough'. He went to hospital and was diagnosed with infectious hepatitis; the only reason the doctors let him go was on the understanding that he was on a flight straight back to England. The doctors had told Phil that he had to stop drinking for good, but he told the band he'd just have to give it a rest for a year—which he did, taking some delight in now being able to remember how out of it everybody else was—and next day, relaying back all the gory details.

They were gearing up for another crack at the USA, when on November 23, the night before they were due to fly out, Brian Robertson's hand was cut following a brawl at the Speakeasy Club. By his own account, Brian was not actually drunk that night but had gone to the club for a meal. Once there, he saw singer Frankie Miller, his friend, falling-down drunk and about to get bottled by the lead guitarist of Gonzalez. Miller had been jumping onstage during their set demanding to have a blow. Brian rushed to intervene, got in between bottle and Frankie and the next minute, there is blood all over the place from Brian's sliced artery. But Brian being Brian didn't just retreat at the point; he broke the guitarist's leg, bust somebody else's collar bone and nutted a third. Brian went home to Glasgow to nurse his wounds. A doctor told him he would never play again. Scott Gorham recalls that 'Phil was beyond livid, beyond being able to speak'.

Morrison and O'Donnell flew out to New York to meet with the record company, make some decisions and see if there was anything they could salvage from the mess. As luck would have it, Queen were due to start a US tour in January and wanted Lizzy as their support. So, who do you call? The irony of Gary stepping in for Brian who had been glassed would not have been lost on those who knew what had happened back in 1974.

Gary reckoned that Phil had been contacting him even before this happened to check out how things were going with Colosseum. As Lizzy tour manager Frank Murray says, 'If Phil had a choice between Gary and Brian in the band, he would have picked Gary. Brian's playing was impeccable, but I think Phil believed that Gary had more possibilities and then, of course, the hassles Robbo caused.' Gary was never far from Phil's mind; on the *Jailbreak* album there is a song called 'Romeo And The Lonely Girl' with the lines 'For all his good looks there were scars that he took / And a lesson to be learned'. Phil would tease Gary that Romeo was an anagram of Moore.

If Phil wanted to check out how Colosseum were doing, a look at the respective recording success would also have told a salutary tale. In April 1976, *Strange New*

Flesh was released with a whimper rather than a bang, while in the same month *Jailbreak* was a Top 20 gold-disc-awarded album on both sides of the Atlantic. For Gary, this was another well-timed opportunity. Unlike his low-rent experience in the States with Skid Row, here was a chance for some major profile-raising with a band on the up, playing support to a world-class act in front of audiences in the tens of thousands. This was the kind of situation Lizzy relished; the chance to give a main act a real run for their money. As Scott said, 'Our motto was leave the stage covered in blood and watch the headliners slip all over it.'

How did Scott react to the arrival of Gary Moore? 'We had a short rehearsal time, no more than a week and we'd never played together. But you could see it was going to work and work really well. Gary's style was a lot different from Brian's and I'd never really played with another guitarist. But when he started to play, it was, like "Oh-oh, this guy's fuckin' good and I gotta get my game together." But what made it so easy was that Gary was right on the ball. He did know the songs and anything he didn't know he got—just like that. "Which part are you playing? Okay. I'll do the harmony bit." Go through it once, got it and we're outta there.'

Beyond Gary's sheer musicianship, Scott says, 'it was the happiest I'd been for a long time. Brian had been getting out of control, he and Phil were arguing the whole time about stupid little things. Phil would have a go at Brian for growing a beard: "I'm the only one allowed to have facial hair." You kiddin' me? Crap like that. When Gary came in, it felt fresh, with new energy and no arguing. Just heads down and everybody pulled together.'

Given Thin Lizzy's *modus operandi* with headliners, backstage tussles with Queen's slick organisation were to be expected. There were arguments over soundchecks: how long Lizzy would get, or even if they would get one at all. Would Lizzy be allowed to fly their logo and if so, where on the stage would it hang? How long would Lizzy play for? There were certain no-go areas of the stage out into the audience where Lizzy were banned from performing. Gary took absolutely no notice of that at all and just ran straight to the audience and gave them the full Gary.

As Scott recalls with some relish, 'The Queen audience certainly seemed to know who we were. We were getting encores; people were pumping their fists. We were in San Francisco and I remember going over to Gary's side of the stage and the audience just lifted off their feet. And this wasn't your regular audience; there were hot pants, spangles, glitter and all that—and that was the guys!'

At the start of the tour, Chris O'Donnell says he was buttonholed by former

Hendrix tour manager Gerry Stickells, now working with Queen: 'Be good,' he said, 'but not too good.' Gary told Mark Putterford, 'Apparently Freddie was very intimidated by our band. People would tell us afterwards that Freddie would be stomping up and down his dressing room while we were on stage going, "Listen to that applause! Get that band off NOW!!" One night Freddie's boyfriend … came into our dressing room and said, "I just want to tell you guys you were wonderful tonight," before scurrying out of the door. He told us later that Freddie would have killed him if he'd known he'd been in to congratulate us. We thought it was hysterical.

'I think the tour was the best thing Lizzy ever did from the point of view of raising their profile. And for me it was all very fresh—much better than my first stint in the band. Some of the shows we did were brilliant … we actually did an incredible amount of shows in three months (42) and the travelling was very gruelling. The weather was awful—it was the worst winter they'd had for years … There were certainly a few interesting flights on that tour …'

Gary and the Colosseum management had made it clear that once the tour was over, Gary would return to promote the new album *Electric Savage*. Scott reckons this made life a lot easier: 'I knew Gary wasn't a permanent fixture and we talked about that quite a bit on the tour. There was that magic circle, we'd done tours and albums and had quite a bit of success and I wanted to keep that continuity going with Brian Robertson. My thinking was, *If you start changing things around, you'll break the magic circle*. And because Gary was only helping out, anything anybody was unhappy about they could swallow, and it was easy for Gary to take orders and he was fine about it.'

Phil couldn't do anything but accept that Gary was once again only temporary, but he wasn't above playing some mind games in the press to put the pressure on, to suggest the area in which Gary could really shine: 'I can't say to him, "Hey man, this is going to be far more successful that Colosseum." I gotta respect him for playing what he wants. I mean I think Gary Moore is the best living rock'n'roll guitarist in the world today, but he's in what I consider to be a jazz-rock field. In that field, there's a lot of great guitarists. Like the competition is *heavy!* That's basically the paradox that Gary is in, but all the great guitarists go after that. You either do what Clapton has done and go simpler and become a songwriter or you do what Beck is doing and chase it into the realms of where it becomes musicianship.

'That's what Gary is doing. He's just ahead of his audience. When Gary Moore was playing rock, the audiences should have been there to hear him. But it might be down to Gary. "I've got this down. I want to play rock again." He has these two sides to him all the time; the musician side and this basic energy side where he just wants to go out and boogie, and he gets that chance occasionally to blow out as a rock guitarist with Lizzy. But with Colosseum, he satisfies a much more demanding need, playing with excellent musicians like Jon Hiseman.' Or, as Chris O'Donnell puts it rather sardonically, 'You're either in a rock band or you're a musician. You can't have it both ways.'

Brian had not been fired from the band but was allowed only a bit part on the album *Bad Reputation* (which didn't include having his picture of the front cover). He knew he was on borrowed time, to the extent of planning a band with his flatmate bassist Jimmy Bain to be called Wild Horses.

As 1977 gave way to 1978, the situation with Brian was becoming impossible; he was forever getting into drunken fights and there was talk again of replacements so that when it went wrong with Brian again, as everybody knew it would, they'd be prepared this time and not caught on the hop. Chris O'Donnell says, 'he was given an ultimatum by a doctor who said, "If you don't stop drinking, you'll be dead inside three months." I rang his dad to say we were sending Brian back and his very words were, "Christ, you don't get what we Glaswegians do. We're hard drinkers. That's makes us creative." No, it doesn't, it makes you a drunk.' Talking to Mark Putterford, Brian was completely honest: 'I was really out of control, a complete asshole … [As well as speed] I'd be on two bottles of Johnny Walker Black Label a night; half a bottle at the soundcheck, half a bottle before going on stage and the other bottle during the gig.'

Eventually, even Scott, who had done everything he could to keep Brian in the band, had to concede defeat. 'I defended him so many times, but I couldn't do it any longer because of what he was actually doing to the band. We'd been working too hard to have one guy bring the whole thing down.'

Come August 1978, with Colosseum at an end, Phil turned to Gary yet again, ahead of their first tour to Australia and once again he agreed. 'We didn't even think of anybody else,' says Scott.

This time, Gary signed a contract, which became a contentious issue. Gary said he would agree to sign if he got equal shares with the rest of the band, while Chris O'Donnell and Scott both say that because such an arrangement would have been unfair to the others, Gary was not a member of the Thin Lizzy company, but instead had an open-ended contract as an employee. Both can be right; it was perfectly reasonable for Gary to expect equal shares of forthcoming gig money (and royalties on any songs he wrote or contributed to) but not to receive, for example, royalties due to the band for recordings that he had nothing to do with.

Even so, he could still have walked away from a contract and, as obvious a choice as he was, there was still lingering doubt in the Lizzy camp that he would really stay this time. Phil's distrust of him left Gary a bit bemused: 'We were good mates, but we would always fall out. There was another side of Phil that I didn't really get. I think he was always insecure. He'd want to fuck you before you could fuck him. I could never understand it.'

In truth, Gary's return to Lizzy was more like a slow train coming. In January that year, he was at the Ramport Studio to help Phil lay down tracks for Phil's projected solo album, *Solo In Soho*. Shortly afterwards, Gary secured a deal with Monty Babson to record what would become his second solo album after *Grinding Stone*, to be called *Back On The Streets*. Recording took place at Morgan Studios and was in effect a coming together of all Gary's musical activity since 1974. Tracks were split between the jazz-rock style of Colosseum while the rest primarily represented the hard rocking Lizzy style with Phil and Brian Downey. Gary's original idea was just to do a jazz-rock album, but he soon realised that all he would be doing was recreating Colosseum II, so he began working up some ideas with Phil to somehow balance the album out.

Back On The Streets was co-produced with Gary by Chris Tsangarides, who was making the grade as an engineer at Morgan Studios and had been the tape operator for *Electric Savage* and *War Dance*. 'So, when it came time to do Gary's album I said, "I'd like to do that," and it was okay because they weren't looking for a "big noise" producer and, anyway, producers were not in the same league as they became in the 1980s and 1990, plus of course I was cheap!

'Believe it or not, I do remember coming out with that classic line, "You play it son, and I'll record it," and, to be fair, Gary let me do what I wanted because he didn't have any more of a clue than I did. There was only so much you could do with a recording then, anyway. We went for a good feel and a nice balance and that was pretty much it.

'Gary asked me if I knew any drummers, so I got Simon Phillips in, who was only a young kid at the time, but who I had worked with on a Jack Bruce album, and we did the bulk of the album in a week, all jazz instrumentals. Then Gary came in with this ghetto blaster and played me a song done with a drum machine, keyboards and a guitar solo. "What do you think of this?" "Oh, that's lovely," I said. It was "Parisienne Walkways" and he said that Phil and Brian were coming in to record it.' The song started out as an instrumental written by Gary and Don Airey during Colosseum II days called 'Biscayne Blues', which itself was similar (if slower) to a hard bop/bossa nova style song composed by jazz trumpeter Kenny Dorham and appropriately titled 'Blue Bossa'. Gary told the story of what happened next:

'I remember I came to Phil's house one night and he was sitting in bed, it was about seven o'clock in the evening and he said he didn't want to get up too early that particular day. I went to his bedroom, where he had an old beaten-up acoustic guitar and I was sort of saying, "I got this melody." I think I played the lead line. I was just singing and playing. He said, "It sounds really French that, let me put some lyrics to it." So, he kind of went away and he wrote the vocal parts to it, because up to that point I was convinced it should be an instrumental. I never thought for a moment of putting lyrics to it. He came up with this great vocal part, which was, of course, "I remember Paris in '49," which was actually very ambiguous lyrics because his father's name was Parris and Phil was born in 1949.'

Chris explained to *Sound On Sound* how the track was recorded: 'I set up the sound and then it was just a case of one, two, three, off we go. It was captured in no time at all—one or two takes—maybe three at the most—and what surprised me was that Gary left a gap for the long, big note [which began the solo about two thirds of the way through the song] and then they started up again. I couldn't understand how he knew where the band would come back in. There was no click. However, the solo you hear on the record was captured live in one take and he got it in perfect time. There's a double track and a harmony and all I added was an echo plate. Unbelievable.

'In terms of the other overdubs, Phil pumped the accordion and Gary played it and Phil also played the song's descending intro notes on the upright bass. It was an electric one and we had to put chinograph marks on the fretboard so he knew where to place his fingers. Gary played a Solina string synth to imitate the sound of a mandolin and a Rickenbacker 12-string guitar.'

Gary always contended that what happened next took place during the mixing of 'Parisienne Walkways', but Chris Tsangarides reckons that the song was mixed in Studio 1 at Morgan while the following incident happened in Studio 3 during the mixing of 'Song For Donna', a ballad destined for the album, which Gary had written for his girlfriend.

'I'm sitting there at the desk getting on with it and in walks Ozzy Osbourne,

Bill Ward and Geezer Butler. And they all sit down and say, "Ooo, play that again, Chris, that's luverly, that is." Then Bill Ward throws up in the bin, meanwhile Ozzy starts chasing my tape op round the room with his pants down, "Oh, I lurve you Vic, I wanna fuck you, come here." And then he starts doing this aeroplane business into the wall. I mean serious, running the full length of the studio and boosh—right into it. Thank God it was padded, you know. Half an hour later, Tony Iommi's on the phone, "What have you done to Ozzy? Stupid sod is numb, he can't feel anything from the neck down." So, I told him and he said, "Oh, that stupid fucker." So, he's off to the hospital and we are all proper worried. He comes back about half an hour later bouncing off the walls. What happened? Nothing to do with the wall. He'd taken so much coke he couldn't feel anything. Meanwhile, I'm trying to mix this beautiful song, he's standing next to me, taps me on the shoulder and there's his dick on my shoulder—which was a famous Ozzy trick.

'We also did "Fanatical Fascists" and "Don't Believe a Word". And it all seemed to take forever, because on some days, we'd be working on Phil's solo album.'

'Don't Believe a Word' was something of a contentious issue in Thin Lizzy. Phil had written it originally as a 12-bar blues, which both Brians thought was, to put it bluntly, 'shite', as they said. Brian R added in a guitar riff while Brian D speeded the whole thing up with a quick tempo shuffle beat. Chris was much taken with the version he recorded. As he told *Sound On Sound*, 'I loved the simplicity and emptiness of it … it was a sort of Peter Green/Santana "Black Magic Woman"-type vibe. Ironically, Peter Green, who was making one of his famous comebacks at the time, was in the adjacent studio to us at Morgan and he popped in to see Gary. So, I played him this song and went, "How come we don't sound as good at that?" I remember Phil looking at me, me looking at Gary and Gary looking at Phil all with big cheesy grins as if to say, "We've got the thumbs up from God!" It was amazing.

'I was dead lucky really,' says Chris, 'me just starting out and look what I had fallen into—a rare talent like Gary and all those great songs. You'd have to be really stupid to mess that up so it made me look good. Everything came from Gary's fingers, from his heart and soul. He had faith in me to handle that album when I was just a kid.'

That was a start of a long-standing professional and personal relationship between Gary, Chris and their families (they became godfathers to their respective children). Chris went on to work mainly with hard rock and metal artists, including Judas Priest, Yngwie Malmsteen and Black Sabbath, but also Tom Jones and Depeche Mode. 'It was a strange album, though,' concedes Chris. 'Colosseum II, Thin Lizzy and a bit of punk coming in because Paul Cook and Steve Jones shipped up and we did a few songs with them, which never came out.'

Gary was round at Phil's one night when Gary Holton of the Heavy Metal Kids was staying there (more on him later) and they got into a conversation about the appeal of just going and playing a gig, collecting the cash and walking away—no agents, record companies, managers, no business, just play and go. Phil came up with the name for this hypothetical band, The Greedy Bastards, soon shortened to The Greedies—and the idea caught fire among the younger musicians on the burgeoning London punk scene. A debut gig was planned for February with Phil, Gary, Gary Holton, Jimmy Bain and Dammed drummer Rat Scabies, but that fell through. Instead, they played the Electric Ballroom in north London, managed by ex-Lizzy tour manager Frank Murray, on July 29, the day before Gary was officially announced as Brian Robertson's replacement. On stage were Gary, Phil, Scott and Brian Downey, Steve Jones and Paul Cook from the Sex Pistols, plus Jimmy Bain and Chris Spedding.

Phil had this idea he wanted to stay in touch with 'the street'; he didn't want Lizzy to be lumped in with the bands of the 1970s, now dismissed as 'dinosaurs' by a new generation of club goers and record buyers. But while Phil loved all the trappings of being a rock star, Thin Lizzy were never going to take themselves so seriously that their music took on the pomposity and self-importance bedevilling some of their contemporaries. Lizzy were rock hooligans and could easily find common cause with the brash and thrash of the new wave. When The Greedies played together, the set list was far more Lizzy than Sex Pistols, but it didn't matter, because in the end it was still guitars, bass and drums—it was still rock'n'roll. However, Phil didn't fully embrace the punk aesthetic; he was absolutely not up for being spat at. The audience was probably a mix of fans, which prompted Phil to shout out, presumably to the Lizzy faction, "If anybody starts fookin' spitting, give them a fookin' wham from me!"

Some commentators have congratulated Phil on being shrewd and engineering a great career move. Well, not really. Phil's aspirations for Thin Lizzy being an international headlining band playing in big arenas like Queen were never going to depend on the grace and favour of a handful of devotees on the UK punk scene. And there was a fatal downside to this marriage. As well as being in the vanguard of new music, some of the big names on the punk scene were also early adopters of an escalating drug habit—heroin.

Up until the late 1970s, heroin use in the UK was primarily restricted to older drug users on the London scene, who had come out of the middle-class, bohemian jazz scene of the West End. They were injecting heroin imported from the Far East; few people wanted to inject their drugs and if you tried to smoke this form of white heroin, it would just melt. Then a new form of heroin began appearing on the streets of London, imported from the Middle East—brown heroin you could smoke. No needles meant the earlier taboo, that injecting heroin put you over the line, was gone. People started smoking heroin off tinfoil—chasing the dragon. They quickly realised that most of their money was literally going up in smoke. A far more cost-effective way of smoking for this new breed of young working-class users was to inject. By which time, they were hooked.

Phil had already been warned off drinking, but while on Lizzy's US tour in September 1977, he was taking increasing amounts of cocaine and then trying to sleep off the effects with tranquilizers. Brian Robertson had been dabbling with heroin and now Phil's own house was fast turning into a shooting gallery for the detritus of the London punk scene, who viewed heroin use as some kind of romantic, anti-establishment 'outsiderness'. Phil would complain that Sid Vicious would come round, drop needles on the floor and then pick them up and inject himself. Donna says that once, when she and Gary were there, 'Nancy Spungen was wandering around naked while Paula Yates was slumped on the sofa.' Not wishing to appear 'uncool', Phil just let this go on around him, until he too began to sink into the heroin quagmire.

With Gary now fully signed up, they were about to embark on yet another US tour, this time headlining over AC/DC and variously supporting Kansas, Journey, REO Speedwagon and Blue Öyster Cult and then on to Lizzy's first trip to Australia. Out of the blue, Brian Downey—Mr Dependable—threw a hefty spanner in the works by saying that he was totally exhausted and couldn't make the trip. He headed off to Ireland to follow his favourite form of relaxation, away from all the stresses and strains of the music business—just him, a fishing rod and the quiet of the Irish countryside.

Although Phil was aghast at losing Brian, the band were due to fly via Los Angeles for a few days rehearsal and the feeling was it shouldn't be that difficult to find a replacement drummer there. The auditions came down to former Zappa drummer Terry Bozzio and Mark Nauseef, who had seen service with Ronnie Dio's Elf and The Ian Gillan Band. The official story is that Mark got it over Terry, who was supposedly asking for too much money and wanted to bring his wife on the tour. An insider rumour also circulated that one member of the Lizzy entourage (and surprisingly not Phil) got a bit too friendly with said wife, causing Terry to beat a hasty retreat.

According to Frank Murray, 'America did seem to bring out the worst in Philip at times' and trouble seemed to swirl around the band and the crew, who were constantly getting into punch-ups. Sound man Peter Eustace said that Phil made sure that the crew and the band hung together and partied together. He would conduct the interviews for prospective new crew members himself and his first question was 'Can you fight?'

His latest escapade was to try and track down Jerry Lee Lewis as he had heard that the rock'n'roll legend didn't take kindly to black people. Gary said that they were waiting for the limo to come round and pick them up and watched in horror as it swung across the road, aiming to cut through a gas station, when another car blocked him in and the limo driver proceeded to start ramming into it. Out of the car steps a man mountain waving a gun. The driver screeches across to the band, tells them to jump in fast and the chase is on. 'At one point,' said Gary, 'the other car pulled alongside our car, the guy wound down the window and started waving his gun at me!' They jumped lights, drove through the car parks but the guy stayed right on their tail until they eventually managed to shake him off. And they never did find Jerry Lee.

Phil managed to get into two fights in the same bar on consecutive nights and then was nearly busted for coke coming back into the US from a trip to Mexico. Gary had his moments too; a Thin Lizzy fan, Mike Flanagan, saw the show on September 23 at the Uptown Theater in Kansas City. Expecting to see Brian Robertson, he had no idea who Gary was: '[He] was jaw-droppingly good ... He was absolutely on fire ... I'd seen the likes of Iommi, Blackmore. Brian May, Buck Dharma, Ted Nugent, Alex Lifeson and ... Van Halen four times in one year, but what I saw out of Gary Moore had convinced me that he was as good if not better than all of them. BUT I have never seen anybody get so angry on the stage as he did that evening ... Thin Lizzy had a very rough night ... they were having technical difficulties ... Phil's bass didn't sound right in the mix, [and] not once but twice, Gary's guitar cut out while he was soloing.

'The first time it happened he was visibly angry, but a roadie got things squared away. The second time it happened, during his extended solo on "Me And The Boys", he became unglued. He literally took off his Les Paul and threw it at the roadie ... hard! ... and he walked off stage and let the band finish the song. The roadies got things squared away again and he came out, but they wrapped up the show quickly from there.'

While Gary and Phil didn't argue on this tour, nevertheless, Gary was always on the look-out to wind Phil up, especially if it meant puncturing his carefully cultivated media image. On the flight to Australia, Phil got extremely agitated when Mark Nauseef took a picture of Gary spoon-feeding Phil while he was asleep and then during the press conference, Gary made literally an 'off-colour' remark when Phil replied to a journalist that he thought he had some relatives in the country. 'Yes,' said Gary, 'a tribe of Aborigines who live up the road.' Everybody in the room was laughing—except one.

The highlight of the short Australian tour was the concert in the shadow of Sydney Opera House in front of an enormous crowd estimated at around 300,000. The police, who had probably never seen so many people in one place before, stood nervously by waiting for the riot, which never happened. The show was a triumph; Gary played through his party piece with no power failures this time and threw in a few bars of 'Waltzing Matilda' as a nod to the audience—a little trick he repeated in different countries over the years.

Back home, there were three more Greedies gigs, one in London and two in Dublin, and then the traditional end of year gig at Hammersmith Odeon to thank the Lizzy fans. However, although the band welcomed back Brian Downey, it didn't go well with poor sound, mistakes and another Gary moment. He was handed a guitar with no strap, right before his big solo moment, first London gig back in the band and the guitar clatters to the floor. Gary chased the roadie off the stage and used the guitar to demolish a mike stand. What should have been a celebration of a very good year for the band, turned into a mess, a harbinger of what lay ahead.

06

DAYS OF SMACK AND ROSES

—

Gary's solo album *Back On The Streets* was released in September 1978. The playing throughout was exemplary, the young Simon Phillips in particular exploding across the album and with the title track, Gary had come up with real barnstorming crowd-pleaser. He was very comfortable in the studio surrounded by musicians he knew, like Don Airey: 'It was always a challenge for him to find musicians who could keep up with him. It was great music, wonderful ideas. Gary was a genius, really. In the studio he could make something out of nothing in a minute.' Yet, as Chris Tsangarides remarked, it was something of a hybrid, which ran the risk of falling between stools, very much the fate of both Skid Row and The Gary Moore Band, although the material on this new album was streets ahead in accessibility over Skid Row.

Gary himself admitted to *Melody Maker* a few months later that having got Phil involved in what turned out to be some of the best tracks on the album, and knowing how poorly Colosseum II recordings had fared, 'I'd like to have removed all the instrumental pieces. I think it demonstrates two sides of my playing very well, but it's not consistent. You don't really get any credit just for being versatile.' The reviews were guarded: they didn't warm much to Gary's voice or the writing, but generally agreed that depending on your tastes, there was something here for both fans of Thin Lizzy and Colosseum II. And that was the point, really; Gary had yet to build to his own solo profile and have a strong fan base to sell to, so the album managed no higher than seventy in the UK album charts. However, like *Grinding Stone*, the album has risen in the overall assessment of Gary's output.

Five of the eight tracks are jointly credited to Gary and Donna (Campbell). She maintains this was all part of Gary wanting to look after her; they had been together for four years, no mean feat in the notoriously fickle world of rock'n'roll romance. Donna had spells in hospital, where she says Gary did his utmost to care for her, and they even got as far as wedding invitations, until Donna backed out at the last minute. Less charitably, it has been suggested that Gary was advised to do this for tax reasons, akin to a businessman putting the house in his wife's name. Donna says she was offered a lot of money for her share of the rights, but eventually sold out for a much lesser sum to Monty Babson. Donna, incidentally, is the girl on the front cover of the album waiting for her man to come out of prison and on the streets again.

However, by the time the album came out, their relationship was over. Gary was interviewed by *Beat Instrumental* in January 1979, where talking about Phil he says, 'At the moment we're living together again while I'm looking for a new place.' So, what happened? Gary received his fair share of female fan mail, some of it pretty explicit. Instead of just ripping it up, though, he would stash it under the carpet of their flat. The inevitable happened; once when Gary was away, says Donna, 'my friend found this letter and photo, which he really didn't want to show me'. It was from somebody called Lisa with a photo attached of a young blonde girl. This was Lisa Franklin, whom Gary had met out in Australia on the Lizzy tour: 'I had a job with Chappell Music Publishing in Sydney. I went out to dinner with some friends, one of whom knew Gary. He was very offhand over dinner, but as I got up to leave, he followed me out and invited me to the show next day. But we never met up and then he phoned me to say he had sent a roadie to look for me. So, we went out for dinner again and I finished up back at the hotel. But he really wasn't my type, to be honest—the tight trousers, the heavy metal look.'

Lisa lived in Los Angeles; when the Lizzy Australian walkabout was finished, instead of going back to London with the band and crew, Gary flew to LA (with Mark Nauseef) to see her. When Donna got wind of what was going on, she confronted him with the evidence. Despite Gary's desperate pleading that it was a one-night stand—and, says Donna, trashing a guitar in the dressing room when she subsequently announced she was leaving—there was no going back.

There is a song on *Back On The Streets* called 'Fanatical Fascists', by Phil Lynott– a punk song about the political situation in the UK where extreme right-wing groups like the National Front were growing in popularity. Talking to Mark Putterford many years later, Gary said, 'I seem to remember there were a lot of people around at the time who were interested in stealing that song. Gary Holton from the Heavy Metal Kids was one. I just managed to get in first.' Gary Holton might have missed out on a song, but he did manage to steal Donna.

As well as leading the HMK, Gary Holton was also actor, most famous for his role in *Auf Wiedersehen, Pet*, a very successful UK TV comedy drama about a group of British construction workers who go to work on building sites in Germany, where, unlike home, there are jobs and money. Unfortunately, Gary Holton was a chronic heroin user; he married Donna in 1979, but they split in 1981, albeit remaining friends. Holton died of a heroin overdose in 1985, midway through the second series of *Auf Wiedersehen, Pet*, but the producers used body doubles and clever editing of dialogue already recorded to allow the series to be completed.

Coming off the back of the platinum-selling *Live and Dangerous* album, which got to No.2 in the UK charts, there was a lot riding on the next studio album. As well as a lyricist, Phil was a published poet and well versed in Ireland's strong poetic traditions. The centrepiece the new album, titled *Black Rose: A Rock Legend*, was a poem by James Clarence Mangan called *Róisín Dubh*, a patriotic poem disguised as a love song, about the Spanish fleet coming to rescue their Catholic brethren from English oppression, during a time in the nineteenth century when expressions of nationalism in Ireland were banned. Phil name-checks the great figures of Irish literature—Joyce, Yeats, Wilde and Brendan Behan.

Built around this song, which combined traditional Irish melodies and new compositions, is an album acclaimed as Thin Lizzy's finest studio offering and, in chart terms, certainly their most successful, owing much to Gary's input throughout. He showed what a difference he could make to the musical maturity and intelligence of the band.

Writing for *Sounds* in April 1979, Gary Bushell underlined that Lizzy were a cut above the average hard rock band: 'Lizzy are head and shoulders above any of yer recycle a riff and scream about "gunna ball ya all nite long" toss-off "competition". Lizzy write songs. They have energy, they have hooks, and at their best they have perfect rock dreams … Even the sexuality, the "macho stud" bit, is more healthy animalism than any avid "inadequates" fantasising.'

Many years later, Gary talked to Lizzy chronicler Martin Popoff about the work he did on the album. Gary has three song credits: 'Toughest Street In Town', 'Sarah' and 'Black Rose'. About the first song, Gary said, 'That was a riff I had before I joined the band and we built it up from there. And the middle eight riff was a riff that Scott had hanging around. And the title was mine, I kind of lead off on some of the lyrics. I would write some of the lyrics for the first verse and a chorus and Phil basically filled in all the holes for me … But the main idea was something I had. I think I wrote it in New York … Good place to come up with a song like that.'

Gary reckoned that 'Sarah' (written about Phil's baby with Caroline Crowther) was destined for Phil's album *Solo In Soho*. 'I wrote most of that song … and [Phil] wrote most of the lyrics. But … it was my idea that it should be about his kid which is a really weird thing to have happened.' The song was recorded at Morgan Studios back in 1978, with drummer Mark Nauseef and Huey Lewis on harmonica. Lewis was in a band called Clover, who had supported Lizzy in the States. Nobody else in the band thought it was right for a Lizzy album, a point echoed by Harry Doherty in his review for *Melody Maker* when he called it 'oddly out of place'.

Gary recalled an impromptu guest appearance with Huey Lewis and Clover in the States. They were both travelling in their respective buses and met up on the road: 'He invited me to come and play with him next night. They were doing "The Boys Are Back In Town" in their set at the time and I came on stage and it was the weirdest gig. Because I remember all the guitars were in their flight cases because he wanted it really, really quiet onstage … And he had the mayor and all his family sitting there … it was like a Cliff Richard gig in England … it was all so polite and everything was so low key backstage. And I thought, *What happened to rock'n'roll, you know?* Very strange, but he was a nice guy Huey, I always liked him.'

Gary composed 'Sarah' on acoustic guitar, with added drum machine, 'and we added a lot of stuff after that … it was put together over quite a long period of time. So that was completely different from any other track Thin Lizzy ever recorded … [and] is probably the best showcase of my playing on that record.'

Gary said that 'Black Rose' was his favourite track on the album: 'I wrote the Irish sounding, Celtic-like jig type pieces in the middle. I got very involved in the arrangement of that song with Philip. We worked pretty closely on it … I think [Phil's] idea was to represent the different people in the band. Because Brian Robertson was Scottish, he thought of doing it with him at one time, so there's a bit of "Will You Go, Lassie Go" in there … a traditional Scottish song … plus a bit of "Shenandoah", which represents Scott. But then it was also an Irish Celtic legend sort of thing … [Phil] was very into Irish poetry and Irish legend.'

Over and above his direct compositional input, Gary's professionalism was felt right across the recording process, which took place under the control of top producer Tony Visconti at (for tax reasons) EMI's Marconi Studio in Paris. As Tony said to Scott Gorham biographer Harry Doherty, 'I thought Gary was a great influence on the music. He was an incredible technician.' Interviewed in turn for this book, Doherty said that during the recording, Phil would be in bed for 'days at a time. Both Gary and Tony were concerned about that downward spiral. But it turned out to be a very good album and you can put that down to Gary's quality.'

Scott also acknowledges Gary's positive effect on the band: 'Before Gary, we were a pretty loose kinda band in the studio. We didn't give a shit. But with Gary coming in, his work ethic was completely different. He was into everything being clean and absolutely in tune, the vibrato totally in time. We really worked harder, a lot of rehearsal time, a lot of thinking about the songs, how we were going down. And he was a really different guy to work with in the studio. He was hearing things that sort of weren't there. With Robbo and everyone, it was "Hey, well, we can fix that later." With Gary, it was "Hey, let's do it again, c'mon."

'He might not have been in charge, but he was certainly listened to because you knew how good this guy was. Gary didn't seem to want to take over anything, just put in really great, valid ideas. And it was a really substantial album, probably the first one that had a substantial feel to it. Everything just tightened up. It was his first album with Thin Lizzy and, by God, he was going to make it a good one.'

Scott says that Gary was also good for him personally: 'There's a run in "Do Anything You Want To", and I don't do scales like that. But we just sat down and worked it out until we got it right. He was coming up with guitar parts that I didn't know if I could actually play. But that's where Gary was really good for me. He forced my hand to become a better player, which I'll always appreciate about him. He made me step up. You have to play with really good players to become a good player yourself. You can't be afraid. People ask me if I was 'afraid' of Gary Moore. Hell, no, what's the point of being afraid of somebody who you want to learn from? And he would show me and we would sit down and work things out because he wanted to be surrounded by good players himself.'

Tony Visconti had a solid working relationship with Gary, which not only contributed to the success of the album but was probably instrumental in getting the album done at all, because he was becoming very frustrated at the dissolution gaining force around him. Phil would come in, spend hours and hours on vocals, changing lyrics as he went along and then reveal these were just guide vocals and they'd have to be done properly later. The main reason why it took so long to get the vocals right was the impact of cocaine on Phil's voice, making it sound very nasal. Scott admits that in Paris, 'the partying started in earnest, this was where the wheels started to come off … it was the beginning of the downfall of Thin Lizzy.'

'Got To Give It Up', on the album, was Phil's attempt at an anti-drug song. But there is an old saying in storytelling that goes, 'Show, don't tell'—and clearly, whatever Phil was writing about the perils of drugs, he wasn't taking his own advice. He admitted as such to Harry Doherty at the time: 'How many times do you say you are going to give something up and then you don't?' According to the engineer Kit Woolven, cannabis, coke and Courvoisier were all to hand while Phil was trying to record this song, which was almost the last straw for Tony. But matters were getting worse; in Paris, both Phil and Scott were dabbling with heroin—not strung out yet but heading for that slippery slope.

They had found common cause as drug buddies; this sets up a whole sub-set of intrigue and secrets, a different level of communication, excluding anybody not part of the inner circle. Scott says he and Phil 'were always hanging around each other, drugs, going to clubs. Gary wasn't doing anything like that. I don't even think he was drinking at that point. We didn't even bother to call him up. We just be liquored up, drugged up and having a great old time. I think there was quite a bit of Gary being jealous of me and Phil, of the relationship we had. He was only really being paid attention to when he had the guitar on—beyond that, it was "Don't even bother knocking on Gary's door." Looking back, we probably should have done more to integrate him into the fold.' Having produced Lizzy's *Bad Reputation* album, Tony Visconti could see that Gary didn't fit in with the whole Lizzy rolling caravan of dissolution. He turned to Gary one day and said, "What the fuck are doing in this band?"'

Gary flew Lisa in from LA and she spent some time in Paris and says that at the playback party for *Black Rose*, heroin was doing the rounds: 'For Gary, it was like being sober at an alcoholic party. He was always on the outside of that.'

Despite all the cracks in the edifice, 1979 was shaping up to be the most important year in the band's history. They had important promotional tours to undertake, including the States, which had all the potential to finally break them as a major band, so long as they could get through a whole US tour without ten types of disaster. But as Scott says, 'You never let your guard down because something is going to fuck up. It's the curse of Lizzy. That's the way it is.'

In March, they went out to the States for a short tour supporting Nazareth. From the end of March, for the next few weeks, they toured the UK and Europe, although the last few dates in May were cancelled officially because Phil had contracted food poisoning from sour milk. The real reason was of course, drugs, which, says Lisa, 'really pissed Gary off'.

Brian Downey flew back to Ireland, while the rest of the band, Mark Nauseef and Huey Lewis flew to the Bahamas to do more work on Phil's solo album and for Gary to record the follow-up single to 'Parisienne Walkways', called 'Spanish Guitar'. Even here, Gary was seemingly out on a limb. Scott says, 'it was blazing hot, we were all lying round the pool drinking, and up comes Gary in black t-shirt, black trousers, black boots, sitting under an umbrella looking so white. "For fuck's sake, Gary, come in the pool. What ya doin'?" But he didn't want to know.'

On the Nazareth tour, during a stop-over in New York, Phil and Scott began injecting heroin in the company of Willy DeVille from Mink DeVille. For the first time, the thorns of the Black Rose drew blood. From Gary's perspective, the drug/drink situation was manageable in the studio while they were recording the album. He often sat with Tony Visconti when the other guys weren't there, working to make improvements across the whole album. In the studio, you can always re-do parts, in theory, as many times as it takes to get it right. Onstage, you only get one shot: increasingly, the after-show party began before show time and for Gary that became too much to bear.

Gary related one story to Mark Putterford where he says that Phil was so late getting ready for a gig that the limo left without him: 'Later he arrived at the gig and I could tell he was pissed off in a big way. He'd been doing amphetamines the night before and he was "coming down" and that made his mood worse … So that night we went on stage and Phil was still in a foul mood. By this time, he was beginning to make a lot of mistakes on stage because of the state he was in; he'd forget words, miss bits out and once he even sang through my guitar solo. I was screaming at him on stage and he had his back to the audience and was screaming back at me. We were both going "FUCK YOU!"'

Gary said the guys in the front row were shouting out 'You suck!' and then Phil split his leather trousers and had to scuttle behind the drum riser to change. The crew were killing themselves because he had been really awkward with them earlier. Reflecting back on this later, Gary called the whole mess 'comical', but he certainly wasn't laughing at the time.

Scott admits that Gary was not wrong to point all the mistakes that were happening onstage; because he and Phil were in seven sorts of disarray, 'we came up with some real stinkers'. It was a real affront to Gary's own professional standards. He would remonstrate to whoever was listening. Nobody was, not least because most of the crew were just as wrecked. And nobody, other than Gary, was going to challenge Phil. He could be an intimidating figure; he was also the band leader, and in a position to get anybody fired.

Chris O'Donnell was shocked when he found out about the heroin use; Phil had issued instructions that this should be kept secret from the management. 'But anyway, you couldn't tell,' says Chris, 'not in the slightest.' And it is true that users can be very adept at hiding their habit; Phil was not falling down all over the place.

Even so, the general view inside the camp regarding Gary's complaint would have been: 'Lizzy still managed to get through most of their European tour and the first section of the US tour, the records were doing very well, fans were generally none the wiser and, hey—this is Thin Lizzy not Barry Manilow, so get over it and stop rocking the boat.'

That was never going to wash with Gary. They arrived in LA and Gary and Phil spent time in a studio in the few days leading up the first gig so that Phil could lay down some vocals for 'Spanish Guitar'. But said Gary at the time, 'the vocals were so bad, the engineer asked me if he had a cold'. Brian Downey went down to the studio to hear what was going on: 'I found the vibe very weird, pretty bad. I think something must have happened between them at that studio session.'

While Gary and Phil were tearing each other apart in the States, back home was the evidence of how powerful they were as a creative team. Between March and June, *Black Rose* reached the second spot in the album charts, 'Do Anything You Want To' was in the Top 20, while 'Waiting For An Alibi' and 'Parisienne Walkways' both cracked the Top 10, the latter giving Gary his highest ever singles chart position as a solo artist. Back on the road, the band got through the first four gigs supporting Journey. Scott still felt at the time that what was happening really wasn't that terrible, it was fixable, nothing bad was going to happen. And then it did.

On July 4, they played Bill Graham's Day on the Green Festival at the Oakland Stadium in front of 50,000 with Journey, The J Geils Band, UFO and Nazareth. In Gary's words, 'we were doing this huge gig in front of thousands of people. He [Phil] gets up, forgets the words again, kicks the mike over and has a strop on stage … and that's when I thought, *That's it. I can't do this anymore.*'

There was a major shout-up backstage and Gary stormed out. He went off to the Le Parc Hotel in West Hollywood where he was staying with Lisa: 'He told me he wasn't going on the rest of the tour and I said, "You can't do that." Then they are ringing to find out where he was and I had to make something up like "We overslept."' In fact, Gary wasn't even there; by the time people started wondering where he was, he'd literally headed for the hills to Northridge, some thirty miles outside Hollywood and the home of former Deep Purple bassist and singer Glenn Hughes. Glenn had been in the Hollywood studio at the same time as Gary and Phil. Mark Nauseef had introduced them and they really hit it off. Gary told Glenn the same story: 'He told me he was going to leave,' says Glenn 'and he said, "I wanna form a band with you." Well, I said, "That would be fantastic, but you've got to finish the tour first." And then, maybe next day, about three in the morning the phone rings and it's Phil: "If you're fookin' hiding him up there, I'm gonna rip your fookin' t'roat out Hughesey." Now, Phil was somebody you really didn't want to cross. I'd never had a fight in my life and I wasn't from the streets of Dublin.'

They were due to fly to Reno for a gig on July 6. Eventually, Chris O'Donnell got Gary on the phone; Phil was in the room with Scott, who recalls: 'Gary was over at Glenn's and he was going on about getting no respect in the band, so Chris is going "Yeah, yeah, you get no respect—now, when are you getting over here?" But Gary was going on and on and, eventually, Phil just said, "Fuck it. Fire him." So, I'm thinking, *Errr ... what does this mean?* "We'll do it as a trio," says Phil. "Whaat?? This is a two-guitar band. I can't play all the parts. What are you talking about??" "No, no, man, you can do it. It's not a problem."' Gary later refuted that conversation, saying Chris O'Donnell asked him point blank whether he was in or out and Gary say he was out. There was another garbled version of Gary's departure told to *Melody Maker* in September, which had Gary missing two gigs and being told in between how well the band played as a trio and then being fired.

An announcement was required. The music business is generally loath to wash its dirty laundry in public, so some excuse could have been made about Gary being 'ill' and unable to continue—as they had done with Phil at the end of the European tour. But the management and Phil were beyond angry: they just let rip, saying Gary had been sacked because he was 'unreliable'. The media had a field day. Headlines proclaimed: 'Lizzy give Gary Moore the boot', 'Thin Lizzy sack Gary Moore', 'Thin Lizzy—Shock Sacking'. Chris O'Donnell says there were so many interview requests that for telephone interviews, unknown to Phil (who usually spoke for the band), he ended up impersonating Phil, who was getting fed up with all the calls. 'When the *Miami Herald* called, I said, "We never let the circumstances control us. We always control the circumstances." It was the headline in the weekend edition and somebody brought it to the dressing room to show Phil who scratched his head and said, "I don't remember saying that," to which I replied, "No, I did." "Right," he said, "I'll do the interviews. I don't need you putting words in my mouth."'

For his part, Gary was incensed; he knew he had resigned rather than been sacked and they must have guessed that he wasn't going to sit on his hands over this. Chris O'Donnell now agrees that was the case but argues that because Gary had a contract, which he had broken, they had to go through the process of sacking him. But there was no 'process'—it was an announcement made in the heat of the moment. Naturally, the media came to Gary for his side of the story, and he was only too happy to oblige. He told BBC Radio One, 'I've never been sacked from any band. I left Lizzy about two weeks ago. It is true that I failed to turn up for a gig, but I was very, very upset at the way things had been going at the time. There were a lot of personal problems between Phil and myself. I didn't feel he was performing up to the standard that the band deserved ... plus personal things that I don't really want to go into. The reason they are saying that I was

DAYS OF SMACK AND ROSES **125**

fired because they are annoyed that I walked out in the middle of a tour. The thing between Phil and I is just very intense. It's either very, very hot between us or it's not so hot … I'm very sorry for the fans, but as a musician I have certain standards to keep up and there is no way I could have gone on with what I was hearing next to me on stage. I think that people who pay to see a band deserve higher quality music than they were getting.'

Gary spoke to another journalist, Ronnie Gurr from *Record Mirror*, who, after Gary had complained about how the partying had got out of hand, asked him if 'the stereotyped role of the rock philanderer holds no attraction for you then?' Gary answered, 'I guess I'm weird like that. My fun is getting up there and playing and as far as I'm concerned, the rest is just preparing for that. I'm just very serious about what I do and I don't see why I should be held back.' He went on to say that 'if I was leader of Thin Lizzy, Phil Lynott wouldn't have lasted a week in the band. He was making me make mistakes.'

And for Gary, 'preparing for that' included proper rehearsals. Gary took rehearsals equally seriously, as we have seen with The Gary Moore Band, and it would be a hallmark in his future career as a solo artist and band leader. It is possible that the rest of the band took a somewhat more cavalier approach to rehearsals—and some might not have been in much of fit state anyway, but it certainly grated with Gary. 'We were playing in front of the biggest audiences on the Journey tour and they allowed us full use of lights, PA and our effects. Now if that isn't an opportunity I don't what is. We blew it because we just hadn't rehearsed enough. We hadn't played for two and a half months. Four or five days rehearsal for a major US tour is a joke.'

Thin Lizzy played five dates as a trio before Midge Ure was drafted in to play his first gig in New Orleans and finish the tour. Gary is on record as saying that whatever his contribution to the band, he always regarded the line-up with Scott and Robbo as the classic Thin Lizzy. If asked, he was always contrite about leaving the band when he did, always admitting he should have at least finished the tour. But if Gary had cause to remember Parris in '79, it would have a reflection full of anger and regret. Phil and Gary didn't speak for another four years.

07

JET FORCE

Consequent on Gary leaving Lizzy, there was a certain amount of tit for tat business swordplay. It was reported that Warner Bros, Lizzy's US label, were planning to stop the release of *Back On The Streets* in the States because of the prominence of Phil's vocals on 'Parisienne Walkways' and 'Don't Believe A Word'. Apparently, Phil objected to this, but Gary took Phil's vocals off the second song and no more was heard about it. Phil's vocal also came off the October '79 single release of 'Spanish Guitar', although by mistake 1,000 copies with Phil's vocal were released in Sweden, which became something of a collector's item.

Then Lizzy's management said they loaned Gary £30,000 to buy a flat in Fitzjohn's Avenue in Hampstead, an upmarket area of north-west London, a bridging loan against getting a mortgage. Gary said it was payment for services. The management retaliated by putting a lien on the property, stopping him from selling it and, according to Gary, even sent somebody round there to change the locks while he was in the States. Inevitably, it all ended up in court, where Gary won because there was no documentation detailing the status of the money. This all played out over the subsequent months of 1979, but still in July, Gary had walked out of Thin Lizzy in the middle of a major US tour. What next? Was Gary left high and dry? Gary's business manager Colin Newman, also representing Monty Babson's production company Mr Sam Music, did a deal with another client, Jet Records, to release *Back On The Streets*. Jet Records was owned by the one and only Don Arden.

The story of Don's mercurial and controversial career in the music business is well documented. Born Harry Levy in 1926, the fiercely independent youngster dropped out of school at 13 and spent most of the 50s living the dream in the entertainment business as a stand-up comic, singer and impresario. He switched to concert promotion bringing over (and then managing) Gene Vincent and arranged tours for Jerry Lee Lewis, Little Richard and Sam Cooke. When The Beatles changed everything, he moved from rock'n'roll into pop first as agent for The Animals, then signed The Nashville Teens, Amen Corner, The Small Faces, The Move and The Electric Light Orchestra to management contracts.

Jet Records was established in 1974 and scored an immediate hit with Lyndsey De Paul's single 'No Honestly'. But it was ELO—selling millions of albums worldwide and breaking into the US market—who established Jet Records as an international player and enabled Don to open an office in Los Angeles. Don had mixed it with some notoriously shady businessmen and outright gangsters, where violence and intimidation were often just a wrong word away. So, he was convinced rock'n'roll was a man's world. His daughter Sharon would prove him wrong. Just as feisty, ruthless and uncompromising as her dad, Sharon wanted her share of the cake. While Gary was signed to Jet Records for recording, he was signed to Sharon for management, her first foray into the world of rock.

Why Gary? Obviously, he was an outstanding guitarist, but not just that—after a period in the doldrums, the guitar hero was coming back into fashion, and the main catalyst for that was Eddie Van Halen.

The band Van Halen's first two albums were worldwide hits straight out of the blocks, essentially setting up the heavy rock explosion of the 1980s and introducing Eddie's ground-breaking guitar technique. Gary first came across Eddie on the 1978 Thin Lizzy tour; apparently, having watched him for the first time, a rather worried Irish guitar player went straight back to the hotel to try out this two-handed tapping business. But, although in interviews Gary could be a bit indifferent about Eddie's playing in so much as he didn't feel moved by Eddie's flamboyant style, they certainly appreciated each other's technical skill. Eddie was sometimes spotted at Gary's concerts, hopping up and down with delight in the wings as Gary would reel off a lick, look at Eddie and they would both laugh.

The other appeal of Gary for Jet was the success of 'Parisienne Walkways', which, while it did nothing in the States, showed that Gary had the potential to compose the sort of power ballad that brought significant chart success for bands like Foreigner and Styx, heralding so-called pop metal as another fashionable genre on the US market for the next decade.

The process of signing Gary to Jet was not without its bizarre aspect. Lizzy manager Chris O'Donnell says he was called to a meeting with Sharon and a lawyer at the Beverly Hills Hotel to negotiate Gary's release from Thin Lizzy. A somewhat bemused Chris says he told them, 'There is nothing to negotiate. He's left the band.' Chris's 'take' on this meeting—which Sharon cannot recall—was that 'I think he must have suggested to the Ardens that he wanted to sign to them for management. As they thought he was a permanent member of Thin Lizzy, they might have imagined he meant he could bring Lizzy with him. So, Lizzy would sign to Don as a band and then Don does a solo deal for Gary with Warners, Lizzy's US label.' But there is no evidence that Gary had any management deal lined up before he left Lizzy, although if anybody seriously thought that with two solo albums to his name, Gary was in Lizzy for keeps, they were fooling themselves, even if he had stayed for the rest of the tour. And on signing up for *Back On The Streets*, Jet threw a massive party for Gary, which must have caught his attention.

For her part, Sharon reckons that Gary leaving Lizzy 'was one of the worst mistakes of his career. Lizzy were just breaking, and they were gaining momentum in America. It was the perfect tour for them, and he just fucked it up. And you never get that momentum back again.' And she was right, they didn't. But whether all the blame for this can really be laid at Gary's door, when Phil and Scott were in such a state, is highly debatable.

Gary had a deal—now he needed a band. Gary and Mark wanted to play together; Gary had told Glenn he wanted to form a band with him; Mark knew Glenn from playing on Glenn's 1977 solo album *Play Me Out*. The stars were aligned. This was clearly a Gary Moore solo project: the band was originally titled Moore but for some reason Jet thought this would be confusing, so the name changed to G-Force after Gary told Mark that at school he was known as 'G' by some of his friends.

'The band was clearly built around Gary and his playing,' says Mark, 'and they were mostly his tunes as well. I reckon this trio was unique; there was Gary's playing, Glenn playing Fender Rhodes with Taurus bass pedals. It was like power soul. Really killing. We got together every day and were rehearsing and writing in rehearsal places around LA and went into the Record Plant to demo what we were writing.'

'But it bothers me to this day that this trio didn't happen. The management dug the band, Sharon was right behind us. They took good care of us, spent a lot of money—crew, rental cars, retainers and other expenses, but were never breathing down our necks. They'd just come down to the studio, check it out and leave.'

Unfortunately, Gary was walking from one chaotic bass/vocalist situation into another. In short, Glenn Hughes was a mess. Or, as Sharon now expresses it in her own inimitable fashion, 'He was out of his fuckin' mind. All you got out of him were sheep noises.'

'There were very few people in the industry who weren't doing coke,' says Glenn, 'and Gary was one of them—he hated that drug. I just adored Gary and we were becoming really, really good friends. He never spoke about the coke directly, but if we were at the Rainbow Bar and Grill and people were snorting coke off the tables, you could tell Gary didn't like it. During that time when Gary was going to stay with me, just before he left Lizzy, I thought, *He's going to be a guest in my house. Surely I can stop this for a while?* And I did.

'But anybody who is an addict or an alcoholic can only hide their addiction for so long before they start digging back in the bag. I was a bit high maintenance, and I didn't realise I had a problem. My lifestyle was really not marrying with their lifestyle, which was more of a drinkers' club—Sharon and David (Arden, who co-ran Jet with his dad), Mark and Gary were all drinkers and if you are an addict in that set, it can rub against the green. Eventually, it will spoil the party.

'It would have been in August 1979, my twenty-eighth birthday, and Sharon had a party for me at La Dome on Sunset Boulevard. I got really drunk that night, fell into the cake trolley and dislocated my shoulder. Sharon was laughing her arse off and I got really upset and angry and apparently I said I was leaving the band—which I don't remember saying, by the way. So, the next day, I got a call from Sharon about 11am and I asked her what time we were starting, and she said, "Well, we ain't because you left the band." I tried to back down and say I didn't mean it, but Sharon can be pretty brutal and she said I needed to get my shit sorted out before I did anything else. So that was the first time *ever* I'd lost a gig due to my addiction.'

Glenn talked about being 'high maintenance' (no pun intended) and this would have been the coke talking. As much as Gary would have hated heroin, he would have despised coke just as much because it makes people completely obnoxious and impossible to deal with. In certain industries, and the music business is a prime example, part of the job description is to be the baddest guy in town, to be in people's faces, in control and on top of your game. Coke will do that for you in spades—at first. And then all sorts of anxiety and paranoia sets in and, in the end, everything can fall apart, nobody wants to know you—and that can happen in months rather than years.

So, explains Mark, 'we are in a spot because we knew we weren't going to get another guy like Glenn that does all the singing and playing at such a high level. He was writing as well. He had been working with Ray Gomez and Narada Michael Walden; they had cut some things, so Glenn was bringing some great tunes—a kind of white power soul thing—hard and heavy, but very melodic and soulful too.' In other words, a perfect complement to Gary's playing and his approach to composition. But they had to start looking elsewhere.

'We auditioned all kinds of people down at Frank Zappa's place,' says Mark. 'It was a real nice room. All of them were really good, but we weren't sure what we were looking for except we would know it when we heard it. I remember Doni Harvey, bass player from Automatic Man, coming down and John Gustafson (the bassist who had played with Mark in The Ian Gillan Band) flying in from London. We also tried a few keyboard players who played keyboard bass.'

'We both knew Tony Newton from Tony Williams' Lifetime with Allan

Holdsworth—an absolute killer bass player. He'd played with John Lee Hooker at sixteen, backed the Supremes at seventeen, he'd been the musical director for Smokey Robinson, toured with the Stones and Stevie Wonder. He'd also been on a record called *Sunshower* by a German pianist Joachim Kühn with Jan Akkerman and Ray Gomez. I called Tony up and he came down to check it out. He brought a tremendous energy out of Gary. He had a double-neck bass with drone strings on it—he really went for it. Tony could sing, but he didn't want to be an 'out-front' singer like Glenn and Gary didn't want to be the lead singer either, so he could play more.'

Sharon reckons it took about eight months to get the album together and, in a re-run of Colosseum II, *the* main issue was trying to find a singer. 'It's so hard to find a lead singer for a band,' she says. 'The great guitar player and the great lead singer—that's your winning combination and it's like gold dust to find it.'

Gary and Mark finally looked in their own back yard: 'That album, *Sunshower* had two vocal tracks on it, which was Willie Dee. So, when Gary and me were talking to Tony, we mentioned the singer because the vocal tracks were good. Willie came down and he was in that same blue-eyed soul tradition. And there we were.'

Willie Dee (born William Daffern) had been in the third incarnation of a cult 70s hard rock band called Captain Beyond, originally formed from ex-members of Iron Butterfly, Deep Purple and Johnny Winter's band. He joined the band for their third and last studio album *Dawn Explosion*, released in 1977. The band broke up about a year later.

If getting the new band together was one headache, finding the right producer was another. They had cut some demos at Cherokee Studios with the house engineer, but then went through a number of producers, including Eddie Kramer and Roy Thomas Baker, before eventually deciding to produce the album themselves (mixed by Dennis Mackay, who'd produced Jack Bruce among others), to which Jet agreed.

While they were putting the new band together, there was a very belated appearance in American record shops of *Back On The Streets*. There was no band to tour the album, and in any case, it was music out of time because Gary had moved on. But the critics could only review what they had in front of them and so while Gary's guitar playing was highly praised, there were the inevitable comments about an album of two halves. But *Cashbox* called it 'one of the more listenable efforts this year' while another paper proclaimed that 'the album is brutal. Moore has a command of his guitar that ranks with the great ones. He challenges all forms of contemporary energy music.' There was an interesting if hilariously erroneous comment in the *Rocky Mountain News*, whose reporter opined that Gary was 'a guy in terror of success', citing as evidence the fact that he left both Skid Row 'when the Irish group made its London breakthrough' and Thin Lizzy twice 'because of that band's success'. Gary was always anxious about his career, about what the next step should be. But what the reporter took for 'terror' was Gary wanting to do his own thing, play his music on his own terms, even if not always in his best interests. G-Force was arguably a case in point.

Mark Nauseef reckons 'we had tunes from the time we recorded *Back On The Streets* at Morgan and in the Bahamas plus the material we had been working on with Glenn that was already in shape—this power soul direction—which maybe had the potential to be even more powerful because we now had Tony. And then somewhere in there, they started to sound like pop—staccato eight-note things— and it was Gary that was bringing that in. Then the material started to change to fit that and I thought we were starting to lose our way here.'

Listening to those demos, including three from the session with Glenn, what you hear is a band shaping up towards being a no-nonsense hard rock band, but without sacrificing the melodic content inherent in Mark's view of where the strength of the band should be. Although Sharon says 'you couldn't tell Gary what direction to take his music, he told you'—even so, Sharon and Jet were looking for a sound that would appeal Stateside. Gary himself seemed unsure of what to do, as he told the UK paper *Musicians Only* in July 1980 after the album's release: 'I just wanted to get a band together that was a great band. I wasn't really thinking about the direction or anything. I think at the time I was directing it at the American market.'

The eponymous album, released in May 1980, had much to commend it and was an important staging post in Gary's career, eschewing the lack of coherence that had undermined his earlier work. Overall, *G-Force* was a comprehensive package of early 80s pop metal with high-grade musicianship, plenty of inventive and catchy riffs from Gary (especially on 'Because Of Your Love') and vibrant arrangements. They foreshadowed both Gary's own career for the rest of the decade and more general developments in music. 'White Knuckles' (which segues into 'Rockin' And Rollin'') appeared to be an answer to Eddie Van Halen's 'Eruption' and became a routine part of Gary's repertoire. There was a marriage of pop sensibilities and aggressive rock guitar across the album, which didn't really capture the public imagination until 1983, when David Bowie released 'Let's Dance' (solo: Stevie Ray Vaughan) and Eddie Van Halen added a solo to another pop hit in the same year, Michael Jackson's 'Beat It'. Coincidence? Maybe. Then again, perhaps somebody had been inspired by what Gary had served up.

There was also a view that perhaps the album was over-produced, too many nods to ELO in the string arrangements, and that Gary had made a mistake is putting his guitar straight through the mixing desk using a DI unit—giving it a synthesized, fuzzy sound rather than the hefty, crunching sound from a regular amplifier. Gary was quite proud of this; as he told *Musicians Only* in the same interview, he had first come across the sound working on Phil Lynott's 'Sarah' and on the G-Force album: 'I was trying to get a distinctive sound and I think I have. I didn't use amps on any of the solos, it's all DI-ed. The guitars have gone through over-drivers and things, but no amps. I found it was a really good way to get a sound that was upfront. You could do anything with it. And it's all totally flat with no EQ added to it.'

The choice of single was also debatable; it should have been the Tony Newton/ Willie Dee composition 'You Kissed Me Sweetly'—probably the most realised marriage of pop and driving rock styles on the album and Dee's best vocal performance—rather than Gary's 'Hot Gossip'.

This song is worth a second look because, according to Gary's girlfriend Lisa, the sentiments expressed exactly match what was going on in their relationship. Once again, Gary was becoming obsessively jealous:

> *I don't mind you going out with your friends, if it's to places where we've both been. But I don't like you going with him, don't wanna have to say this again. I don't mind you going out to a show, if it's with people that we both know. But I don't like you going with him, I'm gonna stop this before it begins.*

Even as early as March 1979, Lisa said that Gary had asked her to marry him, but she had written to her father to say that she wasn't going to do anything rash. 'He was so jealous; if I was staring out into space in a pub, he'd accuse me of wanting to fuck some guy he thought I was staring at. He actually said, "I don't mind you going out with your friends to a movie or a restaurant while I'm away, but I want to have seen the movie or been to that restaurant first."' Lisa also claims that Gary told her the whole G-Force album was about her 'fuckin' around'. Impossible to verify that claim, but certainly there are Gary compositions on the album that speak to the notion of a desperate infatuation, and on 'She's Got You' there's a woman 'so blond / it tears you apart'.

In the company of Sharon Arden, Gary and Lisa were certainly living high on the hog. This was still what Don Arden calls, in his autobiography, Sharon's 'wild child' years: impossibly expensive shopping trips, extravagant gifts of cars, furs and jewellery. She bought Lisa a black convertible sports car—mad parties at Don's multi-million dollar, Howard Hughes-built home, ludicrously overpriced meals in hip LA restaurants. Jet was also covering all of Gary and Lisa's daily living expenses and all the expenses of the band during the long recording process of the album. Sharon was right behind the band: 'Gary and Sharon got on famously,' says Lisa, 'the same sense of humour; both very witty and very naughty. Hysterical, really.'

It wasn't all bad between Gary and Lisa: 'We would go into a Mexican restaurant where there would be a guitar entertainer and Gary would ask to borrow a guitar and it would be, "Oh no, no, no," because Gary looked like some kind of punk rocker. But then he would insist and play the most amazing Spanish guitar. And the whole restaurant would be like, "WHO'S THAT?!" And that gave me the chills, "Oh my God, he's so talented and he's mine."'

However, Gary and Lisa were not meant for each other; she was a party girl who enjoyed her freedom: 'I couldn't breathe. He was so jealous. It was awful. I thought if we got engaged, he might lighten up. So, he bought a ring on Sunset Boulevard and we got engaged. Really, though, I was in love with Steve Jones.' As Glenn said, much of Gary's LA social life was in the drinkers' club—and that could easily get out of hand between Gary and Lisa, who was also rather fond of the coke. Their relationship was volatile, paranoid and dysfunctional; Lisa claims there was violence; she retaliated by cutting all Gary's clothes up, causing thousands of pounds of damage. Speaking to Chris Welch in 1982, Gary mentioned a Spanish guitar that got busted up by a girlfriend—and this could easily have been Lisa. Sometimes she would go and hide out at Sharon's place: 'She would let me stay but told me I had to go and sort things out.'

Things were no better when Gary moved back to London and the flat in Fitzjohn's Avenue—more fighting, tears, food thrown against walls, desperate attempts by Gary at reconciliation. But Lisa's approach to life and her lifestyle just made him too insecure and nervous. Eventually, she fled back to LA and that was that.

Gary had been here before; the last time he was trying to lead a band, there was all sorts of emotional turmoil in the background and here he was again. And like before, the band itself was starting to unravel.

Strangely, for a band whose material was attempting to win over American music fans, there were no gigs in the USA at all—none of the material was road-tested, no private or low-key gigs anywhere. Tony Newton says there was discussion about the band doing some gigs under a different name before the album came out. Instead, it was decided that the band would debut in England on tour supporting Whitesnake.

Bernie Marsden was in Whitesnake at the time and said he convinced everybody to put Gary on the tour: 'I couldn't believe it, nobody knew who he was, but they weren't too pleased when Gary opened up and nearly blew the audience to hell and back with the volume.' But they couldn't have been that displeased because Neil Murray says that in 1982, with the departure of Bernie Marsden and Micky Moody, David Coverdale was giving serious thought to asking Gary to join the band.

The album provided the bulk of the live set plus 'Back On The Streets', 'Parisienne Walkways' and 'Toughest Street In Town', one of the very rare occasions when Gary performed a Thin Lizzy song. They went down really well; many fans compared them very favourably with the headliners. 'We kicked ass on the tour,' says Tony. 'I think it was a matter of exposure; we had the musicians, Willie was singing his ass off, it had all the components. We were going for our own sound and, as far as I was concerned, we did a good job. Lots of hard work and energy went into that project.'

Gary later described the band live as 'a disaster', but that had to be more a reflection of his personal problem with Willie Dee because live bootleg recordings belie any assertion that this band could not deliver the goods. Stripped of the LA studio pop gloss, they were a ferocious live act: Mark and Tony had that rhythm behind Gary totally locked down and gave Whitesnake a run for their money.

Ultimately, though, nobody has a concrete explanation as to what happened, although there were strains and stresses that would have contributed to the demise of G-Force. Certainly, Jet's enthusiasm was waning; Don prided himself on how much he would spend on a band to make it successful. His investment in ELO, for example, was enormous, especially with their stupendously extravagant stage show. Jet had invested in G-Force in all departments but so far had seen no return. Mark Nauseef views it in very practical terms: 'I think the answer as to why Jet pulled out of G-Force has a lot to do with Gary's solo situation. Jet had signed Gary as a solo artist and released *Back On The Streets* in the US. So, after the G-Force tour, I think that Jet concluded that regardless of what they thought of other musicians in the band, they had to focus on Gary. I think for them G-Force was draining energy from Gary as a solo performer. Of course, Gary would need a band to continue touring and recording, but it didn't need to be a band on retainers, et cetera.'

G-Force were supposed to play the Reading Festival, but apparently there was some problem with visas for the American musicians, while Gary had moved back to the UK. Gary would have known that Jet was not going to pay for him to fly backwards and forwards. This was his way of signing off on the band without having to endure a sit-down meeting.

Sharon too was beginning to put her considerable energies elsewhere—towards John Michael 'Ozzy' Osbourne. Sharon and Ozzy first met in 1974 when Don took over management of Black Sabbath. When Ozzy was kicked out of Sabbath in 1979, he signed with Sharon for management. Trying to launch Ozzy's solo career, she enlisted the help of G-Force. Mark recalls, 'we tried out some material with him, got him up and running, trying to get the first album together. We wrote some material, rehearsed it at Zappa's place—and Frank was in the mix to produce that first album. We were really slamming behind him and he was up for working with us. Gary would start with an intro and as usual he would really go for it, playing like it was his last day on earth—and then we would get to the vocal and Ozzie would just stand there and say, "Now what do I do?" He was so sweet and humble, just standing there listening to the way we were playing. We said we could lay back a bit, cool it down and he said, "No, man, this is great." He was so positive about it all. And then I'd see Sharon in the evening, put a cassette in the car and she'd go "Yes, this is it."'

But wanting to see his kids, Ozzy suddenly jumped on a plane and headed back home, which put an end to their collaboration. Mark says, 'We got paid, got given handmade luggage as presents, but we were disappointed that we weren't going to be involved in recording the album.' However, the thought of Gary trying to work with Ozzy on any sort of regular basis makes you wince. He quite rightly turned down the offer to be the guitarist in Ozzy's band, the spot taken by Randy Rhoads. There was an in-joke among Gary's Jet Record label companions that if Gary had got closer with Sharon, his future career may have panned out very differently.

So, Ozzy may have helped distract Sharon both professionally and emotionally away from G-Force. Then there was Willie Dee. He was finding the whole environment very challenging. Interviewed for a Captain Beyond fan site, he said, 'I went through all this fiasco with Sharon and G-Force ... it was a real nightmare because Sharon wanted to do really pop stuff. And I really didn't want to do pop stuff.' He went on to say a lot of songs weren't used because they weren't 'pop' enough for Sharon's taste. He claimed too that 'me and Gary hated each other'— and the whole situation drove him to a nervous breakdown.

Pondering on this, Mark Nauseef observes: 'Whatever his beefs were/are with the G-Force situation, I think he was offered a reasonable opportunity and no doubt there was a lot of attitude in that band, but I'm not sure how and why he perceived his situation to the point of "nervous breakdown". Gary could definitely have some edge and he would sometimes push the musicians he worked with. He also had no hang-up about letting others know that he wasn't pleased with their contributions. But I think he only did that with the musicians he thought had the potential to deliver. He simply wouldn't take the time to challenge someone who didn't have the goods or he didn't respect. Willie sang great on the record and that was Gary pulling it out of him.'

But Mark also suggests that with Gary—and with Tony, given his pedigree—maybe there was an overdrive to perfection that Willie found hard to handle and was thus uncomfortable with the pressure. In any case, if the singer, the frontman, is not the leader of the band, then there is every chance that the leader—in this case most definitely Gary—would be telling him what to do and how to perform—none of which would sit easily with most singers.

Mark talks about 'attitude in the band' and, for sure, Tony Newton, with all the depth and breadth of his experience, wanted his say: 'My understanding was that it was a group project rather than Gary's band per se.' Tony goes on to vent his criticism at the way the album sounded because of Gary's insistence on how the guitar would be recorded: 'He was thinking that it would give it a unique sound—and it did give it a unique sound—a horrible, scratchy, piece-of-shit sound. Going through the board destroyed the fidelity of the album.' Gary himself backtracked in another interview saying that while to his ears it sounded great in the studio, 'it didn't transfer too well to vinyl and I was a bit disappointed in the end result … it wasn't warm enough and sounded totally detached from the backing tracks'.

Tony is also quite critical of some of the musicians Gary subsequently had in his band, saying that he and Mark Nauseef were at a different level to those he describes as 'generic' sidemen. He goes onto to say: 'I was surprised that Gary didn't have great musicians in his band, that he didn't have the wisdom to know that if you do that, you're better. I think maybe he just didn't know how to deal with people like that.' In Tony's opinion, because of that, 'he was a fantastic composer and guitarist who rose to greatness, but my take anyway is that he didn't reach his potential'. And given Gary's clashes with star musicians, who were band leaders in their own right, like Phil, Glenn and later Cozy Powell, he might have a point.

The band didn't so much end as fizzle out. Tony says they were all on a weekly salary, 'and it just stopped. But nobody got a call. I eventually got in touch with Don Arden, had a meeting and he said he didn't know what he was going to do with Gary.'

Sharon looks to Gary for an explanation: 'Gary and I spent a lot of time together, socially. I can't remember any specifics, but Gary was always dissatisfied. Not finding the right singer was a big stumbling block for Gary. But in the end, he didn't need a frontman—he was the frontman. And he wanted to be bigger, he wanted to be more. Nothing was ever right and that's being an ambitious musician. He wasn't where he wanted to be.'

While Don might have been at a loss in relation to promoting a pop metal band called G-Force, as Mark points out, he still had the guitarist known as Gary Moore under contract, which would never have been for just one album. There was more product to deliver.

Back in the UK, Gary gathered around him a new band more in keeping with the heavier side of *Back On The Streets* and *G-Force*. Recruited were archetypal heavy rock double bass drummer Tommy Aldridge, formerly with Black Oak Arkansas and the Pat Travers Band; ex-Lone Star vocalist Kenny Driscoll; blues-rock bassist Andy Pyle; and Gary's friend from Colosseum II, keyboardist Don Airey, who had gone on to Rainbow and would soon be in the Ozzy Osbourne band. Before any touring, Gary wanted to record a live album. Calling on the services of *Back On The Streets* producer Chris Tsangarides, the band—just called Gary Moore and Friends—played two nights at the Marquee in early November 1980.

The album was almost a re-run of the live G-Force set and by choosing tracks like 'She's Got You' and 'Because Of Your Love' it underlined the power of G-Force in full flight for those who never saw them on stage. Gary added in what he announced as a new song, 'Nuclear Attack', plus the rather dark 'Run To Your Mama'. Overall, it was a template for Gary's direction in the years ahead. Unlike the controversy surrounding the recording of Lizzy's *Live And Dangerous*—how much of it was really live and how much fixed—Chris Tsangarides says this album was 'a proper live album'.

But Jet didn't release it at the time. Then, over January/February 1981, Gary took the band—exchanging Driscoll for Charlie Huhn (ex-Ted Nugent band)—plus another bass player, Jimmy Bain, into Morgan Studio to record an album, *Dirty Fingers*. Gary included some eight new but mostly unremarkable compositions, but did include another anti-nuclear anthem, 'Hiroshima', and 'Don't Let Me Be Misunderstood', the first of Gary's highly effective reworking of classic songs to suit a heavy rock style without detracting from (and perhaps even enhancing) the original. Much of the rest, though, sounds like contract filler material—'Really Gonna Rock' is 'Rockin' And Rollin'', 'Dirty Fingers' is just an abstract of 'White Knuckles'. Nor, says Chris, was the album even finished: 'We got to a point, did a quick mix and that was that.' On the plus side, there is a certain appeal in the rawness of the album as a slab of early 80s heavy rock, even without all the final touches and added finesse that Gary would have insisted upon. When these albums were finally released to cash in on Gary's growing international success, *Dirty Fingers* was preferred by some of the HM critics to Gary's contemporary releases, exactly because there were none of the pop synth sounds so detested in unreconstructed metal circles.

None of which made Gary any happier with Jet's actions—the debacle with *Dirty Fingers* coming to epitomise for Gary his whole Jet experience. He told *Sounds* in 1984: 'I'm annoyed. It wasn't good enough for them four years ago when it was originally written. Now they've released it as a rough demo. The songs are OK, but they were never properly recorded or mixed; the whole album's just been thrown together … its release has nothing to do with me.'

By 2001, though, Gary's views had mellowed. Talking to *Classic Rock* he said, 'Actually I don't have a ton of regrets about Jet. [After G-Force broke up] I was gonna get something together with Cozy Powell and Tim Bogert but Jet sabotaged it. They weren't paying bills for anything. Eventually I bought my way out of the contract, but I don't have a problem with Don Arden. I'm sure a lot of famous things did happen, but he was always OK with me. I've been at his house, been pissed with him and seen him get sloppy and sentimental. We've never argued in our lives.'

So why were the albums not released at the time? From this distance, one can only speculate, but Jet couldn't have predicated Gary would have the success he later did, which would warrant hanging back on releases. So, the reasons must have been more immediate to Jet's situation. According to Chris Tsangarides, even before the studio album was recorded, Jet was trying to do a deal with Geffen Records by promoting the new band as Britain's answer to Van Halen. Perhaps Jet was sending a message to Gary that they weren't prepared to bankroll another band for him.

Wholly backed by Warner Bros, Geffen had only been established in 1980, set up by former Asylum Records boss David Geffen. Donna Summer, their first signing, gave them a gold album *The Wanderer* and they also had John Lennon.

On December 8, 1980, two weeks after *Double Fantasy* hit the charts, his first album in five years, Lennon was murdered in New York.

David Geffen hired John Kalodner as the label's first A&R executive. Kalodner was regarded as the King Midas of A&R having signed Foreigner, AC/DC, Peter Gabriel and Phil Collins to Atlantic Records. 'So, a week after Lennon's death,' recalls Chris Tsangarides, 'Geffen sends over John Kalodner. We set the band up in the studio with PA, lights, everything. Nobody really liked him, especially when they told us he was having a hair transplant, "so don't laugh".' Nothing came of this: any hope of a deal evaporated.

Jet may have been trying to cut its losses (which must have been significant) or were just trying to offload Gary because he was too strong-willed or they were disappointed with the lack of interest in G-Force—probably a combination of all three. Maybe, too, Don's extravagance was beginning to catch up with him and he was also spending a lot of money on lawyers, fending off one lawsuit after another.

According to Chris, they were trying to do the two albums on the cheap and he says that once the Geffen deal collapsed, nobody got paid, or paid enough. If the studio bills weren't paid, then Monty Babson at Morgan would not have released the tapes anyway. By now, Don Arden's financial situation was such that during the year, he would sell his prize asset, ELO's publishing rights. Jet then may have had little choice but to sit on the albums, in the hope that one day they would find a buyer. This left Gary and the band with no money and when Tommy Aldridge was pinched for Ozzy's band—adding to Gary's displeasure with the Ardens—it was goodnight Irene. Although he was learning all the time, Gary couldn't but regard this as yet another failed attempt to get a solo career off the ground.

With no regular source of income, Gary was happy to work on other projects as an 'axe for hire'. Back in 1979, he had recorded a track called 'The Killer' for Cozy Powell's first solo album, *Over The Top*, which teamed him again with Don Airey. More importantly, though, this was his first meeting with Jack Bruce, who became a close friend over the years. The album also featured a song written for Jeff Beck called 'The Loner'. The original composer was keyboard player Max Middleton, but later Gary reworked the song to the extent he was credited as joint-composer.

In the summer of 1981, Cozy went into Britannia Row Studios to record his second album, *Tilt*, with almost the same line-up, to which Gary contributed 'Sunset' (an extended, even-paced solo composition that is almost an instrumental version of G-Force's 'I Look At You') and 'The Blister' (co-written with Don Airey). There was a rumour that Gary wanted to take out a band with Cozy, Jack and Don but Jet wouldn't finance it. Shortly after the recording, Gary took a call asking him to come down for a studio session with Greg Lake.

Emerson, Lake and Palmer came to epitomise the bloated excess of 70s arena rock—a legion of road trucks, an army of touring staff including their own doctor, Greg standing on a genuine Persian rug. But it wasn't the New Wave that killed the band –it simply ran out of steam after the release of *Love Beach* in 1978.

This left Greg with something of an identity crisis and a deep uncertainty as where to go next. Rather than staying in a comfort zone, he took off for Los Angeles to try out some new material with the members of Toto and guitarist Snuffy Walden, who had been in a band called Stray Dog signed to ELP's own Manticore label and who went on to compose the music for *The West Wing* among other film and TV credits.

Still without any real sense of direction, he came back to the UK and undertook further recordings in different locations including Abbey Road. The turning point for Greg was the arrival of Gary Moore.

'I'd co-written a song with Bob Dylan called "I Love You Too Much". It was a 12-bar feel and the effect I wanted was a blistering guitar solo. I said to my manager, "Who does that really well?" And he said, "You know, the guy who would be perfect for this is Gary Moore."'

Much to everyone's surprise, Gary turned up a full half hour early for the session. 'He walked in, wearing this long black coat and carrying a Strat,' says Greg. 'His road manager had been in earlier and put up a Marshall amp at the end of the studio. We said hello—and Gary was very sweet and charming and quite shy. So, he said, "Shall I go and get tuned up?" I could see he was a little nervous and I thought it was to do with coming in to do a session, but actually he was just quite shy.

'He went into the studio, put the guitar case down, took the guitar out of its case, round his neck, plugged it in and started fiddling around, tuning up. He put the phones on and said, "Do you want to run the track then?" I said okay—and when I do that, I always put it on record, because you never know! So, we ran the track and well, it was just incredible to listen to him. Without ever hearing it, he just instinctively knew what to play. And that's what's on the record. At the end of the track, everybody in the control room just stood up and applauded. And I think that's what he liked to do. Just walk in and obliterate everybody.' What Gary assumed was the warm-up was done and dusted in a moment of brilliance.

Having heard what Gary could do, Greg certainly did not want Gary just packing up his guitar and walking out. After years of playing bass, Greg wanted to get back to playing guitar: 'Gary was like manna from heaven. Who better to get back into guitar with?' Greg needed to put a band together to tour the album, so he invited Gary to join him, drummer Ted McKenna and keyboardist Tommy Eyre for a UK tour scheduled to start in October and November, finishing off in the States in December. Gary told *Kerrang!*: 'Greg has this way with words—he'd make a great politician—cos he's very good at convincing people that what he thinks is right. So, before I knew it, I was in a band with him.'

'I've sat with Gary in a studio, just me and him playing guitar, and he's had me in tears, such was his ability. Gary could open up and suddenly he's Hank Marvin, then he'd play something Irish, then Elvis, then country & western. And I don't just mean a few licks. You name a country song and he'd play it. He nurtured me back into playing guitar in lots of ways.'

'He would always have a guitar round his neck to the point where sometimes it got irritating. You couldn't even talk to him sometimes—"Gary, Gary, could you stop playing for just a second? Please. This is important!" I said to him one day, "Don't you ever get fed up doing it?" He said, "You know what, Greg? If I walked into a hotel and on the bed was Bo Derek naked and a Stratocaster, I'd pick up the Strat." And we were both guitar fanatics—guitars, guitar playing, amplifiers, strings. The music was almost a chore! There would always be a conversation going on. Obsessive would be the word.'

Greg was so taken with Gary's playing that he even included 'Nuclear Attack' on his own first solo album. Apart from 'Love You Too Much', Gary also features on 'Retribution Drive' and other tracks alongside Steve Lukather from Toto. But if they found common cause over a hot fretboard, Gary and Greg also shared an anxiety and confusion about musical direction. Gary once said about Greg that he would go half-way round the world to borrow a cup of sugar from next door. The self-titled album, released in September 1981, demonstrated the same lack of cohesion heard on Gary's earlier work. Says Greg, 'The album sold few hundred thousand copies and Chrysalis were disappointed. They were expecting ELP and sales of two million.'

Out on the road, though, Greg had a great time: 'Lovely people, great players, funny, very funny. Gary had a great Irish sense of humour.' The show at Hammersmith Odeon on November 5 was recorded for a live album and delivered its fair share of fireworks, mixing up Crimson, ELP, new material from the solo album and Gary's compositions 'Nuclear Attack' and 'Parisienne Walkways'. About that tour, Gary later told Chris Welch, writing for *Kerrang!*: 'We went to America and we were unlucky … the Stones and AC/DC were on the road at the same time, so we weren't selling half the tickets we could have sold. But some of the shows were just a joy … And for me it was a big, exciting thing because I'd never had a chance to play in America in that way … I played in America with Thin Lizzy as part of the guitar team, but never in the normal style. It was great for me and I made quite a few friends out there. Most of them had never heard of me before.'

Reviews of the album and the concerts ranged from puerile abuse straight from the pens of punk hacks to those who were encouraged by the strength of the stage show. One *Melody Maker* writer, though, just let his imagination run away with him by suggesting that 'the bourgeois romanticism of Greg Lake sits ill at ease besides the proletarian machismo of Gary Moore'.

At the time, Gary and Greg were both searching for a way forward. Gary's previous experience with frontman bassist/vocalists (Brush, Phil and Glenn) had been highly creative, but personally fraught. But here was somebody clearly on Gary's wavelength, with whom he shared a geek's interest in all things guitar, and who, like Gary, was a strong composer possessed of a highly tuned lyrical sensibility, whose admiration for Gary as a player knew no bounds. Could they have made a go of it?

For sure, Gary was an integral part of Greg's follow-up album *Manoeuvres*, playing all the guitar, composing one song and co-credited on two others. But Greg was still floundering. Interviewed later, he said he should have followed Sting's path—basically, playing the same mix of reggae/jazz/pop and world music material but without The Police. Or in Greg's case, some progression on from King Crimson and ELP that would pass muster in the 1980s. As it was, the album took a battering from the critics and sank with all hands on deck. Some of the material, though, hinted at the AOR style of Asia. When John Wetton left that band, the call came for Greg, which effectively derailed his quest for a solo career. Eventually, he found his way back to ELP.

Mark Nauseef is unequivocal in his praise for Sharon and the effort she put into getting G-Force off the ground. Tony Newton agrees: 'She had one of the smartest minds in the business and she was excellent for the band and cared about it—no doubt.' And if it all ended in tears, she was at least able to do one last favour for Gary. She introduced him to Steve Barnett, who became Gary's manager and turned his fortunes right round.

08

ROCKIN'
EVERY NIGHT

Steve Barnett began his music career in 1970 as an agent working for Gerry Bron, dealing with Colosseum and Uriah Heep. He became an agent for NEMS Enterprises, the company originally formed by Brian Epstein, and represented artists such as Elton John, Black Sabbath and Deep Purple. In 1980, he teamed up with ELP and Greg Lake manager Stewart Young to form the management firm Part Rock. Steve took on Gary's management (his first artist) early in 1981 and it was through the partnership that Gary got the gig with Greg.

The imperative for Steve was to get Gary a decent recording contract. But he started with a publishing deal. He had a good contact at Virgin Music Publishing, Richard Griffiths. Richard was AC/DC's first agent outside Australia and the agent for Paul Kossoff after he left Free: 'I was a wet behind the ears, know nothing, but enthusiastic. Steve was also an agent then and he took me under his wing.' Richard moved to Island Records and then Virgin. Gary was signed to Virgin for publishing and then Richard persuaded Simon Draper, co-founder of Virgin Records, to sign Gary to the label.

From its creation in 1972, Virgin Records had gone through various iterations. Starting life as a progressive rock label with artists like Tangerine Dream and Mike Oldfield, they gear-shifted to the Sex Pistols and then, in the early 80s, came out as a new wave pop label, launching the careers of Culture Club, The Human League, ABC, the re-invented Phil Collins and later Simple Minds. So, while Gary was preparing for his first album for the company, Virgin were doing very nicely. Richard Branson and Simon Draper wanted to expand and create another label for other kinds of artists, which they called Ten Records because it debuted in 1982, the company's tenth anniversary.

To secure the Virgin Records deal, Gary had to get some demos together ahead of forming yet another new band. Reflecting on all his experience so far, it couldn't have been a prospect he would have relished, even if the pot at the end of the rainbow was a recording contract with a high-flying label.

Early in 1982, Gary went into London's AIR Studios with bassist Kenny Aaronson and the mercurial, but brilliant drummer Bobby Chouinard, both on loan from Billy Squier's band (another Part Rock client) to record demos of virtually all the tracks that would appear on Gary's first album for Virgin.

The next item of business was to find the right producer. Gary remembered meeting the American producer Jeff Glixman who had produced four albums for Kansas including their two biggest chart successes *Leftoverture* (1976) and *Point Of Know Return* (1977). 'I came over to the UK to work with Magnum' says Jeff, 'who were signed to Jet Records. I was in the office and in walked Gary Moore. Don Arden introduced us and I told Gary what a big fan I was of his work with Thin Lizzy. We talked a bit in the hallway and that was that. Then it's 1982 and I get a call from Steve Barnett.'

Steve played Jeff the demos which had been recorded at the sessions, plus another one recorded on February 8, a song called 'End Of The World' also recorded with Billy Squier's rhythm section but with vocals by Jack Bruce, whose soaring cadences marked him out as one of the most distinctive voices in rock. Having heard what Gary had done so far, Jeff took a deep breath, 'I said, honestly, apart from this track with Jack Bruce on it, I would start over. I wouldn't know where to go with this. Steve said they only had enough budget left for 21 studio days. They had guide tracks, overdubs, some of the arrangements were wacky. I said, 'let's just go into the studio with a real cool band and basically cut it live because Gary can do that—and if Gary is ready, let's get the singer as well. So, we talked it through with Gary and he was interested in doing it this way. Meanwhile I went off to work with Triumph while they worked it out. Then Steve called again to say they wanted to do it.'

Who was going to be in this 'real cool band'? Jeff said he'd really like to work with Ian Paice: 'Gary asked me if I knew him and I said no, but Steve said he would work it out.' The reason Gary stood any chance of getting Ian was by a huge slice of luck, David Coverdale decided to put Whitesnake on hold for personal reasons which left the rhythm section of Neil Murray, who Gary knew well and the internationally renowned drummer looking for work. Gary added another friendly face, the highly talented Tommy Eyre on keyboards and there was his band. The new band rehearsed at E-Zee Hire through the second half of June. Jeff arrived to be greeted by an anxious looking Gary: 'He said, "I'm a bit worried about Ian. He just sits in there with a single bass drum and a snare and a hi-hat and just taps out the songs."

'So, we went in there, worked through the songs, did two days and they'd already been at it for three days. On my second day, Ian suddenly shows a spark and whips off this terrific snare roll and I went to him and said, "That's great. Some more of that would be good." And he looked at me and said, "I know what you're thinking, mate. I've been doing this a long time, made a lot of records. I'm just getting the arrangements in my head. When we get to the studio, it'll be fine." And it was. He was just learning the songs.'

Probably for the first and only time in the history of his band, Gary had a player with a far more established reputation than his own. But Ian acknowledges the reality of that situation, 'Gary was the boss; it was his name on the marquee. I would have been on slightly more than the other guys, so it was like a partner/ junior partner thing which I was totally comfortable with because I didn't want any serious involvement which might scupper anything else which came along and it was Gary's baby.'

Ian's view on not being locked into the band was very much in tune with Gary's when he left Thin Lizzy for the first time in 1974 to avoid signing anything that would tie him down contractually. Ian too, wanted to keep his options open and didn't see this as any kind of long-term arrangement. Neither for that matter did Gary, who told Chris Welch, 'It's not a permanent band. I've just put this line-up together for an album.'

When Chris asked Gary about the name for his new band, he replied, 'Gary Moore And His Expensive Friends. We pay each person a certain fee for the period of work. Each one negotiates his own fee. Whoever is the smartest gets the most money out of me. Are you out there, Ian?' … If you look at the cars that arrive at my rehearsals, you'll see who is getting the most money. I came on a bicycle—ha, ha.'

According to Neil Murray's diary, the bulk of the recordings were done at AIR Studios in July with some work at Virgin's own Town House Studios. Still, however, the issue of the vocals had not been resolved. Jeff reckons Glenn Hughes was once again in the frame, 'but when I heard Gary in rehearsal, I said, "You can sing this thing. You know, just do it." And he said, "Well, I can't always sing and play at the same time." "Okay, we'll just come back and put the guitar in where we need to." So, we went in and it was incredible.' Virgin were not keen on a different lead vocalist either: they had signed Gary as a solo artist, they wanted one voice, his voice, to run through the recording.

With a limited budget to focus the mind, they sprinted through the recording. 'A couple of solos were overdubs, but mostly it was there,' recalls Jeff. 'Gary had said to me he often didn't get on with producers, but he was great. Some artists have a definite idea of what they want to do and people find them hard to work with, but I find them great to work with. I've done two records with Tony Iommi and three with Yngwie Malmsteen, who's supposed to be the most difficult person in the world. With Gary, I just tried to create an environment to protect him and allow him to be the most Gary Moore he could be.'

Gary was at a pivotal point in his career; by 1982, aged 30, he'd been a professional musician for nearly fifteen years and had built up a fearsome reputation as a guitarist with Skid Row, Colosseum and Thin Lizzy. But after two false starts at running his own band, he was now anxious to make that step to the next level. When asked about the 'game plan' for Gary, Steve Barnett explains that 'the idea was to go out, build a following. He wanted to be the guitar hero he had always wanted to be, going out under his own name. We all agreed that was what we were going to do and we tried to surround him with the best players we could. Because he was such a great player, everybody wanted to play with him—something of a superstar band. That helped the whole proposition and that was the beginning.'

Gary reiterated the point in an interview: 'I know you can only get a long-term following by gigging and gigging. Look at AC/DC and all the bands that have made it on that level for the last five or ten years.' In effect, he was saying after all those years as a professional, to make it as a solo artist, he was virtually starting again. And remember, he had gone to the States with Greg Lake only the previous year and found that nobody knew who he was. He had to be realistic in his aspirations for the new album. He told *Sounds*, 'we're not banking on this album being a massive success, It's solely to re-establish me.' Gary called it *Corridors Of Power* after a political novel by C.P. Snow about the problems of abandoning a nuclear weapons programme and trying to find an alternative approach.

Gary had already addressed the issue of a nuclear Armageddon in 'Nuclear Attack' and 'Hiroshima' (*Dirty Fingers*). It surfaced again on the album in 'End Of The World' and was a theme Gary would revisit. Although he took some stick for what was regarded as a shallow piece of posturing, remember, Gary was a child of the 50s, when the threat of nuclear war was very real. Gary would have been only nine when the world was brought to the brink by the Cuban Missile Crisis. Jack Bruce has very strong memories of being on the London Underground on the way to a jazz gig and seeing how worried everybody was. As a committed opponent of nuclear arms, he would have been very much in tune with the sentiments expressed in 'End Of The World'.

Following on from his reworking of 'Don't Let Me Be Misunderstood' on *Dirty Fingers*, Gary chose to cover Free's 'Wishing Well', but admitted he had to wait a while so that people 'forget the original almost'. He went to explain to *Sounds*, 'I always liked the song and stayed quite faithful to the original version. A lot of people said to me that they prefer my version to the original. The only thing I can say about that is that it's probably a lot heavier. Recording techniques have improved, so the sound's going to be a lot better. I'm sure if Free recorded it now they wouldn't do it the way they did.'

Inevitably, all concerned were keen to get that hit single; they tried and failed with 'Always Gonna Love You', released in September 1982. Virgin tried again with 'Falling In Love With You' the following February—Don Airey and freelance bassist extraordinaire Mo Foster were drafted in for the remix recording.

For all his promotion as a dour-faced, snarling axe hero, Gary had strong melodic and pop sensibilities and he was genuinely irked that he couldn't get airplay. Interviewed by *Kerrang!*, he noted, 'we've got good material, but it has to get played on the radio. And if the single we put out ("Always Gonna Love You") had been played, I'm sure it would have been a hit. We just haven't had that opportunity … I look at the charts and if there are still things in there I can relate to, why can't I have a song that's up there? Why can't I have a place in the charts. I think we deserve one as much as anybody else. I'll try and beat them at their own game.'

For the single, Culture Club producer Steve Levine was at the desk to craft the level of pop gloss that might have made a difference. Gary was keen to work with Levine: 'I love the songs that Culture Club have recorded—they're very catchy and reach a lot of people. I want to give the guy a free hand and see what he comes up with. He says we can do it how *we* want, but I want to see how *he* works. Times are changing and it will be good for us to work with someone of the moment.' Ian Paice observed drily, 'It'll either work incredibly well or it will be a shambles'. 'It's an experiment,' insisted Gary. 'Everything is changing. We've got to change too.' In the end, it was neither incredible nor a shambles; just not enough people heard it.

Another ballad was recorded, 'Love Can Make A Fool Of You', which remained unreleased until the 2002 remastered version of the album. The track was reportedly offered to other artists, including Abba's Anni-Frid Lyngstad for her Phil Collins-produced solo album (as 'Frida') *Something's Going On* (1982).

Arguably, the strongest and most dramatic track was the sweeping anthem 'I Can't Wait Until Tomorrow'. More than any other of Gary's autobiographical compositions, it summed up his restless searching, his enduring frustrations of not even being totally sure of what he was looking for, or whether he would be content when he found it. The search had underpinned not only his career to date, but in retrospect, a poignant and prescient trope for the years ahead. As if to underline the point still further, and maybe with a nod to the album title as well, Gary had told Donna that he often dreamed about walking down a corridor with many doors and being unsure which door to open.

As Jeff remembers it, 'Ian had fun with Gary on that track. There's a timed open space, at the start of Gary's solo, they were looking at each other like who's going to draw first and make the first move—and they both hit it exactly at the same time. There was another moment when Jack Bruce was in the studio and Keith Emerson stopped by and they were just playing free form and it was just amazing—Ian just had fun with it.'

Jeff had a good time with English musicians too, 'because they took the attitude, "Hey, that's your side of the glass. This is mine. You do your thing." And Gary just wanted the right sound; he was much more concerned with the production side than the engineering side—that the songs and the music played matched his ideas as the songwriter.'

On its release in September 1982, the critical response to the album was very positive; Gary had clearly planted a flag in the rock landscape. Writing for *Kerrang!*, Chris Welch called it a 'marvellous album, the finest of his career'. The fact that the album had been recorded relatively quickly paid dividends: 'the result is a series of performances that have a spontaneity and freshness.' Heading the list of pleasant surprises for Chris were Gary's vocals, 'unpretentious, soulful and as passionate as his guitar work'. And then maybe the finest accolade any guitarist could get, especially from such a seasoned and respected music journalist: 'the outstanding feature … remains Gary's guitar which brings a smile, such is the mix of enthusiasm and virtuosity unleashed. His improvisation is full of unexpected leaps, twists and spirals and he talks through his guitar in a way that has not been heard since the great days of Jimi Hendrix … A five-star album that deserves to go into the hall of fame.'

Dave Roberts for *Sounds* was less effusive (especially about Gary's vocals) but still gave the album a four-star rating and paid tribute to the fact that Gary took some care about the songwriting, 'combining HM power and energy with true melody'. Surprisingly, in amongst all the heavy rock *sturm und drang* both reviewers cited 'Always Gonna Love You' as their favourite track, making the case for its place as an FM radio hit alongside the best that Journey or REO Speedwagon could offer. Roberts thought that Gary had yet to produce his 'defining statement', a point it would be hard to argue with, 'but meanwhile this is a rock showcase of HM/HR, accentuated by fretwork of frightening superiority'.

Although expectations for the album had been modest in Gary's camp, Richard Griffiths from Virgin Publishing was unhappy at the lack of promotion in the UK: 'I remember having a massive argument with Simon Draper the day we got the first chart position. I went over to see him and we had this huge row and he got so pissed off, he walked out of *his* office and just left me standing there fuming.' It did actually achieve a respectable spot at No. 30 in the UK album charts and probably sold about 250,000 copies worldwide over time. Although Virgin were always very supportive of Gary right into the 90s, they were essentially a label geared towards pop success and, certainly in the early days, really didn't know how to promote Gary. As Steve Barnett says, it was essentially a question of getting out there and for Gary to repay his dues over again to establish himself as a headlining solo artist, which was going to take more than just being an outstanding guitar player.

In mid-August, they went into E-Zee Hire once again to rehearse for the first leg of the UK tour, which would take them to Christmas. Gary was able to retain the services of Ian Paice, Neil Murray and Tommy Eyre. But while Jeff had just about convinced Gary to do all the vocals on the album, he was still not comfortable playing and singing live.

Speaking in mid-1984 to *Chicago Sounds* when the problem was still around, he said, 'I've always worked with bands where there was a real strong lead singer. I've never felt that I should be the singer. In Thin Lizzy obviously Phil was the singer and with Greg Lake, he did the singing, so I was doing backup vocals … I don't really want to be out front. My guitar playing is the "frontman", that's the way it works out … I don't mind physically standing behind the singer at all: I love it! I can have a great time out there … then I don't have to worry about who's singing what.'

In another interview with *Music UK*, talking about singing and playing at the same time, he said, 'You don't realise how difficult it is until you've got to do it. I must improve my breath control because I've been in situations where I've leapt off the drum riser after a particularly emotional frenzied solo and when I get back to the microphone I'll start singing out of pitch, out of tune or whatever … The other problem is learning how to operate all my effects foot switches without looking down at the ground because as soon as I do that the vocals disappear. I have to a degree simplified my whole effects set up and racked them, so I now have less pedals to cope with on the floor and it seems to be working out OK.' So, for the 1982 tour, Gary turned once again to Charlie Huhn.

Gary was pleased with the rehearsals, as he said to Chris Welch: 'We've only been rehearsing for ten days and it's very tight already. They are so quick at picking things up. They learnt all the songs I had written in about five minutes.' Not surprising, though, as most of the set was drawn from the new album, which had been rehearsed and recorded by all of the musicians except Charlie, leading Ian to ruminate on how it was all too much: 'He was a stickler for rehearsing things (unlike say Ritchie Blackmore) and sometimes we just rehearsed things to death. You left the first three or four shows in the rehearsal room and you got sick and tired of playing it before you played it for real. But it was important to him that the details were correct, even if it drove everybody else nuts.'

They played the two warm-up gigs at the Marquee and a final one at the Reading Festival, dogged by atrocious sound, and that was the final curtain for Charlie Huhn, who took up an offer from Geffen Records to go back to the States and write for Trevor Rabin. 'So I'll have to learn to sing and play,' Gary told Chris Welch. Well, not yet. Neil Murray played Gary some demos of a band he'd been in called Badlands, which featured former Lone Star and Uriah Heep vocalist Jon Sloman. Gary liked the voice, hired Jon and also replaced Tommy Eyre with Don Airey, which meant almost another two weeks of rehearsals, before the start of the tour proper on November 24 at Surrey University.

They picked the highlights of the show to play a 35-minute set for German TV as the last show before Christmas. Watching this on YouTube, one can see the inherent problems for Gary of having a frontman lead singer—Gary's willingness to undertake *some* lead vocals, but not all of them. This meant that Sloman had to be on stage so he could sing lead as required. At least he could play keyboards, but even that was unnecessary because Don Airey was in the band. A second keyboard player was completely superfluous. Asked by Chris Welch for *Kerrang!* why Jon was playing keyboards as well as Don, Ian Paice hit the nail on the head: 'Well, he shares the singing with Gary and when he's not singing, he's either got to stand around with a tambourine looking like a pillock … so he might as well do something constructive and looks a little different.'

It also made for a confusing stage presence; Gary was clearly the frontman—not just because the guitar was the focus of the show, but because he was taking on lead vocals, unlike say Jimmy Page or Eddie Van Halen or most of the other big name rock guitarists who left all that to their shaggy-haired, chest-baring singing partners. For that German show, the whole singing saga reached a new depth of silly when Jon Sloman came out from behind the keyboards to take over singing Gary's most personal song 'I Can't Wait Until Tomorrow', in which Gary summed up his whole attitude to his career—'Okay, done that, what's next?' Jon Sloman delivered this and other songs, especially 'Rockin' And Rollin'' in a style that can only be described as excessively melodramatic. And when it came to the instrumental 'Hurricane', Jon just left the stage, leaving Gary and Don to fire rockets off each other as they did in Colosseum II before steaming full pelt into Ian's solo.

Although it was unclear exactly which way Gary would jump, once the tour was over in early 1983, the honeymoon period with Jon Sloman came to its inevitable end. Gary told *Kerrang!* that Jon would now be concentrating on his solo career, 'as we kind of knew he would'. He continued, 'Now we don't have that terribly uncomfortable thing of where he had to fit in, what he should do onstage after he'd sung and I was playing a long solo. Did he walk around, shake his arse or whatever? I think he was very uncomfortable with the whole thing.' Gary even admitted that listening back to the tapes, he realised Jon was no more comfortable singing these songs than Gary himself, 'so I realised there was no point in having a singer who's not going to do it better than I could. Also, as a songwriter, you envisage the way you want your songs to be performed. If you hear them performed that way, you get very picky and say, "Why don't you sing them like me?" But if you are saying that then you quickly get to thinking, *Why don't I just sing them myself?*

It does seem, though, that Jon and Gary came to a mutual agreement over this without any undue animosity, because shortly after Jon left, Gary (and Neil) were helping him out on some demos at Barge Studios as he started to get his solo career off the ground.

But that *Kerrang!* interview took place several months later. While Gary was helping out Jon, Don Airey was busy convincing Gary to give it a go: 'I told Gary he could sing better than all the other guys we had tried put together.' On March 16, they played the Paris Theatre where Gary, for the first time, performed all the vocals, followed by a series of festival dates in Europe, at which Gary really put his singing on show in front of an estimated total audience of around 100,000 people.

Gary was given the chance of a major US tour supporting Def Leppard, a band in the vanguard of the New Wave of British Heavy Metal, whose third album, *Pyromania*, produced by Mutt Lange, shot to No. 2 in the *Billboard* charts and sold over ten million copies. But he would have to do it without Don Airey. Don's wife was pregnant; understandably, Don didn't want to embark on a long US tour. But when Don was ready to come back, he instead joined Ozzy Osbourne's band to record *Bark At The Moon*.

This was normal business for a freelance musician like Don, but Gary predictably took it more personally, saw it as a kind of betrayal and lashed out a bit through the media, suggesting in one interview that Don wasn't right for the band anyway because he was too technical and Gary wanted a more rock'n'roll rather than classical approach. Moreover, he claimed the pregnancy was just an excuse because Don wanted to join a more successful band and so on. But it all blew over; they remained friends and worked again together, as we shall see.

Gary's choice of replacement for the US tour was quite inspired. Keyboard player, guitarist and singer Neil Carter knew Gary through his time with Brian Robertson's Wild Horses, who had the same management as Thin Lizzy. 'Later on, one of my friends, who was a roadie for G-Force, invited me down to a rehearsal,' says Neil, 'and Gary ordered me out! We laughed about this many times.'

At the time of his abrupt dismissal from the studio, Neil was with UFO: 'I went from one band of heavy drinkers to something even worse; they could have taught Brian Robertson and Jimmy Bain many things, but definitely not about music. It was chaos.'

Gary's guitar tech at the time, Dirk Sommer, had been tour manager for Wild Horses and brought Neil in because he thought this would take the pressure off Gary 'and sometimes second guitar would fit better than keyboards'. Neil was aware of what Gary needed, 'a keyboard player to replace Don but also somebody who could play guitar too—and not many people did that. It was rhythm guitar, really; I wasn't a frustrated lead anything. The role I had in Gary's band was perfect for me—a very supportive role, some guitar, some singing; the keyboards were not really the main thing. I got landed with it. I never felt completely comfortable with the idea I was a keyboardist, but I took it on with Gary, although I'm not in same league as Don Airey.'

Neil went to the Pink Pop Festival gig in May so that Don could show him some things, leaving the new member concerned he wasn't up to snuff because the set still contained some of the more complex jazz-rock elements: 'I was never going to be able to get anywhere near that,' he says. So, they formulated a much heavier rock set; they were only due to play 35 minutes on the Def Leppard tour.

It worked very well; Neil could come out front, help out with backing vocals and play guitar, so there was none of the 'semi-lead vocalist with nothing to do' problem. Neil also had a strong stage presence, but without the risk of overshadowing Gary and the guitar.

The Def Leppard tour was a significant opportunity for Gary. Unfortunately, they were third on the bill behind Krokus, but the Swiss band's latest album *Headhunter* had gone platinum in the States. For Neil, even playing second support for Def Leppard was slightly demeaning, as Def Leppard had supported UFO and, further back, had even carried in the amps for Wild Horses. As Neil Carter acknowledges, though, 'there was a real aura of success around Def Leppard, [but] there was a sense of something happening around Gary too, that he was on the rise. Everything was well organised; Steve Barnett was a good manager and Gary wasn't going to put up with rubbish.'

Ian supports the notion that Gary was being both professional and realistic about the tour: 'Those bands had big albums in the States and everybody in the business knows it's not about being the best, it's about who the audience want to come and see. And if you are trying to make a statement about yourself, the more people you play before, the better the chance you have of doing it. Def Leppard were pulling up to 20,000 people a night, so not a bad tour to be on—and we had a great deal of fun with those guys. They knew who the better musicians were, but it was their name up in lights and it never really bothered Gary that he wasn't headlining the really big US gigs. He was not a stupid man.'

Even though *Corridors Of Power* didn't chart in the States, the local disc jockeys were full of praise for Gary's music, and he was getting airplay. Tom Starr from WOUR said, 'The phone stories on Gary Moore are gospel. If you doubt it, just give "End Of The World" a spin and watch your switchboards go wild.' Nikki Stevens reckoned the song had listeners to KSJO 'in varying degrees of aural orgasm', while the song was the number one request on WDVE. Sky Daniels from WLUP declared more generally that 'Gary Moore is finally getting the push a guitarist of his finesse deserves'. There was one article based on a discussion between Dave Meniketti of Y&T, Eddie Van Halen and others sitting round talking about guitarists and the question came up, 'Who's the best guitarist in rock?' Dave said, 'Well, the best one isn't here. He's over in England and it's Gary Moore.'

But just in case Gary needed any reminding of where he was in the pecking order, they finished the tour in July playing as headliners, but to small club crowds of a few hundred in Dallas, Houston and Austin.

After a rest in August for holidays, they started about two weeks of rehearsals at John Henry's rehearsal place in London in preparation for recording the next album at Sarm West Studios on October 3. But the next two weeks were fraught, the recording process being nowhere near as straightforward as for *Corridors Of Power*.

For a start, the studio, based in Notting Hill, west London was undergoing refurbishments, so there was a lot of drilling and banging going on. Gary was planning to produce the album himself but changed his mind at the last minute and recalled Jeff Glixman. Gary started to have problems with the way Neil Murray was playing bass. 'Gary's view was that he wanted a platform for the drums and bass with no surprises,' says Neil, 'and he didn't want anything he thought would disturb him, just absolutely solid and safe. When we were doing *Corridors Of Power*, playing "Wishing Well", I said that I would play it like it was done by Free with a couple of very simple bass runs. Quite nice. "No," said Gary, "don't do that, do this," which was more boring. But when we did "Parisienne Walkways" live, the whole end section of that I would do a lot of embellishments, playing off what he was playing and he would not necessarily stop me from doing that. What I was required to do on the album anybody could have done, which is a shame because I could have brought more personality into it.'

Neil says he didn't get on with Jeff Glixman either, who naturally sided with Gary, and it was even worse for him on the new album. Jeff confirms that Neil found it hard 'to take direction and always wanted to embellish' and it would go something like this: 'Gary might say to Neil, "You're off there." "No, I'm right with the drummer." "But you're not with me." "But the drums are playing the downbeat." '"Yes, but I'm pushing and I want the bass with the push." "No, the bass goes with the drums." "Not in this case. I want it to go there."'

Jeff observes that 'Gary would really have loved to play with Felix Pappalardi. That would have been great. Jack Bruce was in many ways perfect too because he addressed the bass like a guitar. He could be very solid when he wanted to be, but he heard it like a guitar player.'

For his part, Ian Paice says he really enjoyed playing with Neil: 'He was a really fine bass player and I like those little notes; that to me makes a bass movement work. But Gary wanted to be the guy 100 percent and if the bass player is taking up 50 percent, that's 50 percent less for Gary. I play to patterns and I can play to different bass lines, it makes no difference at all. If Neil's bass lines were too busy for Gary, it doesn't mean to say they were wrong; they just weren't what Gary was hearing in his head.'

Ian continues: 'There are no hard and fast rules. Any collaboration of four or five musicians in a rock'n'roll outfit where nothing is scripted except basic arrangements is simply a chemical blend of how the players work together, whether it is happy or uncomfortable. It's not like working from a score. It's all about balance and if one guy plays in a way that doesn't fit in with the lead guy's concept then it has to change.'

And change it did. Neil records in his diary that he was informed that Mo

Foster would be re-doing most of Neil's bass parts. Another bassist, Bob Daisley, was also brought into the studio. Bob had come out of the Ozzy Osbourne band having been fired just before the release of *Bark At The Moon*, resulting in a tortuous legal wrangle over writing credits. Gary even played some bass parts himself, so who played what on the final tracks is impossible to say with any certainty. Neil and Gary parted company on October 23.

Gary was then forced into another change from a most unexpected quarter; astonishingly, Ian Paice suddenly announced he couldn't play properly and couldn't carry on with the recording: 'Drummers have a clock which is their timekeeping— and I lost my clock. I couldn't keep tempo. I told Gary he needed to bring in somebody else because at that moment I didn't know what I was doing. It started to go awfully wrong on that second album; obviously, it's more critical in the studio when tempos are slipping. We didn't have click tracks, so it had to be right—and I didn't know what was wrong. It took me about four or five months to work out what was going on. Basically, I was hitting too hard, using muscles instead of technique.' Neil Carter recalls that 'it took ages to get the drums right and this is where Ian just lost his mojo'. Gary was able once again to call upon Bobby Chouinard, who appeared on four of the eight tracks—and so, despite all the problems, the album titled *Victims Of The Future* appeared on schedule in December.

While the album did not mark any musical progression from *Corridors Of Power*, there are significant points to note. It was heavier than its predecessor, located more in the mainstream of heavy rock albums of the period. Prime examples were the title track, the semi-autobiographical 'Teenage Idol', 'All I Want', an expertly judged makeover of Jeff Beck's/The Yardbirds' 'Shapes Of Things' and 'Law Of The Jungle'—the latter straight out of the Led Zeppelin/Sabbath 'mammoth stomping through the ice' song book. Ozzy Osbourne was slated to sing 'Jungle' (the original title of the album) but either touring commitments or illness (depending on which account you read) prevented his participation. There was a guest appearance, though, by Noddy Holder doing back-up vocals ('very loudly,' says Neil Carter) on the 'Shapes Of Things' chorus, recorded, according to Gary, in Town House Studios' toilet to get an echo effect.

Gary always denied he was a heavy metal guitarist, usually on the grounds that he had far more strings to his guitar than just pounding riffs and lightning arpeggio runs. One good example was the solo on 'Shapes Of Things' where, as Jeff Glixman explains, 'it was something Gary wanted to execute in a certain way. We did that one in sections, not several takes of the whole solo—Gary would make sure one section was just how he wanted it before moving on to the next.' Another prime example of how his imagination went far beyond the standard expectations of guitarists of the genre was 'Murder In The Skies'.

On September 1, 1983, Korean Air Lines Flight 007 was on a scheduled flight from New York City to Seoul via Anchorage when it was shot down in the Sea of Japan by a Soviet fighter plane. All 269 passengers and crew aboard were killed. The incident sparked international outrage and prompted Gary to express his own view, which, while perhaps lyrically simplistic—and with vocals that verged too close on screaming (although maybe appropriate in this case)—nevertheless made him a national hero in South Korea. In the song, Gary used the guitar to help tell the story, especially at the end, exploring the sonic possibilities of the explosions and tearing metal of a plane being shot out of the sky and spiralling down to its horrific end.

David Coverdale remarked that it wasn't the kind of song that makes him write lyrics, it was the kind of song that makes him want to cry. Gary gave that view short shrift telling *Kerrang!*, 'all [people like that] do is write about themselves. It's so egocentric to go onstage and sing about your prick!'

On the album, along with all his other attributes, Neil Carter revealed himself as a songwriter; 'Empty Rooms', which became a concert favourite, came from turmoil in Neil's private life: 'I was in a bit of a mess, I'd just split up from my wife. Gary, me and Neil Murray were at the studio when I came in with a multi-track I'd done—and they were really mean and taking the mick. Gary didn't like my wife very much. I wrote the song in a hotel room in Texas. The version I have from UFO sounds quite similar, but Gary must take full credit for the melody and overall finish.'

And finally, as part of the career-building plan, the album started making some chart impact around the world; only modestly in the States, but a Top 20 album in the UK (12), Finland (7) and Sweden (15), with strong sales in Japan. But they were still searching for that all-important hit single. There were several attempts to lever 'Empty Rooms' into the charts and while it stalled just outside the Top 50 in the UK, it was Gary's best showing since 'Parisienne Walkways'.

Virgin were clever in that they virtually invented the 360-degree deal where you signed to them for recording, publishing, recorded the album in their studios (Gary often used the Town House), so it was largely out of one pocket and into the other, but it did allow artists the freedom to build careers and not have everything riding on the success of one album. This meant they could afford to be more generous with the advances and recording budgets, but not that much more.

Enter Steve Barnett, of whom Virgin's Peter Price says, 'he was one of the greatest managers of the time and certainly knew how to squeeze every penny out of everybody. I'd get a call from Steve to say, "We haven't got enough money to do this or that." I'd say, "Steve, there is nothing left in the budget." So, he'd call Richard Griffiths and ten minutes later I'd get a call from Richard saying, "I've approved the extra budget."'

It was industry practice for companies like Virgin to do licensing deals with other labels to secure worldwide distribution. But it was Virgin's Ken Berry who had the vision to push the idea that if Virgin were going to have international hits, why shouldn't they have them on their own label? Virgin started opening offices worldwide and Gary's appeal in territories like Scandinavia, Germany and the Far East became very important to the label. He was just about their only artist who could establish significant Virgin presence in places where playing heavy rock in tight trousers was still a huge money spinner.

Ian got it together in time for the start of the 1984 *Victims Of The Future* tour, but Gary still needed to find a new bass player. In the surprisingly small world of heavy rock, Craig Gruber knew Mark Nauseef when they both played in Ronnie Dio's Elf. Craig went on to be in Rainbow twice—which at various times also included Dio, Don Airey and Bob Daisley—and he replaced Geezer Butler in Sabbath for about nine months. His own band Bible Black didn't work out so he moved to London looking for work. He had a shot at Ronnie Dio's band because he had heard things weren't working out with Jimmy Bain, but in the end called Steve Barnett and got an audition with Gary. One of his songs, 'Blinder', was recorded during the *Victims Of The Future* sessions, never made the final album, but did feature in some of the concerts.

Craig recalls he was thrown right in the deep end: 'That first show was a televised show for the BBC. And we weren't even supposed to be playing it. It was a Whitesnake show, but Gary called to say that David Coverdale was ill and said, "Do you want to play Sunday night?" I said, "Are you shittin' me?" And this was Wednesday and we weren't ready. But he said, "Fuck it, I think we should do it, man. It's gonna be televised and we've only gotta play an hour." Gary's voice wasn't really ready, it was cracking badly, and he didn't really hit the notes until we'd done about ten gigs, but we didn't make one mistake.'

Craig was clear about his role in the band: 'I was the foundation; Gary wanted somebody to play bass with a pick. I played with a pick in Rainbow too—you get notes that are clean and distinctive rather than muddy. The pick articulates the note, you get a sharp punchy attack, more powerful tone and you can get really tight with the drummer, really lock into the bass drum.'

After more UK radio and TV appearances, they went off to Japan for Gary's second visit, a year after the first. Given Deep Purple's profile in Japan, having Ian in the band was good promotion, but Gary's fan base out there was also growing. The first album sold about 60,000 copies, the second would rack up sales around 80,000 and if the reception he received in 1983 was enthusiastic, by 1984, it was nuts.

As Craig recalls, 'When we landed at Norita airport about four in the morning, there were three to four thousand fans there waiting for us. The Gary Moore fan club had made life-size images of each of us—haircuts, clothes, full-size dolls. It was creepy. What were we supposed to do with these things? We thanked them profusely, of course. The Japanese are very conservative—you should have seen the look on the faces of the hotel staff when we brought them in. I took mine up to my room and it was like talking to myself.'

And that was just the start: 'We couldn't sign into the hotel under our own name. They attacked the cars, tried to climb in through the windows. It was crazy. Gary said, "I can't believe this. I've never had this kind of reception. I don't know what to say. It's just like The Beatles."' Neil Carter too was quite unprepared for all this adulation: 'Gary and Ian set me up by asking me to meet the fans in the hotel lobbies', where he was subsequently trapped signing autographs for forty minutes.

Gary Bushell from *Sounds* was travelling with the band and also fell for the hotel lobby setup. He wrote: 'Steve Barnett thrusts a bundle of Gary Moore postcards into my unsuspecting mitts and suggests I dish them out to keep the fans sweet. The first lot I approach tilt their heads uncomprehendingly until they suss that I'm not hawking, selling or pushing and when they clock the cards, their boats light up like I'm doling out fivers. Suddenly a strange squawking sound starts building up from the other ranks, followed by the frantic stamping of stampeding feet … they're coming from all directions … and just when I think I'm going to drown in damsels (worra way to die) Gary Moore is spotted making a sneaky get-away.' Neil remembers the same group of girls would follow them everywhere: 'They'd get on the train and follow you to the next gig—they were always very respectful—but always there.'

Gary said to *Sounds*, 'It's a bit embarrassing really. It's silly. You shouldn't put people on pedestals. A great guitarist is no better than a great plumber … Still,

I should complain. This is what we all strive for … Trouble is I reckon I'm more scared of them than they are of me.'

All the gigs sold out including the 14,000 capacity Budokan. Japanese gigs can be strange for Western bands; for example, to ease out the chaotic rush-hour crush on the Tokyo subway, Budokan concerts start at 6.30 with no support, so many of the audience come straight from the office in suits, carrying briefcases. They sit very politely during the songs, leaving the band to think they have bombed—and then go berserk at the end. Craig recalls this last gig was a complete triumph— 'everything really gelled at that point. It was a great sound, we were loud, we pummelled them, it was thunderous'—and, uncharacteristically, so fired up were the audience they were clapping through most of the gig. Screaming for an encore, they were treated to the single 'Hold Onto Love', not normally part of the set, but which, according to Gary Bushell, had the legendary Japanese promoter Mr Udo 'bouncing on his feet in delight'.

Bushell offered this assessment of his namesake: 'Most rock and pop is really about minor talents supporting major egos. Gary Moore is an exception to that rule of dumbness being both a major talent—one of the very few guitar heroes worthy of the name—and a nice guy, a real rough diamond. He deserves to be the star he's becoming internationally, but he doesn't act like one.'

They came back to do a full schedule of European dates in March in preparation for another assault on the States in May, this time supporting Rush, when Ian pulled out of the tour, because his wife was expecting their third child. However, during that period, the classic Deep Purple line-up were offered an eye-watering amount of money to reform, which meant Ian was not coming back. Bobby Chouinard was once again the go-to guy. Gary really liked Bobby's playing—on *Victims* he had stood in for Ian, got straight off the plane and straight into the studio. As he told *Modern Drummer*, in 1985, 'I love that kind of a challenge. It's nice to be able to help your friends out. I just have an intuition with Gary, having worked with him, knowing the way he plays and what he wants to hear. I sort of helped bail out the project for him.'

When Bobby got the call again, the new Billy Squier album was being mixed, but the tour rehearsals weren't due to begin until July, so he was free to tour with Gary. They did a four-day rehearsal with Bobby then into the first gig in Albuquerque, New Mexico, a punishing near forty-date tour playing 20,000-plus stadium venues. 'And everywhere we played, people turned up to watch the shows,' says Craig, 'Whitesnake, Jeff Beck, Eric Clapton, Eddie Van Halen—and

Neal Schon played a night with us in San Francisco.' Gary reported to *Kerrang!* that 'the place went crazy. In fact, we were so hot that Alex Lifeson really had to go out and blast away with what Neil and I had done. It was the first time I'd seen Alex giving his tremolo arm stick.'

'American audiences just loved Gary, he just slayed them,' says Craig. 'If you played a guitar and you knew who Gary Moore was, you were there. After the shows, he was just flooded with guitarists and fans from all over the world. I remember these Japanese girls we saw at almost every gig—it didn't matter if it was Tokyo, LA Forum, Castle Donnington, some gig in the Midwest: they were there. I brought them backstage and we gave them records and T-shirts and they just freaked.'

Craig was very impressed with the way they were treated by the headliners: 'On the first night of the tour, we walked into the dressing room and there's fruit baskets, wine and champagne welcoming Gary on to the tour. And they came up to us and said, "We're such fans of you guys, we love you so much. We really wanted you on this tour." It was like family. Unbelievable. We were stunned.'

Everybody loved Bobby Chouinard too, but, as Neil recalls sadly, he was 'a complete maniac, such a shambles of a man, very sweet, but just hopeless'. And here's why: as Craig puts it, 'all Bobby did was drink and do lines of coke. The tempos were really shaky and off. He would go out of rhythm and Gary would turn round to me and shake his head. He screamed at him one night, "Listen, you know, I'm fuckin' paying you. This is a professional band and we're on tour."' It didn't do much good though. 'He would do a line,' says Dirk Sommer, 'and say, "There goes the condominium"; another sniff, "There goes the Ferrari."'

After the US dates, Bobby went back to the Billy Squier band. Once again, Gary was urgently looking for a new band member—barely a month away were prestigious dates on the Monsters of Rock Festival. Following some intensive auditioning, the unexpected choice was former Roxy Music drummer Paul Thompson.

Maybe it was an omen of troubles ahead, but while, as Ian Paice observed above, being the best player around was no guarantee of commercial success, it certainly got Gary out of a tricky spot at the first Monsters gig at Castle Donnington. As the band went for the first song, there was deathly silence. Awful moments followed, until Gary spotted a loose cable at the side of the stage, rushed over, pushed the squabbling roadies aside and kicked the cable back in place. But this was a time when drunken metal fans had taken to throwing beer cans at the big festivals and fuelled by alcohol, the mood started to turn ugly against Gary.

Don Airey (still with Ozzy Osbourne) was standing at the side of the stage: 'The reaction was awful and I was really feeling for Gary out there; there was still a strong spiritual and musical tie between us. He was still my friend. And then he got to the solo on "Empty Rooms" and out in the audience you could hear a pin drop. Everything came to a halt backstage too—musicians, crew, guests, management—everyone stopped what they were doing to listen. I can hardly do justice to how stunning that solo was and what a pivotal moment in Gary's career it came to be. It still rings in my ears thirty years on.'

A young Irish fan, interviewed for the *Emerald Aisles* video, who saw Gary at the same concert remarked he was 'just an ordinary guy who plays guitar with a bit of maturity rather than idiots like Kiss and Mötley Crüe who can't play at all. Saw them at Donnington, they were appalling. Gary destroyed them in every single way ... totally wiped out Van Halen and Jake E. Lee (Ozzy Osbourne) and all those guys ... much better ... the best.'

There was a touring and recording lull through the early winter months of 1984, leading up to some extremely important gigs for Gary. Apart from a couple of Greedies gigs in Dublin, he hadn't played in Ireland at all for ten years. That would have been enough to put Gary into a state of high anxiety, added to which the gigs—one in Belfast, the other in Dublin—were due to be filmed and it began to create tensions within the band, not helped by the fact that, from Craig Gruber's point of view, Paul Thompson was not really working out.

'The dynamics of everything changed; Gary started to get real short with people. We still had Paul on drums and it wasn't the same without Ian—we didn't have to even look at each other. It just worked, whereas Paul and I had to grind it out, working out almost every bar. Gary was really stressed out and rightly so because the band wasn't sounding good, it really wasn't. [Despite all the problems] Bobby was a powerful rock drummer, Paul just wasn't; Roxy Music wasn't known for that. Paul was out of his element, he would ask me to turn down, so Gary would turn on him and tell him to play louder. It just wasn't working. I said I would stay if I had to, I wouldn't leave them hanging. But I couldn't really say "Fire Paul Thompson". By contrast, although he admits he was surprised Gary chose Paul, Neil Carter says, 'I was equally surprised how well it worked.'

Although his time with Gary didn't end that well, Craig is at pains to emphasise the positive: 'I became a better musician, a better bassist, a better writer. My technique improved greatly; it really did. When I left Gary's band, I was not the same bassist who joined. I grew so much; it was the discipline and precision of it all. I didn't play badly, maybe three bad notes in 18 months—and he heard every one of them. Even if I just slightly mis-fingered and played right on the fret—so, not so much a wrong note—he still heard it.'

Craig goes on to explain how different it was playing with Gary than in his other bands: 'The druggies, drinkers or party guys would not have worked out in that band. You know, like you're in Rainbow, we'd be booked for a rehearsal on Monday. Ritchie would turn up on Thursday at 4.30pm, come in with that "death ray" look, we called it, like he was pissed at everybody. Ronnie [Dio] would say, "Where the fuck have you been for the last three days?" and they'd go at it. Then a glass of Scotch would be thrown at the wall. Ritchie's Stratocaster would hit the floor and he'd be gone again until Monday. Our road manager would have to go find Ritchie and baby him; Ronnie would drive off and I'd just drive back to Malibu Beach and drink. It was awful.

'Gary, on the other hand, was easily the best band leader I've worked with—laser focused, totally organised, there was structure and discipline. We knew exactly what we would be doing every day of the week. Rehearsals were Monday to Friday, 10–6. Everybody was on salary. In the other bands I was in, the tour manager was pretty much the leader. With Gary, he was 100 percent the leader in charge of the band, the crew, hiring new people. They would do duties for a day to try them out. But even the most humble person on the tour he would treat well. That's a sure sign of character, of who the person really is. It didn't matter who you were, Gary shook your hand, said hello, always took the time. Behind the scenes he was a very caring person.' But as others have remarked, 'as soon as he put that guitar on, it was all business, there was no bullshit—"Okay, we're working now, guys, you are pro musicians, you are not allowed to make a mistake, you can't drink, you can't do drugs, you can't act up and run amok."' Bob Daisley stepped into the breach for the Irish gigs in December. Meanwhile, Gary was building bridges with another bass player he vaguely knew.

Living in London, visiting the same pubs and clubs, knowing some of the same people, seeing the same bands, it was inevitable that from time-to-time Gary and Phil Lynott would be sharing the same space: 'I'd bump into him in various nightspots,' Gary recalled years later to Mark Putterford, 'and we'd do our best to ignore each other. It was stupid, really. One night I was in Dingwalls with Jeff Beck and a couple of girls and we were having a great laugh. Phil was sitting in the corner sulking and you could tell he really wanted to come over and join the crowd, but he wouldn't because I was there. It was really sad but quite funny as well.'

Then, sometime late in 1982, Gary was on his back way from Germany, Phil was en route from Dublin and the two met up at Heathrow—or rather, the two crews saw each other first. Each was pointed out to the other by a respective crew member and then everybody stood back to see what would happen next. But they were too deep in each other's heart and soul for the feud to go on any longer— four years was enough.

Thin Lizzy had one final tour planned for 1983 with one big reunion gig featuring all the guitarists to take place at the Hammersmith Odeon on March 12. There was only one way for Gary to play; he was the only one sweating after the soundcheck. Phil was late arriving, but when he arrived on stage, he made straight for Gary, all laughs and handshakes. Everyone went through their paces, but all the guitarists took a back seat on 'Black Rose' as Gary was the only one who could play the tricky parts—and he even had to remind Phil how to play the bass lines.

With Phil winding down Lizzy and Gary out on tour through 1983, their paths didn't really cross again until late 1984, when Gary invited Phil to join him as his guest for the Irish dates. There is a saying that you can't be a prophet in your own land, but you certainly can be a guitar hero and one can only imagine what Gary must have been feeling as he walked out on to the stage at the Ulster Hall in Belfast on December 17 for the first of two shows in front of a wildly ecstatic audience. He'd stood right there back in 1967 watching Peter Green wide-eyed and telling a journalist that The Who on stage there had been so powerful, Gary and his friends felt like they had been beaten up. He would have remembered being told off by a teacher for daydreaming about rock stardom. And here he was—not with one guitar, one set of strings and an AC 30, but striding in front of thirty-two tons of equipment, his own band, his name on the posters, drilling his young audience into the ground with the sheer force of his sound.

Even though the band just played their standard set, with no reference to the Troubles, there were songs that could be easily re-framed in that light—Gary being 'Back On The Streets', his audience being 'Victims Of The Future' and wondering if it really was 'The End Of The World'; 'Wishing Well' exhorts people to throw down their guns and look towards a brighter future while 'Shapes Of Things' continues the military theme.

And there was 'Out In The Fields'. It looks like it was only played in Dublin, not Belfast; it might have been deemed too dangerous to play the song north of the border. Although Gary denied the song was written with the Troubles in mind, because of the later video, it became associated with violence in Belfast. In fact, Gary would have had every reason to write about the trouble in his home town. It would not have been exploitative or gratuitous because the husband of his beloved aunt Phylis was shot dead by the loyalist Ulster Volunteer Force (UVF) on May 27, 1976 in a sectarian killing while on October 29, 1983, his cousin George, aged only twenty-three, was murdered by the same group. George was shot in the head and then had his throat cut. George was himself a member of the UVF; apparently it was all a terrible mistake. George was drunk one night and accidentally offended another UVF member who took his revenge. His killer was never caught, although, as was often the case at the time, many people knew exactly who he was and Phylis says he is still walking around.

Gary was overwhelmed by the response; young fans clutching albums and autograph books surged around Gary wherever he was signing and when the band and crew repaired to the Gresham Hotel after the Dublin gigs, Gary's room was just awash with people. He was cornered in the bathroom, having had a bit more to drink than he should have. Bemused by what was going on around him, he was left staring like a rabbit caught in the headlights.

After a hard year's touring promoting *Victims Of The Future*, Gary had hardly caught his breath when he was back in the studio early in January 1985, looking to start work on the next album. But if the recording of *Victims* proved troublesome, it was an easy stroll through the park compared with the jigsaw puzzle sessions comprising what would be aptly named *Run For Cover*.

By the time the album was done in June, Gary had used four and a half producers (Gary did some himself), three drummers plus sampled drums, three bass players (plus some from Gary), three traditional keyboard players (including contributions from one of the producers), synthesisers, three lead singers (including himself)—but of course, only one guitarist.

The story of *Run For Cover* really hinges around Gary's relationship with two bass-playing singers, both in states of continuing disarray. After his unceremonious departure from G-Force, Glenn Hughes was left still high, but not dry and was frittering away his talent, until he met up with Pat Thrall, whom he first saw sharing lead guitar work in The Pat Travers Band. Once Thrall left that band, he contacted Glenn to see what he was up to and eventually they got together in LA to record some demos. What emerged in 1982 was the *Hughes/Thrall* album produced by the legendary Andy Johns, a huge-sounding album awash with Thrall's synthesised guitar sound, which successfully married pop and rock sensibilities. And while it didn't gel with the record-buying public, the industry was much taken with the album, which is credited with influencing the sound of American AOR through the rest of the decade.

It certainly caught Gary's attention and he called Glenn up out of the blue: 'He was coming into town opening for Rush. By then Hughes/Thrall had broken up; we were supposed to do another album, but that wasn't going to happen now. So, what was I going to do now? And here's Gary saying right off the bat, "We've got to get together again, join my band, write songs or sing on an album."'

Most likely, *Hughes/Thrall* had proved to Gary, perhaps naively, that Glenn could hold it together and he was very keen to use Glenn's voice because he was such a great singer, 'and it was a great honour for me to hear Gary say these things'. Glenn came to London to start recording and was given a smart flat in Maida Vale for the duration of the sessions. If Gary was looking to recreate the sound of Glenn's album, it might have made sense to bring in Andy Johns as producer. But perhaps because of availability, it was decided to engage the services of American producer Beau Hill, who was relatively unknown until the chance came to produce Ratt's debut album *Out Of The Cellar*, which sold three million copies stateside and propelled Hill to international status.

The first songs laid down with Hill in January, 'Out Of My System' and 'Nothing To Lose', were by way of an experiment, to see how Glenn and Gary would work out in the studio. Dante Bonutto, reporting for *Kerrang!*, asked Gary if he knew much about Hill: 'Oh, just the first Ratt album. Funnily enough, the one thing I didn't like about the production … and I said this to him—was the guitars which I didn't feel were loud enough on the solos. He said something about them being "an extension of the energy of the track" all that kind of shit, but I just thought, *Fuck it, I want my solos turning up*, so there was a bit of conflict over that. I guess it's just a matter of opinion; I like to hear my solos clearly, make out all the notes.'

Although both Neil Carter and Paul Thompson appear on the album and had been part of the touring band, Gary didn't seem to have in mind that they would be the main keyboards and drums. It was all new material (with one exception), so Gary wanted all his options open. The initial focus was on Glenn, despite behind-the-scenes objections: 'There was so much opposition to me getting together with Glenn; my management warned me against it and my record company didn't want to know. I fought with so many people just to give it a shot. They all said, "You'll be sorry!" but I just went, "Well look, that's my problem. Let's see how it works out."'

Peter Price of Virgin Records recounts that 'Gary insisted he wanted to be in a band with Glenn Hughes, he just kept on about it. Eventually, I found a number for him in America. I told Steve that Gary had got me to call him and Richard Griffiths sent me over to America. We met up and I asked Glenn if he was sure he was free, that he hadn't signed anything with anyone else. "No, no, I'm free. I can do this." So eventually I went to see the Virgin America lawyer. I walked in, Glenn's in the corner and on the desk, a big pile of papers where Glenn had signed away parts of his life over the last five years, which he couldn't remember much about anyway.'

Meanwhile, it wasn't working out with Beau Hill: 'We spent about five days in the studio ... but when we heard the mixes later on, we weren't very happy with them because everything sounded so dull. Plus, I wasn't too keen on Beau's attitude towards my guitar playing, which was not exactly negative, but kind of non-committal. He wasn't really interested in what *I* wanted to do with the guitar. I'd be laying down a solo in one room and he'd be off in another putting his keyboard overdubs on. He was more interested in keeping the band out of the room and getting on with his own stuff, so I got a bit pissed off with that and figured it wouldn't be a good idea to continue using him ... I guess we're just not right for each other.' The final straw was Hill's dislike of 'Out In The Fields'. As he puts it, 'I did think it was kind of wrong for him anyway ... it's more a frantic English sounding type of thing I suppose. I wanted to give him something he could really put his stamp on which is why I went for "Nothing To Lose" and "Out Of My System".'

Virgin managed to engage Andy Johns, the *Hughes/Thrall* album producer, and he came over to the UK (along with that band's drummer Gary Ferguson), to produce 'All Messed Up', 'Reach For The Sky' and the title track 'Run For Cover', which Gary admitted very much took its inspiration from the *Hughes/Thrall* opener 'Got Your Number'—even taking one line of the lyric ('don't run for cover') for the title of his album.

Because 'Empty Rooms' had been so popular with American audiences on the Rush tour, it was decided to re-record the song for a tilt at the US single charts. During a break in the tour, Gary took the band into Union/Western Studios in Los Angeles with Peter Collins. He produced two albums by mod revival band The Lambrettas plus their Top 10 UK hit, a cover of the Leiber and Stoller song *Poison Ivy*, and the 1982 Musical Youth No. 1, 'Pass The Dutchie'. The song did nothing in the States, but Rush were so impressed with the sound they grabbed

Collins for their 1985 album *Power Windows* (and three more albums thereafter), putting Peter out of the running to produce all of *Run For Cover*, which Gary had hoped he would do. But there was time for Peter to have another go with 'Empty Rooms' for the new album, this time trying to create a very 80s pop sound with just Gary (and Neil on backing vocals), synthesizers and the engineer Jimbo Barton handling drum samples. Released yet again as a single, it did get to No. 12 in Ireland and broke the Top 30 in the UK, so there was a degree of satisfaction in the Virgin camp that they had persevered with it, although the rock critics thought it smacked of a dearth of ideas.

Of much more significance, though, was the Peter Collins-produced 'Out In The Fields' where Gary invited Phil to be on the recording. Since the break-up of Thin Lizzy, Phil had been going downhill; the drink and drug use was spiralling out of control, and he was fast becoming a complete liability as far as the industry was concerned. Irish DJ Smiley Bolger was full of praise for Gary: 'All credit to him—when nobody else would touch Phil with a bargepole because of his reputation for all the wrong reasons. Appearances on television would get cancelled on the day because Phil would turn up and he would be all over the place. It's a small industry and stuff like that spreads like wildfire. He couldn't get a deal for his band Grand Slam and it nearly killed Phil not getting Live Aid, a real kick in the bollocks. At least Gary put him back on the map.'

But it wasn't Gary who would have to sort out the messy details. 'Steve Barnett and I had to go down and sign Phil up,' recalls Peter Price. 'We got down to his house on the Kew Road with these big red gates that a tank couldn't have run down, in case there was a drugs raid. We sat there, waited half an hour. Three girls came down the stairs followed by Phil looking pretty bloated and not very well.' Phil was still technically managed by the Thin Lizzy company, which was less than happy when Phil signed to Ten Records for £5,000 cash-in-hand, which probably found its way into a drug dealer's back pocket.

Despite the inauspicious start, what came out of Gary and Phil's latest collaboration was a hit single, backed by a video with the boys in military jackets against a backdrop of a devastated city. Released in May 1985, the single was a Top 5 hit in four countries, including No. 5 in the UK, destined to be Gary's best ever showing in the UK single charts. They milked the success for all it was worth, appearing together on top UK TV pop shows.

Although some people at the time and since have praised Gary for giving Phil the chance for a comeback, he never saw this in terms of doing his friend a favour:

'Even though ["Out In The Fields"] was written long before Phil got involved, it was his packaging of the whole thing which helped to make it such a bit hit. The military uniforms we wore during the promotion were his idea. He had a gift for marketing, a great sense of how to sell something to an audience.'

The video shoot was part of the *Emerald Aisles* promotional video shot by NFL on the Irish tour at the end of the 1984, plus the promo shots for 'Out In The Fields, 'Empty Rooms' and another song by Phil on *Run For Cover* called 'Military Man', originally written for Grand Slam.

Tony Platt, who co-produced the live album *We Want Moore!*, some of the backing tracks for *Run For Cover* and production and editing work on the video, was very impressed with NFL's professionalism and creative ideas: 'It was stroke of genius on Steve Barnett's part, really—instead of just doing some boring old film. These NFL guys are good at spotting interesting things coming up and capturing action spontaneously. They were also incredibly innovative; they had these technicians who were always building new bits of kit. One guy had made a 35mm camera out of an old tank camera that could clamp on the top of Gary's guitar. There's a strange shot down the strings; Gary moves, the background moves, but the neck stays still. And they were the guys that first came up with Sky-Cam, a camera tethered by four steel cables on four sides of the auditorium, and you fly it round the arena. That was the first time it was ever used.

'We went through a proper film process: storyboarding, editing, post-production. We had to be careful in the editing because Gary had a few Strats, but they were all different colours. So, if you weren't careful, you could go from one colour to another and back again all in the same songs because we filmed quite a few concerts. There was the Irish music from The Chieftains, dialogue and narration, so it was innovative in that it wasn't just a documentary about a rock guitarist.'

By the time Gary got to recording *Run For Cover*, the songwriting did need a lift, and Phil provided that. But while Gary still hoped that Glenn was getting it together, he was under no such illusion with Phil. There was nothing he could do to swerve Phil away from his drug use (although there was a rumour that Gary paid for Phil to go into rehab one time), but at least he could rebuild some of his friend's shattered self-esteem. Gary did know what he was dealing with, though—he had a security guard frisk Phil before he would let him in the studio; then the studio staff would helpfully smuggle him some whisky to take the nervous edge off. Yet despite their renewed friendship and resulting studio success, going out the road again was never an option. Gary told a Swedish radio journalist, 'We don't work very well in that kind of situation. We end up fighting and then it breaks up … we're different people, but we work well together in the studio. We always come up with something that people like, so there's definitely some kind of chemistry between us.'

What Gary wasn't expecting, though, was the imploding once more of his relationship with Glenn. Having gone to the barricades to get Glenn involved, ignoring all the warnings, Gary was bitterly disappointed with what transpired and, true to form, vented his spleen to the rock press. Apart from the drug problem, Glenn was very much overweight. Some of his time in the UK he spent at Gary's house, where Gary claimed he ate him out of house and home: 'We were going, "Come on Glenn, you've got to get yourself together." And he'd say one minute "Oh! I've been running," and the next minute, you know, we'd drop him off at his flat and then catch him sneaking into a sweet shop to buy about six Mars bars!' Gary went on to claim that if they all went out to an Indian restaurant, Glenn would eat twice as much as everybody else, the relish tray, everything. Gary had also expected more from Glenn in the studio: 'After we'd done the first two tracks with Beau, Glenn went back to LA while I was working away with Phil, but he didn't do anything, he just sat on his arse. He had so much time, I thought he would come with a few things for the album, but it didn't happen—and then the only song of his that we *were* going to use, "Still The Night", we found tied up on the publishing side, but we fought tooth and nail to get it.'

The reason they didn't get it was another sore point with Gary—Glenn's simultaneous involvement with a Bronze Records concept album *Philomena* with Cozy Powell and Neil Murray, among others. The album was a total dud, as Gary knew it would be, 'and for that reason I didn't want him involved. I wanted him to wait until the *Run For Cover* came out so people would go, "Oh great, he's really done something special here." But he wouldn't listen. He was so desperate to get his name in the papers, so desperate to prove to everybody that he's still a big name—which of course, he isn't at the moment … I wanted him to come out shining, it was all for *his* sake, but he thought I was trying to hold him back.'

The crunch really came when they began planning for the tour to promote the album. 'He wanted me to call it the Gary Moore Band featuring Glenn Hughes, but I just said, "For a start, it's not called the Gary Moore Band, it's just Gary Moore and you can't have Gary Moore featuring Glenn Hughes plus Neil Carter" … he had this idea in his head that name really counted but he couldn't sell out the toilet in the Marquee if he went out on his own, *that's* the reality of the situation.'

Gary really liked Glenn as a person, 'underneath he's a really nice guy', but his analysis was that Glenn never got over being in Deep Purple and was now forever surrounded by hangers-on and so-called friends, who would massage his ego and who kept ringing him when he was staying at Gary's house. Gary reckoned that one of these calls came from two guys who had been promised a job on Gary's road crew by Glenn if they flew over from LA.

Gary said he was serious about helping Glenn get his career back on track, maybe get him a solo deal with Ten Records if the album and the tour worked out. But Steve Barnett had known Glenn from way back when he was the agent for Trapeze and especially gave Glenn a hard time for the chemical indulgences, 'and rightly so,' says Glenn. For insurance purposes, Steve Barnett required Glenn to have a blood test before there was any thought of taking him on the road. Glenn knew what would show up—so he ducked the test and was back on the plane home.

Speaking now, Glenn says that he found Gary's comments very hurtful, especially the remarks about eating: 'Well, I went down one night and made a sandwich. I wasn't some monster in the attic.' He also reckons that what Gary really railed about to the press was the coke use, but that got changed to Mars bars presumably for legal reasons. Glenn also observes that Gary's anger went way beyond him not pulling his weight and being out of it: 'I've never known anger like that before. It was almost like I was his big brother and I'd done something terrible to him.' The similarity with Phil's situation must have screamed out to Gary.

For Glenn, though, hurtful as the comments were, they also acted as a wake-up call. 'When I was in my cups, I wasn't a guy you could trust ... when we recorded the album, there were weekends off, that's when I could do what I wanted to do. I was hanging with Lemmy at the Embassy Club and you know what's going to happen there! I never used drugs using the week, but going back into the studio on a Monday morning ...'

In fairness to Gary, it seemed that his press tirade was in response to something that Glenn had said once he was back home—to justify the break up—that somehow he and Gary hadn't clicked musically, which incensed Gary because he knew that just wasn't true.

What with all the musicians and producers involved, *Run For Cover* could have ended up being a dog's breakfast. Fortunately, Mike Stone came in—he had a long history as engineer for Queen in the 1970s and he scored major production hits with Asia and Journey. He mixed the whole album (and produced two tracks from scratch) and very nicely pulled all the disparate pieces together, producing a seamless result.

By his own admission, Dante Bonutto was not a big-time fan of Gary's music, but he wrote of the new album, 'I find myself drawn inexorably towards the album with a sloppy grinning enthusiasm bordering on the juvenile. Like a child let off the leash on a Yuletide Hamley's sprint, the riches on offer are quite overwhelming and can lead to tantrums, purple faces and serious fits of pique if not absorbed measure for measure under parental control.' Steffan Chirazi of *Sounds* was less effusive, wondering about having only six brand new compositions on a nine-track album, while commenting with suspicion about what he and others saw as the overuse of synthesisers and keyboards and the drift to 'dumb commercialism' at the expense of Gary Moore guitar fan expectations. But while he thought Gary could and should do better next time, he predicted that the album 'will joyfully jump into the charts and it is worthy of success'. And he was right: gold album status in the UK and Sweden and decent chart and sales showings across many territories with the ominous exception of the States. Gary still couldn't catch a cold out there and refused to tour stateside through 1985 and 1986 to promote the album, declaring to *Kerrang!* that 'it's stupid to go where you are not wanted'. The band settled down to be Neil Carter and Bob Daisley with drummer Gary Ferguson staying after the album sessions and some guest appearances by Phil on three UK dates.

Mark Putterford reviewed the Edinburgh Playhouse concert at the start of the tour, making the point that Gary always chose great musicians to back him and that you were always guaranteed a slick, tight show with plenty of staggering guitar work. He reiterates too, that for all the guitar pyrotechnics, it wasn't just about the speed, 'as the slow 'n' sleazy "Cold Hearted" and the startlingly beautiful "Empty Rooms" proved, this Belfast boy's playing isn't all blurred fingers and flashing plectrums—it has real depth'. The album was finished in June, the tour in September. The period in between was time off—to get married.

* * *

Kerry Booth from Lincolnshire was just seventeen when she came to London in 1981 to try and make it as a model; she shared a flat with another model, Susan, who was married to Paul Thompson, then still the drummer for Roxy Music. Kerry's dad, Dave, was the successful manager of Grimsby Town FC from 1982–85.

'Paul had a circle of musician friends and we went to a club one night and a mutual friend of ours, a guitarist, was obsessed with Gary, always talking about him. Susan looked round and said, "Oh look, over there, it's Gary Moore." We met up and he came to a party at the flat and after that he kept calling me up. I was not really that interested, there was quite a big age gap (about eleven years). Then he went to New York and, completely by chance, I met his manager Steve Barnett. Steve phoned Gary and said, "I've just met this girl who I think you would really like." Quite bizarre. Just one of those things.

'When he got back from New York, he called me again and again, he just persisted and eventually we went out for lunch. At that point (c.1981/82) he was drinking an awful lot; when he arrived at that first party, he was completely drunk, and it was not where I was at—at all. But when he came back from New York and I saw him in the daytime, it was just lunch and it revealed more of who he really was—really sweet and protective. He knew I was surviving on very little money from modelling work. I wasn't eating, so I was really thin and he was concerned about that, took me out to eat. So, I got to know him and it was very exciting; he was very busy, surrounded by music business people—not my world at all. I was very green and naïve. I think his manager was very keen on Gary being with me because I think he thought I would be a calming influence. A few people did warn me away from him. He did have a pretty bad reputation for drinking and his fiery temper.'

Kerry moved into the flat in Fitzjohn's Avenue that Gary had bought with Thin Lizzy money, which they then sold and bought a house in Highgate, moving on to a rented house in Maida Vale. Gary took her out on the road with him on both the Def Leppard and Rush tours and he didn't want Kerry to work because then she wouldn't be available to go on the tours. Gary was often quite lonely on tour; he wasn't a party animal, certainly not the sort of parties favoured by Thin Lizzy. While he would laugh and joke with the band and the crew, he often didn't hang out with them because he was the boss and not many people fancy a night out with the boss.

Kerry did all the planning for the wedding but observes that 'even though Gary absolutely wanted this, he still felt trapped and restricted and whenever he had that sense, he would try and run. I could see what he was doing. A couple of nights he didn't come back. Phil was back on the scene, but he was not in a great place; his house was party central, and Gary got sucked back into that a bit. One night Phil was having a party, so we both went, and the house was just full of undesirables. It got to about 1am and I said I was going home. Gary wanted to stay. So, Phil says, "Well, I'll come back with you." Very typical Phil. "No, that's not going to work, Phil …"'

Gary and Kerry got married in July 1985, in the Lincolnshire village where Kerry's parents lived. Phil was obviously invited; Peter Price got a call from Chris Morrison's office: 'They called and asked if we would take care of Phil. So, the train's going at 9am. Me and Richard (Griffiths) are there with our wives. No sign of Phil. Just as the whistle blows, this shambling mess appears with a roadie who shoves him on to the train. He looked as if he'd been up all night. As the train moved off, I said, "Anybody fancy a tea or a coffee?" Phil's standing behind me at the counter and I said, "Do you want anything?" "I'll have six brandies." "Phil, it's nine o'clock in the morning." "Okay, five." When we got the small local train, Phil went to the toilet. The train must have lurched because he came out with a line of coke across his sunglasses.'

Phil got sidetracked because, according to Kerry, 'he arrived halfway through the service, very dishevelled. Gary said he always had to steal the limelight.' Gary recalled the arrival of his friend to *Record Collector* in 2008: 'He turned up the church is a pair of fucking skin-tight black jeans. He'd bought a suit, but thought the trousers were too baggy and you couldn't see his knob or something.' Gary, Phil, Neil Carter and Gary Ferguson played and, according to Gary, Kerry came up at the end of the first solo and asked him to turn it down, 'and then Phil shagged the bridesmaid, of course—and I am not joking'. In answer to the question did the bridesmaid get the bouquet, Gary replied, 'She got something long and colourful, but I'm not sure it was bouquet.' Phil's version of 'congratulations' was 'Well, you fucking done it then!' The last time Phil and Gary played together was on September 28 at the Hammersmith Odeon as part of the *Victims Of The Future* tour.

As the year drew to a close, those around Phil say, in retrospect, that they were looking at a dead man walking; he was in poor shape. On Christmas Day, his mother found him unconscious at his house on Kew Road. He finally got to intensive care in Salisbury Hospital via a circuitous route involving a private London 'script' doctor and a Wiltshire-based rehab centre called Clouds House. He remained in hospital for about eleven days, looked to rally, but lost the fight and passed away on January 4, 1986. Years of chronic drug and alcohol use had left his body defenceless against the infection that finally claimed his life.

Gary and Kerry were in Tenerife when the call came: 'Gary absolutely loved Phil, absolutely loved him. That night it was really odd, there was a real sense of

Phil being in the room. Gary said to me, "He was here, he was absolutely here." Gary never made it to the funeral on January 9; Kerry maintains 'we literally couldn't get back, though; there were no flights'. But Gary told Lynott biographer Mark Putterford that he went down to the beach, 'and the awful realisation kept coming over me in waves. It hit me so hard I didn't know what to do. Then that night we went to this bar and "Out In The Fields" came on the video jukebox … I was like a zombie, I just stood there in a daze. It took me ages to get my head together and I couldn't face coming back for the service.'

Jeff Glixman says he had seen Phil with Tony Iommi at the Rainbow Grill in LA in November, 'And then I get this call from Gary in January to say Phil had died. He just sat on the phone and cried for about five minutes—no conversation and then he talked about "Parisienne Walkways" and "Out In The Fields". "I just had to tell you, man," he said, "those great days are over."'

The following May, around 30,000 fans gathered in Dublin for the Self Aid concert in aid of the unemployed, where tributes were paid to Phil—and Gary took part in a Thin Lizzy reunion. But by then, Gary's more lasting tribute to his soul mate was already in the planning.

ABOVE Gary (*top row, far left*) at his first school in East Belfast, Strandtown Primary. **LEFT** Gary and friend with the catch of the day.

ABOVE Gary with his first guitar—a cello-body Framus—sometime around 1960–62.

LEFT Gary aged fourteen in 1966 with The Barons.
BELOW Platform 3 with Dave Finlay and Colin Martin—Gary's last band before he left for Dublin.

Gary in his most carefree days on
Dublin's hippie folk scene, 1969.

TOP Down on the farm with Noel Bridgeman (*left*) and Brush Shiels in Skid Row. **ABOVE** Thin Lizzy 1974: the start of Gary's fiery relationship with Phil Lynott. **LEFT** Gary and Gibson with Skid Row.

Onstage with Skid Row: maybe the
first shot of Gary giving it the full Gary.
© Jorgen Angel

Gary Moore Band

COLOSSEUM II

ABOVE Gary's first professional band as leader, 1973: Phillip Donnelly, Gary, Pearse Kelly, Jan Schelhaas, Frank Boylan.
LEFT Gary with Colosseum II, 1976.
BELOW The Gary Moore Band, 1982–83: Jon Sloman, Neil Murray, Gary, Ian Paice. Jon was the last vocalist in the band before Gary took on the role himself.

GARY MOORE

ABOVE & LEFT Two shots of Gary's G-Force, a band that promised much but was never given the chance to deliver. This was also the era of fashion-disaster guitars.

ABOVE Gary in pensive mood, psyching himself up before a gig in 1982.
RIGHT Two Celtic soul brothers, Gary and Jack Bruce, 1982. © Neil Murray
BELOW RIGHT Gary recorded and toured with Greg Lake in 1981, when both musicians were looking for their next moves.

THIS PAGE Gary chilling out in Japan, where he earned himself a huge and wildly enthusiastic fan base, in 1984. **BELOW** With Ian Paice.

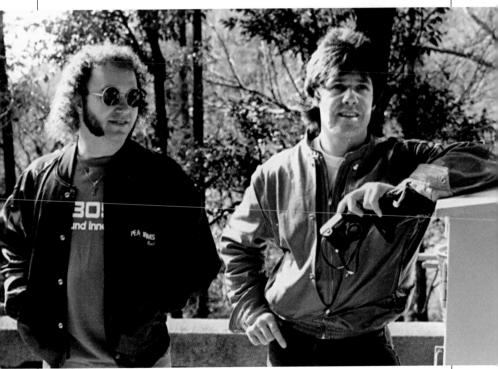

RIGHT A still from *An Evening With The Blues* at the Hammersmith Odeon, May 1990. **BELOW** The Thin Lizzy debacle now history, Phil appeared on three dates of the *Run For Cover* tour in 1985. © George Bodnar/Iconic Pix

Gary jamming with Carlos Santana
in Konstanz, Germany, 1987.

ABOVE Gary with Mr 'Icepicker'
himself, Albert Collins, at the
Montreux Jazz Festival, 1990.
© George Bodnar/Iconic Pix
LEFT Gary and Albert King, 1990:
King declared that Gary and Stevie
Ray Vaughan were his sons and could
really play the blues, although he
warned against thinking you have to
play all the notes.

LEFT Gary with Belfast friend Ian Hunter. **BELOW** Gary onstage with George Harrison for the launch of Harrison's National Law Party, 1992. © *Richard Young* **BOTTOM** Gary's dream come true: BBM with Jack Bruce and Ginger Baker. A band that burned fierce but short. © *Al Thain*

ABOVE Scars with Darrin Mooney and Cass Lewis, 2002: a brief return to the heavy power-trio format. **RIGHT** A sublime blues meeting with B.B. King, performing 'The Thrill Is Gone' at the Town & Country Club, London, 1992.

LEFT The words say it all: Gary's induction into the US Blues Hall of Fame, 2015. **BELOW** The classic Les Paul/Marshall combo.

Fans pay tribute to a guitar legend gone
far too soon. © Geoff Swaine/Avalon

09

HAIR TODAY, GONE TOMORROW

In one of his last interviews, recorded in December 1985, Phil Lynott told a Swedish journalist that in January he was going into the studio with Gary to record a new single, a follow-up to 'Out In The Fields'. The song was 'Over The Hills And Far Away', but instead of becoming their next potential hit collaboration, it was the jump off point for Gary's next album, a tribute to Phil, *Wild Frontier*.

The prodigal return to Ireland in 1984, the reunion with Phil and his subsequent death, later reinforced by the Self-Aid concert in Dublin all served to rekindle Gary's thoughts of his Irish roots. Maybe too, the genesis of the idea that you could play to that romantic, mystic and martial Celtic tradition with all the fire and rampaging, buccaneering spirit of Thin Lizzy, but without the chemically-induced shenanigans and temper tantrums.

Yet if Gary was looking back into the past, he was also looking to the future in his admiration for all the new technologies that were coming onstream. His melodic imagination had already taken him past the limitations of most heavy rock guitarists of the period. His growing confidence as a singer and his proven ability to write songs way beyond the banalities of 'cock rock' added up to a musician who, while still corralled by fans, journalists, and the business within a certain genre, was determined not to be confined by it.

Between January and the end of May, Gary began work on some new songs and started thinking about producers. As a fan of Billy Idol, Gary was in discussion with producer Keith Forsey, and also with U2's Steve Lillywhite and with Pete Smith, who worked on Sting's *The Dream Of The Blue Turtles* album. The sessions started with Smith behind the desk and the band out front working on three new songs with the addition of session drummer Charlie Morgan.

The first song was a medium-paced Celtic roots rocker and up-front political statement on the troubles in northern Ireland, 'Wild Frontier', with Thin Lizzy-style harmony guitars and a very specific and poignant reference to Phil in the lines, 'And I remember a friend of mine / So sad that he is gone / They tell me I'll forget / As time goes on.'

While the guitar would always be at the head of the mix, Gary's intention on the new album was to keep the solos quite short and snappy as he did on 'Take A Little Time', a homage to Billy Idol's 'Rebel Yell'. This was another autobiographical song based around the idea of respect, reflecting Gary's tirade against Lizzy manager Chris O'Donnell as they argued on the phone about Gary leaving. The song shows Gary held the notion of 'respect' in high esteem. As he explained enigmatically, 'it's about somebody who has taken you for granted—it's actually about somebody

I know … but nobody famous like Glenn Hughes … it's just saying, "You're not treating me with the respect you should be treating me with."'

The third new song was the anti-heroin 'Stranger In The Darkness'. From its early beginnings in the late 1970s, the UK was now in the grip of a full-on heroin epidemic. The government had recently launched Britain's first anti-drug media campaign called 'Heroin Screws You Up'; The Who's Double O charity was funnelling funds to drug treatment centres, while rock benefits were raising awareness about the dangers of heroin and additional funds for treatment.

The focus for Gary's song, as he explained, was on 'the kids who come to London and get caught up in the whole Soho thing and turn to heroin to escape the pressures of living, when you are sixteen years old and unemployed. Some end up turning to prostitution to pay for their habit. It's quite heavy. Not one to play the vicar! … It's something I felt very strongly about after Phil died … kids have to be told that it's not funny to die when you are eighteen and it's not fashionable to be lying in a heap in some Soho street. I had a girlfriend who almost died from that, and I've actually seen somebody turning blue in front of me and having to be rushed to hospital … Heroin is a very selfish drug, because it not only ruins your life, but it ruins the lives of the people around you.'

During this period, Gary also worked on an instrumental called 'The Loner' about Jeff Beck and written by Jeff's main keyboard player Max Middleton, although the guitarist never actually played it. The song was first heard on Cozy Powell's album *Over The Top* featuring Clem Clempson. Gary reworked it sufficiently, taking part of the middle section and moving it to the front and writing a new middle eight, to be able to claim co-writing credit. 'I always loved melody … and wanted to do it more like "Parisienne Walkways" type of thing rather than the jazzy way it was done on *Over The Top*. I'm really pleased with it. It's the first guitar instrumental I've done in a long time, so it was nice to do something a bit emotional like that.' It was to become a concert favourite.

On the summer concert circuit of 1986, Gary road tested the new material. For the first time in about four years, he managed to hang on to the same line-up for consecutive tours. Gary Ferguson was still the favoured drummer and working well with Bob Daisley, about whom Gary said, 'When the thing with Glenn Hughes didn't work out and Bob became available, I jumped on that like a shot. I couldn't wait to get him in the band. Bob's definitely one of the top bass players around, he's just got that sound that really fits with what guitarists play … he's got that really fat sound under the guitar, it's like a modern Jack Bruce, a very aggressive dirty bass sound which I've always loved ... most people want to play funk bass under rock-based things which doesn't fit. It's too clean and such a bright sound gets in the way of the guitar ... it's just wrong for this type of music [because] it makes the guitar sound like mud ... it needs a low bass to support it. That fits in with the way Gary [Ferguson] plays which is a very wide sound.'

Gary was also cementing his relationship with Neil Carter, especially when it came to writing: 'Neil contributes a lot of things; he's not credited with a lot of the ideas that he's put into this band. On [*Run For Cover*], he didn't play on that many of the things, but he inspired a lot of the ideas because he was around when I was writing the songs. He wrote "Empty Rooms" with me ... he comes up with great riffs like the riff on "All Messed Up", that's a typical Neil Carter riff. He's very prolific—he's never without his little Fostex [a multi-track recorder], always writing and there's always some good stuff which we end up using.'

The band had a series of large venue dates set up including supporting what would be the last tour that Freddie Mercury would undertake with Queen. They started in Sweden at the 35,000-capacity Råsundastadion and walked straight into a political storm. Several journalists refused to attend the press conference in protest against Queen playing at Sun City in South Africa during the apartheid era, when many other artists had boycotted the country. Gary took it in his stride, as he told *Kerrang!*: 'If anyone listens to my songs, they'll *know* how I feel about the South African situation.' You don't need to look any further than 'Out In The Fields', where Gary expressed that it didn't matter if someone is black or white; 'all I know is I'm here to play for my fans and probably half of those who've bought tickets will be coming along to see us because we know we can pull 10,000 people in this city without too much problem. I wouldn't play Sun City, but I *will* play Stockholm.'

The band hit the stage in the pouring rain and the sound wasn't the best, but Neil caught the attention sporting a lime green two-piece suit, white shirt and shoes and a diamanté neck brooch with a plastic Pac A Mac to round off the ensemble.

The small summer tour would be Gary's only outing for 1986 as the rest of the year was devoted to recording the album. In the early stages of recording, Gary made one of the most controversial decisions of his recording history to date. There were no live drums.

Often because of budgetary constraints, but also because he had firm ideas of what he wanted, Gary tended to write at home and bring songs quite fully formed into the studio. For the first time, Gary started using his own drum machine outside the studio, which, given that he was an absolute stickler for tempo, was a revelation. Working with Pete Smith on the early demos had introduced him to the late Roland Kerridge, the drummer from the new wave/synth pop band Re-Flex. Kerridge transferred Gary's drum parts on to a powerful Linn 9000 drum machine as Gary didn't know how to use one. Gary took some of the machine's own snare sounds, known as Park Snares, as they were recorded at Park Gate Studios in Wales, also incorporating overdubbed live hit-hat and tom-tom sounds provided by Kerridge himself.

'In the past,' said Gary, 'it's always been done the old way of recording where you'd get your ideas roughly in shape them go into the studio, bang the drums down, hopefully end up with a backing track that's hopefully steady and then have to compensate afterwards for all the drummer's mistakes and all the things that aren't in time. You can't really play in total confidence over a track that's [all over the place] and that's always been a problem of mine even before all the machines came along and there was an alternative. I used to give drummers such a hard time, trying to get track steady and sometimes you'd end up with tracks that were steady, but by that time the drummer was so frightened to try anything that you'd get very rigid and sterile sounding track that had lost all the feel.

'Sampling has become important to me. Programmed drums, triggering samples. I work in a completely different way. The band doesn't play together in the studio ... [Recording the album] wasn't like going in with a band and things changing and therefore losing the essence of the songs. This way, everything ended up a lot closer to the way I envisioned it all. In the past, I've lost my direction just by getting other people involved too early and not having the songs completed myself. That's something to think about for a songwriter! If you go into rehearsals with a song half-written and everybody else starts throwing in their idea, things get confused.' If ever there was an articulation from Gary himself as to why the band was billed simply as 'Gary Moore', that comment to *Metal Rendezvous* would have left nobody in any doubt.

It also left Gary Ferguson completely out in the cold; at first, says the drummer, 'we had Gary, Bob, Neil and Pete Smith helping with production and engineering. After we learnt the tunes, we went in to record them. Everyone seemed happy. A little time went by and a recording schedule was faxed to everyone. I was excited and called management and they told me Gary had decided to do the album with programmed drums. So, this sort of ruined the *Wild Frontier* album for me and I left.'

Having lost producer Peter Collins to Rush, Gary managed to secure his services to produce the new album—a strong guiding hand that Gary welcomed and somebody who would be prepared to push him down a more adventurous path in the studio. As Gary explained, 'During the mixing of the single version of "Empty Rooms", we were running through the first verse and [Peter] took out the drums to check something or other. I was listening to the sequencers with no drums going and I said, "Maybe we should leave it like that and have no drums in the first verse." He said, "Are you sure about this? It'll be very brave." So, I said, "Right, we'll be fuckin' brave. Go for it!" … He's very clever because he appears to be doing nothing and yet he's taking everything in all the time. If there's the slightest little thing wrong with a track, he'll spot it very quickly. Or in a song, I might add, because he's one of these people who is not averse to telling you to rewrite parts if he doesn't like them.

'The original chorus of *Wild Frontier* was completely different and when he heard it, he said it was a good song, but he didn't like the chorus. I was devastated 'cause I thought it was really good, but the way he put it to me made me determined to come up with a better one. It took weeks and weeks, but eventually it came and he said, "Right, that's okay. We'll do it." He wouldn't go into the studio until he felt it was right.

'Peter got me into this new way of working and I think I've taken it a lot further than he thought I might—I've caught the disease as he calls it, of the machines and of wanting everything to be in perfect time all the time.'

Gary was also experimenting with guitars. Engineer James Barton recalls that Gary's guitar tech, Keith Page, 'would build guitars for Gary on the floor of the control room. He would start in the morning with bits all over the floor and by one or two in the afternoon Gary would be playing it.' While Gary was still using his Strats and Les Pauls, he was also in a phase of playing Charvel guitars, going back to the recording of the G-Force album in 1979, including a fur-covered leopard-skin model. Around the time of recording the new album, Keith Page took a basic model, changed the scratch plate and the pickups and added a neck from a different guitar.

Building kit guitars was all the rage then, to create a one-off guitar, most notably Eddie Van Halen's Superstrat. According to Graham Lilley, who succeeded Keith as Gary's guitar tech, 'most new guitars then were mostly crap, so a custom model was a draw. They only lasted a short time, maybe one or two tours before the latest thing took over. This was typical of all musicians; they are in a constant search for a better or different sound, tone or look.'

So, armed with his latest favourite guitar and locked into the recording process with Peter Collins, Gary worked away on the album for the rest of 1986. Collins explains more on how he helped Gary develop his vocal sound during the sessions, something both Gary and his producer were taking care over. For the first time in his recording career, Gary wasn't trying to find that elusive right singer for the band.

'This was hard because there was a certain sound I was looking for from Gary's vocals. There was an area of his voice that I did not like, a sort of plummy, thick quality, which to my ears was uncommercial and I tried to clear up his diction. But there was a great timbre that could be achieved, and he was happy to work with that. In those days you didn't have the tuning facilities and the ability to play around with the vocals as you can now. I would be very, very selective about which key the song was in. And sometimes, from a guitar standpoint, it wasn't so good—so we had a bit of a barney on that one! But I would always insist on that.

'He would come up with fantastic ideas and I'd insert them where I felt they were most effective—vocalising, background vocals and arrangement ideas. I'd say things like, "We need a breakdown here, this hook to happen there, I need something sensitive and quiet here to set up a very powerful section," or I might say, "Something needs to happen at this point in the song that's very different to anything that's happened before"—and he would come up with stuff, just great ideas.'

Continuing the Celtic theme, Gary and Neil wrote the powerful 'Thunder Rising'. Neil explains, 'I got a lot of history books recently and got into the legends about Ireland. The old Irish warriors used to go out and cut off their opponents' heads and hang them from their horses! I'm not too keen on preserving the cartoon aspect from Irish mythology, but I love the spirit of those times and the Irish people are very warm-hearted by nature, although you wouldn't think that by watching the news. In fact, they are a very friendly people and they've always loved music and poetry.'

Finally, there was Gary's plaintive tribute to Phil, 'Johnny Boy', written as an Irish ballad and played live in the studio with The Chieftains' Paddy Moloney on pipes, Don Airey on keys and Gary on acoustic guitar.

For his cover version track, Gary made the unusual choice of The Easybeats' hit 'Friday On My Mind': 'It was one of those songs I grew up listening to, and although a few people like Bowie have done it, I thought instead of taking another Yardbirds song, I'd do that and try to put my stamp on it by writing something new into it … because I don't think there's any point in doing a cover version of anything unless you take somewhere else … This version I think is sufficiently different and modern enough to justify our covering it.' Talking about the presence of a sitar on the track, he said, 'Yeah … one of those things you hear on all the old Tamla Motown stuff and we thought we'd put it in there because it was so stupid. When we were doing the sitar overdubs we were pissing ourselves laughing, because it made the studio sound like an Indian restaurant. We should do a 12-inch Tandoori mix, I suppose.'

Speaking about writing the album in the wake of Phil's death, Gary told *Juke* magazine, 'the whole period was kind of strange, you know, because you don't get over something like overnight … So, I was very emotionally distraught at the time, I was very depressed … it pushed me, 'cos I thought, *What would Phil have wanted me to do?* There were all these kind of things in my mind at the time and I felt that I'd like the album to be something that Phil would have been proud to be a part of.'

Released in March 1987, *Wild Frontier* was Gary's most successful album of the 1980s, earning platinum, gold and silver sales in Sweden, Finland and the UK, respectively, and was a Top 20 seller in at least half a dozen other countries, while 'Over The Hills And Far Away' was a No. 1 single in Finland and Norway, and together with 'Wild Frontier' and 'Friday On My Mind', charted well in several territories.

Headlining his review 'A Bouquet of Black Roses', Paul Elliott of *Sounds* gave the album a five-star rating: 'At its most reflective, *Wild Frontier* is full of melancholic charm. At its rowdiest, it's as uplifting as rock has ever been. Pleasingly, Moore has relieved his music of its old, slightly cumbersome metal plating to let it breathe in more warmth and colour. He's also feeding off his Irish heritage like never before, a sense of tradition spreading through the folk jig feel of "Over The Hills And Far Away" to a new lyrical maturity. You have to go back to '79 and Thin Lizzy's *Black Rose* to find Gary's roots showing strongly through the songs.'

But despite all the obvious echoes of Lizzy running through the album, 'this isn't the shameless, self-indulgent, sentimental plunder that it might sound. Moore has simply slipped out of his rusty metal shackles to grasp that emotive quality which made Lizzy unique.

'*Wild Frontier* is possessed of a burning yet never gushing romanticism, at its clearest on "The Loner" and "Johnny Boy". I've never been one for virtuoso rambles, but during "The Loner"—a misty-eyed instrumental with, dare I mention it, a delicate Parisian flavour—that guitar *talks*. And by that I don't mean that it babbles the kind of gassy gibberish with which Eddie Van Halen and his imitators are still fiddling frantically.

'After years of muddling, Moore has at long last found a style of his own which isn't a vice on his exceptional ability … *Wild Frontier* smokes, soothes, rocks, rouses and satisfies. It's the kind of record that might have made a certain old rocker very happy.'

A worldwide tour was planned for 1987 to promote the album, but first Gary had to sort out a new drummer to replace Gary Ferguson. In March, Bob Daisley had played bass on the new Sabbath album *Eternal Idol* and recommended to Gary the American drummer on that session, Eric Singer, who had replaced Bill Ward in Sabbath in 1985. 'I was always a big fan of Gary. I used to play *Corridors Of Power* and *Victims Of The Future* to death. Jeff Glixman produced both those albums and both the Sabbath albums I worked on. The audition went well, but they said there was another guy Gary wanted to check out. So, I went back to my hotel room to learn some more songs from a cassette, like "Thunder Rising". I went back next day to John Henry's and they said at the end that I had the gig. Only thing was that my drums were stuck in a warehouse at Heathrow, but I couldn't get them out because the Black Sabbath management hadn't paid the bill. So, I borrowed a kit from Cozy Powell and was touring with "Cozy Powell— Whitesnake" all over the flight cases.

'We rehearsed for a month before we started that tour, which was really good for me because it meant I got really comfortable with the material and got in playing shape because this would be the biggest tour I had ever done. Bob and Neil were living in Brighton, so they had to catch a train home after rehearsals, but Gary just wanted to carry on playing, so we'd just stay and jam on Lizzy songs. He would just solo indefinitely and never run out of ideas. It was always fresh.'

The tour started in March; the band steamed out the blocks. A *Kerrang!* review by Paul Henderson, of their concert at the NEC arena in Birmingham, only their second date of a seventy-date world-wide tour, was effervescent in its enthusiasm:

'While the vast majority of the "old school" Guitar Heroes are either retired, hibernating or in various states of suspended animation … the new breed of high-speed technophiles … is increasing in number at an alarming rate. Gary Moore occupies a unique position … able stylistically to slot neatly into place in either camp and at the same time bridge the divide with an effortless ease of which no other currently active player I can think of is capable.

'Moore is a remarkably engaging guitarist to listen to—incredible control, confident in his ability and with a more or less unique mix of speed and "old fashioned" feel. On the current tour he has also proved something to watch, abandoning the tired but still *de rigeur* backdrop of either wall-to-wall Marshall cabinets or "concept" structures. Instead, he has moved forward with the clean lines of a "cubist" stage set, the equipment neatly tucked out of sight, and an equally modern lighting design which uses tasteful washes.

'Gary took to the stage wearing a black jacket bearing the gold arm stripes of a high-ranking officer and proceeded to marshal his small but highly effective unit through a tough and vigorous set that more than lived up to his reputation. Blessed with a crystal-clear sound, they opened up with "Over The Hills And Far Away"—piercing guitar flurries buttressed against elegant, sampled sounds of Celtic instruments and precise harmonies, new boy Eric Singer's twin bass drums thundering through the NEC like explosive charges. Every song retained the crafted structure of its recorded counterpart.

'Gary himself was masterful and at times mesmeric, alternating between high-speed pyrotechnics and a more delicate approach that occasionally brought to mind the grace and control of the wonderful Jeff Beck. Particularly on a short section which preceded the main body of "Empty Rooms" and during "Wild Frontier", Moore showed a side of his playing—one of style and feeling—that is often overlooked. Elsewhere he applied the aural pressure with vicious intensity. "Military Man", the crunching riff of "Victims Of The Future" and "All Messed Up" displayed the heavyweight ferocity that he is able to bring to his soloing, while for "Shapes Of Things", he scaled a podium and dipped deep into a potpourri of guitar styles that was a treat to listen to.

'After finishing the set with an intense and note-perfect "Out In The Fields" … the band came back with blistering versions of "Rockin' Every Night" and "Wishing Well". Most groups would have left it there—finishing fast, finishing loud and finishing heavy. But instead of knocking the audience into final submission with a frenetic finish, Moore went for something of more cerebral appeal by playing the beautifully elegant, "The Loner".

'It was a parting shot that flew straight and true, piercing the collective Brum heart and leaving the NEC awash with emotional liquor that will take some time to evaporate.'

Henderson was probably unaware of the significance of the comment 'Every song retained the crafted structure of its recorded counterpart'. Gary was very particular about how he wanted the songs rendered live, right down to the tiniest detail of cymbal beats, as Eric Singer recalls: '"Over The Hills" is in 6/8, almost a shuffle. It was very fast and had to be played with one hand on the cymbal and sometimes I would cheat and play with two hands, crossing over, doubling up. But Gary would say, "No, no, I want it played with one hand." So, I would still try and play with two hands, then if he turned round to see how I was playing—I'd switch to one hand.

'A song like "The Loner" could be anything from eight to twenty-seven minutes. When he got into an extended jam or solo like that, I'd get into some improvisation, grab each other like that. But he didn't want you slinging your whole arsenal in there, like "I want your meat and potatoes, but not the kitchen sink and all the utensils as well. I want to know that you've got that stuff in the drawer, but I don't necessarily want you to use it." That seemed to be the overriding theme with the players he chose. And if Gary did think you were over-playing, rest assured you would hear about it even on stage in the middle of a gig.'

But this was Gary, and you either went with the flow or you didn't. This line-up did—and as the band rolled across the UK, Japan and Europe—where they were outselling Prince—they delivered that same level of high-quality performance night after night in front of thousands of people cramming sizeable venues. A good flavour of just how wrench tight this line-up was, how well Gary was playing and the level of confidence he exuded can be seen online with the NFL film of Gary's triumphant concert at Stockholm's Isstadion on April 25.

Despite his reticence over playing in America again, Gary had every reason to believe that this band playing a highly successful album could finally crack it. Many of the US regional press reviews were very positive, most declaring at last that Gary was due his rewards. But although 'Over The Hills' made it into the Top 30, the album didn't make the Top 100 and when Gary saw the list of dates—all bar two being just club dates, playing to a few hundred people, his heart must have sunk.

Gary's production manager on the tour was Gerry Raymond-Barker: 'The only place of any size we played as headliners was the last gig of the tour at Paradise Theater in Boston, a couple of thousand or so. Virtually all the other places were sleaze-ball little clubs. The local promoters there couldn't give a shit who you were. The organisation wasn't there. I was constantly calling the agents in America and they didn't want to know because they were putting other acts in there and didn't want to upset the venue owners. So, although they are taking a percentage of the fee, they are not backing you up. The catering was shit, local labour was shit. Gary was not impressed AT ALL. And he didn't like the arse licking you have to do in America when you have to speak to every radio station two or three times a day non-stop. And yet he could see himself as a bloody good guitar player, playing the sort of places he'd left behind years ago in Britain and Europe.'

They did play one other larger gig, the Metal Mania Festival at the Sam Houston Coliseum in Texas, where they were down the bill behind the likes of Y&T, Ace Frehley and TNT. Gary's caustic remark summed up what he felt: 'There are a lot of opening acts here tonight.'

The main reason Gary even agreed to do those penny ante US club dates was because he was in the middle of what is known as 'a year out'—having to remain outside the UK for at least ten months in the tax year (in this case April 1, 1987–March 31, 1988) to reduce the tax bill. Gary hated it. As he complained to *Juke* magazine, 'You're kind of forced into taking a holiday, which is a real drag because you want to be at home and you're forced into lying on a fucking beach when you could be back writing the next record or something. I mean lying on a beach probably sounds pretty good, but it's different when you haven't got a choice. It's like being in a prison really, because although you can go where you want and lie in the sun a lot, you get sick of that after a while. I mean, I'm sick of that bloody sun right now … I want to get back to England and see some bloody rain!'

The situation was further complicated as Kerry was pregnant with their son Jack. 'I had gone out to the States when I was six or seven months pregnant because Gary wanted me out there, but I had to come home in the end.' Meanwhile, once the tour was done, Gary went to Ian Paice's place in Spain and Kerry joined him once Jack was born. Towards the end of the year, he went off to Ireland to start work on the rapid follow-up to *Wild Frontier*.

None of the band were on retainers, it was a 'pay to play' arrangement. So, Bob Daisley flew to LA to record tracks for the latest Yngwie Malmsteen album and Bill Ward's solo project before salvaging Ozzy Osbourne's album *No Rest For The Wicked*, not only playing, but writing some of the music and all of the lyrics, and then briefly stood in for Geezer Butler on a Sabs US date. Neil Carter, on the other hand, commuted back and forth to Dublin for about three months starting in January 1988, working with Gary on a new set of songs.

Gary had struck a vein with *Wild Frontier*; audiences and the record buying public really warmed to the Celtic vibe. The link with Phil meant Gary drew the music from his heart and people responded to that sincerity and conviction. So, although he was telling the media that the new album to be called *After The War* was not meant to be a follow-up to *Wild Frontier*, Gary couldn't really help himself: that influence was bound to creep in. The tracks 'Dunluce' (Parts 1 and

2) and the autobiographical 'Blood Of Emeralds', which charts Gary's move from Belfast to Dublin, were written out there. Once the process moved into Puk Studio in Denmark, the writing took a more mainstream rock approach, although Gary's other trip down memory lane with 'Living On Dreams'—about growing up in Belfast, dreaming of rock stardom while losing his bus fare to the toughs outside the Maritime Club—could easily have come from the Thin Lizzy songbook.

While in Dublin, Gary had recorded another version of 'Emerald' with Brian Downey and asked Brian to join the band. But his ex-Lizzy band mate declined, so with the intention of re-introducing live drums to this album, Gary turned instead to the heaviest drummer on the scene—Cozy Powell—who had decided he'd had enough of joining bands and would simply make himself available as a drummer-for-hire. There was still a fair bit of programming on the album from Andy Richards but backing up Cozy were Simon Phillips and Peter Collins's go-to session drummer Charlie Morgan. Peter Collins recalls that even the best of them can have tricky moments: 'There was a very fast double kick drum pattern on "Blood Of Emeralds". While we were recording the track, Simon's legs cramped up and the track just ground to a halt. He just asked everybody to leave, to take a break and leave him alone. And we heard him in the studio doing drills, very slowly and then building the speed up. About forty minutes later, he called us back and he had it down perfect.'

Gary was never shy about taking a public swipe at the music business, current trends or even individual players and bands. This time, the track 'Led Clones' was a dig at the band Kingdom Come, with German vocalist Lenny Wolf, who had taken flack for being so close to Led Zeppelin that on first hearing some thought Zeppelin had reformed. Gary took his cue from press comment dubbing the band 'Kingdom Clones' and also at criticism of David Coverdale for trying to sound like Robert Plant on his multi-platinum album of 1987. The track was quite cleverly executed, woven through with Zeppelin's 'Kashmir' eastern tones and Ozzy doing a very passable Robert Plant wail. On cloning, there was more than a passing similarity between 'Thing Called Love' and 'Hot For Teacher', although when questioned, Gary was adamant he'd never heard the Van Halen song.

Gary intended to include a cover of a Roy Buchanan song on the album, tried it out and decided it didn't work. Then in August 1988, during the recording of the album, Buchanan was arrested for being drunk following a domestic dispute and tragically committed suicide in his cell. In tribute, Gary covered 'The Messiah Will Come Again'.

Peter Collins was once again in the production chair and recalls an early hiccup in the recording regarding the engineer: 'Puk was a residential studio near Aarhus in northern Denmark, very popular—George Michael had recorded there. Everyone had their own small house. We hired this engineer who had done a lot of work with Pink Floyd. Gary thought he'd be good because he liked the Floyd guitar sound. But the engineer turns up with his wife and there was an unwritten rule about that. She was sitting in the control room on the first day and Gary was very uncomfortable and asked me to ask the engineer if his wife could *not* be in the control room while we were working. So, I asked and she left. Later we all had dinner; Gary and I were working after that and he came up to me and said, "I don't think this is going to work out. I just have this feeling that it won't work." Anyway, we convened next morning—and there's no engineer. He's gone. We're in Denmark in the middle of a field, Gary and the band all ready to go—and no engineer. We put through panic calls to Virgin and they came up with Ian Taylor who'd done Kansas and Cheap Trick. We'd never met him, but we were desperate, and his track record was such that we had to give it a shot. He came over and instantly it worked—he was fabulous, great to work with, a nice man and he got these great fat, warm analogue sounds which we loved. He was the guy.' And it turned out he would be 'the guy' for Gary on more albums than any other engineer/producer.

Gary was keen to make the guitar once again the focal point of the album. He was becoming more self-confident to the point where he didn't want Peter around when he was recording his solos but would get Peter to sign off on them. He was also trying out new angles; 'Living On A Dream', for example, had double-tracked bottleneck guitar while the solo on 'Led Clones' comprised six bottleneck tracks and backwards echo.

The return to a more front-and-centre guitar style was also a statement by Gary at his dismay over what he saw as a new breed of guitarists all playing off the same hymn sheet. As he explained to *Guitarist* (March 1989), he didn't get the same feel from modern players as he did from Hendrix, Clapton, Green or Beck: 'What we have today is a set of very generic guitarists who have been through this process known as the Guitar Institute of Technology and I am not a big fan of those, to be honest. I think a lot of people are going to say, "Yeh, bollocks!" and think I've got some sort of axe to grind. But the thing is that all the players from that background sound so similar; they haven't been encouraged to show off their individual talents … this sort of "conveyor belt" production line of guitarists really haven't got a lot to say for themselves ... I mean they are talking a lot and there are a lot of notes coming out, but there's no real humour to the playing ... I hate the records these guys make—half of them sound like a demo tape for Ibanez and the others sound like guitar tutorials ... it just sounds like all these scales stuck together.'

Despite having a British producer and engineer, the decision was taken that the album should be mixed by an American—Duane Baron, who had mixed and engineered for Quiet Riot, Mötley Crüe, W.A.S.P., Krokus, Poison and Ted Nugent. The intention was clear—you need the album mixed by an American who had worked with the same bands that Virgin believed Gary should be aligned with—and somebody familiar with US radio broadcasting sound.

The album was released in January 1989 and picked up a UK silver disc plus gold in Sweden and Germany, but overall sales were not a marked progression from *Wild Frontier* while the improvement in the States was marginal. Before the album's release, Gary told *Raw* about touring stateside: 'We went out there last time and did a club tour which really didn't do us any good and I'm not prepared to do that again. If the record does well, we'll go out there, but if it doesn't I'm not going back there just to lose money again.'

Peter Collins had told Gary he thought the guitarist was repeating himself, which didn't go down too well, although Gary had to agree in the end. Reviews were mixed; rock journalist Valerie Potter gave the record a maximum five stars proclaiming it 'a killer' and praising 'its incredible live feel ... freshness and impact', with 'great songs and the superb playing'. 'My first review of the year,' she concluded, 'hope they are all going to be this good.' By contrast, the usually supportive *Kerrang!* headlined their review 'Don't Mention The War', slating the album as Gary's 'weakest solo effort to date, suffering badly from a lack of memorable songs, a coherent musical direction and pretty much everything else needed to drag an album from the grasp of mediocrity' ... and ending with a death knell comment on Gary's attempt to swim in the choppy, fickle waters of hard rock: 'And when compared to the rich and inventive albums fashioned by those young and vibrant bands, *After The War* is shown up as what it is—average and ultimately forgettable.'

There was another stab at humour on the album. 'Ready For Love' was supposed to be a pastiche song about the rug-chested medallion men of Los Angeles. Trouble was, a song like that written for an already sexist hard rock genre could easily be construed as 'serious'—which it was by some reviewers, who clearly didn't get the joke.

Gary was now having serious misgivings about the whole way his career was going. Being quite superstitious, if he was looking for omens about the future, his anxieties would not have been assuaged by events in the run-up and early part of the 1989 tour.

With Cozy so familiar with the material, it made sense to take him out on the road—or at least it made sense on paper. Remember, Gary would insist that the songs would be played live in the same way as on the record. From the very start of the rehearsals, Bob Daisley could see the troubles ahead: 'Cozy would do a fill and Gary would go, "No, no, there's no fill on the record, so don't do that. But there is one here, so do that." Cozy had no free hand, really. By Friday at the end of the week, I phoned Gary at home and said, "I don't think this is going to work out." I could see the clash coming. But Gary said, "Don't worry, it'll be fine, he'll settle in." So, I didn't push it, but in the end Gary was phoning me telling me, "I think you're right."'

Bernie Marsden said Cozy rang him the night he left the band: 'He said, "I'm not putting up with it anymore." I said, "What have you done?" "I'll tell you what I've done. I've put him in his fuckin' place. I'm sick of him telling me what to play. I'm Cozy fuckin' Powell."' He left the band with less than a week to go before the start of the tour in March—and then went public in slightly more measured tones.

He told the press, 'You don't hire a drummer like me and then tell me what to play … [drummers] see a song in a different way. I just had this problem with Gary Moore … he wanted me to play the tracks his way. There's nothing wrong with that, but I didn't feel able to do it out on the road … when you are playing live you have to be able to do your own thing … and I felt that Gary was unhappy with my interpretation of his numbers … there wasn't a problem with the whole show, just certain numbers. I just didn't feel it the way he wanted. It was sad the way it ended, though. I still respect Gary as a player, he's a great guitarist, but the way my departure was handled was possibly a little undiplomatic, shall we say. A lot of fans out there who'd bought tickets for the shows will be a bit disappointed with the way it turned out.'

The comment pointed to another unarticulated issue going on behind the scenes; Gerry Raymond-Barker reckons 'we were ordering up loads of equipment for the tour that you thought Cozy couldn't possibly need—and then we got to hear that he was doing some sort of separate merchandising deal for himself and that didn't go down too well either. Gary's response was "Fuck this. This isn't the Gary Moore/Cozy Powell show," and that did push things over the edge.'

The hunt was on for a new drummer. As Graham Lilley recalls, 'We'd finished rehearsing at John Henry's and we were going up to Elstree to one of the big sound stages for a production rehearsal. We had to move all the lights and PA and do a couple of days run through before we went off to Edinburgh and Sheffield. I'd dropped back into John Henry's to pick something up. I was in reception talking to the receptionist and then Gary's on the phone asking for Ted McKenna's phone number (ex-Alex Harvey, Greg Lake). So, I'm thinking, *Oh-oh*, and by the time I get back to Elstree, Cozy's kit's been packed away. Then it turns out that Chris Slade is coming in (ex-The Firm and David Gilmour). He stayed locally with various tapes and they put it together with Chris in the three days we were in Elstree. It was a lot to learn for Chris. "Blood Of Emeralds" was a hell of a track—it had taken Simon Phillips a day and a half to record it and that was with pre-learning it. We had to cancel those first two gigs in Edinburgh and Sheffield.' (They were rescheduled for later.)

Although not surprisingly a little rough round the edges, the second date in saw Gary back in Belfast for yet another triumphant return to his hometown, this time with the reviewers in step saluting the full-blooded, air-punching, honest delivery of those songs that had such resonance and poignancy for a Belfast audience.

On March 12, the band played a huge gig at Wembley Arena—which almost didn't happen. Graham Lilley revisits what he calls 'the nightmare', providing an insight into how the most unexpected technical problems can occur on a major gig:

'The venue had redone the hall and moved the old stage slightly further back, so they could increase the capacity. What they didn't say was when they moved the stage, they hadn't really rewired the place and the story was that they had moved the old power point where the touring productions plugged into the house three-phase mains supply. But instead of cutting back the cable, it seemed that they had coiled up the slack, and covered it over with a new floor, creating a large induction coil!! So, the touring production set up that day, the lighting rig dimmer racks were in their usual place, on the floor, upstage right corner of the hall, on top of the coiled house mains. So as soon as we finished setting up the band equipment, we discovered an almighty hum/buzz on the guitar equipment.

'We spent the rest of the day trying to find the cause of the problem, but nothing could make the hum less, or at least quieter than the guitar signal. The nature of Gary's gear set up on the *After The War* tour, meant it was very loud and had a lot of gain in the signal chain, combined with a selection of vintage guitars, which picked up any external noise or "dirt" on the mains supply and made it very much louder.'

Gary was very particular about soundchecks; however big the venue, absolutely nobody was allowed to be there, other than the band and technicians—a major headache for whoever in the crew was charged with keep the curious away. With this problem still unresolved at soundcheck, the situation for Graham was even more stressful than usual. 'We ended up moving the guitar amps across the stage from where they had been on the tour in an effort to get away from what we had since been told was a huge induction coil, radiating the hum. And with it being "The Big London Show" the pressure was on Gary to go ahead, as a lot of guests, record company and media were due in. I think Gary was backstage while we were still trying to sort out the problem, well after the doors opened and the audience were in their seats. David Gilmour had a word with Gary, something along the lines of, "So what? Make the best of it and enjoy yourself," or some other encouraging words.

'By this time, we had got the support band from Germany, called Victory, set up, but as soon as they switched on their guitar radio system, the hum made them unusable. More running around trying to fix things and time ran out for their opening slot. We ended up taking them back off the stage and resetting for Gary's stage time, which was delayed further as we were still looking for a fix.'

While Graham was trying to sort out the guitar problems, Gerry Raymond-Barker had his own problems: 'The audience were waiting to come in, the doors were being held, experts were called in. Steve Barnett had been talking to Gary and they decided to completely switch the stage around, but the cabling wasn't long enough, so we had to completely strip everything out. The support band were going berserk because this was their big chance, and they had all their record company people out there.'

'Quite a bit later,' says Graham, 'Gary hit the stage and played most of the show with one guitar fitted with low impedance/active pickups, which didn't amplify as much of the hum as his other guitars.'

Despite all the delays, Gary instantly won the crowd over. He gave special mention to Chris Slade and turned what promised to be a car wreck into a great night out, rewarding the audience for their patience with the ever-popular 'Parisienne Walkways', the first time he had played the song live possibly since the 1985 *Run For Cover* tour.

The '89 tour was all big venue dates including the 16,000-capacity newly opened Stockholm Globe, where Gary's was the first official concert following a gala opening by Bob Dylan. The Hammersmith Odeon gig, after half a dozen

Japanese dates, was one of the best of the tour. But Gary did not enjoy the long-haul flight to Japan and, says Graham, 'he did get ill out there, blew out some promoter and record company dinners. There was one show out there where he had this look on his face like, "Why are you making me do this?"' There was a definite change in the air.

With sell-out tours, high-charting albums and singles producing gold and silver discs, critical acclaim, adoring fans and a worldwide reputation among his peers, it might seem ridiculous to ask the question 'So what was going wrong?' But it *was* going wrong—or at least, not as commercially right as Virgin and Steve Barnett expected from a musician who could stand tall beside any contemporary guitarist you care to name. True, each album did better than the previous one, but sales were stuck around an average half million mark where those bands that might be considered Gary's main rivals were racking up multi-million sales. The failure to crack America lay at the heart of the problem. There isn't one answer—and some of the problems were not unique to the States, but the USA was the big prize—and teasing out some of the strands, it tentatively goes something like this.

Frustrating as it may sound, being a great musician is absolutely no guarantee of commercial success; factors like timing, image and style often trump virtuosity, even genius. Gary himself acknowledged this when he said of guitarist Allan Holdsworth, 'You have a true pioneer … [but] who the hell has heard of [him] outside a handful of people in the States and a few people in the jazz scene over here? He's a real artist; he kind of suffers for the rest of us. Look at what he's done and then look at all the people who have taken credit for it—endless! And there he is in his house, pretty well having to pay to put out his own records. It's pretty unfair really.'

Being in the right place at the right time playing the 'right' music is all. Some accidents of timing you can't help; Gary was born too late to be ranked (as he surely would have been) alongside the Great British Guitar Giants like Clapton, Beck and Page, but too soon to enjoy the kind of post-disco heavy rock New Guitar Messiah roles heaped on the shoulders of the likes of Joe Satriani, Steve Vai and Yngwie Malmsteen. As we have heard, Gary had no love anyway for a rather pompous and overblown guitar style that thought it was bringing gravitas to the world of rock guitar by hanging on the classical coat-tails of Paganini, Bach and Liszt. Instead, it delivered an endless stream of similar sounding albums peppered with unaccompanied arpeggio noodling. It was for the most part an empty, soulless virtuosity that deadened passion—the complete antithesis of what Gary was all about. Gary's face-pulling was not just for showtime—it was rehearsals, recording, soundcheck, any time. Even so, Gary did seem to be out on a limb; a reviewer cited above talked about Gary being 'a bridge' between peaks of guitar god reverence; he could also be regarded as having fallen between the gaps.

On timing, Gary was quite late to the party in terms of the territory he was trying to inhabit. From being a teenage prodigy in the late 60s, he had taken until the early 1980s, treading a difficult and uncertain path, to even begin making his name as a solo artist. Even *Corridors Of Power*, Ian Paice regards as 'the wrong album at the wrong time'. By then, the American heavy bands like Kiss, Aerosmith and Van Halen were well-established big hitters; likewise, the more AOR bands like REO Speedwagon, Journey and Styx, where Gary also looked to compete with his more melodic power ballads. In the UK, too, Gary found himself up against the young guns of the New Wave of British Heavy Metal like Saxon, Iron Maiden, Judas Priest and Def Leppard.

Another strand was that search for the killer lead singer. But a duel front-line of top-flight guitarist and flamboyant, 'out there' singer was—as Sharon Osbourne remarked earlier—almost standard operating procedure, the essential DNA, for the successful rock band: the Stones, Zeppelin, Sabbath, Purple, Whitesnake, Aerosmith, AC/DC, the list goes on. Journey only really took off commercially when they switched the emphasis from instrumental virtuosity to Steve Perry-led pop metal ballads. That was a problem Gary never resolved—and it was also difficult for Gary trying to be a 'solo act' in the world of heavy rock/metal. There is a kind of tribalism inherent in the genre: the (mostly male) fans like to see 'a band', to be able to relate to different individuals and build that relationship over time.

The idea of the 'band', especially one that has grown up together, is very appealing in a kind of 'we're all in this together', band of brothers, 'everybody hates us and we don't care' sense—even if the band all drive off to their luxury hotel afterwards. To be sure, there are conflicts, tortuous internal dynamics and occasional departures—but the core, usually the singer and guitarist, remain (even if they constantly argue too) to keep the train rolling on while the show, the press and PR and the merchandising all help retain the illusion. Of course, there are exceptions like Alice Cooper and Ozzy Osbourne, who thrived as a solo artist, but only after establishing himself in Sabbath. In Gary's case, it was always only ever about Gary—he was out front doing it all, his name, his face and his voice alone. This was down to his personality; the only way he could operate and feel comfortable.

Mention of Ozzy brings us to the thorny issue of image and style. Would Jimi Hendrix have been as successful and popular if he had relied solely on his extraordinary talent? If he had just stood there in jeans and T-shirt and played? Timing played a huge role here too, coming to London at the height of the Swinging 60s when London was the centre of everything cool.

But Jimi's style—honed from the lessons of black blues artists and playing behind the likes of Little Richard and the Isley Brothers—made him the complete package: the playing, the voice and the songs backed up by the clothes, hair, sex appeal, onstage pyrotechnics and auto-destruction. Simply being an internationally famous black artist in a white world was a novelty. Eventually, he said he was tired of 'playing the clown'—but it was a psychedelic straitjacket that he and Chas Chandler wove.

Alongside a ferocious touring schedule and underpinned by an increasingly extravagant stage show and that unique trademark style, Kiss made twenty albums between 1974–84 and with virtually no airplay, fifteen went gold and thirteen platinum. And that was all before MTV—the real game-changer for the music business and probably the single most important reason why the industry went from slump to boom in the 1980s. The right image was now critical for any artist hoping for commercial success in the US market. The bands with the best MTV image were the heavy rock/metal outfits—all heroin chic-thin, big hair, make-up and Spandex: Mötley Crüe, Ratt, Twisted Sister, Quiet Riot. Just pick your Poison. Millions of albums were sold without the need for radio friendliness. From 1983–84, heavy metal album sales jumped from 8 percent of total US album sales to 20 percent. In 1986, MTV's *Headbangers Ball* attracted 1.3 million viewers a week. In June 1987, with U2 at the top of the US album charts, the next five slots were filled by Whitesnake, Bon Jovi, Poison, Mötley Crüe and Ozzy Osbourne. By 1989, when Gary's latest album went on sale, 40 percent of records sold there were classed as heavy metal, prompting *Rolling Stone* to declare that heavy metal was 'the mainstream of rock'n'roll'.

And every time Gary released an album in the States, he came up again multi-platinum competition like *Pyromania* (Def Leppard), *Slippery When Wet* (Bon Jovi), *Master Of Puppets* (Metallica) and David Coverdale's 1987 breakthrough album *Whitesnake*, which owed much of its huge success to input of one John Kalodner and the co-production work of Mike Stone, who worked on *Run For Cover*.

Everybody had an angle: the horror cinema sets of heavy metal; big production sound but with blue-collar rootsy appeal from Springsteen, Tom Petty and John

Mellencamp; Bon Jovi's anthems of conscience fronted by the clean-cut, film-star looks of Jon Bon Jovi—fashionable with all the sound and fury of hair metal but without the violence and sexism.

So where did Gary fit into all this? He didn't—and he hated it. His heart just wasn't into trying to compete with all this hoopla—whether it was the soul crushing touring, the 'crummy videos' (as he wrote in 'Led Clones'), the make-up, biting the heads off bats or trying to squeeze himself into air-gasping clothes. And as good as some of his songs were that could compete at an AOR/radio level, he couldn't get the radio play either, because he wasn't MTV-friendly and so couldn't land that big hit. Trying to be this heavy rock star with the huge show and cool videos in order to shift albums and singles was never going to work for him. He just wanted to play—and if people were prepared to come and see him and buy the music he had on offer, so be it. If not, well, knock yourself out. It would be on Gary's terms or not at all. He became increasingly disillusioned with the rock treadmill and the emphasis on style over content. Talking about the compromises he felt David Coverdale made to break America, Gary said: 'He had to make certain cosmetic changes to achieve that—*cosmetics* being the operative word—and I'm not prepared to do what he's had to do; they'll (Americans) have to take me as they find me or not at all. Obviously, you have to compromise to a certain extent otherwise we'd all be walking around in old T-shirts and slippers; and you've got to make your stage show something worthwhile for the people who pay hard-earned money to see you. But the image will always be secondary.'

Gary did hire professional advisers to draw up plans and models for the stage set, and as production manager Gerry Raymond-Barker admits, 'We had elements of Spinal Tap going on, but not to any great extent—with Gary's guitar playing we didn't need that much by way of effects. But because it's a rock show, you have to have a bit of pyro, a few flashing lights and a stage set that resembles something or other.' But as Gary said, 'if somebody comes up to me at the end of the show and says, "The lights were great," I know I'm in trouble! Plus, if you get into the big theatrical production rat-race then you are entering the Pink Floyd syndrome and you have to come up with something bigger every year. I don't want to be taking twenty trucks out with me because you'll never earn any money that way. I remember Greg Lake telling me how ELP took an orchestra on the road … he went out the back one night, saw twelve trucks full of gear and thought, *I'm fuckin' paying for all this??!* Next day, they fired the orchestra.'

Then Gary really hit the nail on the head:

'The sickening thing is that so many bands go out there and hide behind their stage gimmicks. Rock is the perfect game for bluffers and over the years, plenty of people who can't sing or play have made a lot of money out of it ... everything these days is manufactured, "Let's get in a hairdresser, let's wear these clothes let's do the big video ..." What about the music?

'When you are talking about videos and the importance that's attached to them, then I'm sick of watching them ... I have to do them. If I don't make a video then I shouldn't make records because you must compete. The best video is the one by Prince where he isn't even in the fucking thing. I am not an actor. People don't want to see me walking down the street hanging out with some girls in their underwear. Whatever I do in a video, I must be performing with a guitar.' Gary didn't feel he was an actor on stage: 'Some are, like those designer rock bands. You get one side of me on stage, the extrovert. I get all that out playing live. I must be there, otherwise I wouldn't be doing this. But I do try to stay as close to *normal* whatever that is, but I do get this kind of ego thing when I'm up there. It's a good place to let your frustrations out.'

Gerry Raymond-Barker confirms that 'Gary was not interested in the lights, so long as he was lit. He wasn't interested in the merchandising side either and to be honest there was nobody there with the artistic flair and interest to critique what was being put out. Gary was not interested in 'artistic direction' in that sense. When there was down time with Gary, I did stage managing for George Michael for the *Faith* tour in 1988. George wanted to know everything about everything, right down to brochure design, artwork, stage setup, camera positions, everything to do with the show, down to the nth degree.'

It all started very quietly one night in April 1989, with the band in Germany. As Bob Daisley remembers it, 'Gary and I used to sit in the tune-up room and tinkle about with various bits and pieces, bits of blues, the *Blues Breakers* album. That night in Germany, I happened to say to Gary, "Hey, why don't we do a blues album? It'll be the biggest thing you ever do."'

10

THE BLUES
IS ALRIGHT

According to engineer Tony Platt, Gary's desire to do a blues album went back as far as 1984 and the recording of *Run For Cover*: 'Gary was getting disillusioned with everybody wanting him to be a pop star. He and I had several late-night chats over a few beers. I said to him, "For fuck's sake, Gary, why don't we make a blues album?" He said he'd love to do it, but the management wouldn't hear of it. We tried a few times to pitch it, but nobody would listen.'

Five years on and Gary was dropping hints all over the place. In yet another interview where he railed against what he felt was soulless guitar shredding, he said, 'It makes me laugh really because you put on a B.B. King record and it makes the stuff sound meaningless.' To *Guitarist* (March 1989), he was extolling the praises of the new young white blues guitar hero on the block, Jeff Healey: 'There's so much coming from the guy, it doesn't sound like other people … it's him and there's nothing stale or old hat about the way he plays. It's fresh and he's 22 years old … It'd given me inspiration to hear someone like that come out.' Gary mused on the idea that this could start a whole new blues revolution in England, because as he said, 'It's all happening in America right now.' This was a reference to the apparent resurgence in interest in the blues stateside; Jeff Healey's debut album *See The Light* had been released in 1988 to wide acclaim, while John Lee Hooker's career enjoyed a major critical and commercial boost in 1989 with *The Healer*, so too had that of Bonnie Raitt, that same year, with *Nick Of Time*.

Guitarist and journalist Neville Marten probably interviewed Gary more times than anybody else and talks about Gary's deep knowledge of music: 'He shocked me a few times. I remember asking him once about a Larry Carlton song, "Do you know any Larry Carlton?" And he just played me a song, "It Was Only Yesterday"—and he played not only the jazzy chords, but he was improvising the solo over the chords like Barney Kessel or Joe Pass might. And I said, "Why don't you ever do that on record?" He replied, "That's not what they expect of me. They want the Marshall flat out and the Les Paul screaming at the top of the neck."'

Neville recalls a guitar jam night at the London Astoria, again in 1989: 'I was backstage and I heard "Hideaway" coming from the room upstairs. It sounded exactly like the record—and it was Gary, and he ran through another famous blues song, "Need Your Love So Bad". He played both onstage—and "A Whiter Shade Of Pale" with Gary Brooker on vocals and keyboards and "Wide-Eyed And Legless" with Andy Fairweather Low. He played phenomenal solos [on the last two], among the best I heard him play. And when I heard those blues songs in the dressing room, I said, "You really should do that, that's you, that's where you are."'

That same night, Chick Corea's guitarist Frank Gambale was there and Gary confounded his expectations too by sitting with him and trading Chick Corea licks. Picking up on the jazz theme, Gary was rethinking his whole approach to playing: 'The frame of mind I'm in at the moment means that I'm into the more simplistic way of playing—like the blues style … I like to listen to all kinds of music, but, for instance, if I was to listen to anything jazzy now, it would be more traditional jazz guitar playing, rather than the 70s fusion type of thing … I did enjoy listening to Bill Connors … he was a very emotional player and he had a style that nobody else had.'

So, knowing neither jazz nor straight blues was something 'they expect of me', Gary tentatively raised the whole issue with Steve Barnett during the *After The War* tour: 'I remember saying I'd had enough of all this. It's like a fucking big circus out there. Every time we go on stage, we've gotta have Andy Pandy's playroom up there, you know, and bloody big cubes with people jumping off things and flash bombs up your arse all the time and you know what's happened to the music? And I said, "I'm thinking of making a blues album," and much to my amazement, he said, "Great idea."' Gary speculated that Steve's enthusiasm may have derived from the new interest in the States; but whatever, at least Steve hadn't just laughed it off.

At the beginning, though, it was all very low key. Despite Gary wanting to turn his back on hard rock, this would nonetheless be a small side project, a non-contractual album. In very typical Gary fashion, a new musical direction meant a new band, but without explicitly dissolving the existing one. While Neil Carter didn't relate to the music he heard coming from Bob and Gary in the tune-up room, he says he did feel rather 'cut adrift … it was a bit raw even though I understand Gary had to do something different. It was all a bit awkward—not bitter, just a bit odd.' For Chris Slade, it was 'have sticks, will travel' and he went off the join AC/DC. A tad more aggrieved than the others was Bob Daisley: 'When I said, "Why don't we do a blues album?" I did mean *we*, the band we had at the time.' Although it was Bob who suggested Gary listen to 'Oh, Pretty Woman' in the very early stages of collecting material, he never got to play on it.

Gary began looking around for what he felt would be the right musicians for a blues band. His enduring love of Fleetwood Mac led him initially to think he might even contact Mick Fleetwood and John McVie to see if they would be interested in the idea. Snowy White was mooted as a possible second guitarist, with Mac's original producer Mike Vernon at the desk. While still mulling on that thought, he contacted Andy Pyle, with whom he had rehearsed in the early days of Colosseum II, and Andy brought along a drummer Graham Walker and keyboard player Mick Weaver. Gary was also trying to mix and match players, so Brian Downey, ex-Jethro Tull drummer Clive Bunker, Bob Daisley and Jack Bruce were invited to jam on the blues in different combinations over the course of about a week of try-outs at John Henry's rehearsal studio. Gary also rang Don Airey, who would play a crucial part in Gary's new direction over the next couple of years.

'I'd just been recording with Judas Priest in Provence. Gary phoned and said could I meet him in E-Zee Hire near John Henry's place. I had a bit of time before the flight back, so I had a coffee in the Promenade des Anglais in Nice. I met Gary in a café and there on the wall was a big picture of the Promenade des Anglais where I'd been sitting that morning. I thought, *This is a good omen*. It was just a skeleton of an idea; he was in with Andy and Graham and after about a couple of hours Andy said, "Okay, we sound like a band now."'

Gary was in his element. As he said later, 'It was great. We'd just go into the rehearsal room for a couple of days a week and bang out some old standards. We just worked on some things we liked. And as we were playing through these old songs, I got a couple of ideas for original tunes … It was nice to just go into a room with people and play for the sake of it, rather than having to rehearse for a tour and worry about anything.

'It was like re-learning. It was like stripping everything down including the whole sound, you know, getting away from this huge wall of amplifiers, playing through little amps in a rehearsal room and just taking it right back to the essence and going from there again and rediscovering all the things you'd forgotten over the years, all kinds of nice things—all the reasons you started playing in the first place. I think a lot of musicians fall into the trap of, you know, they get on this big treadmill and the more success they achieve, the further away they get from the reason they wanted to play in the first place—and hopefully it wasn't for the money, it was for love of the instrument, the love of music.'

The basic trio plus Frank Mead (harmonica and sax) and Nick Payne (sax) went to a studio in Wokingham, Berkshire to record some demo tracks with engineer Ian Taylor who had worked on *After The War*. Cozy Powell had mentioned the place during the recording of that album, Gary already played a session there for Mo Foster and it wasn't far from where Gary was now living with Kerry out at Shiplake, near Henley-on-Thames.

The first tracks they laid down were the old Mac track 'Stop Messin' Around',

Jimmy Rogers's 'Walking By Myself' and two of Gary's compositions, 'Midnight Blues' and 'Look The Other Way'. They also went for a studio try-out at Sarm West, where they recorded demos of 'Still Got The Blues (For You)' and 'Oh, Pretty Woman'. Everything was very relaxed, because at that point, Gary thought he was just doing a side project, not 'The Next Gary Moore Album'. Ideas were flowing like water; as Don Airey recalls, 'there are 47 reels of 24-track tape lying around somewhere, different ideas, different takes'.

Gary played the demos to Steve Barnett, who thought they needed a bit more work on them before they went to Virgin, because as he says, 'there was something really special about the song "Still Got The Blues (For You)", but I thought the whole idea should be better formulated before we went to the record company, because it was a very dramatic shift in style and focus. I left it a few weeks and when I saw him again, he had properly demoed the songs and the whole idea was coming together.'

Steve went into see the company and play them the demos: 'Everyone who heard the song "Still Got The Blues (For You)" thought it was a "moment"—it redefined who Gary was and they were very supportive.' Virgin A&R executive John Wooler confirms the view that 'initially, Virgin were thinking this would be a non-contractual album, sort of "Let Gary get this blues thing off his chest." And then when they heard the demos, people who were not into blues reacted really well and thought this had more commercial potential than a straight-up blues record. The thinking was that the playing is great, so that will appeal to the guitar fans and the songs are melodic, so that might appeal to a wider audience. Then they were committed to a full-blown album with a reasonable budget. It was at that point that Gary finally decided that he would use his own band of musicians rather than some kind of "back to the roots" concept album with Mike Vernon and Fleetwood Mac.'

Now they were rolling. But who would produce the album? Peter Collins was Gary's current go-to guy, but Gary thought this really wasn't for him. Instead, he suggested to Ian Taylor that they could produce the album themselves. Sarm West was the chosen studio; Ian Taylor set to work: 'We didn't have a huge budget and Sarm West was quite expensive, so we didn't book a lot of time and aimed to do it in a month, or maybe less. I set everybody up in the big room there. Gary's amps were in one booth, but Gary was in the room himself with the musicians to get a live feeling—we wanted musicians playing together in the room rather than ripping it all down and doing lots of overdubs.'

As Ian reminds us, when it came to the recording, 'it was all about Gary and the guitar. Gary liked to work with me because I could get his guitar to sound good. I understood where he wanted it in the mix and I made his life in the studio as comfortable as possible. I always had this thing about making the signal path to his guitar as simple as possible. Don't fuck with it too much, use good microphones and put them in the right places. I could get a sound very quickly and it allowed him to go into the studio and not have a lot of fucking about. I could capture something quite quickly without Gary getting moody or upset. Everyone arrives, he's in a good mood, so right, let's get up and running. When he had the guitar in his hand he became a slightly different person, he became very charged and that's what would happen in the studio. He'd come in all relaxed, but as soon as he's got the guitar on, everything's got to happen or the moment is lost.

'He didn't want any surprises from his backing band. He wanted the landscape clear so he could do exactly what he wanted to do. What he didn't want was the bass player or the drummer putting in fills when he wasn't expecting them. Graham (Walker) and Andy were ideal; steady and simple and certainly not vying for attention.'

Of the twelve tracks from the original CD release, half featured the basic group of musicians originally gathered for the demo sessions: Graham, Andy, Mick Weaver and Don Airey—playing those early songs with the exception of 'Look The Other Way', which remains unreleased. This same line-up recorded the final version of 'Still Got The Blues (For You)' where the solo was done in one take: 'We went back on that track,' says Ian, 'and dropped in two notes where the tuning wasn't spot on. Such a small thing to fix. Gary was really tough on his own playing, really tough. At the time, I don't think he knew how good that solo was; it was like "Okay, that'll do for the time being." But when we listened back, it was obvious—that was the solo.' Like all of Gary's greatest solos, it was symphonic in structure, built up in careful sections underpinning an enduring song of simple grace, intensity and the sustained emotional power inherent in the classic falling fifth chord progression.

The eponymous track featured strings and Gary introduced a brass section to his line-up to get that big band blues sound—and here, Don's technical skill was invaluable as he conducted the strings and scored all the arrangements for strings and brass. When they undertook the promotional tour, Don was the official Musical Director. Gary knew well enough that even if he recorded a blues album, there was always going to be a hard rock element in the playing. Bringing in his crunching sound would be Gary's signature blues style, which would differentiate him from the original blues sounds of Peter Green or Eric Clapton. But Gary also knew that playing with a horn section would be a whole new ball game for him.

Having a larger band came from the idea of engaging some of the top American bluesmen—Gary wanted to record 'Oh, Pretty Woman', so why not bring over the man who made it famous, Albert King? Virgin's enthusiasm had seen a nice bump in the budget, which would make this possible.

'He's always been a big idol of mine,' said Gary, 'since I heard him on this little transistor radio that we had at home—the song was "Cold Feet". Nobody can play like Albert King with that attack of the thumb and big, long bends and when I heard him I thought, *Who the hell is this guy?* It just totally blew me away.' Gary referenced the influence of Albert King on Hendrix (in particular 'Foxy Lady') and that Eric Clapton's playing on 'Strange Brew' was a straight lift from Albert and on through to Stevie Ray Vaughan, 'so to get the chance to work with someone like that on that song was just amazing for me'.

Coincidentally, John Wooler had pitched the idea to Virgin of starting a blues subsidiary to be called Pointblank. He had connections in the US blues community and specifically had been talking to Albert about being the first artist on the new label: 'Gary asked me to approach him and I ended up speaking to his lawyer in Arkansas because he didn't have a manager, and eventually we worked out a deal.

'Albert was due to fly over First Class and I was due to meet him at Heathrow, take him to the hotel and then to the studio next day for the recording. So, I'm down at Heathrow at midnight—no sign of Albert. In the morning, I get a call, it's Albert, "Where have you been?" Turns out he caught a different flight but didn't think to tell me. It's ten in the morning and he says, "Come and pick me up. I want to start recording." Now, normally, Gary would come in around two in the afternoon. So, I'm frantically trying to call Gary and Steve to tell them that Albert doesn't want to hang around; he wants to get down to the studio. Gary lived some way out, so I went to get Albert and tried to delay things by taking him to breakfast, and anything I could think of to try and slow down the process.

'Albert's track was due to be recorded at Metropolis Studio in Chiswick, west London. After I had phoned, Gary got there early and we cut the session around midday. For Albert, it was all about getting down to the studio, doing the song and going home.'

Albert was very non-committal about this venture. Gary told *Guitar World*, 'it was very tense. He didn't know me from Adam, he just came over for the money originally, you know. He walked into the studio and said, "What have you got?" And I said, "Well, we've got a version of 'Pretty Woman' from your *Born Under A Bad Sign* album." And he said, "I want to hear that!" and he was really belligerent. We put the tape on and got as far as the second line in the first verse when he jumped up and said, "Stop the tape! Stop the tape! The line is supposed to be '*sure* is the rising sun'—not '*she* is the rising sun'." Now, I'd spent like a week trying to figure out these damned lyrics which were buried in the mix anyway and I got this one word wrong! And he roasted me for that for the rest of the day. Every time the tape would go by, he'd look over his glasses like an old schoolteacher and say, "*Sure* is the rising sun, *sure* is the rising sun.'"

Albert had every right to be sceptical; he did hold a generalised grudge against white guitarists whose careers he regarded as having been built on ripping off his style. Interviewed later, he confessed about Gary, 'I thought he was just another kid trying to get into the guitar blues world. But once he started playing, it started gettin' better and better all the time, you know wha' I mean? And I started watching him and I was gonna play, I had some ideas—and I forgot 'em watching that kid play (laughs). Boy, he was playin' the wildest things! Golly Moses—where did he come from? That guitar was hotter than pepper pudding.'

Albert could see that Gary wasn't some uppity blues wannabe, 'the kid' could really play. As far as he ever could, Albert mellowed a bit, but not before he freaked everybody out by tipping a load of bullets on the table in search of his pipe-cleaning knife. Turned out back in his home town of Memphis, Albert was a county sheriff's deputy—if you called Albert at home and he wasn't there, you could get him in his patrol car—and he produced the badge to prove it. It may also have been a subtle way of saying that at six-four and nearly eighteen stone, you didn't mess with Albert King.

There was great anticipation at Albert's arrival; everyone was waiting to see the legendary Gibson Flying V known as Lucy. Imagine their shock when Albert King walked in with his guitar in a cardboard case tied up with a rope. It turned out not to be the original guitar; even so, they couldn't believe he didn't have a decent case. He clocked Gary's case, and Gary then asked Graham Lilley if he could get Albert a new one, 'but it had to be lightweight, so he could carry it; Gary's was 9mm ply with an outer card cover edged in metal with big knuckle corners. But the company, Chandlers, did a lightweight aluminium one. So, I contacted them and they managed to get one to him in time—the guy worked over the weekend. And it turned up, foam-lined and the guitar fitted perfectly.' But says Ian Taylor, 'Albert didn't like the colour of the foam inside or something like that and he didn't want to pay for it—even though he was being paid a whole load of money—it was never meant to be a present.'

Ian Taylor remembers trying to get the track done with Albert overdubbing on the basic rhythm track: 'He takes his guitar out and tunes it up roughly. Graham Lilley says, "Do you want to plug into a strobe tuner?" Albert says, "No, I'm fine." And then we try to play with the track and he's miles out of tune. And then it's, "Well, you need to be in tune with the track, Albert." "No, no—you need to be in tune with me"—because he is used to playing with his own band who had to be tuned to him, not the other way round. If he isn't in concert pitch it doesn't matter. If he says it's in E and it isn't in concert E, but its Albert's E, then it doesn't matter—everybody tunes to him. We tried running the tape at a different speed. Then we spent a couple of hours going through the solo note by note and we fiddled around. Then Gary looked at me and said "What are we doing? It doesn't sound any better and it doesn't sound like Albert. Let's forget it and go with what we have."'

John Wooler and Gary were having discussions about what other blues artists they might involve. 'We had been at the rehearsal studio, and I was giving Gary and Steve (Barnett) a lift back and we were talking in the car. I said, "Have you heard of Albert Collins? I'll play you a great track. You'll love his guitar playing." And I played him "Too Tired" and Gary said, "That's incredible. Never heard of this guy in my life." So, I made Gary up a tape.' It so happened Albert Collins was around in London to play at The Forum. He came into the studio, and they got 'Too Tired' down in three takes. Albert Collins was the easiest guy in the world to work with—no muss, no fuss.

Albert Collins then invited Gary to come and play on his gig. As Gary told *Blues In Britain* magazine in 2006, he was amazed how relaxed Albert was before a gig: 'I got to the gig and the band were going on stage—they always do that thing where they play a song or two before the main guy comes out—and he was up in the dressing room just holding court and there were all these people in there. He had a bottle of vodka, had his guitar just laying there on the bench. He was so cool. If that was me I'd be so nervous, nobody would come near me before I play … He was just having a little party in the dressing room. Next thing he picked up his guitar, put it over his shoulder, said "See you down there, Gary," and off he went. I have to admire him.'

Although much of the album was cut live with the basic band, Gary did want to mix up the feel. So, on 'As The Years Go Passing By' (which Duane Allman had speeded up to create the 'Layla' riff), Gary used Bob Daisley and Brian Downey, but it was also a chance to play with mates. Bob was the one guy who could make Gary laugh all the time—a master of the one-liner, which made for a very relaxed atmosphere.

There was one very special guest on the album—George Harrison. When Gary and Kerry moved out of London to Henley-on-Thames, they became part of what Kerry calls 'the Thames Valley gang'—an enclave of musicians and their families including Ian Paice, Mick Ralphs, Dave Edmunds, Jim Capaldi, Alvin Lee and George Harrison. 'There were dinners and parties and jams,' says Kerry, 'but they were all very cautious about who they let into their circle and they weren't sure if they were going to allow Gary in. George was especially cautious for obvious reasons. One day, we went round to Alvin and Suzanne Lee's place and Alvin had this studio and they were all jamming away. Gary got up and literally blew them all away. That was his induction and so we became part of that set. He was accepted.'

Despite his initial caution, it was George, says Kerry, who got closest to Gary: 'They struck a chord with each other. There was something they both had and they found a comfortable groove with one another, a real easy way of being around each other. It was really lovely. George would just laugh when Gary played, he thought it was hilarious. And Gary always thought George was an incredible guitarist, but not necessarily in the way you would think about a guitarist. Gary said that whatever George did was so precise and added to the song, a genius at putting the right piece in the right place. So, there was a professional appreciation of each other, but more than that, they used to talk about everything. There was no hierarchy with George, he was very down to earth and funny—and Gary wouldn't have taken any of that anyway—Beatle or no, Gary had a big enough ego of his own; he was very confident in his place in the scheme of things.'

Gary said later of George, 'He was like most people, you know. He had different sides to him. George was a character and he was a very charismatic and special person. He was kind and had an incredible sense of humour … he was like a naughty schoolboy with a glint in his eye … I had some great times with him. I also had some embarrassing moments, like the time he played me the opening chord to "A Hard Day's Night". It wasn't the way I played it all those years. I said, "Is that right? Are you sure that's right George?" He looked at me and went,

"Yes Gary, it's right." I felt like shit, like the earth was swallowing me up. At least he showed me the chord … Actually, when he showed me it made perfect sense because the arpeggio at the end … is that chord broken down.

'It was great being around him and playing all those Beatles guitars that were hanging up on the wall in his home studio. He'd take the Rickenbackers down and the one Clapton gave him after "While My Guitar Gently Weeps", that red Les Paul, as well as the Gibson acoustics and stuff. It was like being a child in a toyshop.'

For Gary's album, George wrote, played and sang on 'That Kind Of Woman', also performed by Eric Clapton later in 1990 for the *Nobody's Child: Romanian Angel Appeal* led by Olivia Harrison. On the *Still Got The Blues* album, Nicky Hopkins provided some beautiful piano for the track recorded at George Harrison's studio, although the piano was slightly flat even though it was regularly tuned. Ian suggested they got the track in tune with the piano, slow it down, record it at a slow speed, and then get it back to the right speed, rather than waste time getting the piano tuner in.

While Gary might accept and even celebrate 'imperfections' in Albert King, he certainly couldn't stomach his own playing not being spot-on. A good example on this album was 'King Of The Blues'. Graham Lilley remembers Gary's frustrations: 'It was all "What if we did this?" and "What if we did that?" We ended up going out to Hook End, recalling the mix on the desk, changing this and changing that and it still wasn't right from Gary's point of view. It still wasn't coming back at him how he was hearing it.' On 'Texas Strut', his homage to the famous blues guitarists from that state, he never quite got the Stevie Ray Vaughan walking melody line exactly how he wanted it to come out. Virgin wanted some more B-sides, so they cut extra tracks that didn't appear on the album: 'The Stumble', 'Mean Cruel Woman' and 'Left Me With The Blues'.

Ian Taylor got a first hint of what they might have achieved when he went to master the album at Abbey Road: 'Chris, their mastering engineer, was one of their older guys there. He did various bits and pieces to it, then you play it in real time to master it on to vinyl. Chris turned round to me and said, "This is a really good album, you know." Here is a guy who is listening to albums all day. That was the first time it occurred to me, because when you go to master it, you are listening to the whole album. In the studio, you are still fixing things, fiddling with the order. About two weeks later, Steve rang me and said, "This is going to be a big record."'

Meanwhile, there was a promotional tour to arrange for the now-named

Gary Moore & The Midnight Blues Band. Drummer Graham Walker was on tenterhooks: 'It took ages for Gary to decide who was going to tour the album. I was happy just to have done the album, so when I got the call to do the tour, I was delighted.' Gary decided on the core band with Andy and Don plus the brass section. Starting with a warm-up gig in Folkestone en route to the port at Dover, the band set off for what was slated to be a three-week European/UK tour. 'Oh, Pretty Woman' and the album were released in March with the single 'Still Got The Blues (For You)' following in April, just as the tour was getting underway.

There were early signs the album was doing quite well. They were in a hard rock-style place in Copenhagen where they heard the whole album played and seemingly out of every truck stop jukebox came 'Still Got The Blues'. But it wasn't until towards the end of June, when they played the Park Pop Festival in Holland, that the band realised something very unexpected was happening. Graham Walker says, 'We came off the stage, there were all these TV cameras and a red carpet with a fence on either side and the bus had motorbike outriders. We were absolutely shocked, couldn't understand what was going on. You kept tripping over record company people.'

What was 'going on'? Success had crept up behind Gary and tapped him on the shoulder when he wasn't looking. Before the album's release, he had been intensely worried that he would lose his rock audience while the blues community would just think he was faking the blues. Record sales told a different story; they eventually topped three million, he picked up platinum, gold and silver albums across the globe including a ground-breaking gold album in the States where the single broke into the Top 100. This time, against all the odds, Gary had the right album at the right time. Blues was undergoing its periodic fashion peak while all the big hair, big riff, big production rock bands of the 80s were dropping off the radar in droves in the face of the stripped-back sounds of Nirvana and Guns N' Roses. Audiences were ready to be reminded of the timeless simplicity of the blues, delivering pure emotion with taste and control, not swamping it with manic shredding.

Gary needn't have feared the critical response either; while not all the reviewers (especially from the metal publications) were totally convinced by the album, headlines and comments like 'Flying in a Blues Dream' (*Guitar World*, July 1990), 'most breath-taking and succinct soloing ever' (*Guitar*, September 1990) and 'this album burns like a house on fire from start to finish' (*Billboard*, June 30, 1990) were more typical of opinion. In its review of the '50 Best Albums of 1990', *Q* declared the album 'one of the surprise hits of the year … as [Gary] lays down the most scorching licks of his career'. It was a genuine breakthrough moment for Gary, who had been increasingly convinced that as you trudged through the treacle of the rock business, marketing would trump music every time.

Both in album and concert reviews, the more astute journalists were writing that Gary was finally being true to himself, way more comfortable in his skin than he ever seemed in the 1980s—and that audiences recognised the sincerity and honesty in what Gary was doing. The cover of the album he dedicated to Peter Green told the story. On the front, a young Gary Moore look-a-like sitting in his bedroom practising his blues licks, an old record player on the floor surrounded by a slew of blues albums with Jimi Hendrix looming large on the wall. On the back, Gary sitting alone in a hotel room as he often did, still practising, the detritus of room service littering the floor, with blues albums like Mayall's *A Hard Road*, almost a metaphor for Gary's own winding journey, lying next to the CD player.

Don Airey had been playing with Gary on and off over the past fifteen years, 'but his playing on that tour was unbelievable. Sometimes I couldn't believe what I was hearing. While we were on tour, Jon Lord came up to me and said something very complimentary about my Hammond playing. But then he said, "Don't take this wrong. But it's not surprising given what's going on out in front."'

Now it really was all about Gary and the guitar. It was a blues show, not a rock show. There were no tribal expectations about 'a band'. Blues guitarists Muddy Waters, B.B., Albert and Freddie King through to Eric Clapton, Rory Gallagher and Johnny Winter among many others had their name in lights. The rest of the band, however competent—and The Midnight Blues Band were outstanding— were largely anonymous to the general audience. Vocally, Gary was far more comfortably in his range than trying to scream over the top of heavy rock songs.

Symbolically, too, it was the ideal landscape for Gary to traverse; the iconic bluesman cut a lonely figure, back against the wall, facing down the world, as Eric Clapton once said about his own journey. Back in the 60s, John Mayall had recorded an album called *The Blues Alone* while Gary, in Skid Row, had done his own solo spot in homage to Duster Bennett, the one-man blues band. But unlike Mayall and Clapton, Gary was no blues scholar; as a schoolboy, hearing Eric did not send him in search of Robert Johnson or Muddy Waters. Instead, Gary was responding purely to the sound of the music, like an electric shock to the brain, hearing what was possible with a Les Paul and a Marshall and drawing his inspiration from that emotional jolt.

But he was under no illusions that he had nothing left to learn—quite the contrary. If recording with great blues artists wasn't a thrill enough for Gary, he was overjoyed to get the chance to share a stage with them. Albert Collins joined the tour for some of the June dates and for Gary's first appearance at the Montreux Jazz Festival in July. 'Every night he would come out,' said Gary, 'and play songs like "Too Tired", "Cold, Cold Feeling" and "Further On Up The Road" and a lot of the time I would just stand back and watch him play. I had nothing to contribute. I was sort of feeling like just to be on stage next to this guy was enough for me.' Albert Collins was a real sweetheart; cool, relaxed and loving every minute of his time with Gary. In the brief period they had together, they struck up a good friendship.

With Albert King, it was always going to be master and disciple—he flew back to London for just two nights at the Hammersmith Odeon. John Wooler takes up the story of the rehearsal: 'Albert was extremely competitive and he always played really loud. But as he got older, he couldn't deal with the volume. The first thing he said to Gary in the studio was "You've got to slow down and turn it down!" And he was yelling at the horn section, telling them what to do. Same in rehearsals, trying to take over a bit. They were having a discussion about "Stormy Monday". Albert says, "What key do you want it in?" "Anything but A flat," says Gary. "Can't stand that. It's the worst key." Albert walks on to the stage at Hammersmith to do "Stormy Monday" and shouts out to Gary, "A flat!" and goes straight into it. The look on Gary's face! A classic moment.'

Gary said that he felt inadequate in Albert's presence, 'totally out my depth, but he was most encouraging I must say. He taught me quite a lot about guitar playing in just a couple of days … he said to me, "Nobody's going to shoot you if you don't play for two seconds" … He was going to the airport and his car arrived and I said, "Thanks for everything, Albert." And I went to give him a hug and he said, "Now listen, I want to get on your case about that loud playing … you and Stevie Ray Vaughan, I can't stand it. You and Stevie Ray are my godsons. Now you understand that?" He was giving me a lecture!'

The tour was a huge success lasting not three weeks but spread over six months to early September. Towards the end, they were playing large festivals including one in Denmark where, in front of 300,000 people, Gary was presented with a platinum disc for sales in Denmark alone—and they backed Tina Turner on her *Foreign Affair* European stadium tour. Success breeds success, and offers were pouring in from all over the world. Here was a chance for Gary to finally break

America and tour extensively in Japan, Australia and New Zealand. And then the bombshell—Gary said no.

Back in January 1989, Gary had told *Raw* magazine that 'I wouldn't mind putting together a blues band just so I could play a few clubs and be the Peter Green of the 80s for 24 hours'. But once the album came out and the band were on the road, Gary felt he was being dragged back into the whole rock circus he was trying to get away from. Even though he had a top-notch organisation behind him, he didn't want to do the big tours with all the travelling, the complicated logistics, hotels, and soundchecks. For Gary, his anxieties and the drive for perfection would require serious rehearsals, even though they had road tested the material inside out and backwards. Being away from home also meant being away from Kerry and Jack, now a toddler.

On top of that, Gary was beginning to have problems with his ears. He was noted for playing at a phenomenal volume even in rehearsal, as Graham Walker recounts: 'When I first had a blow with him, I went into this little room in John Henry's and I thought World War III had broken out. The whole room was shaking. And he said, "Oh don't worry, tomorrow I'll have a smaller amp—and to be fair, he did."' Production manager Gerry Raymond-Barker tells a similar tale: 'I remember being in the studio once with Gary. It was already blisteringly loud in the control room and he turned to the engineer and said, "Oh, turn it up a bit." So, the engineer whacks it up and it's like somebody stuck a dagger in my head. And Gary just stood there and went, "Yes, that's better." I could never stay on stage in front of his gear when he was soundchecking.' His musicians used to call the stage area between Gary and his amps "the dead zone."'

However, the intense volume was taking its toll. Gary had powered down on the amps and had taken to wearing earplugs but suffered repeat ear infections. Don Airey first became aware of the problem on the blues tour: 'We were in Munich at the Deutsche Museum. A few days before we had played the big Hockenheimring Festival and Gary was having trouble. He was sitting in this park in Munich having a coffee by himself. I wandered past and he was so upset.'

Talks were underway about touring the States as support to the Vaughan Brothers, but then on August 27, 1990, Stevie Ray was killed in a helicopter accident and the whole impetus for touring drained away. Even though the album was selling very well, it might have been risky going out as a headliner rather than as support to an established American blues artist in case Gary finished up on the dreaded club circuit again. There was a tragic irony about Stevie's death because

Albert King had not only wanted his 'godsons' to turn down, but he also said that he hoped to be alive long enough to see them play together, which undoubtedly would have happened if the tour had gone ahead. Who could have guessed that he would outlive Stevie? Although sadly, at the time, Albert King was not in the best of health. He died of a heart attack in December 1992, followed a year later by Albert Collins, who succumbed to cancer aged just 61.

The puzzle of Gary not wanting to tour at least the States was all the greater because by late 1990, he was actually living there. It was very convenient that the blues tour had been extended because from April 1990, Gary was on another tax year out and made the decision to move to Connecticut with his family. Kerry had a friend, Lesley, who was married to Deep Purple bassist Roger Glover and they were living close by in Greenwich while Gary's manager Steve was in the throes of setting up a US office in Philadelphia. There was also another video to edit, shot by NFL Films called *An Evening Of The Blues*, a recording of the May 11 Hammersmith Odeon show.

Yet Kerry says that once out there, even though he had his family with him, he fell into a depression: 'It was hard to know what was going on, it was like a self-sabotage. He was poised to crack America, the record company were right there ready to back him, but he just couldn't do anything. Before we left, he'd done the second [Traveling] Wilburys album, he was Ken Wilbury. When we were out there, Gary was invited to LA to do the video for "She's My Baby", but he said he wasn't well and didn't go. Bob Dylan asked him to be in his band too. Gary didn't like to be pressured into doing anything. He'd been on the road for years and he sort of collapsed and didn't want to do anything. He was just happy to hang around. The Gulf War made it difficult to fly home, everybody was panicking; not that we could stay long back home anyway.' Despite having flu, an ear infection and not wanting to fly to LA for the video shoot, everybody around Gary thought this was, in Graham Lilley's words, 'a totally, totally missed opportunity' to put Gary front and centre of the US rock audience. And more generally, it was very frustrating for Virgin and for Steve Barnett who says diplomatically (and echoing Sharon Osbourne's comment about Gary and Thin Lizzy) that 'in the world we operate in, when you have that opportunity, you really have to strike'.

Eventually, though, Gary managed to climb back on the horse and started thinking about the next album—that difficult second blues album—because of course now Virgin were eager for the follow-up to *Still Got The Blues*. Ian Taylor, who was lined up to produce, wanted to take the pressure off Gary by telling him (quite reasonably) that there was little or no chance that the next blues album would be as successful as the first, so don't get too anxious. Gary, though, was keenly aware of the task ahead: 'It's always hard to follow up something that's been successful because people have such high expectations of what you're gonna do next and also if you're anything like me you have very high expectations of yourself, so you tend to be over-critical and not just get on with it. You can never repeat the experience. You can't just go in and make another album like *Still Got The Blues*—it's done so well and made in virtually total innocence. You can't go in there and be as free as you were with the music. You lose that spontaneity, not just in the playing, but in the whole approach, the writing, the performance.' So, while Gary had escaped to the blues as a way of freeing himself from the pressures of being a heavy rock axe hero, he felt he had fallen straight back into it—as a successful blues musician.

Graham Lilley started looking round for a studio: 'The original idea was to do it in Florida, maybe at Criterion, but make a road trip out of it—me, Gary, Kerry and Jack in a 4x4, drive down from Connecticut, and see some of America. So, we drove down through Virginia, Georgia, went into all the local guitar shops and the clothes shops. I don't think we ever got as far as the studio—the area didn't really live up to the brochure. They finished up in the Ritz Carlton while I was in a little beach hut hotel getting details of studios faxed to me from (Steve Barnett's) Philadelphia office. They all had to be checked out; rooms with recording booths, certain desks, pages and pages of faxes coming through.'

As Gary was out in the States and away from both the familiar recording environments and the musicians he was most comfortable working with, this next album was never going to be as straightforward as the last. 'We did some demos at Soundtec and then we came up with Beartracks Studio in New Jersey,' says Graham. They flew Graham Walker and Andy Pyle out there and Tommy Eyre, who was already living in New York, came in too. But early on, says Graham, 'it didn't go that well. The tunes were not quite formed, and the covers weren't quite right and in the end Andy and Graham went home.'

In February 1991, Gary got a spot on *The Late Show With David Letterman*, playing 'Still Got The Blues (For You)' with the house band of Anton Fig (drums) and Will Lee (bass). Gary was excited by their level of musicianship and they went into the Carriage House Studios in Connecticut to do some demos and laid down Little Milton's 'The Blues Is Alright' with Albert Collins. In a promotional interview for the album, Gary recalled that he and Albert had first heard the track in a Swedish café on the *Still Got The Blues* tour: 'We played it as an encore number for the rest of the tour.' Will and Anton then came to the UK, to Hook End, to carry on under the production control of Ian Taylor, who recalls this funny little incident: 'It was Wimbledon week and George Harrison phoned up and said, "I've got John McEnroe here. Can we come down to the studio?" Now, Gary reckoned that if they came down they would want to jam and he wasn't that keen, so he asked Graham to pack all the guitars away and just leave him with one. George and John come down, we all have dinner at the studio and then George says, "Why don't we all have a jam?" We all looked at each other and then Gary says, "Oh, that's a pity. I've only got one guitar here." "That's okay," says George, "we've brought our own." So, we all went back into the studio, Anton and Will are all miked up and in the control room are Gary, George and John and they get into this blues thing and each take a solo. It was just a throwaway for Gary and George, but John was like a twelve-year-old, nothing like his image as a tennis player—and he played like a fourteen-year-old!'

The recording process continued to be very much 'stop/start' because Gary and Kerry relocated early back to England to visit singer and friend Vicki Brown, who died of breast cancer in June 1991 (and to whom the new album was dedicated), which disrupted the schedule. Because of the 'year out' regulations, Gary recorded most of his parts in Paris and while it is true that most of the tracks were done with a basic four-piece band, exactly which four musicians contributed what bits is a moot point. So, for example, on one track, 'Story Of The Blues', Graham reckons there were six different bass players with Gary in the end playing it himself—and he was still not happy with it. If you look on the cover, Andy Pyle, Bob Daisley and Willie Dee are listed as main bass players on the album, but there are also thanks to Mo Foster and Kuma Harada. Add in Gary, that makes six. It was indicative of the difference between the two blues albums. *Still Got The Blues* had been recorded quite quickly: Gary had little time to worry and fret over the recording. Now he had the money and the time to indulge his indecision, especially when it came to the mixing. As Ian Taylor says, 'he had real difficulty in saying, "Yes, that's great."'

Still Got The Blues was really a homage to the great British blues guitarists who had inspired Gary back in the day. On the new album, *After Hours*, and in an attempt not to repeat himself, Gary was going for a more Stax-inspired soulful sound, using the famed Memphis Horns as well as the Midnight Horns who had recorded and toured the last album. He said he had been immersing himself in a recently released Stax box set. He explained that he was going for a more integrated sound with the horns and, as the writing progressed, realised a role too for female backing singers: 'Unlike before where the horns were added later, I was thinking about horns parts while I was writing … on "Story Of The Blues" [whose lyric is made up of little snippets of classic blues songs], the horns play the melody line and the guitar answers … and the direction the writing was going, there was a need for harmonies, not just one voice like on *Still Got The Blues*. With the song "Separate Ways", the girls sing the lead lines going into the chorus … it was the girls and the Memphis Horns that made [the song] work for me because up to that point the song was almost a goner. I had it hanging around for a while and I wondered how to make it work with the rest of the songs on the album. Everyone wanted it on the album, but I wasn't sure. But having the horns doubling the guitar riff, the vocals doing the chorus line and me answering back, it all took off for me. [The song] was safe then, it got its gig back!'

On *Still Got The Blues*, Gary had focused his writing on the ballads and he followed the same path with *After Hours* because he reckoned you could knock yourself out trying to write those up-tempo blues numbers and they'd never be as good as the large repertoire of classic covers you could choose from. Yet he pulled off a neat trick in writing 'Since I Met You Baby', which was not only in that vein, but sounded like a B.B. King song—so who better to come in and join the session?

'He'd bought the *Still Got The Blues* album and we'd been trying to do something for about a year. I sent him a tape of "Since I Met You Baby" and he could just manage to get away from his touring schedule for about one day to come over and do this. Those guys are always on the road, that's why it's so hard to do anything with them. They live on the road even at that age. They don't sell that many records, so they have to tour constantly. He flew in one night. I'd already done my bits. He came in the afternoon, did his guitar, did his vocal and that evening we did the video together. It was like a dream; it happened so fast. I can't believe he's done it. He was a really, really charming guy, very easy to work with, didn't mind how long it took. Really professional.'

The interview revealed another aspect of the creative process: the running order. Admitting that he was old fashioned in this respect, Gary was still thinking in terms of side one/side two and deliberately placed 'Separate Ways' where it might have come at the end of side one of a vinyl record as a way of winding down to set things up for side two. This was in contrast to the first track, the tough sounding 'Cold Day In Hell', where Gary says he played tough too in order to 'retain the excitement—it wouldn't be me otherwise', contrasting his style with the 'safe, clean guitar sound of some I could mention'. This was almost certainly a sly reference to Eric Clapton, whom Gary felt had lost his edge as blues player, a view he had aired with far less subtlety. On the running order generally, Gary believed that if you got this element wrong, 'you can lose the whole dynamic of the record. You don't want two songs following each other in the same key, you want different kick off points from song to song—even the gaps between the are important [and he left an extra-long gap after "Separate Ways"]. Believe me this one had several running orders. People think you're crazy for spending so much time over this, but it does make the record sound better I think.'

After Hours was released in March 1992 and as predicted, the album was nowhere near as successful in sales terms as *Still Got The Blues*—in some countries, including the UK, where the album went gold, it actually achieved a higher chart position.

The Hard Rock Café in London played host to the launch party where Gary and B.B. King teamed up for 'The Thrill Is Gone' and 'Since I Met You Baby' with the Wilbury crew of Harrison, Petty and Lynne in attendance. Then on April 6, it was George Harrison's turn to invite Gary to a launch—a benefit concert in aid of the newly formed Natural Law Party, a political party founded on the principles of transcendental meditation, whose techniques Gary had learned from George.

Gary was down to play some tracks from his recent blues albums with 'The Hijack Band'—so called because George had swiped Eric Clapton's band for the evening. George wanted Gary to play on 'While My Guitar Gently Weeps'. During the rehearsal, Gary stepped forward for the solo and gave it the full Gary at which point George went to the mike, shaking his head, 'Gary, Gary, it's "While My Guitar *Gently* Weeps".' Gary turned traffic light red, repeated the solo and nailed it. On the night, the YouTube clip shows George turning to show his appreciation as Gary finishes the solo.

The band flew to the States to combine holiday with pre-tour production rehearsals. Gary stayed in Disney World in Florida and then played the Universal Amphitheatre in Los Angeles and New York's Beacon Theatre—the last gigs he would ever play in the States—before starting of the tour with a storming gig at the Hammersmith Odeon on June 7.

At the end of the first month of the tour, they took time out for a special event—being the house band for National Music Day fronted by Mick Jagger at the Hammersmith Odeon with Mick, Ron Wood and Charlie Watts (but no Keith because allegedly Mick wouldn't pay for him to come from Canada on Concord with his entourage). Blues legends Jimmy Rogers, Buddy Guy and Pops

Staples were there; Otis Rush played a great duet with Gary on 'So Many Roads'. Graham Walker fills in the background: 'We went to see the Stones while we were on tour in Europe in 1990. Me, Gary and Andy went backstage to meet them and had a bit of a jam. Albert Collins was with us, and the Stones were very keen on Albert, "What strings do you use?" and all that kind of thing. And they really liked the *Still Got The Blues* album and that Gary was doing blues. So, when Mick asked us to do the show, we flew in from Switzerland, and went straight to the Hammersmith Odeon for the rehearsal with all these different people.'

Unfortunately, pretty much all the dates in August were cancelled because of Gary's continuing ear problems, but not before several shows were recorded and filmed for later release in 1993 as *Blues Alive*. What the recording showed was that, despite his misgivings and anxieties, Gary Moore had reinvented himself as totally credible blues artist—taking up the mantle from the blues heroes he worshipped as a teenager and now standing shoulder to shoulder with the world's finest. There was no better example of that than his breath-taking duet with B.B. King at London's Town and Country Club on November 11, his last gig of the year. It's all there on YouTube, a performance from both players of sheer artistry and diamond-hard precision. But on a darker note, the sentiments expressed in the song they chose to play, 'The Thrill Is Gone', would come back to haunt the Moore family in the months ahead.

11

AROUND THE NEXT DREAM

Gary was off the road (and hardly in the studio during 1993) when he took a call from Jack Bruce, who had just lost his guitarist Blues Saraceno to the glam metal band Poison. Jack had a couple of August gigs coming up in Esslingen, Germany, where his wife Margrit was born. Steve Topping was down to play the first night, but couldn't do the second so Jack asked Gary if he fancied stepping in.

Gary Husband was Jack's drummer at the time: 'I was immediately pretty impressed by Gary's "lightning strike" impact as a guitarist. He meant every note and that means a lot to me. For most of the time we were playing Cream material, which wasn't my favourite endeavour with Jack because I always hated trying to fill someone else's shoes in a very particular and personally formed way of playing. Gary, on the other hand, came in and literally 'owned' those songs, seemingly from moment one, almost as if he had been the guitarist in the original group. It was always very impressive how he did that.'

As Gary told this author in 2009, 'That gig in Esslingen went so well, I asked Jack if he fancied doing some writing together because I was planning the next Gary Moore album.' Gary had tried to set up a studio in his own house in Shiplake. He experimented with the changing room of the outdoor pool, but it didn't work, so he rented a house nearby that would serve as an office and an 8-track studio. Gary said, 'Jack would come over and would work with me during the day. I'd written some songs, but it was kinda weird because the songs were moving more his way and I was starting to think of Jack singing them.'

At the beginning of November, Jack celebrated his fiftieth birthday with an all-star concert over two nights in Cologne featuring many of those musicians he had played with over the years including Ginger Baker, Simon Phillips, Clem Clempson, Dick Heckstall-Smith, Pete Brown and Gary Husband. Gary was invited to take part.

On the day, the musicians gathered to be taken by coach to the venue; Gary disappeared into a limo amid mutterings about 'bloody big-headed rock stars'. The limo was following the coach, but when the coach pulled up outside the E-Werk in Cologne, the car vanished and Gary with it. He arrived about an hour later; it turned out he was very nervous about this important gig and had instructed the driver to park up away from the venue while he sat in the back with the guitar and practised. __

With Clem Clempson doing lead guitar duties on the first night, Gary stepped up for the second. He began with Jack and Simon Phillips playing Jack's frantic 'Life On Earth', a revved-up version of the 'Tales Of Brave Ulysses' riff played at break-neck speed. For the past three years, Gary had been retraining himself in the art of blues restraint. Now he was off the leash—Gary Moore: rock guitarist, red in tooth and claw, harking back to the frenetic fusion workouts of Colosseum II. Jack was loving it; they faced each other, exchanging riffs and smiles, driving each other on. Simon finished off with a drum solo, while Jack and Gary stood to the side, arms round each other.

Ginger Baker followed Simon on to the stage. Gary must have thought all his Christmases had come at once. They started with 'NSU'. When he played this song as a kid nearly thirty years earlier, in front of hordes of amazed Belfast teenagers, could he possibly have imagined that one day he would be playing the Eric Clapton role in front of a packed German audience—where Gary had a large and enthusiastic fan base—alongside two thirds of Cream? They carried on with 'Sitting On Top Of The World', 'Politician', 'Spoonful' and 'White Room'. It was a bravura performance by Gary—truly owning the songs, as Gary Husband observed. The years between Ginger and Jack fell away, they were as powerful as ever and even Ginger Baker could be spotted smiling in the back. From that came the latest and most unexpected twist in the tale of Gary Moore.

Early songs that Gary and Jack worked on included 'City Of Gold', 'Waiting In The Wings' and 'Can't Fool The Blues'. The project was still geared towards Gary's next album, which, on the strength of the songs he was writing, wasn't planned to be another outright blues album. Gary Husband had been told the project was in the offing and that both Jack and Gary wanted him involved. But the weeks went by and the drummer heard nothing, so by the time the call actually came to go into the studio, this multi-talented musician was already committed to an album as Billy Cobham's keyboard player. Jack suggested asking Ginger. Said Gary, 'Are you sure about this??' They had managed to get through a one-off gig with no traumas, but the Jack/Ginger love/hate relationship was legendary. Could it possibly work as a band? Jack had no such qualms, 'Yeah, yeah, it'll be great. Don't worry.' Now with Ginger involved, they were looking at a very different beast. Realistically, it could no longer just be Gary's next album with Jack and Ginger as 'backing musicians'. This was a whole new project and they needed to secure an album deal as a band in its own right.

Steve Barnett had moved to the States to establish Hard to Handle management, as the US end of Part Rock. This worked fine for Gary when he was living in Connecticut, but it was much more difficult once he returned to the UK and so day to day management passed to Steve's UK partner, Stewart Young. Meanwhile,

Gary had a new tour manager, John Martin. During 1993, John found himself thrust rather reluctantly into the role of manager, as the arrangement with Stewart was not working out. But Steve was the deal-making wizard and he flew in to negotiate with Virgin.

He presented to Virgin that much maligned concept, 'the super group'—one with a very topical edge. In January of that year, Cream had been inducted into the Rock and Roll Hall of Fame. They played together in public for the first time since Cream broke up in 1968. Hugs and glad-handing all round created a major buzz through the business that Cream were going to reform. However, it was always Eric's call because he had the organisation behind him to make it happen. But probably with one eye on his own solo career, he didn't want to do it. Now, with the industry still talking about Cream, Virgin were presented with the chance for two thirds of Cream to combine with their star guitarist in what the German show had already demonstrated was a potentially monstrous band. The deal was struck for a 'non-commitment' album, not part of Gary's main deal with the company.

At that point, John Martin had yet to officially take over from Stewart Young. 'I remember driving back with Steve to Heathrow,' says John, 'and telling him that Gary had asked me to manage him. Steve's expression suggested it wasn't going to be a day at the beach. He said to me "Are you really sure you want to do this?"' John's initial foray into management would be something of a baptism of fire.

It all started out calmly enough. They went into the large residential studio at Hook End and as a present for Ginger, Gary's team managed to track down his old Ludwig double bass drum Cream kit on sale in a drum shop in north London. 'Ginger walked in,' said Gary, 'and it was set up and he just freaked when he saw it. But he didn't end up using it because it didn't sound as good as his modern kit.' Gary did have concerns, though, when Ginger first arrived, as producer Ian Taylor explains: 'Ginger had been paid a lot of money for the session, flown in from America business class and so on, and he turned up with hands full of cuts and calluses. Turned out that Ginger had been building fences for his horses and his hands looked like a stockman's. He also had a whopping great bump on his head where he'd fallen off a roof. But it didn't seem to affect his playing.'

After they ran through some Cream songs to warm up, 'we started putting down tracks and it was very easy', said Gary. 'There was no problem at all. It was really fun and I got great insight into the chemistry between Jack and Ginger. It wasn't what I thought at all. They weren't at each other's throats. I think Jack really looks up to Ginger and Ginger knows it, so he'll never tell him he's any good. They are like two brothers, just winding each other up. One day I said to Jack, "Can you ask Ginger to play the hi-hat pattern like he did on 'Born Under A Bad Sign'?" "No way, I'm not fuckin' asking him. You ask him." I just pressed the button in the control room and asked him to play that pattern and he said, "Yeah, sure man. No problem." And Jack looked at me speechless. They were just like an old married couple. It's just the way they were.'

Ian Taylor agrees that for the most part, given the egos on display, it was remarkably plain sailing, though 'we did have one problem over timing with Ginger. For some reason, we were using a click track on "Where In The World" and Ginger just couldn't or wouldn't get on with it. It can be a problem for the older drummers. I remember doing a session with Gary and trying to get Cozy Powell to play to a click track—it was terrible. But Gary was a bit fanatical about timing and eventually we used Arran Ahmun on drums—but apart from that it was fine.'

The band needed a name. They came up with Driver's Arm, Rocking Horse, Herbal Remedy, Worldwide Cargo, Mega Bite, In + Out, Piece of Cake, Thrilled to Bits, Tit Bits, Fantastic Three, Grand Three, Expanding Universe—which was the front runner for a while, unlike Ginger's 'The Pope's Wank', which never really got out of the starting stalls. Nothing stuck, though, and eventually they just settled for BBM—although not before a band called Bang Bang Machine tried to kick up a fuss.

Once the album was in the can, they started thinking about the cover. John Martin says they used David Shineman as the photographer, 'and we did a session all day of them individually, Jack playing cello and so on. At one point, David asked Ginger to stand in front of some angel's wings that had been used for a fashion shoot. When we got the contact sheets back from Virgin, it was such a strong image.' The most amazing juxtaposition stared out from the photo; rock's Grade A curmudgeon in a long black coat, smoking a fag presented as a heavenly celestial being. A classic rock cover.

The album entitled *Around The Next Dream* was released on May 17, 1994 at the start of the tour. The whole vibe about a possible Cream reunion and the fact that half the songs clearly had their Cream antecedence gave the critics ample ammunition for comments along the lines of 'They couldn't get Eric, so they got Gary instead', which was a world away from the truth. Gary recalled that one interviewer actually asked him, "'Have you always wanted to be Eric Clapton?

And now you can be." And I thought, *No, fuck off.* And then Ginger chimed in with "Gary plays like Gary. Eric plays like Eric."' Jack found the ersatz Cream jibes very irksome: 'We deliberately wanted to nod towards Cream. It was around the time when Oasis were copying The Beatles, so I thought, *Why shouldn't I do a copy of me?!* It was very deliberate and I thought it worked very well.'

Some reviewers did buck the trend; *Q* concluded that the album was 'satisfyingly well rounded … which proves that BBM are not Cream reformed with one notable omission, but a credible band in their own right'. Even the ever-astringent Charles Shaar Murray, writing for *Rolling Stone*, felt that improved recording techniques gave this band a sound that was 'bigger, cleaner, rounder and more defined than the often fuzzy, scuzzy over-compressed Cream ever [had]' and thought Gary had out Gibson-ed and out Marshall-ed his illustrious predecessor. Despite all the carping, the album sold well in Europe, reaching No. 9 in the UK album charts.

However, the reviews came out once the tour was under way, and it was BBM on the road where the whole project began to fracture. BBM played a 'worst kept secret' warm-up gig at the Marquee and the band almost folded there and then. With Cream, the sparring was between Jack and Ginger with placid Eric staying out of it or trying to act as peacemaker. Now, whatever label you would want to pin on Gary, 'placid' would not be one of them: a Celtic band leader in his own right came up against Jack, another fiery Celtic band leader hewn from the same rock. The studio and the stage are two totally different environments. Onstage, you are in front of a paying audience, there is a 'performance' going on, no retakes or overdubs, somebody has to cue songs in and out. It was all about who was the leader onstage.

They rehearsed at Peter Gabriel's Real World Studio down in Wiltshire, drove into London for the soundcheck at the Marquee and all seemed fine. But when it came to the gig, according to Gary, 'I was only using a small amp because it's only a small place, so I thought I'd better not play too loud. I used a 50-watt Marshall, but Jack had about three bass rigs and I think he turned them all on at the same time and nearly blew me off the stage. So I'm screaming at the roadie, "What the fuck is going on? All I can hear is the fuckin' bass." And then I said something to Jack afterwards and he gave me this filthy look, "I don't like to discuss gigs after the gig. I have a rule." I then said something really bad back and he was really upset. Ginger was outside having a fag and says, "See Gary, that's what broke Cream up."'

Jack did say later that 'Ginger really did unsettle me that night. He was in such a bad mood'—and according to John Martin, there was the usual row between Jack and Ginger over volume. But for once, Ginger was more the bystander in all this. At any rate, Jack and Ginger walked out onstage for the encore—Gary walked out of the building with John Martin. They finished up at the nearby Groucho Club. And so it started.

The next gig, the opening night of the tour in Gary's hometown, was cancelled. Depending on who you talk to, it was cancelled to let tempers cool or it was cancelled either by Gary and/or encouraged by John to show Jack and Ginger who was the high-profile name of the moment. The tour proper opened at Barrowlands in Jack's hometown of Glasgow and the reception was so good that, as Jack said, 'it gave hope for the band much as the gig with Lifetime there had'. Not so the very next gig—the Virgin twenty-first birthday party at the Manor in Oxford. For Gary, 'that was hideous, they kept changing our set list and then we went on stage and nobody was even looking at us, just standing with their back to us drinking and chatting. We were really angry about that.'

For the most part, though, once they were on the stage, BBM absolutely tore places apart—they were a superb live act and fulfilled all the promise of Jack's fiftieth birthday concert. Gary especially enjoyed the gigs in Spain, 'they were the best ones. We got into jamming a lot in the Cream tradition—it was a very magical band.'

Once John Martin had taken over as manager, he recruited Ian 'Robbo' Robertson to fill the tour manager role. An ex-member of the parachute regiment, Robbo had already acted as a security for the Natural Law Party's Albert Hall concert. That night, he had roped in a friend of his, another ex-serviceman and full-time fireman, Darren Main. Looking back, Robbo says, 'I think the greatest service I did for Gary was to employ Darren.' He began as security for Gary, but quickly morphed into a long-standing, multi-tasking personal assistant, friend and confident who (a bit like Radar O'Reilly in MASH) knew what Gary wanted almost before Gary knew himself.

Gary acknowledged that for all the extraordinary musical telepathy there was between him and Jack, there was a 'political' dimension to their relationship: 'You have to remember there were three, not two leaders in that band—put them together and it's very hard for them to compromise beyond a certain level. I think Jack felt it was more my thing and wanted to get back to being in charge of his own music, although I was trying to keep things as equal as possible. To be honest, at that time, I was probably the most popular of the three of us—I could sell out very big venues all across Europe. I think Jack felt he was being pulled along by me, but I didn't want it that way at all.'

Putting the politics aside, they were the best of mates. Post-gig, Ginger would repair to his room for tea and a spliff, while Gary and Jack would hit the bars with attitude: 'We'd be sitting in a bar and some guy would come up and talk to me and I'd just sit there while Jack answered every question, just taking the piss. We'd drink brandy and get really pissed and he'd suddenly say, "Shall we go home?" And it was like four in the morning and we'd just get a flight home.'

Darren was often left to pick up the pieces after a raucous night on the town; there were times when he would literally make sure they were both tucked up. On one occasion, when Jack wanted serving after the hotel bar was closed, he threatened to heave over a marble-top table until, under Darren's watchful eye, he assessed the weight of the thing and was gently dissuaded from further action.

'We were in a nightclub in Spain,' recalls Darren, 'there was me, Robbo, Jack, Margrit and Gary. I glanced across and saw there was an argument going on and it was escalating to bottles being shown and glasses thrown. Gary, Jack and Margrit were dancing in front of the DJ watched by Robbo, while I was keeping an eye on the fight. Then somebody picked up a chair and it started getting a bit close. I said, "Another couple of feet and we have to go." Then it was time to go and we got out through a door just as the table went over—and then off to another club.'

When Gary talked of flying home, he made it sound like he and Jack surfed the net, booked some tickets and off they went. But this was 1994, so no online booking—and they certainly weren't going to plough through all the flight schedules bound in huge paper timetables to work out how to get home and back again for the next gig. Enter Robbo: as tour manager, it was up to him to make sure the demands of these demanding performers were dealt with as best he could. Mostly any tour manager can take this kind of left-field request in his stride. By his own admission, Robbo wasn't *that* experienced and as yet didn't have the rhino hide you needed for the job. As a seasoned tour manager, John Martin reckons 'you've got to be a complete asshole to do that job and you cannot let all the shit get to you'. But as Robbo concedes, 'that BBM tour was the worst of my life. There were nights on that tour when I was on my own in my room in tears.'

Then there was John Martin, again a newly minted manager—a very different role from tour manager. As a tour manager, you are dealing with very tangible items: have we got enough hotel rooms? Does the plane leave on time to make the connections? As a manager, the decisions are very different: is this the right single to release? Is this the right date for the album release? How much should I ask for an advance? It is a very different skill set. As the manager, you are also at the beck and call of the act, often over very trivial matters, and at any time of the day and night they chose to call. The BBM tour was complicated because while Robbo and John were trying to keep everything sweet with the musicians, they were also negotiating with Ginger's wife Karen and Jack wife's Margrit, who were managing their respective husbands and were obviously going in to bat for them when issues arose. Ample opportunity for yet more friction.

The tour carried on, plans and budgets were drawn up for a US tour with some very lucrative opportunities in the offing. Eventually, though, the band ground to a halt because much of the latter part of the European tour was blown out by Gary, who said he was having ear problems. 'We tried all sorts of things,' says John Martin. 'I talked to Pete Townshend about it, audiologists, we tried new attenuators.' Ginger was pretty fed up, complaining that Gary continued to play at full volume and then cancelled gigs because of ear trouble. They also had to pull out of the Le Zenith gig in Paris because Gary said he had damaged his finger on a dry-cleaning staple. Jack found this all a bit odd: 'I've played with fingers hanging off, you know. Gary was very insecure onstage. He wanted a rehearsal for the gig at Brixton Academy and Ginger was furious because he didn't want to rehearse and blamed me. I could hear him coming down the corridor shouting "I'm gonna kill that Jack Bruce!" But Gary had insisted. He kept a lot of things to himself, even with me. We had some really good conversations, but he never really opened up and it seemed important that he kept these things to himself.'

There was certainly one thing Gary wished he could have kept to himself, something that added hugely to the toxic mix of ego, emotions and politics engulfing and finally sinking BBM. On November 23, 1993, *The Sun* and *The Daily Mirror* exposed Gary's affair with the Moore family nanny.

Kerry freely admits that Gary never seemed content: 'I remember one particular day and we'd had Jack and it was just the most beautiful day. We had a beautiful house, lovely friends, everything was just, you know … and he was just miserable. And I remember saying to him, "What would actually make you happy? If I asked you right now what you want that would make you happy, because we have all this and you are clearly still not happy …" And he said, "I don't know that I'm not happy." He really, really wanted to be happy, but he didn't know how to be.'

Kerry says they both had itchy feet—she comes from a Romany gypsy background, while Gary may have felt a bit rootless having left home so young without much in the way of fond childhood memories. Kerry says they always looked at houses, wherever they went. And while Gary craved the idea of a secure family environment, another part of him could feel trapped at the same time. George Harrison admitted to Gary the same feelings; both were brought up on tough working-class urban streets. For all the trappings of the rock star lifestyle they both clearly enjoyed, they expressed to each other a feeling of imprisonment behind the walls of a gated community and all that it meant for the 'wild child' they both still harboured.

Kerry notes that Gary could feel quite isolated: 'He didn't have friends much outside the business. And it was quite a pressure at home, that transition period from coming off the road, being at home with all that time on your hands. You are used to having your day mapped out for you and you don't quite know where you are. I had to get him to learn to drive when we moved out to Shiplake.'

As far as the marriage itself was concerned, 'there weren't massive problems, but a series of things happened over a period of time. When we came back from our year out in America [1991] I fell pregnant again but lost the baby at six months. I went for a scan and they told me the baby wasn't alive. Gary was in the studio with B.B. King and he couldn't leave when I was having the operation. Then we had to wait a year before we could try again and I needed to go to London for blood tests every week, so it was quite a stressful period. Then I fell pregnant with Gus [born in 1993] and we were out at lunch, my waters broke, things went a bit wrong and I had to have an emergency caesarean. Gus and I were both pretty ill.

'Camilla had answered an ad in the local paper and came to work for us as a nanny. On a couple of occasions, she had said to me, "Oh, I want your life," but the warning bells didn't go. She left because we didn't need her anymore. Gary could feel quite sorry for himself, he needed your 100 percent attention, he wanted me to be there for him, but clearly I couldn't be there in the same way. Apparently, he bumped into Camilla about year after she left [she lived locally] and Gary got sucked into all that because here was somebody who offered the attention and the flattery.'

Camilla Harding-Saunders was 23 at the time, to Gary's 41. Kerry says she had no inkling of what was going on until confronted by Camilla's boyfriend, who spoke to her through the front gate intercom. 'Gary was there when the guy came to the gate. He said that none of it was true, "I'll go and sort it out." Then he drove off and that was that. It was very unresolved, really. He rang me later to tell me it was all true and that it he wasn't coming back. There was no discussion, he just went. But that was Gary, back him into a corner and he'll run.'

Gary left home at some point in early November 1993 (the newspapers had a shot of him and Camilla pushing a supermarket trolley) and moved into the place where he had his office and studio. Virgin's Richard Griffiths recalls seeing Camilla at Hook End during the recording of the BBM album and she was on the tour too. But both papers claimed that the affair started while Camilla was still employed by the Moores, which all sides said was untrue and led to the intervention of lawyers. 'Gary phoned me to say he wasn't at home anymore,' says John Martin. 'That was a difficult time. But we went to see Brian Carr at Compton–Carr who I knew because he was the lawyer for The Clash and Spandau Ballet. You wouldn't want to fuck with him. He's good. Letters were written, there were negotiations with Tom Crone (then legal affairs manager for the *Daily Mirror*), and we got a retraction, damages and costs.'

But the damage went deeper than tabloid misinformation. Gary walked away from his connections with the 'Thames Valley Gang' because he was too embarrassed at what he had done and Kerry says that although he did try to make some kind of reconciliation, it was all too late. 'I wasn't in a place to be too welcoming,' says Kerry. 'He knew how I was about that sort of thing. I had quite strong morals—it was a very black and white area. He had crossed the line and there was no going back. The trust had gone. But he was impulsive; he'd do things on the spur of the moment and then live to regret it.'

Kerry is adamant, though, that Gary 'was a great dad, he'd come round all the time to see the boys and to his credit never lost touch with them'. Once Kerry sold the house in Shiplake and moved out of the area, Gary would follow first to London, back to Henley and eventually to Brighton just be near Jack and Gus. But even though he had done the leaving, Gary nevertheless told Kerry that he didn't want her dating anybody he knew.

'I went to a friend's party and Eric Clapton was there. I left the party at the same time as Eric and one of the paps noted this. I got a call from a paper to say they were going to run a story about me and Eric and because at the time Gary was doing BBM, it was going to be like "Gary stole Eric's band, so Eric stole Gary's wife." I phoned Eric's manager to sort it out; it didn't get in the press and Eric sent flowers because he'd heard how upset I was. But Gary didn't believe I wasn't seeing Eric.

'About six months or so later, after we split, Gary and I were kind of okay and arranged to have lunch. I arrived at the restaurant before Gary and who's sitting there—Eric Clapton, having a meeting with some woman. I was thinking, *Oh God, this looks like a complete set-up.* Gary walked in and didn't even notice Eric, who was mouthing to me, "Are you two back together again?" And then as Gary was leaving he noticed Eric who just said, "Hi"—and Gary was convinced I really was seeing Eric and he was there to keep an eye on Gary. But it was just a ridiculous coincidence.'

Despite all the hassles, Gary said he took nothing but positives away from playing with Jack and Ginger, whom he regarded as 'the finest drummer I ever played with … they both helped me to be a better player for sure. They changed my rhythmical feel, [and like the blues guys] taught me to lay back a bit more and not be so frantic. And Jack is one of the few people I would call a genius; I was crazy about his solo albums; Phil Lynott and I used to listen to *Songs for a Tailor* all day long. The music he was coming out with was just astonishing, so otherworldly, nobody was writing music like that. He made it flow so beautifully melodically. I was quite in awe of him.'

With the collapse of BBM and his marriage, Gary pretty much disappeared off the scene for the best part of a year, although he must have taken some heart from the results of the 1994 *Guitarist* ten-year anniversary readers' poll, which awarded him third Best Album for *Still Got The Blues*, second spot Blues Guitarist behind Stevie Ray Vaughan, an overall third in the guitar slot behind SRV and Eric, and third Best Act behind Pink Floyd and Queen.

As there would be no second album from BBM, there was talk of a Gary Moore 'best of', which John Martin says was originally conceived of as a four-disc box set going right back in history, 'and we tried to get a release on "Checkin' Up On My Baby" and "Going Down", which was done with the Stones on National Music Day'. This never happened and the box set idea was scrapped to be replaced by *Ballads And Blues 1982–1994*.

The title made it plain this collection was not majoring on 'Gary Moore: Fret Melter'—but whatever Virgin's commercial thoughts might have been, it was a useful reminder to the record-buying public of Gary's track record as a soulful songwriter and in retrospect began to lay the ground for Gary's excursions to come into uncharted waters. But before Gary would push the boat out once more, he made the decision to honour his greatest inspiration.

Peter Green had all but disappeared from public view. During the *After The War* tour, Graham Lilley saw Peter in Richmond Park: 'There was this strange old guy sitting on the far side rubbing the side of his head with the palm of his hand, quite forcefully. I could see his long fingernails from where I was. He was quite dishevelled. And then I realised—it's Peter Green.'

Peter had made an abortive comeback in the late 70s/early 80s with a series of indifferent albums and a sub-standard outfit called Kolors only to disappear once more, laid low by mental illness and the attendant medication. There was no indication he was coming back any time soon when Gary—having dedicated *Still Got The Blues* to Peter—began to think about recording a whole album in celebration of Peter's music.

It is hard to overestimate the impact Peter made on Gary. Reminiscing about the early days, Gary recalled that 'Peter plugged into a Selmer at Club Rado and got this most beautiful tone from it and proceeded to kill everybody in the audience with this amazing sound and playing. What impressed me was the clarity coming off the stage, the incredible depth of his tone, the walls and the floor resonating at the same time.'

Peter went to an altogether different place from his contemporaries, a unique player with a unique sound. When he played, it felt like he was trawling in such a dark well of emotional, weary and almost spiritual yearning—manifesting in songs like 'Man Of The World', 'Oh Well' and 'The Green Manalishi (With The Two Prong Crown)', poems of the melancholy, fatalism and superstition marbled deep into the Jewish psyche. The effect on the young Gary Moore was volcanic and Gary owed Peter much—perhaps most importantly, in the way the guitar should serve the needs of the songs, the call and response with the vocal, the interaction with the rhythm section. From this, came Gary's insistence on feel and emotion in playing, not just drowning every song in sonic onslaught. Speaking to *Record Collector* in June 1995, Gary said of Peter, 'his style has not been brought to the attention of younger guitarists and that's affected the way guitar playing has gone. Guitar playing today is so lacking in taste, so lacking in dynamics and so lacking in subtlety. You need someone around like Peter to show people another way.'

Ballads And Blues 1982–1994 had been released to keep up the momentum of Gary's profile, but still with no new recordings planned and his career now very firmly in the blues firmament, it seemed an opportune time to realise a long-nurtured idea. Except that Bernie Marsden beat him to the studio.

'I booked some time in Silvertone, which was the old Morgan Studios in Willesden, and I was working with Tony Platt and Chris Tsangarides who had both worked with Gary. My idea was to do a John Mayall "guitarists" album.

Everybody raves about Clapton, Green and Taylor, but the real hero is John Mayall. He found them all and was pivotal for my generation. I was going to call it *Waiting For The Mayall Man*. I rang up a few lads [including drummer Steve Dixon, who later toured with Gary], told them what we were doing. Tony had got some cheap downtime over two weekends. We did it, got a great old fashioned Chicago blues sound and it was really buzzing in the studio. Then Tony suggested we put some horns on. So, I phoned up the Midnight Horns, Gary's horn section, and they all came down.

'On the Monday after the second weekend, Gary was in rehearsals. The Midnight Horns went down there.

'"Hi guys what you been up to?"

'"We just had a great session."

'"What did you do?"

'"We've been with Bernie Marsden at Morgan all day Sunday."

'"Oh yeah? Doing what?"

'"He's done these Peter Green songs."

'"What??? I've been planning to do that for two years!"

'"Well, he's done it."'

Not quite. Bernie's album, eventually entitled *Green And Blues*, remained more of a respectful acknowledgement of the 60s British blues that was so influential than a direct homage to Peter. It included 'Hideaway' (Eric) and 'Snowy Wood' (Mick Taylor), although half the album was taken up with Peter Green songs.

For his album, Gary recalled Andy Pyle, Graham Walker and Tommy Eyre for what could reasonably be called a faithful recreation of the Peter Green sound—crafted by Gary and Ian Taylor with love and affection and a real attention to detail, rather than simply a celebration. Gary explained his dilemma here: 'You have to approach it respectfully because it is something which for me personally, it's been with me for a long time, so it's almost written in stone this music. I try not to stray too far from it, but at the same time, I want to put myself into it as well, so getting the balance between those two things is a challenge.' Gary did manage to pull this off with great skill, even to the point of refreshing some songs like 'Long Grey Mare' and 'I Loved Another Woman' coupled with a superb reinterpretation of 'Looking For Somebody'. He told Neville Marten for *Guitarist* (April 1995) that he was aiming for a much sparser approach to the blues than had been achieved with his previous two blues albums: 'I've gone back to that very bare feeling. "Merry-Go-Round" is just done with bass and drums; it's very dry and very pure. It's got that essence of what Peter was about, which was that very stripped down, minimal way of playing and that was something I hadn't done a lot on record before, but something that I really enjoy listening to.'

Gary's choice of songs was governed by his desire to make sure that Peter got all the royalties and didn't have to share them with his former manager Clifford Davis. In the end, there were two songs with split royalties, plus Little Willie John's 'Need Your Love So Bad'. Even though the songs were chosen with Peter's financial interests foregrounded, Gary was an intelligent man and must have been aware—at a time when his domestic life was still in some turmoil—that he was making some very pointed statements in full public view on record, which only those close to the situation would have understood. A 'Love That Burns' points towards a yearning that love will last. By contrast, 'I Loved Another Woman' laments the loss of a good woman through neglect.

Peter was beginning to emerge into the light once more, so much so, Bernie says, that he had to rewrite the sleeve notes when he got a call from Michelle Reynolds—Peter's manager (and also Clifford Davis's ex-wife)—to say that 'the lost genius' was sitting next to her. When Bernie then played his album to Peter his response was, 'sounds like Fleetwood Mac'. Bernie was aglow and said to Peter how pleased he was at the compliment, to which Peter replied in his usual laconic, disarming fashion, 'wasn't meant to be'. And when Peter heard Gary's album, he thought Gary had simply played over old Fleetwood Mac tapes—again, was this meant to be a compliment?

There were the expected 'Why bother?' jibes from some critics, but the fans received both albums very well, highlighting what an incredible musician Peter was as a player, songwriter and singer—pulling off all three to such a high level being rare. Among the 60s guitar heroes, this trio of accomplishments was a feat matched only by Hendrix. Gary and Bernie's promotion of Peter—and the publication of Martin Celmins's excellent biography, in which Peter remarkably is said to have been 'flattered' by the attention he received from Gary—set the scene for Peter's tentative return to performing and recording.

For the gig launching Gary's tribute album at the Shepherd's Bush Empire on April 27, Peter made a nervous appearance at the side of the stage. Gary too was full of trepidation; he'd been off the road for a year, was performing music his younger fans would not be familiar with and playing a show being filmed and recorded in front of a sell-out crowd. As he remarked with a wan smile, 'How much pressure can you put on yourself?'

There was no proper tour planned, but Gary did play a festival outside Hamburg and made his second Montreux Festival appearance with a blues set majoring on his key blues influences—Peter Green and the *Beano* album—delivering both the toughness of Eric and the subtlety of Peter. But there was no surprise about which song earned the biggest cheer of the evening—'Still Got The Blues (For You)'. There was a lovely moment at the end when Gary held off from the last note while the crowd clapped and roared its approval. He looked happy and relaxed onstage fronting the perfect band for him—Graham, Andy, Tommy and the Midnight Horns—simple, uncluttered and supportive.

The few remaining dates for the year were blown out. John Martin pulled their spot at the Loreley Festival in Germany after a huge row with the promoter. Andy Crookston was the production manager at the time: 'We had to check in with John every step of the way. Eventually, it was called off because of a contractual dispute. I booked Gary into that show. I turned up and he didn't. They put gaffer tape across his name on the T-shirts and blamed me. I nearly got killed. We had a night in Germany, weren't allowed to watch the other bands, so we went and got absolutely slaughtered.' Drummer Graham Walker recalls getting a call from John just as he was waiting for the car to come and pick him up: 'He said, "The bad news is that the gig is off. The good news is that you still get paid."'

John's turn to be fed up. A relationship had been established between Gary's office and the Stones through the National Music Day gig in '92 and John says he put a lot of work into getting *Blues For Greeny* into the hands of the Stones with a view to Gary playing support on some big Stones gigs that summer. Eventually, Mick Jagger heard the record in his car and agreed to have Gary on the tour. But Gary decided he didn't really feel comfortable playing second fiddle to the Stones. 'The gigs were sold out,' says John, 'it was his audience—and it wasn't a money thing. I was more than a little pissed off.'

Nineteen-ninety-six was the start of another series of step changes in Gary's life, both domestically and creatively, resulting in some of his best songwriting while leaving his army of blues and rock fans scratching their heads.

12

DIFFERENT BEATS

—

It's September 1995. Gary calls his friend, producer Chris Tsangarides. 'He phoned me about trying out a band to do this one song for a Jimi Hendrix film. We went into Hook End with basically the musicians who eventually finished up on the album—Guy Pratt and Gary Husband.' Guy was an extremely experienced session and touring musician (and latterly stand-up comedian) most noted for his stints both with Pink Floyd and post-Floyd projects of Roger Waters and David Gilmour. 'Ironically, we recorded the song "The Wind Cries Mary" on September 18th, the day Jimi died,' says Chris. 'I pointed this out to Gary after we'd done this fantastic track—which I don't think was ever used—and we just looked at each other like, "Oh my God, how spooky is that?" We started talking and he really liked the band and he asked me if I knew a cool programmer—and I did—so that's how Phil Nicholas came in. We started work at Metropolis and then back to Hook End and did a load of work there and then Gary had this tax year out.'

The divorce settlement proved expensive, but Gary had been doing pretty well financially. Even though *Ballads And Blues 1982–1994* and *Blues For Greeny* were non- commitment albums (because they weren't new solo albums), John Martin still negotiated substantial advances, a neat trick considering the first album was full of songs Virgin had already paid for and the second was just covers. On top of that was a hefty advance for the new album—the first since *After Hours* in 1992. In the intervening years, Gary, who was always writing, had built up a large cache of new songs.

As ever, though, there was doubt in his mind as to exactly which direction he would be taking. The new album certainly wouldn't be a return to 80s rock, nor did he want to do another blues album. It unfolded more as a songwriter's album where the guitar wouldn't necessarily dominate, but much was still up for grabs. What follows gives an insight into Gary's painstaking creative processes as he effectively toured the world in search of making manifest the sounds he was hearing in his head.

Gary Husband was the go-to drummer for the collaboration with Jack Bruce, so Gary was more than pleased to finally be able to work with him. Husband is not simply a thoughtful and highly intelligent percussionist, but a composer in his own right and had his own views about adding colour to a song. Not for the first time, Gary Moore didn't necessarily see eye to eye with the guy holding the sticks. Gary Husband recalls, 'I remember some big tension creeping in around the time of that particular recording. Actually, it was more of an out and out spat, about the drum fills I chose to play at various stages of the song.' Much of the album was autobiographical, the most obvious being 'Business As Usual'. 'In case it's not obvious to everyone who hears it,' says Gary Husband, 'that song is nakedly about himself—his lingering childhood memories, his experiences and reactions to what was going on around him and about everything he was feeling and his raw fear. I wanted to just react, emotionally, to those words, and how he sang them, and *correspond* to that story, with the drums, but Gary heard one drum fill on run-throughs that I had played and somehow felt very precious about it. In other words, I wasn't to deviate hardly at all. I objected. And would still object! Because you hear it, and there I am playing the very same lead-in to every chorus or verse each time. Still sounds silly to me. I sound stifled … or worse still, like I'm completely devoid of imagination. But there it was. I can tune it out now if I just listen to Gary's portrayal, as, of course, it's hugely emotive and powerful. But I never could figure out why he did that and not just let me react—y'know, just naturally. I guess it was just his mood that day, because I seem to remember him addressing it later and saying, "I'm sorry man, y'know, I didn't wanna make you feel uncomfortable or anything, or hold you back." But that was Gary.'

Gary Husband underlines just how Gary *could* be driven by the mood of the moment: 'The great Gary-style contradiction is in the fact he completely set me free in "Where Did We Go Wrong?" and "Like Angels", and looking back, I played some quite emotional and dramatic things at times in the song that I found it good to do. I never heard one word of criticism against them! Not one! He dug it all, and we kept everything that had been played on those first takes!'

Guy was amused by one of Gary's particular personality traits that popped up a few times: 'He would do this funny thing—like we'd been out the night before getting hammered and then show up at the studio. But Gary would send messages like, "There's a gas leak and I've got to wait in for the bloke," or "The ceiling's fallen in." And it's like, "Gary, mate, you're the boss. You're in charge. We're the ones who make those excuses. Not you."'

Once, they had to work abroad—Gary was on another year out—and went to a southern French residential studio called Miraval, a charming, atmospheric edifice. The studio featured in a Chris Rea DVD about the recording of *Dancing Down The Stony Road* and was well-known to Chris Tsangarides, who had worked there on several occasions. The time in Miraval straddled the start of the year out. Initially, they went back and forth between France and Hook End in two-week blocks.

Then, off to the sun in Barbados to Eddie Grant's Blue Wave studio where

Gary met up again with producer Jeff Glixman: 'I was there working with some Trinidadian musicians. Gary came in and just plugged into an old Fender Bassman amp and jammed with three reggae kids from Trinidad—they were all metal reggae fans and were well into Gary. We started in the afternoon and it went well past midnight. One of the songs we played was "I'm Lost In Your Love", which he'd just recorded. It was almost like Bob Marley's "Exodus"—and it was one of my greatest musical moments with Gary—so relaxed—unbelievable.'

Gary was most welcome in the studio, which was more than could be said for British musicians in general. They had arrived in Barbados, shortly after the Happy Mondays had famously imploded, leaving the place in tatters—or more to the point, says Guy Pratt, the cars: 'Apparently, they went through 18 hire cars including one time when Shaun Ryder wrote one off and came stumbling up to the studio holding a steering wheel. So, all the time we were there, none of our hire cars turned up because all they were told was, "There's an English band at the studio and they need some cars."'

That wasn't the only glitch; in the Caribbean, if something goes wrong in the studio, you can't just call up an engineer to get it fixed—he could be four hours away or in Miami. The album had been recorded using just 16 tracks on two-inch tape, giving the sound more dynamics, more 'headroom'. The band were recorded on that and then all the other sounds on 24-track, so they were running two lots of tapes for every track—and every tape weighed about three to four kilos, so they finished up with hundredweights of tapes to lug around. Then when they got to the studio, they needed a synchroniser box to make sure the tapes played together. The story goes that some assistant in Eddie Grant's studio was sitting with his foot on the synchroniser on a certain button to make sure it was running while the session was underway. Suddenly, the box gives up the ghost and they are stuck. They can't go out and buy a new one—all they could do was sit on the beach until another one was flown in. Meanwhile, the clock was ticking.

After the combined holiday/recording session, they all went back to the UK, where as far as Chris Tsangarides was concerned, it was all over bar the mixing. 'Gary wanted a break over the summer, so we worked round his dates, but neither Phil Nicholas nor I could afford to take three months off, we had to work. So, we went off to Canada to do this album, ready to come back to start mixing. But Gary didn't like that. He started saying, "Oh, you'll be too tired to do the album."'

Although they hadn't worked together since the Jet days, Gary and Chris had remained friends, and their families were very close. Relations got a bit tricky when Gary left Kerry: 'Gary thought we were siding with Kerry, but we weren't siding with anybody; if anything, we were siding with Gary until the truth came out and then it was a bit "Oh dear". But we had that kind of relationship where we would be talking and then we weren't and then we would be again as if nothing had happened. And I thought this thing with the album was one of those times and it would sort itself out, but I didn't really know what was going on.'

The idea that an experienced producer like Chris would be 'too tired' to give Gary's album his full attention was a bit ridiculous and was in fact an excuse because he couldn't face telling Chris that he wanted a different approach. If the budget allows, as it would have done in this case, an artist might often bring in somebody else to mix an album, a fresh ear, so to speak. Gary went a bit beyond this; no doubt being with a girl half his age had introduced him to the new ambient landscape in popular music. More specifically, he had heard the hit album *Walking Wounded* released in May 1996 by Everyone But The Girl, which featured electronic and dance-style sounds. Back in the 1980s, Gary had been saying that music had to change and he warmly embraced new technology much to the dismay of some of his band members, fans and journalists at the time. In the late 1990s, Gary was not alone in trying to update his sound. Programming underpinned Eric Clapton's 1998 album *Pilgrim*, going much further in the same year with the pseudonymous *Retail Therapy (TDF)* featuring trip-hop, techno, R&B and ambient new age music. Bryan Ferry was reportedly working in a similar vein on an album that was never released. The technology-driven sounds of the 90s allowed for the introduction of more complex rhythms at around 130 bpm. Speeds like that sit surprisingly easily under slow bluesy tracks running at half speed, allowing artists like Gary and Eric to refresh their sound without compromising the overall aesthetic.

Once the album was done, Gary explained to *Guitarist* about the influences that had been brought to bear: 'I've been listening to totally different things lately. Everything I've been buying is from now—Massive Attack and Spring Heeled Jack … Music has changed so much recently. Even rock is completely different now, post Seattle. So, I've been listening to a lot of that and a lot of reggae too. I've got into Bob Marley properly for the first time.' And with a possible reference to Camilla, he went on to say that he had been hanging out 'with a lot of younger people who were into the club scene, so I got turned onto that, whereas a lot of musicians of my generation perhaps aren't open minded to that, or simply don't have a way into it'.

Andy Bradfield had mixed *Walking Wounded* and received a call from Gary's office to say they would like him to work on Gary's new album. Gary had gone back to Miraval and that's where Andy started work. He brought with him keyboardist/programmer Magnus Fiennes (brother of actor Ralph Fiennes). Andy and Magnus had worked together at Virgin's Town House Studios. Most recently, Magnus had been co-producing All Saints' debut album, which produced the 1997 worldwide hit single 'Never Ever'.

Gary was looking to Andy for additional production work and programming, adding loops and essentially reworking what he already had. However, says Andy, 'although he had recorded most of the material, we ended up recording more material from scratch, not all of it making the final album. He was very hands-on and decisive about what he wanted, very driven and pushed himself hard. If he had a very specific idea in mind, he would stop at nothing until he got there and even if he *did* get there, it would be "I think we're better off over there." It was a necessary part of the creative process even if it was time consuming.'

Gary repeated the schedule of going backwards and forwards between the UK and the French studio in the time allowed for him to be in the UK, 'then Gary wanted some strings, so we went to Abbey Road and that was full orchestra. But there were a couple of tracks where he wanted an eastern thing, that kind of bendy string motif and the London guys don't really play like that. Somebody recommended these guys—I think they were Turkish or Egyptian. These two dapper old gents came in, played these lead lines and they were amazing. We ended up layering that with the orchestra and it sounded phenomenal. The orchestra were playing the chords and the guys were all doing all the bendy motifs.'

After about a month in Miraval, they went to a studio on the island of Capri, a converted hotel where the drum room was in the old ballroom with a mirror ball still hanging from the ceiling. 'That was the only place we struggled to get a guitar sound,' says Andy. 'It transpired because they had such bad power, when they built the studio, they'd done this workaround where everything was running on a massive battery back-up, which must have cost a fortune. What you were getting out of the AC circuit wasn't a proper square wave, it was slightly clipped, which explained why the guitar amps weren't working properly. They were converting from AC to DC, storing it in batteries, inverting it and then back to DC. That was fine for the digital gear, console and tape machines, but the guitar amp is very reliant on the power that comes down the AC cord. So, we just worked on some programming elements and some vocals and he wanted to go through all the tracks before we started mixing because back then, you had to ship tapes, which was a bit of a process.' And while recording on Capri sounds glamorous, it was less so in November with the rain hammering down.

One of the last songs to be written was 'Afraid Of Tomorrow': 'I actually did one take of it with a Telecaster,' said Gary. 'I just banged through the chords and did all these little riffs which fitted over the chords at the end. Andy put them straight into the computer and did the arrangement with the computer. That way you get the freshness of your original take, each time; and then you can really mess around with it afterwards. So, we superimposed all these little arpeggios over the main rhythm. In the old days, you had to play it and play it and play it and by that time it was sounding tired.'

With the album finally in the can, says Andy, 'there was then a whole discussion of where we were going to mix. There were various studio options, none of which neither Gary nor I had been to, so we were going off spec sheets that had come back plus what other people had said. And it was a big project; in those days, we'd mix on a traditional analogue console—and I preferred an SSL console, so we needed to find somewhere with a decent SSL console. But as you looked at the more out of the way places, it was becoming harder and harder.'

Normally, Graham Lilley would have been doing all the leg work of finding the right studio. But by around November 1995, Graham had become increasingly fed up with the daily demands being expected of him in service to Gary's inability to do simple stuff like write a cheque or get cash out of an ATM. On top of which Gary was flitting from one expensive residence (a house at Stoke Row in Oxfordshire) to another—the Conrad Hotel on Chelsea Harbour—and looking to Graham to rush hither and thither sorting it all out. This harkens back to Jon Hiseman's observation that Gary never accepted he should have to be bothered by the minutiae of everyday life. But Graham, for one, had had enough and decamped to AC/DC; but, just over a year later, in early 1997, he came back.

Meanwhile, Gary and Andy Bradfield settled on Crescent Moon, Gloria Estefan's studio in Miami. They stayed at the very expensive Biltmore Hotel and began the process of mixing. 'Everything was going really well,' says Andy. 'Gary was very happy, but he was saying he wanted to do more stuff. So, Magnus, who had left by then, came out to join us in Miami for about a week and we recorded some new material and also going over old stuff, almost how you would approach a remix. On some of it, we replaced the drums with loops, Gary replayed some bits and played some bass himself.

'Gary was phenomenal musician and a lovely person, but one of those infuriating people who actually would play a completely blinding solo, then say "But I can do better"—and actually *would* do it better. I remember one time in Crescent Moon and he said, "Right, can we have a go at that solo?" So, I set up the guitar, got a really great sound, recorded the solo and he played beautifully. And I stopped the tape and he said he thought he could do it better. "Really? Are you sure?" "No, no, trust me. Keep that one if you want." In those days, it was slightly trickier because you didn't want to lose what you'd got. And of course, we were working primarily on tape (although there was some computer stuff)—so the number of tracks available to you was limited by hardware. Some of these were big songs and quite spread out. So anyway, I swopped tracks, put it in record and he bloody did do it better. I went, "You git." And we both burst out laughing, "See? I told you." He was so in tune with what he did as a guitarist—he had this innate sort of feel.

'There was a new song we had done on Capri with more keyboards. I did a quick rough mix on the desk in about half an hour and then we mixed it properly and I never beat the rough mix, so we went back to it. It was Gary who kept saying to go back to the rough mix and I was saying, "Oh, for goodness sake." But I went back and listened and I had to agree with him. It had a certain thing about it and Gary wanted to stick with it come hell or high water. And it was indicative of the album as a whole—it was bold, whether or not the fans were going to like it. And that is not an easy thing to do.'

Gary had never spent so much time and money on an album; it had to be done by Christmas 1996 and it was touch and go whether they would get to the finish line. They came home for the holidays, went back to Miami for a week in January and under increasing pressure from the record company, it was done. Guy Pratt says he gave Gary the inspiration of the title: 'It was a quote from David Coverdale. "These days, Guy, you either catch some dreadful disease or they slap a lawsuit on you. These are dark days indeed for a cocksman." But the title *Dark Days In Paradise* reflected a far more poignant truth for Gary than the perils inherent in getting your end away. Indeed, in his personality, Gary was as far away from being the archetypal confident, swaggering cock-rocker—as the story of the album photo shoot reveals.

While he was out in South Africa, fashion photographer Stuart Weston received a call from his agent to fly to Miami. He had to travel via Frankfurt and when he got to Miami airport, there was nobody to meet him, so he had to hire a car and drive to the designated hotel in torrential rain and wind, miles from where Gary was ensconced at the Biltmore. 'As soon as I got to the hotel,' says Stuart, 'I get a call from the Virgin guy to go to Gloria Estefan's studio, which was another hour and a half drive away. As we are going up in the lift, the Virgin guy is very, very nervous, telling me how Gary is terribly, terribly shy. So, we go into the engineer's room and there is Gary in a brilliant white T-shirt and white jeans looking very tanned and healthy. Virgin guy introduces us, I say "Hi," and Gary doesn't even look at me, so it was bit awkward. By then I was completely knackered, a bit phased by all of this.

'There was this long, white leather-look seating running right down one side of the wall and leaning up at the end was a really nice-looking cream-coloured Strat. So, I picked it up, said what I thought of it and Gary made a few comments about how some guitar god had given it to him, maybe B.B. King, I can't recall who. Now, I'm a drummer, but I can mess about a bit on guitar and the only thing I knew was this … [proceeds to articulate the sounds of the "Parisenne Walkways" riff]. And you could have cut the atmosphere with a knife. So, I looked up and went, "What?" And Gary said, "You cheeky sod." "What? What are you talking about?" And he just burst out laughing, while the Virgin guy was just choking himself and I really had no idea what I'd done, I didn't remember it was his song. And that really broke the ice. We agreed a schedule and everything and when I got back in the lift with the guy he said, "You're a fuckin' genius." "Honestly mate, I had no idea what I was doing."'

They were due to shoot down at Key Biscayne, but the weather just wouldn't relent. Stuart was only booked for a day, but the time was going past and nothing was happening. However, by now, he was getting on really well with Gary, so he agreed to stay for as long as it took, just for that day fee, providing they paid expenses and moved him to Biltmore to be near Gary. 'What I did learn about Gary was how incredibly shy, sensitive and insecure he was. He was just a lovely sweet, soft guy, But everyone around him seemed to think he was a bit of an ogre.

'He asked me to his hotel suite to get for my opinion on music he had recorded, which blew me away. I mean, he was a legend and he was asking me! His default was the blues, but in that hotel I heard stuff that was way, way above that artistically and intellectually. He was making some fabulous music.

'He confided in me that there was a girl in the video shoot they had done for the album that he thought was fabulous. And he wanted me to get her involved in the stills shoot for the cover. The conversation went like this:

'"What if they won't let me book her?"

'"You're Gary Moore for fuck's sake. *You* tell *them* what you want—after all, you're paying for it."

'"So, what shall I do?"

'"You call her agency. You book her. You go and pick her up in a big fuck-off stretch limo."

'And that's exactly what he did. We got to the first morning of the shoot on the beach. This big Lincoln stretch pulls up next to the location bus and this lovely girl (I can't remember her name) gets in the bus. And Gary completely clammed up. Every time she looked at him, he just blushed. Couldn't say a word.

'We sat out the whole morning and it just wouldn't stop raining. So, I said, "Let's do some shots in the back of the limo." So, I got Gary to sit on the right and the girl to sit on my left, with some distance between them, both looking out the window as if they had just had a row. Then I said to the girl, "I want you to open your legs a little, be a bit naughty." And Gary cried out, "Stuart! You can't say that." But the girl just giggled and she thought it was hilarious. Then I said to Gary, "I want you to put your hand on her leg." He went bright red. He just couldn't do it. He was so embarrassed. He actually did do it in the end, but they didn't use the shot.

'Sometime later, Gary called me. I was in the pub with some mates and he said he'd come over for a pint. When I told my mates who was coming over, they went "Whaaat?" But I did think Gary didn't have any real mates. And it did freak me out a bit because it shouldn't have been like that for somebody like Gary Moore. But I have known a lot of famous people and they don't have many mates because so many people want a piece of them.'

While he never would be specific in public, he often wore his heart on his record sleeve and one of the key themes running through this album—arguably one of the highlights of Gary's recording career—full of invention and surprise—was his relationship with Camilla. Gary gave a promo interview in 1997 in which he said, 'Every song on the album is something to do with what was going on in my life at the time of making the record, so you know, they're very personal songs … they're kinda hard to talk about … they're all true stories … I tell the truth when I write, I don't make things up, I can't do that.' All you need to do is join the dots.

There was one word that kept coming up when people were asked about Gary's feelings towards Camilla—and that word was 'besotted'. The trouble for Gary was that there isn't much evidence these feelings were reciprocated at anything like the same level of intensity. Gary put women on a pedestal and then felt dreadfully let down when they didn't meet up to his vision of romantic love, his maybe unrealistic expectations. Worse still, Camilla's ex-boyfriend, still living in Henley, was heard to remark that in the local area Gary was regarded as 'the goose that laid the golden egg'. And those around Gary were highly sceptical of what was going on. He spared no expense—cars, stabling fees for horses, the finest hotels and restaurants, first class flights—and apparently gave Camilla a hefty chunk of the damages he won from the newspaper libel lawsuit. At one point, Camilla just took off for Africa, and became very ill, so Gary covered all the medical and other expenses to get her home.

Gary himself didn't like the sun, but the main reason they were looking for 'out of the way places', as Andy Bradfield said, in which to record and mix, was because Camilla wanted to be in the sun as part of her recuperation. In the end, she just seemed to disappear; to those around Gary, one minute she was there, the next—gone.

Laid bare in the lyrics are all the twists and turns of the emotional rollercoaster that Gary was locked into: adoration, joy, denial, bitterness, anger, resentment, melancholy and resignation. Often for the artist who wants to express anguish and pain in their lives through their work, there has to be a waiting period of reflection beyond the turmoil before all the trauma can be sublimated in the art. Gary was actually writing songs while mired in his unhappiness, so what you are hearing on the record is pain as a currently lived experience, while at the same time, he was keeping professional control of the whole recording process. In Gary Husband's view, 'Gary seemed to thrive on the turbulence of these uncertain relationships, draw from them, as it were, and pour all that turbulence into his songs and his playing.' Gary appeared grimly obsessed by the thing hurting him the most, hopelessly locked into his own misery.

As we have heard, Gary took inordinate pains over running orders to get complimentary dynamics between songs—so that would have taken priority over a chronology of life with Camilla. You have to hop around the album to piece together the story and some relevant songs never made the final cut at all, appearing only as maxi singles or as extra tracks on the subsequent re-release in 2003. And the title track is 'hidden' at the end and not listed.

The songs were written over a two-year period, starting during BBM days and the beginning of his time with Camilla. 'I Have Found My Love In You'—the first track on the album to introduce those more modern ambient sounds reflects the first flush of romance and the scepticism of others, but also with some later reflection of the subsequent cooling of ardour.

I can still remember
Like it was yesterday
The pain inside my heart
As you turned to walk away

I don't know
I don't care
What my friends all say
I don't know I don't care
Love you anyway.

But reading the lyrics of the seven songs that could conceivably be concerned with his relationship, this was really the only positive reference. 'One Good Reason' finds Gary as a small, trapped voice, before the riff kicks in and the song explodes with anger and resentment, with descending Abbey Road Beatles strings and a 'White Room' wah-wah power chord sequence until Gary is reduced once more to that still, small vulnerable voice. 'Cold Wind Blows' is especially dark, speaking not simply to a deep hurt, but also that this person was inherently incapable of love and warm feelings as he wrote about her 'bad seed'. This is a howling voodoo world blues in the night combining Native American and aboriginal tribal sounds with sitar and a growling fuzz-tone solo. There is real menace in the song, hints of dark forces. Gary was quite superstitious when it came to the occult, and some have suggested that Camilla claimed powers in that direction. 'Always There For You' makes it pretty clear that Gary saw the relationship as a one-way street, while there is a direct reference to Camilla's own travels in 'All The Way From Africa', when Gary asks whether she found what she was looking for.

Symbolically, perhaps, the title track is also the hidden track: beneath the patina of sun, warmth and well-being to be found in an island paradise like Barbados lies Gary's sense of loneliness and unhappiness with his personal life. And while there may be some poetic licence in the lyrics that follow, still you can't help feeling for somebody who, however naively, gives their all in a relationship, only for it to end quite cruelly—although some could be forgiven for thinking this was also poetic justice. By the time Stuart Weston arrived in Miami, around March 1997, Camilla was gone.

I should be feelin' so happy
To wake up each day in the sun
But I can't seem to raise a smile
Since this day's begun.
'Cos when you're feelin' so lonely
There's just one thing you need
Dark days in paradise
Dark days indeed
I followed her to the airport
I got down on my knees
But she stood there smiling
Ignoring all my pleas.
Then she left me so lonely
It made my poor heart bleed
Dark days in paradise
Dark days indeed.

'Business As Usual', on the other hand, makes no attempt to hide its autobiographical inspiration, taking us through Gary's childhood and into the early years of his professional life with Phil, the Stranglies, Skid Row and the influence of Peter Green, before leaping forward to the 'scandal' of his affair with Camilla and the admittance of 'a heart broken, but it wasn't for the first or the last time'.

When people are lonely or depressed and unhappy with their current circumstances they often reflect on happier times. As if to bring those memories back to life, Gary did some recording with Stranglies in 1996. Having not released an album since *Heavy Petting* in 1970, they embarked on *Alternative Medicine: that difficult third album.* The band had done some recording in London and came back to Ireland where Gary joined them at a small analogue studio in a place called Ballyvourney in south-west County Cork: 'It was right in the middle of the peaks area,' recalls Tim Booth, 'and he really liked being there and really enjoyed that we were hanging out together once again. It was a self-financing album and we said to Gary, "What shall we pay you?" And he just laughed, "You couldn't afford me," and he just did it for nothing.' There was lots of joking and laughing.

For a brief moment, Gary could once again be the young fresh-faced guitar slinger who just rode into town, not Gary Moore Ltd with a bunch of people relying on him for their livelihood.

'A while later, he came round to see me after he had done some overdubs for an animated film of mine,' says Tim. 'My partner was running a laundry service. We sat in the house with a bottle of wine and then she said, "Oh, I've got to deliver this ironing." And she looked at Gary and said, "Would you do it? The guy I'm delivering to is one of your biggest fans." It was a chemist who also played guitar. He'd developed some photos I'd taken of Gary in the studio. He'd looked at these photos and said, "Is that Gary Moore?" "Yes, it is." "Oh, I'd love to meet him." So, Gary says, "Yes, I'm up for that." So, he walked into Mark's shop, it was about seven in the evening, with the ironing in his arms held out straight in front of him and said, "Your ironing, sir." And Mark looked him, his jaw just fell to the ground and he ran out the shop to his car to get an album and cassette for Gary to sign.'

In 'Business As Usual', Gary makes a reference to Sylvia, the Tipperary girl who took his virginity and the fact that he had 'three children'—there was Jack and Gus, but of course also Saoirse. So guilty had Gary been about the break-up, he had virtually written her out of his life script, even saying she was simply the product of a one -night stand. At odd moments in her early childhood, Saoirse saw Gary, 'then on my tenth birthday, this taxi arrived with a birthday card and £20, the first time that had ever happened'.

Their first sustained contact didn't occur until Gary had left Kerry and was with Camilla: 'There were lots of phone calls during BBM days,' says Saoirse, 'and we tried to keep it light. We talked about me being at drama college and music but he was obsessed with Camilla and wanted to talk about her all the time. I just let him talk. I was very angry with what he had done [leaving Kerry]. He'd spoken to my mum just before the story broke saying he definitely wanted to be in touch with me and build bridges. Then it all happened and I thought, *Oh, this is never going to change.*

'Then he disappeared for about a year, he changed his number and I couldn't get hold of him, so I was pretty angry about that. Then I got this message on the answer phone, timed at about five in the morning. He was in Miami, but so drunk and in a real mess, heartbroken, and that led to the longest period of being in touch.' But their relationship was, as Saoirse puts it, 'messy and complicated. As we got to know each other, I think he got more ashamed of being absent. If I talked about childhood memories, he would get very uncomfortable and change the subject. I felt I couldn't be myself. It was weird because we *did* start out being ourselves and then it got more difficult.' It was Saoirse this time who says she 'walked away' as she wasn't anything like 'healed' enough not to be angry at Gary's discomfiture. It would be a few more years before they resumed contact.

Lyrically, much of the rest of the album dealt with wider quasi-philosophical and eastern religious themes about our place in the world and the need for peace and reconciliation. A good example was 'Afraid Of Tomorrow', which featured the Egyptian violinists and North African throat singers and was inspired by Paulo Coelho's book *The Alchemist*. An allegorical novel, *The Alchemist* follows a young Andalusian shepherd named Santiago in his journey to Egypt, after having a recurring dream of finding treasure there. Gary's stated intention was to musically tap into the wellspring of all his influences over the years and 'One Fine Day' resonates with a late-60s George Harrison-driven Beatles feel and may also have reflected Gary's recent and close relationship with the former Beatle.

'Like Angels' is a classic Gary Moore ballad, probably the most perfectly realised track on the album and one that Gary knew was special even as he was writing it: 'I did a little demo of it at home just with some keyboards and a drum machine, just very simple. But even at that stage, if a song's any good, you can always tell it's gonna happen, you can tell the first five minutes … it's one of my favourites … I like the whole theme of the song … I did something different on this with the guitar from what I had done before in there … there's a bit right before the solo … this little breakdown which to me every time I hear it, it really makes me … I dunno what it is, something about that sequence right before the solo.'

Gary goes on to explain how he produced a startling effect on the guitar, a ghostly, ethereal cry: 'I wanted the guitar to sound like an angel singing, so I was trying to find a way to do it and I picked up a screwdriver with a really long point, a real thin blade and I put the guitar on my lap and started playing with this screwdriver and it just soared … And then I used it again on the song after that, "What Are We Here For?", it's got a much more eastern flavour to it, not a bluesy kind of slide … you can move the thing around a lot quicker because it's a much smaller surface actually touching the string and it gives you a lot more dexterity that way.'

If there is much autobiography in the lyrics, then Gary also takes the listener on a tour of his musical influences. Going through the album, including the additional tracks, you can hear Hank Marvin, music from the *Grinding Stone* era, Chicago blues as well as sounds clearly inspired by recording in the Caribbean, the paradoxically chilled calypso beats on 'Dark Days In Paradise' and unadorned reggae. But maybe the primary inspiration for Gary in veering away from expectations was Jack Bruce.

Gary reckoned that but for BBM and the chance to work closely with Jack, the new album might never have happened: 'He kind of freed me to go back in this more melodic direction and to start writing more interesting songs.' Gary said that Jack had always been an influence and not just because of Cream, 'but his solo stuff as well. I used to listen to all his solo albums, there was some incredible music on there, you know if people only knew how talented he was … he's like a modern-day classical composer. He doesn't write within the constraints of rock or anything, he does his own thing, he's totally free, there are no barriers there, he writes in all kinds of styles and he makes it work. So, to be around him, I could feel this thing creeping back into the music again and that led me to write these songs, definitely.'

Dark Days In Paradise is a beautifully crafted, sophisticated album of modern composition and a credit to everyone who helped in its creation. While admitting the album was not an unalloyed success, Gary Husband believes that 'Like Angels' and 'Where Did We Go Wrong?' in particular, were 'real, real jewels, lovely and immensely soulful ballads. That's the Gary I remember with a lot of fondness, the soulful, vulnerable and passionate side as represented by his performances there. It was really very nice to have been around and taken part in those recordings. Guy also played beautifully on those two songs and I was really impressed with him and [it was] immediately comfortable for me to play together with him.'

If you had listened to *Ballads And Blues 1982–1994*, you would have realised the album wasn't a million miles away from Gary's inherent soulful lyricism, but it wasn't rock, it wasn't blues and the guitar complimented the material rather than dominating it. So, it was never going to be a Top 10 album, and while the single 'One Good Reason' was quite well received critically, the usual reviewers of Gary's work in the rock and metal press were not impressed. Even so, the album still managed around Top 30 in most of the territories where Gary usually sold well, although it only managed Top 50 in the UK.

The next question was, would Gary tour the album? Gary certainly enjoyed playing with Guy and Gary Husband: 'I've got such a good rhythm section that they can play so steadily on anything so there's no problem with that.' And they all wanted Magnus on the tour too.

What would they play? If Gary was going to tour following the release of a new album, he had to feature some of the new material. How would the audience react? Prior to the start of the tour, Gary joked with *Guitarist* magazine about the set list: 'I've been thinking how I'm going to put a set together from the past that can fit in with this. I could even make up a set of completely new material, but I know there's a few that we'll never get away without playing—"My Way" and "It's Not Unusual"—you know, all my big hits.' But once he got out there, touring mainly the European blues-rock hinterland of Germany and Scandinavia, home to his biggest fan base—things did not go too well.

As Magnus says, 'audiences were expecting blues and rock. They were shocked—not dissimilar to Dylan going electric at the Newport Folk Festival. There were cries of "Blues!" and "Rock'n'roll!" There were some very confused faces when Gary Husband would be hitting Octopads and triggering loops.' Guy agrees: 'There was an unbelievably awkward drum and bass section of the show. We knew what was going to happen and it was like, "Do we really have to do this?" Gary's take on drum and bass was really, really laudable. In theory, it can be taken as a very muso type of music—jazz/funk, complicated drum patterns. But he didn't really understand it is all supposed to be slightly out of tune and played by people who don't really know what the chords are. So, Gary's going for a more crisp, Herbie Hancock-type fusion, which isn't going to work for a drum'n'bass audience and absolutely isn't going to work for a rock audience. We were at the Montreux Jazz Festival. We did that bit and there was just fuckin' silence, tumbleweed and somebody in the audience shouted out, "No, Gary, blues and rock'n'roll!" So, I stomped up to the mike and went, "Yeah, rock me Amadeus."'

Looking at the Montreux concert, the reaction wasn't quite that bad. Yes, there were tumbleweed moments for the more ambient selections, but when performed live 'One Fine Day' and 'Cold Wind Blow' were straight-ahead rock songs and there was plenty of guitar play in 'Business As Usual', which the audience appreciated at the end. And there was a good smattering of the songs Gary would always have to play—even throwing in a rampant version of 'Out In The Fields', all of which naturally earned the biggest cheers.

When it came to re-creating the new album on stage, Gary wanted it played like the record sounded—and was probably even more stubbornly determined than ever in the face of a lukewarm response to the new songs. Magnus could see the inherent conflict here, 'as a musical director, you have a very specific vision of how you want things to sound and you arrange things in a very specific way and you want to be able to replicate that every time, deliver that night after night. You don't want musicians veering off that path too much. But of course, it can be frustrating as a player if you don't get the opportunity to augment and extemporise. On recreating the *Dark Days In Paradise* album, it was very specific and because the rhythms were being triggered by Gary Husband, there wasn't much room for lots of freedom. It all had to work tempo-wise, part-wise, the mechanics of the playback of various elements. So, it took a while to plan out and it was quite meticulous.'

Although he was calling the shots rhythmically for the live performance of the new material, it was the way Gary Husband played a blues standard where the two Garys butted heads again. 'On one occasion, I broke the rules in "Pretty Woman" or something and did something a little different. He glared at me right after it, evidently pretty displeased, and as we finished the song proceeded to notify the audience, "The drummer's played too many nights at Ronnie Scott's! Ha!" Well, I didn't walk off but I was fighting every impulse to! After the concert, though, I went straight to him and warned him that if he ever publicly tried to humiliate me onstage again in front of a packed audience like that, I would not put up with it. I'm not in the business of playing "anti" any song or piece of music. I'm a musician, above everything, and I needed to make a big distinction clear to him. I can't play exactly the same every night, like a computer … and he'd be certainly hard pushed getting someone like Jack Bruce or Ginger Baker to do that. I told him in no uncertain terms that if he wanted a workhorse drummer who never, ever deviated in the slightest and played every single thing verbatim he should just get himself one. Then Gary would go to every possible length to tell me how treasured I was in his band, and how his gig is "tailor made" for me! Oh, man.'

The gigs were nothing if not eventful, most notably when Magnus got lost in the moment. 'We played some biker festival,' recalls Guy. 'Now, Magnus isn't really a live player and he used to get a bit carried away. He'd play machine-gun effects and mime machine-gunning the audience. He was posing so hard that he dislocated his shoulder. So, he just ran off into the crowd leaving us to carry on without a keyboard player. He was running around hoping somebody would pop his shoulder back, but these big bikers were just a bunch of Jessies. Eventually, he found the Red Cross tent, which was full of people having freak outs on home-made psychedelics. He made it back to the stage for the third number looking white as a sheet.'

Offstage, though, the tour went very smoothly. Guy was very impressed with the setup: 'We were very well looked after. Gary paid very well, the hotels were lovely and it was a pretty relaxed schedule. At the end of the tour, me and Magnus clubbed together and bought Gary a really nice Donna Karan puffa jacket as an end of tour present—and you rarely buy the artist a present at the end of a tour.' Much of the credit for the organisation goes to the no-nonsense professionalism of the stand-in tour manager, the future Mrs Moore—Jo Rendle.

Gary's office was based in Richmond and was run by Melissa Fountain. She had been a booker at the Circle Agency, done some production and had many contacts in the business. Melissa was recruited by Pete Brewis, who took over as Gary's guitar technician during Graham Lilley's absence. 'When Gary was abroad,' she recalls, 'we could spend three or four hours on the phone depending on what he was doing and this was before I'd ever met him and we'd have these intimate phone calls. We'd talk about his childhood, which was clearly a tender subject. I was going out with Phil Lynott before he died. His flat was always full of horrible, horrible people. I never told Gary about me and Phil.'

Melissa's husband Richard knew Jo. She was a graphic designer and part of an arty, creative set who hung out in Chelsea. Jo came in to take care of the office one time when Melissa went on holiday. Gary and Richard became very close; Gary presented him with the fringe jacket he'd only worn once for the cover of *Wild Frontier*—it still had the label in it.

Melissa says that Jo and Gary got on really well, 'so when it came to promotional work in Germany for *Dark Days In Paradise*, I said "Why don't you take Jo?" He said yes, and they pretty much fell in love on the plane.'

Because Gary had been out of the country, most of the initial contact with Jo had been down the phone. He got back to ask, 'Who's that girl?' 'When the album promotion came up, he asked me out to dinner and I said no,' says Jo. 'So, he brought it up again in a very loud voice in first class on the plane and I said yes, just to shut him up. We did some dates in Germany, but he didn't want to tour it. He said he was sick of being on the road and the whole Camilla thing had left him pretty damaged and his trust in people was zero.'

Eventually, Gary agreed to a tour on the condition that Jo came along. Gary's tour manager at the time, Andy Crookston, wasn't available, so despite being a complete novice, Jo got the gig. She was very careful to keep everything professional. They slept in different rooms to start with, because otherwise it would undermine her authority with the crew—it would be like Gary's brought his girlfriend on the road. And once the tour was over, Jo played a key role in stabilising Gary, getting him more grounded in the daily realities of life.

This was very important because there were changes afoot in Gary's business affairs. Towards the end of 1996, John Martin quit as manager after various disputes with Gary and Gary's accountant/business manager Colin Newman. Gary soldered on without a day-to-day manager for a while, but felt the loss, and so Stewart Young came back as manager from 1998 for a couple of years.

More significantly, following disappointing sales of *Dark Days In Paradise*, Gary was dropped by Virgin, after a relationship lasting fifteen years. By then, one of Gary's allies at Virgin, Peter Price, was working for Warner Bros in Ireland. He came back to London to start a small Warner label called Coalition and commissioned demos from Gary in the hope of being able to sign him. 'But by the time we got round to talking,' says Peter, 'they fired me and dropped the label.'

This left Gary without a deal or an advance while he worked on the next album. Although more associated with his past recordings, Gary called up Ian Taylor to co-produce, engineer and mix the album. Apart from Gary who played guitar, bass, sang and provided additional keyboards, the only other recognised musician on the album was Gary Husband, who came in for a couple of tracks. Otherwise, it was down to the programming skills of Roger King with some additional work from Phil Nicholas.

Gary installed himself at Marcus Studio 3 for a block booking of five to six months. 'We had the smaller room at the studio set up 24/7,' says Graham Lilley, 'so we could set aside a few weeks at a time, depending on Ian Taylor's schedule, and also take weeks off without moving the equipment or disturbing the recording console. Tracks could be left to come back to after a period of time, do rewrites, etc. It meant a longer recording period, but because Gary didn't have a record deal at the time, it was more of a laid-back process.'

The album lived up to its title of *A Different Beat* as Gary explored the drum and bass terrain far more explicitly than on *Dark Days In Paradise*. Gary was influenced in part by the work of Fatboy Slim, to whom one track is dedicated, and perhaps also the British band Apollo 440, who produced an eclectic mix of sounds including rock, ambient and techno. Gary went in with finished songs, suggesting that much had been written over the same period as *Dark Days*. Lyrically, the new album could be regarded as *Dark Days 2* as Gary continued to exorcise the demons of his doomed relationship with Camilla.

Gary knew full well by flirting with drum and bass, he was on to a loser from the start, 'because the people who liked my guitar playing would have hated those rhythms and the people who liked those rhythms would've hated my guitar playing. And me even more!'

In truth, though, he was doing himself a disservice because while he was right that the club audience would not have been impressed, there was far more to enjoy of Gary's guitar playing on this album than the last. In fact, there was enough appropriate material to regard it as a modern blues album as much as some benighted effort at being cool. The best examples are 'Go On Home', 'Lost In Your Love', 'Bring My Baby Back', 'Can't Help Myself' and especially 'Worry No More'. There is incendiary slashing guitar, raking slide over thunderous beats, the sweeping blues lyricism of 'Surrender' and with 'Worry No More' a compelling mash-up of the spare blues styles of John Lee Hooker, R.L. Burnside and Jimi Hendrix, who Gary honours on the album with a cover of 'Fire'.

There has always been much speculation as to the direction Hendrix would have taken. Probably in the 70s, he might have gone down a jazz-fusion route, but with all the emergent technology of the 90s, Hendrix too would have embraced the opportunity to update his sound while remaining true to his blues roots as Gary does on that track.

Record company executives came down to the studio to hear what they thought might be another *Still Got The Blues* only to leave somewhat bemused. Eventually, a deal was struck with Castle, but as Gary predicted, the album fell between stools and pretty much sank without trace. He said later to Neville Marten that he thought the guitar journalist was the only person who actually liked the album.

For now, the time for experimentation was over, Gary had the rest of his career to think about; and there was family to provide for—Jo was pregnant. The blues train needed to leave the station once more.

13

BUSINESS AS USUAL

Gary was off the road in 1998 while he recorded the album but responded to Jack Bruce's request to play a couple of gigs in a trio with Gary Husband in the north of England. Jack repaid the favour by appearing at a charity gig with the same line-up in Chelsea, organised by Jo, campaigning to save an adventure playground next door to where she and Gary were now living. Gary's nomadic existence at this time was dizzying in its complexity; he seemed to be buying and selling properties with the same regularity as you might buy a pint of milk.

Having left Kerry, Gary had first moved to Pishill, where he had the office/studio he had been renting, then bought a place with Camilla in Henley, selling that when they split. Jo had been dividing her time between Pishill and her own place in Lots Road in Chelsea, so she could get to her art degree studies at London Guildhall. But she found Gary's retreat far too rural for her liking whereas Gary liked the peace and quiet of the countryside and didn't want to move permanently back to London, although he still retained a flat there. The next step was to buy a place in Henley, which needed a lot of work doing on it, so that Jack and Gus could visit at the weekends, as by now Kerry had sold Little Pastures, the gated house in Shiplake, and moved to Marlow.

But Gary's business was in London, and he was spending a fortune in taxis commuting backwards and forwards and paying hefty hotel bills staying at the Conrad Hotel in Chelsea. When Jo became pregnant (Lily was born September 3, 1998), she started getting Gary's feet on the ground, finally persuading him to buy a flat in the Conrad Complex in Chelsea Harbour.

Although it was just a charity gig, here were three musicians who were never going to give less than 100 percent and they ripped into a selection of Cream, Jack Bruce solo and BBM songs including a long jam version of 'Born Under A Bad Sign' and 'Sleepy Time', which Jack dedicated to the song's lyricist, his ex-wife Janet, who was in the audience. It was a highly emotional night for both of them—the first time they had met since the tragic death of their son from an asthma attack in 1997.

The performance from the band that would have formed instead of BBM demonstrated that if it had got off the ground, it could well have succeeded beyond the tempestuous few months of BBM. While egos could still have pulled it apart, it wouldn't have had to deal with the 'second-hand Cream' tag nor the always simmering tensions between Jack and Ginger—and with a band of composers, could have delivered some thrilling music.

The more immediate issue for Gary was a tour for 1999. The name of the game was to re-connect with his blues audience, so Gary was on the look-out for musicians who would provide a sympathetic and straightforward accompaniment to his guitar.

Keyboardist Vic Martin was a seasoned session and touring musician who had a regular gig with Barnes Blues at the Bull's Head pub over in west London. The bassist in Barnes Blues was a veteran of the London blues and rock scene, Pete Rees. Barnes Blues would often invite guests to play. One night, the trio were supposed to turn up but only Gary did, so guitarist Papa George invited Gary to the stage. Afterwards, Jo got Pete's phone number for Gary and from there, Pete got Vic involved, who says, 'the last thing I expected was to be offered a gig with Gary Moore'. Graham Lilley sent Pete and Vic a CD with all the songs—with the exception of 'Fire'—that would comprise a standard Gary Moore blues set.

Walking By Myself
Oh, Pretty Woman
Since I Met You Baby
Tore Down
Need Your Love So Bad
I Loved Another Woman
All Your Love
Fire
Still Got The Blues (For You)
Too Tired
The Sky Is Crying
Further On Up The Road
The Blues Is Alright
Parisienne Walkways

Gary Husband was the drummer for the first few gigs, but doing straight blues wasn't really his scene and he left to join Mark King's band during the period in which Level 42 had disbanded. Gary held two days worth of rehearsals, trying out eight different drummers, including Ted McKenna, with whom Gary had played in the Greg Lake band, and Geoff Dunn (Earth Band, Van Morrison and Procol Harum). The last guy was Darrin Mooney (recommended by Don Airey), who had recently started playing on a casual basis with Primal Scream. As soon as they started playing 'Surrender' from *A Different Beat*, Gary and Graham looked at each other—and Darrin was offered the gig—which, once the Primal gig became official, started a push-me/pull-you for Darrin's services between the two bands. They shared the same agent, so when Primal Scream were off the road, Darrin would be available for Gary. Over the next decade, Pete, Vic and Darrin would provide the backbone of the most stable line-up in Gary's solo history.

Aged just 22 in 1999, Darrin was a talented but relative inexperienced drummer while Pete and Vic too were stepping up from the easy-going, informal world of the London pub rock scene. The rigours of a Gary Moore rehearsal took them somewhat unawares.

Gary wanted to introduce some of the original numbers from *A Different Beat* into the set. They went with 'Surrender' and 'Lost In Your Love', both relatively easy, but also an instrumental that Gary might have had in the can for *A Different Beat*, but didn't use at the time, called 'The Prophet'. 'We soon called this "The Bastard",' says Vic. 'It was complicated, you couldn't busk it, it had to be learnt. And if you got one note wrong, it would just ring out. You had to get it right and we went over and over it until my hands almost bled—and worse still—I had to start it!'

And early on, the young, feisty Darrin found himself caught up in the complexities of Gary's relationship with drummers: 'I had a bit more ego back then. But I look back on it now and it was his gig. I just wanted to do more. I did find a way round it because if you were a weak character you could get intimidated and I've seen bass players with Gary fuck up the simplest of lines because they were feeling intimidated. Gary would hear something he didn't like and he would pick up on it. And I did have run-ins with Gary from time to time, but he was usually right—and I just wanted to be a drummer and hit more things! I was like, "You want more of a Mitch Mitchell vibe, more ghost notes?" "No, no—just play on the hat." But he would let me have a lot more freedom when he was soloing because I would kick him up the arse and he loved that because then he'd go up a gear. I could build it up and do phrases and he'd latch on to them, so the bass player had to be solid. We did have that Jimi Hendrix/Mitch Mitchell thing going in the blues numbers.' Graham Lilley recalls that both musicians 'would bash ten bells out of each other in soundchecks'.

Pete was just astonished at the level of Gary's musicianship: 'We were in rehearsal in Music Bank, just messing around, and he started playing John McLaughlin's *Inner Mounting Flame*. It was a really complicated piece of music and he was just messing about.' Vic on hearing Gary take off says simply, 'I nearly had a heart attack.'

The first leg of what was known as the *Different Beat* tour kicked off with a short UK run and before heading off to Europe. But they had only done four dates in early November when disaster struck. Guitarists who play all the time develop calluses on their fingers, which build up and form protective pads allowing players to bend and pull very thin metal strings without cutting themselves and making it impossible to play. Tour manager Andy Crookston relates what happened: 'We were in the E-Werk in Cologne and Darren (Main) said that Gary wanted to see me. I went to the dressing room and he said, "I've got a problem." The hard pad of skin on the little finger of his left hand had got detached. He said, "Look, this is what happens"—and he pushed the string and the string just disappeared into his finger. We tried everything including superglue, but it just wasn't working.'

The place was sold out, the audience chanting his name, 'Gary got rather panicky about the bad reaction this would cause. I told him to be calm, an announcement would be made and then we would leave to drive back to the hotel. Leaving suddenly would make it look worse. So, I made the announcement and the audience took it well—better than running out the building.' While Gary flew back to London to get medical attention, the band went on to different places in the hope that the tour could resume, but to no avail.

'Gary was very appreciative of the way I handled it,' says Andy. 'Later gave me a very generous gift in the first-class lounge at Oslo airport—it was a Émile Gallé vase—"Crookston—come 'ere"—and it's one of the nicest things I've got—a lovely thing to remember him by.' That finger incident cost Gary and the band the rest of the European tour, although fortunately they were able to reschedule all the dates the following year, in 2000. This was dubbed as the second leg of the *Different Beat* tour where drummer Graham Walker came in to replace Darrin who was on Primal Scream duties.

For the first time in his career, Gary looked east instead of west and played his first gig in Russia. The band played in Estonia, then drove hundreds of miles to the Russian border, where they were kept waiting for four hours before being allowed through. Once there, the roads were atrocious. They were in two cars: a people carrier and a Mercedes. Vic Martin had a bad back while Gary was just getting fed up being thrown around as the Mercedes bounced in and out of the potholes. 'We were in the middle of a bloody forest,' says Pete. 'Gary stopped the car, got out and said he wasn't going any further until they got a decent car. About fifteen minutes later, this big stretch limo appears out of the woods. No idea where that came from. Then we had a police escort, flashing lights and sirens all the way to St Petersburg.'

Once in the New Arena, the army controlled the crowd, which was kept about 500 yards from the stage. Nobody stood up until 'Parisienne Walkways', at which point the army lost control completely and everybody rushed down to the front of the stage.

With the tour over and all the cancelled dates honoured, they went back home to record Gary's comeback blues album *Back To The Blues*. Chris Tsangarides was again producing, working in a control-room created especially for the recording. Graham Lilley explains: 'Rehearsals were normally held at Music Bank in one of the two big studios and the Sony Walkman cassette recorders would always be on to record the sessions. These were great for picking up the room sound, but sometimes the vocals got a little lost underneath the sound of the band. So, I would set up the monitor console in the studio to record to DAT; we just needed to add some room mics and got a few interesting rough tapes for Gary to play later at home. And with chatting over the results of those tapes and cassettes came the idea to use the room to actually record in with a mobile studio parked downstairs in the car park.

'The idea moved on to building a control room in the lounge area of the studio. It had a full-length double-glazed window installed, looking into the rehearsal room, and a "cat flap" to run the multicore cable through, so you could keep the double set of doors to the lounge shut and keep the sound out.

'We had already bought a 24-track digital recorder for *A Different Beat*. Chris had all the mikes, effects and so on—all we needed was a valve desk and to put up some acoustic panelling. We rented the space, did a deal on the day rate—we weren't going to be knocking anything down, just shifting some furniture around. It worked well because we could rehearse and do takes at the same time.' Gary had always liked the idea of setting up his own studio and he and Graham had looked at various buildings over the years, but this was close to making that happen.

Gary's propensity to rehearse and record at concert volume did cause Vic a few problems: 'He used a battery of deafening Marshall amplifiers and always wore earplugs, while I couldn't hear my poor little 40-watt Leslie cabinet acoustically and had to hear via two powerful monitors placed either side of the Hammond. I rarely ever had any problems playing live, however, as we always had great monitor engineers aboard. We recorded the album at Music Bank with all the recording equipment installed in the lounge area. It was very Heath Robinson, but it worked and the recording process, which can so often be like root canal dentistry, was relatively painless.'

In interviews, Gary explained his ambition for the album: 'I wasn't trying to make *Still Got The Blues* again. That was made after coming off the back of playing rock for a long time and there was a lot of overplaying. I think I've got away from that with this record. It's taken me ten years to do it, though. I wanted to show people that when I play blues now, it's a bit different. Because I was using the hollow semi-acoustic, I was getting a different sound, a clearer sound and I wanted the music and the sound to tie in together and be very simple and very direct. I couldn't write very complicated songs because that would have just ruined the whole thing and just taken it somewhere else, so anything that didn't fit in, I just chucked out.

'Chris [Tsangarides] has got this really natural sound and that's what I wanted on the record, so it sounded like you were actually there with the band. We didn't use lots of echo and stuff, we just kept it raw. Even to the point where "Stormy Monday" is completely live, that was a rough mix. Same with "Drowning In Tears"—that was one take, the only time we ever played it. I thought it would be the hardest of the lot, because it's so long, but we all got it right first time … It only took about a month to make the entire record.'

After two albums of dedicated, complex studio work all over the world, Gary just wanted to kick the dust off his boots and let rip. The success of *Still Got The Blues* could have opened up a new commercial platform for the type of lighter blues coming from Eric or Chris Rea, but that was never going to work for Gary. Fans would have been relieved to hear muscular blues and blues-rock tracks like 'Enough Of The Blues', 'Cold Black Night' and 'How Many Lies'.

Gary's influences were never far below the surface; the clipped aggression of the soloing on 'Stormy Monday' echoing Eric's solo on 'Have You Heard' (*Beano* album); 'Drowning In Tears', an extended reworking of Fleetwood Mac's 'Looking For Somebody' from their debut album; and the Roy Buchanan feel on the Eastern-flavoured 'The Prophet'. 'Picture Of The Moon' was a Gary Moore signature ballad echoing 'Parisienne Walkways' and 'Still Got The Blues', while Gary plumped for another Yardbirds cover, this time, Billy Boy Arnold's 'I Ain't Got You.' Released in March 2001 on yet another new label, Sanctuary, the album reclaimed some of Gary's lost chart positioning of recent years, doing best in Sweden.

They toured strongly across the UK and Europe to promote the album: 'The band were particularly tight,' says Vic, 'and because we were only a four piece, the travel arrangements—luxury tour bus—and hotels were always first class. I have some great memories of that tour … Darrin and Pete were always up for a laugh.

On a night off at the Celtic Manor in Newport, we had quite a few drinks. On returning to our rooms, we discovered that the room number plates could very easily and quietly be removed and interchanged. This we did and forgot until the next morning when pandemonium broke out in reception after breakfast. Nobody could get back into their rooms because the keys wouldn't work.'

Venues varied enormously; some places Vic says were 'atmosphere-free' or like the Lea Cliff Hall in Folkestone, which had 'appalling acoustics', although Vic especially enjoyed playing the Barrowlands in his hometown, Glasgow, because the audiences 'were really raucous. We went back to Germany yet again where the metal promoter George Hofmann looked after us as only he can.'

George had known Gary since the Monsters of Rock tour in 1984, in a country that has always been very warm towards Gary: 'Absolutely,' he says. 'The Germans loved and still love him. The German audience is very loyal and expect the artist to come and play on a constant basis.' Looking at the date sheets across his whole career, Gary played Germany more than any other country outside the UK.

'There was no grey area with Gary,' says George, 'people either loved him or avoided him. But he was one of the most straightforward guys I ever met. He never schmoozed around and if he didn't like somebody, he would tell them. But his requirements were never unreasonable, and he always took care of his band mates and crew. He'd never let anybody down who was working for him. On the other hand, he expected 100 percent, no excuses. Gary made his own decisions and he wasn't hiding behind a manager. However, as a promoter, this was brilliant for me, as I could talk directly to him about any business.

'We shared a lot of common interests, both of us were gear heads and it was absolutely fun going into music stores with him. We were in a big store once—it was a Saturday morning and full of people—and there was a Wes Montgomery Gibson model there. So, I grabbed it and Gary started playing traditional Django Reinhardt stuff like you wouldn't expect. And there was dead silence, people looked around, "Who the fuck is that playing?" They all stood around him and the store guy came over wondering why I had pulled a guitar off the wall without asking and then he looked and saw who it was, "Oh, my God. It's the boss."

'I had this 1959 Les Paul and he really wanted it. He offered me about £25,000 and I said, "No. I want £100,000." "But I'm Gary Moore." "Yes, and this is my guitar!" It was never purely a business relationship; he played a major role in my private life too and was part of our family. He was there for me like a brother—and our bar visits became quite legendary.'

Gary fell ill during July and a few gigs were cancelled, but they finished off in September with more UK gigs. In hindsight, a hint of what was to come could be heard on 'Cold Black Night' and especially 'How Many Lies'. This was less blues and more power rock in the style of Jimi Hendrix with Pete and Vic laying a solid foundation while Darrin played the Mitch Mitchell role he craved, roaming all over the music and driving Gary on. Gary explained to a journalist he had been listening to a lot of Hendrix and decided to go down the power trio route. It was in truth a surprise decision—and one that didn't include Pete Rees or Vic Martin.

New Year's Eve 2001 at Gary and Jo's place. Gathered there were Jack (fourteen), Gus (eight) and Lily (three), Melissa and Richard Fountain. 'Gary had bought Jack this small Gibson Les Paul,' says Melissa, 'and we were sitting in his living room and I said to Gary, "I bet you can't play the solo from 'Eight Miles High'," and he just did it, note for note.' But it was a night for the children. 'Jack played guitar; Gus was on drums with Lily singing a song she had written called "Rocking Badger". Gus started singing and Lily turned round and said, "Stop. The drummer doesn't sing."

'Richard and Jo went off to a Chinese restaurant and ordered everything on the menu. It was a beautiful frosty evening, a magical night. Jo and I got up late next morning. Gary and Richard had cleared everything away and Gary had cooked breakfast for everybody.'

Remembering his dad, Jack says, 'he was just a laugh. As well as being a father, you could just hang out with him, have a drink, sit down and play guitar. He was always cool like that. Family time alone was the best time. He loved Christmas— he was a very generous person, loved giving presents, making people happy, very kind-hearted. But he could be a father when he needed to be; if you stepped out of line, you knew it.'

Lily too has good memories; Gary and young daughter would go off into make-believe worlds of their own: 'He was a fun dad. He would make up loads of stories—Mirror Land where everything was in reverse; Silly Billy; the Moon Fairy made of cheese. I would get picked on a bit at school and he had the same. He would always tell me what to say. Mum would say, "No, no, don't retaliate. Go tell the head teacher." But then dad would say, "No, you've got to say this to them. Say something worse." He knew what he was doing. When I said it, it stopped.'

Even though he had already walked away from it once, this was the normal family life that Gary wanted and needed. He kept the tours short, no more than six to eight weeks at a time, so that he could be an everyday parent, doing the school run, going to parents' evenings, family picnics on the beach, meals out, walks. As Lily says, 'I never thought of him being away. He would come back so regularly. I never felt like he was missing.' He was meditating regularly and even went to anger management classes to get his quick-fire temper under control.

Darren Main remembers with affection that Gary 'adored his family and would always talk about them, how they were getting on at school. When the kids came on tour with us, they still had to do their homework. At one point, Gus was learning Latin and trying to get us to help him. We did a show with Ian Anderson and The Bootleg Beatles. It was in a stadium that had a racetrack. After the gig, Gary was running down the track shouting at me, "Come on, let's go, let's go. I'm going home tomorrow." He was in such a hurry to get back to the hotel to get home that I had to remind him that we still had to get the plane next morning!'

Professionally, too, he had another family, a very loyal and well-organised group of people who looked after his interests—Graham Lilley, Colin Newman, Darren Main, tour managers like Andy Crookston and later Steve Croxford and Dick Meredith (with whom he became especially close), his sound guys Robbie McGrath, Andy May and Chris 'Privet' Hedge and the agent team of Barry Dickins and Prue Almond—all working in the service of getting Gary out on stage. Andy Crookston sums it up:

'Gary was really only put on the planet to play guitar; he wasn't very good at the rest of it. You could get really fed up with him and then he'd go out there and play and that was that.'

Gary needed life on the road to be a well-oiled machine, working with military precision—no surprises, everything to hand, set pre-gig routines, almost at the level of obsessive compulsion—and the man largely charged with holding the oil can was, appropriately enough, ex-serviceman Darren Main. When he wasn't on tour with Gary, Darren held down a full-time job as a fireman, but juggling both jobs was made easier as the Chief Fire Officer was a big Gary Moore fan. Darren knew the drill:

'If we were on the way to a venue, we would call ahead to Graham, who would have already set up. We would tell him how far away we were, find out the best entrance to go straight to the stage for the soundcheck. This could be stressful because Gary had a huge dislike of people watching the soundcheck and it was my job to keep people out, which could be difficult if you had a large venue with lots of ways into the auditorium.'

There always had to be a soundcheck, although not always possible at festivals where the audience is already there. But it wasn't for the want of trying. Andy Crookston recalls an altercation with Joe Cocker's crew, who were trying to stop Gary having a proper soundcheck. 'Eventually, it was agreed that we could do this at 11am before the gates opened.' But Joe just started doing one song after another. 'Meanwhile, I'm fighting the guy for the power cable to the backline. Joe Cocker was just about to start yet another song, so I pulled the plug myself.'

Darren makes the point that 'Gary's sound on stage was second to none. Obviously it was pretty loud and to get that right with all the other band members being able to hear what was being played, you had to be pretty good as the sound engineer and all those working for Gary were top-drawer. For about the first ten years I was with him, he would record every show on a DAT. He would listen back to all of them and be very critical of his own playing—he just wanted to do a 100 percent professional job. The moment Graham handed Gary that guitar—that was it, he was gone.' It could be a struggle to maintain that perfection, as Darren explains: 'As the venue fills up, the sound can change from soundcheck to show. Graham could hand Gary a guitar in tune … that wasn't by the time Gary played it.' You can imagine Gary's reaction to that although it was invariably a case of immediate explosion then forgotten—no afters, no post-mortems.

Darren was with Gary in the lift of a hotel in Germany as they prepared to go for a run, 'and Kirk Hammett from Metallica gets in the lift. You could see they recognised each other. Kirk was very pleased to meet Gary and said, "Do you know, man? The sound we want and have always wanted is yours. How do you get it?" And Gary was really very humble and said, "Well, you have to have my guitar and a Marshall amp." He never put himself in front of celebrities—he let the guitar do the talking. He knew he had fans, other artists, young players. But I still don't think he realised just how many people looked up to him.'

One of Gary's legendary touring tics concerned hotels. Any tour manager knew he had to make sure there were no building works going on in or near the hotel. This could easily be consigned to 'rock star-ness'. But the reason was very simple; Gary liked to sleep late and didn't want to be woken up by crashing and banging—and his ears were particularly sensitive to that kind of noise. Also, he insisted on a swimming pool because he wanted to stay fit—and when he stopped that because he said his fingers were getting too soft, a cross-trainer was added to the luggage. Darren dragged the thing in and out of hotels all over Europe. Darren also took with him a flight case wardrobe, Gary's life support system for the whole tour—phone chargers, hairdryer, Elastoplast, every type of personal gadget you could think of that Gary or the rest of the band might need.

Trying to sort out a hotel for Gary almost cost one tour manager his life—only to be saved in the nick of time, by Gary. The man in question was Steve Croxford, who was with Gary during 2002–2003. 'I booked him into the best hotel in Brussels, the Amigo. All the restaurants and a beautiful square are all nearby. We get there and it's in a small side street that you can't get the bus down. Lo and behold, the building opposite has got scaffolding up. And Gary's standing outside the hotel, telling me to get him another one. There I am at midnight, phoning the travel agent in London on a 24-hour service asking, "What else is there in Brussels?" Turned out we couldn't get anywhere else. Meanwhile, I'm standing at the front of the hotel with my back to a parked cab and it started to move. Gary pushed me right across the street otherwise the cab would have run me over. I didn't even see it and said to Gary, "What was that for?" "You shouldn't stand behind taxis that can't see you."'

Once backstage in the moments leading up to show time, Darren would lay out the dressing room just so—it became an automatic routine he hardly had to think about. To settle Gary's stomach and his nerves, the Gaviscon and a glass or two of white wine would always be on hand. Gary had been a public performer since he was a boy, so it is strange to relate that he did suffer from serious stage fright—and it is a condition that can worsen with age. It didn't help that Gary was, by nature, an anxious person, but he had carried with him the weight of responsibility for the success of the show night after night since the early 1980s. Stage fright is not at all uncommon among even the most experienced artists; in a radio interview, Annie Lennox revealed that her stage fright was so bad, she seriously feared having a panic attack on stage. Part of Gary's preparation immediately before a show was to lock himself away in the dressing room for a period of meditation, with only Darren allowed to enter. Sometimes, though, he and Darren would go for a walk to help Gary clear his head: cue tour manager heart attack. Gary left nothing to chance; he was accused of over-rehearsing by some band members. Two hours before a gig, psychologically, he was already onstage.

Gary loved shopping for guitars, gadgets and clothes, so it was fun time when he and Darren would go off during the day to check out the local shops. One of Darren's many tasks was to act as Gary's security—which does sound a bit odd. Gary was unlikely to be mobbed by hordes of screaming teenagers as he walked down the street. But Gary was very shy and wary of people he didn't know and because of this, rather than because of any rock star snobbery, he wasn't overly keen on being approached on the street by strangers, however well meaning. He was fine for an official signing session planned in advance. Many fans have reported how friendly Gary was, willing to sign everything put in front of him, chatting away and posing for photographs. Others said he was pretty abrupt and almost rude because the person caught him at the wrong time or in the wrong mood. Darren would walk just a fraction behind Gary and slightly to one side, so he could see any approaches, 'but then, we'd get to a pedestrian crossing that was just starting to beep, he would race across ahead of me just in time. It was lovely to walk into a guitar shop with him and see the commotion and enthusiasm he generated. You'd see all the people whispering. He knew so much about guitars and he was a pedal freak. If he bought a pedal that he wanted, he'd go and buy two. Nothing was ever thrown away, though—it all went into the store.'

And Gary wouldn't just buy one shirt either—he'd buy half a dozen, all exactly the same. After a show, Darren would wash and iron the shirt from that gig, because he knew full well that Gary would want to wear it the next night— even though he had five brand new ones hanging in the wardrobe. 'He never questioned why that sixth one was always there too, but that's because I made sure it was. If, for some reason, the shirt wasn't ready, he would try one of the other five shirts, but he'd still come back to that one. I don't know if he did that just to wind me up. Eventually, he told me not to keep washing it, but I did and he kept wearing it. It was just so funny.'

Gary seemed to approach each tour like a new beginning; he would buy all new underwear, socks and T-shirts every time. As part of her art course, Jo says she created an installation at college called 'Dark Matter' made up entirely of Gary's socks.

But that was Gary—because he was a creature of habit and didn't like surprises, those around him were rarely caught out either, because they knew exactly the 'what, when and how' of keeping Gary happy and focused, right in the zone where he needed to be. This solid backing and organisation gave Gary the headspace to plan his next move.

Gary was driven by the music, whatever he was hearing at the time, whatever somebody close to him might be listening to. He had been reconnecting with Jimi Hendrix of late, but he was also listening to his son Jack's music, like Rage Against the Machine and the Kings of Leon. While on his last tour, he had started playing rock riffs on a Fender Strat in the warm-up, much as he had played blues licks on the *After The War* tour, which signalled his future intentions. There was so much music in Gary, it just poured out of him, he could hardly contain it and now his mind turned to producing something more in the Hendrix vein, an aggressive rock sound using younger musicians.

Darrin Mooney was still available and he brought in his bass player friend Cass Lewis, fresh out of the recently disbanded Skunk Anansie. Gary was surprised that Cass would want to work with him, 'but he actually turned out to be a huge Thin Lizzy fan and when he came in, it tipped the balance in that heavier direction. I was happy to go with the flow … the whole creative process was very inspiring. The chemistry worked so well; we were a band in five minutes flat. In fact, by the time I got to the rehearsal room on the day we met, Darrin and Cass had already been playing together and were already locked in.'

And a band is what they planned to be: when Gary teamed up with Jack and Ginger, no way could it just be billed as 'Gary Moore'—and neither was Cass prepared to go down that road: 'I was never a session player. I don't just come along and play for you. He said he wanted to do a Hendrix-style rock thing, which is why I agreed to do it. I wasn't interested in just doing a blues regurgitation.' Gary had been scared of losing audience by putting out *Still Got The Blues*; having now established himself as a credible blues artist, he was scared of losing *that* audience by fronting a rock band once more.

So, they had to come up with a band name—but according to Darrin, 'we couldn't think of one and it was getting ridiculous, so Gary just put our names into a computer and it came up with a load of random names, including Scars—a touch ironic because Gary was still sensitive about his face and got upset if anybody called him 'scar face'.

Getting back together with Chris Tsangarides and roaming across Gary's favoured studio haunts of Music Bank, where Chris had the studio established, Sarm West and Hook End, Scars went in to start work on their album. Just like on the road, in the studio too, Gary wanted everything to run like clockwork, which was great for Chris and his assistant, Tim Hole, because they knew exactly what was expected and there was no messing about. 'Some artists,' says Tim, 'would just turn up, hadn't bothered to string their instruments and then we'd be hanging around for three hours while they got enough dope in their bloodstream to be able to perform. It was very different with Gary; we would be in by 11am, Graham Lilley would make sure the amps were warmed up, guitars restrung, all the intonation perfect. Then Darrin and Cass would be in at 12.30, start jamming so they were ready because when Gary came in at 1:00, he would just drop his coat and off we go. They'd play for an hour and a half, then stop for fifteen minutes for a tea break and a sandwich, listen back to what they had done—then off again, tea break at 4.30 and go on until 6:00. Then we'd do the back-ups and be gone by 7:00. Just like a day in the office.'

The back-up was crucial: 'We had about 150 full takes of songs, so much stuff was recorded, and you never knew when Gary might go, "That version we did at twelve o'clock on Wednesday—that was good, let's call that back up." Gary brought songs in that he had written and demoed at home, but he also wrote songs with Cass in the studio and they worked well together. On "Rectify", for example, Cass came up with the riff, Gary was right on it, doubled it and it took off from there—created on the spot.'

Not everything ran totally to plan, though; incredibly, the studio manager walked into the live room during a recording. Chris was right in the zone, 'suddenly there is this godawful racket from the guitar and Gary tore this poor sod a new one is all I can say. I did feel sorry for him, but if there's a red light, you don't walk in—and he was the studio manager. Another time, I had the guitar in this room in Studio One at Sarm West—and Gary played at full pelt in the studio—and even with all the soundproofing, George Michael, who was downstairs, was complaining that the guitar was bleeding into his vocal mike—and he went away until we had finished.'

The album of all band-penned material was released on Sanctuary in September 2002 and has divided Gary Moore fans ever since, with opinions quite literally veering from best to worst album and all shades in between. The consensus view was of a solid album with some good songs, but which didn't really signal any new direction. With 'World Of Confusion' ('Manic Depression'), 'Ball And Chain' ('Voodoo Chile') and 'World Keep Turnin' Round' ('Crosstown Traffic'), the Hendrix inspiration jumped out the speakers, but for Cass, it wasn't really the modern rock album he was hoping for; as he says, 'the blues snuck in'. Photographer Stuart Weston knew Cass even before Gary called him up to Hook End to take the photos for the cover. Stuart and Cass subsequently became best friends and housemates and Stuart could tell that Cass wasn't too happy about the way Scars was drifting and speaks of a 'tense' atmosphere in the studio.

Once they hit the road to promote the album, Gary's standard blues repertoire was very much in evidence. ZZ Top came to Europe in October. Both bands shared the same agent, so Scars were invited on to the tour—not as 'support', mind you (Gary would have vetoed that) but as 'very special guests'—and struck a good deal: Gary got a guaranteed fee plus a percentage of ZZ Top's percentage. Top's manager queried why they were paying Gary so much; they found out when they got to Germany. Billy Gibbons started watching the show when he realised how good Gary was and how much the audience was lapping it up. 'If you can be a special guest on a big tour,' explains Prue Almond of ITB, 'you get so much more exposure. Say you win over 10 percent of a 70,000 audience and compare that with filling a 2,000-seater hall.' ZZ Top's crew were very good to Scars all round, even carrying their gear on their trucks.

The payday for this tour allowed everything to happen in style; on October 14, the band were playing Le Zenith in Paris. Melissa and Richard had just got married and were on honeymoon there. Jo and Gary decided to make it an extra special occasion. Gary invited them to move out of the dump they were booked into and over to Le Faubourg, a very expensive Parisian hotel where the band were staying. Melissa has very fond memories of a great night: 'Scars played on Monday, and we all rode back in the tour bus, then met after freshening up in the Buddha Bar with Gary, Jo, Cass and Darrin, my friend Jean-Jacques, Darren Main and Steve Croxford. Gary insisted on paying for the whole evening. We drank innumerable bottles of Cristale. Richard taught us chair-dancing, as the snitty waitresses would pinch your chair if you left it for a second. And we only had to stumble 100m back to the hotel.'

The band went out again in 2003, but this time just as Gary Moore on the UK Monsters of Rock tour, sharing the bill with Whitesnake and Y&T. There was nothing wrong with the playing, the band was solid—and was well received by the crowd, many of whom would have been only too glad to see Gary back to flying up and down the fretboard. At the same time, he was a hostage to fortune, playing covers from his 1980s songbook, like 'Wishing Well' and 'Shapes Of Things' after expounding at length in the music press about how much contempt he had for Big Hair, Big Arena rock. Journalists were not slow to dump on him from a great height.

The album did not sell well, and the final concerts of the tour were cancelled, including that year's Montreux Festival appearance. In the press, Gary mentioned something about an accident in the shower, but nobody now seems to remember exactly why the gigs were blown out. Gary had told journalists that Scars was meant to be something long-term, but he must have known as he said it that he would never project too far ahead. Scars had run its course. Gary was probably getting bored and looking to move on while he and Cass had a dressing room bust-up when Gary stopped in the middle of a song and glared at him for putting in an unscheduled fill. Cass says they never played together again, 'but he gave me all the songs that didn't appear on the album and we became really good friends. So anytime he was in London he would call, or if I was playing in Brighton, he'd phone and ask if he could come to the gig. He was an axe-wielding serial killer. Top man. And if you could get him out of his skin, make him relax and stop being so guarded, he was the most beautiful man, a lovely person.'

Interviewed by *Guitar & Bass* in 2004, Gary reflected back on that brief swerve off the blues highway: 'it was a return to a far harder rockier sound'. But having got Cass in to get that edge, he concedes in hindsight, 'I think it ended up going too much in that direction, far more than I originally wanted it to. So perhaps I do have a regret about that—but I did enjoy exploring the guitar sonically.' Perhaps this was an unintended play on words: for the Scars trip he was seen unusually playing a white Gibson Explorer, similar to one owned by Chris Tsangarides.

The interviewer raised the issue of the Monsters of Rock tour suggesting that given his recent track record, Gary looked a bit out of place: 'To be honest, I didn't really want to do it in the first place. I didn't want to tour with Whitesnake for a fucking second. That's not slagging off David Coverdale, it's just a genre thing. I actually really like David and he asked for us to be on the tour, which was really kind of him. But my statement in the 90s was that I left all that behind in the 80s. I didn't want to get lumped in with it again.' To which the journalist reasonably responds, 'So why do it?' 'We got offered ten big dates with the opportunity to play in front of thousands of people every night. We love playing, Scars wasn't doing anything, so it seemed like a good idea. Plus, we got featured on a live album and the DVD as well. Oh, and we got paid a lot of money!'

The piece went on: 'Moore was also unhappy with the reaction from some of the rock press who criticised the absence of any blues. "It was like being in *Kerrang!* again, getting a slagging off if the reviewer didn't like your shirt. We weren't on the tour because we played blues, it was the Monsters of Rock, not the Monsters of Blues."' But in fairness, there was an equal amount of criticism about Gary doing well worn covers like 'Wishing Well' and 'Shapes Of Things' and, from the reviewers' point of view, going through the motions. But Gary would have known only too well that he would struggle to get a favourable review.

Gary also had a pop at including Y&T on the bill, concluding that they needed a bigger third act to draw in the crowd. The interviewer then went into pious mode:

'This somewhat cynical approach is hard to defend, yet at least it's honest. But it does give fuel to his critics. If he didn't want to do rock, why release the very rock sounding Scars album and then take the Monsters tour, do it for the money and then complain about the reviews from the very people and the genre he sought to distance himself from?' As he says, Gary was honest to a fault, even if it didn't always serve his best interests, but as far as the cash is concerned, Gary was a professional musician who needed to earn a living; it stands to reason that if a lucrative offer came his way, he was obliged to give it serious consideration. Yet, Gary had already turned down huge offers to tour *Still Got The Blues* all over the world. It wasn't always about the money.

But the message of Scars and his experimental albums was clear—having worried constantly about being accepted as a bona fide blues artist (he even sang unnecessarily on the *Scars* album 'Wasn't born in Chicago / But I can play the blues)—he was now universally accepted as exactly that, and even criticised if he hit the boards and didn't play blues. So, the road ahead was clear and he got back on the blues trail with a new album called *Power Of The Blues* recorded with Darrin and Chris Tsangarides and his old mate, bassist Bob Daisley.

Reminiscing in his autobiography *For Facts Sake*, Bob writes that he was back home in Australia watching a programme called *Air Crash Investigation* and thinking how glad he was not to be flying again when the phone rang and it was Gary, who said, 'I start recording my new album next week in London, do you fancy playing on it?' 'I didn't have to think about it. I'd always thought so highly of Gary, so I immediately agreed. It was good to hear from him and have a chat. I'd seen Gary on several occasions when I'd returned to England, but we hadn't worked together for over ten years.'

Bob flew into London and met up with Gary to discuss the album because Bob wasn't just a bass-for-hire—he was a songwriter and arranger: 'The plan was for it to be a more spontaneous, raw, rough and ready record without having the shine polished off it.'

They went into Sphere Studios in Battersea, south London and as soon as they were underway, as just a trio with Darrin, 'it felt and sounded natural and comfortable from the off. Gary could sometimes be demanding and pedantic, which is not necessarily a bad thing. But for this album he was more relaxed, loose and open to freedom of expression and was playing like an uninhibited demon himself. Each song was arranged, quickly rehearsed and then it was, bang, get it down straight afterwards. It was a great way to record—rhythm guitar, bass and drums with a guide vocal, all done together. It captured the live, fresh, vibrant and spontaneous feel of everything and there was certainly plenty of vibe and support happening between us, just what Gary was looking for. A good portion of the album had been written by Gary,' continues Bob, 'he was pretty self-sufficient in the songwriting department. But I co-wrote "Getaway Blues" and the title track, "Power Of The Blues".' They worked through from Monday to Thursday and then back for a second week, by the end of which they had twelve basic tracks that Gary was happy with: 'I remember him saying, "It took three months to get to this stage with the last album." Two songs didn't make it onto the new album, "How Blue Can You Get" [by B.B. King] and "You Know My Love" [by Willie Dixon] ... but my favourite was "That's Why I Play The Blues", written by Gary. We recorded it live together in the studio with keyboards and horns, although the final mix was without the horns, which I preferred.

'I for one enjoyed every minute of the nine days that we spent in the studio, the work had been full-on and concentrated, but the end results as very satisfying. Gary was *moore* than happy too.'

And he had every right to be. In some respects, *Power Of The Blues* was probably the album he had hoped *Scars* would be—a trio power blues album, allowing the guitarist freedom to roam, backed by an extremely versatile drummer like Darrin who would take the initiative to drive Gary on, all underpinned by Bob's utterly reliable, heavy-end bass playing.

Gary came of age on this album as a blues guitarist—he had learned his lessons from Albert and B.B. King, adding his own signature aggression and grit, those shards of ice at the heart of the blues. There are some quite superb solos on this album—'There's A Hole', 'I Can't Quit You Baby' 'That's Why I Play The Blues' and 'Can't Find My Baby' being worthy of special mention. Gary often included tracks that frankly outstayed their welcome, but not here—short, tough and tight—in, out and goodbye.

This time around, the critical response was very positive. *Classic Rock* wrote, 'And the power is strong with Moore. As he's proved since 1990's *Still Got The Blues*, he has an almost preternatural facility for the form ... it's the sound of dues having been paid in full. He's rarely been in such fine form.' *Powerplay* opined, 'After last year's harshly criticised live set, many wondered what direction Gary Moore would take next and thankfully he's gone right back to basics with easily his best album since ... *Still Got The Blues*.'

Refreshed and energised, Gary was in discussion with Bob about touring the album in 2004. In June, they played two gigs supporting Bob Dylan in Ireland, followed on July 2 by the Østfoldhallene in Fredrikstadt, Norway, the first date of a projected European and UK tour. And then, by the cruellest stroke of luck, Gary had a serious problem with his hand—so serious he thought he might never play again.

Those closest to Gary admit that he could be a bit of a hypochondriac at times; he had been complaining of a hand problem and received an injection from a specialist to try and deal with it. Then, he and Jo went on holiday with Melissa and Richard in Rimini for a few days before the next scheduled gig of the tour, in Romania. While they were on holiday, Melissa's dog had a modest chew on Gary's hand. Next thing, Melissa gets a call from Jo to say all the gigs were off including the one they were all going to, the Pistola Blues Festival in Italy, because Gary had an infected hand. Melissa was shocked; she thought, *My God, I've broken a guitarist*. But it was an infection derived from the steroid injection back in London. Gary's hand started swelling up, he was taking anti-inflammatory drugs, but nothing was working. He went straight back to the UK, by which time his hand was enormous: he could hardly hold a fork, let alone a guitar.

They had to cancel the rest of the tour—and then came the hammer blow from the tour insurance company: they deemed this injury to be 'pre-existing' to the tour and refused to pay out. This left Gary with huge bills. The financial formula of the shows is they recoup all your costs and leave you with a profit. And the budget list is long: pre-tour production costs, musicians and crew wages, hotels and travel—an average tour budget for the UK and Europe could be at least £50k. On top of that there were costs to insure promoters against cancellation—the list goes on.

Of itself, this might have been manageable if Gary's income had been healthier. But purely in terms of record sales and royalties, his star was on the wane; he never got close to repeating the success of *Still Got The Blues*. That could have mitigated by touring: he was still in demand all over the world, especially in regions where he had never been seen or not seen for a long time—Central and South America, Japan and the Far East. But there was one major barrier to potentially lucrative globe-trotting: Gary had a crippling fear of flying and it was getting worse.

While flying is still reckoned to be one of the safest forms of travelling, if you are, by necessity, a frequent flyer, then those of a nervous disposition will calculate that the more you fly, the odds of something happening are increased. This explains why Gary wouldn't tour *Still Got The Blues* as far back as 1990 and why he hadn't returned to Japan, whose fans absolutely worshipped Gary. So, any journalist critical of Gary for doing the Monsters of Rock tour just for the money might have wanted to dwell on the fact he turned down a £150,000 *profit* for one show in Korea, where he was still a hero, for writing 'Murder In The Skies'.

Neither could promoters in Mexico, Brazil or Dubai tempt him with hefty offers.

Travel arrangements for a Gary Moore tour were often a logistical nightmare—matching show dates with short-haul flights only broken up with long-distance road travel. Agent Prue Almond says, 'he used to give me such a hard time—but only on the answer phone. He'd leave me a long great message and I'd call him back, "What's up, Gary?" "Err … err … well …" and then in a few seconds you'd have brought him round again. I never worried about calling him back. He had an endearing lack of confidence. It just took one other person and he'd agree—and he'd be very kind and very grateful.'

To persuade Gary to go to Russia involved spreading the maps out on the table to work out how they could break the journey in places, fit in some gigs to make the stopover worthwhile and then move on.

And Gary knew his planes, as Scars tour manager Steve Croxford explains: 'He wouldn't get on a small plane. He would rather do a 400-mile drive. Before you booked anything, you had to tell him not only how you were getting there, but what plane you were trying to book him on. And he knew every plane there was, so nothing with a prop, nothing with less than three seats in a row. And he had to sit between rows 2 and 5 because Business Class normally finishes after row 5. And you couldn't book him into row 1. And here's why. One of the first flights out with him, I was sitting a few rows behind and we were both in aisle seats. As soon as the plane took off, he dropped the tray and his left hand never let go until they told him to put the tray back up. Row 1 doesn't have a drop-down tray.

'With Gary, you had to be 110 percent on the ball; if you lied to him or things changed and you didn't tell him, he'd look at you and throw a shit fit. But if you explained everything, told him what the reasoning was—he was a very clever, very understanding person—he would listen.'

One time, Gary and Darren Main were the only people left in the departure lounge: 'There were no staff, no passengers, no crew, nobody and I was pleading with Gary to come out of the toilet. Eventually, we got to the plane on time, but I went ahead and urged the pilot to put out a favourable weather report to the passengers to keep Gary from getting off—he actually came out to speak to Gary in person. Although there were times when Gary did leave the plane—doors shut, seatbelts on and then Gary says, "Sorry, can't do this," and we're off the plane.'

This happened in August 2002 at Billund Airport in Denmark. Scars had just played Smukkeste Festival and were headed for the Bulldog Bash in Gloucestershire. At the last minute, the airline changed the type of plane and Gary was off. They spent £250 on a taxi to Copenhagen, then a BA flight to Heathrow and another car across country to the gig. Gary got there just in time.

What with insurance problems, reduced record sales, turning down large pay-days and ordinary living expenses (including maintenance payments), Gary was building up a mountain of debt. Gary and Jo discussed in all seriousness about what he would do if he couldn't play: there was talk of writing children's books based on the stories he made up for Lily and they wondered whether this was the time for Gary to write his autobiography. He did manage the odd guitar outing; using custom ultra-light strings, he turned in a thrilling version of 'Red House' on his battered pink Strat at Fender's fiftieth anniversary concert in September—which earned him a standing ovation. He played Roger Daltrey's charity gig in support of Teen Cancer at Ronnie Scott's in October plus a guest appearance with John Mayall in November, but that was it. Gary was moving towards a momentous decision, one still spoken of in guitar circles to this day: he decided to sell the Peter Green Les Paul.

All sorts of claims and counterclaims surround the sale and subsequent history of this guitar—some of it played out in the courts. There were a handful of people involved down the line, each with their own version of events and nobody with a good word to say about the other guy. Delving into the truth is also compromised by 'confidentiality clauses' about sums of money, which is faintly ridiculous when you consider that works of art valued at tens of millions of pounds go on sale in public auctions. The buyer may be anonymous, but the sale price certainly isn't. When you hit the internet and delve into the guitar forums, wild rumours, speculations and insults fly freely. But as far as can be ascertained, this is how it went down.

The Peter Green 1959 Les Paul Standard Serial No: 92038 was no doubt a legendary instrument, whose mystique and therefore value had grown over time. Gary had toyed with the idea of selling it before the injury because it had become too valuable to take out on the road, although he was still using it right up to the recording of *Power Of The Blues* and possibly on the handful of dates he played in 2004. 'I'd get it out of store for a day or so,' says Graham Lilley, 'and it would go straight back again, sometimes on the same day. I even had it with me overnight sometimes if we were staying in London, just in case.'

But despite its pedigree, the guitar itself was hardly the original Peter had sold to Gary, having a different headstock, tuners, bridge, knobs, back plate, jack plate, screws and neck bindings. Over time, too, it had taken a fair battering. Gary decided he was going to handle the sale himself (in hindsight, maybe not the best move) and began discussions with a west London guitar dealer. Gary was a private person, and since the tabloid exposure of November 1993, had been especially keen to avoid any adverse publicity wherever it might rear its head. He thought he might attract a certain amount of criticism for selling the guitar, which, in any event, was a big emotional wrench for him. With all this in mind, he stipulated at the outset that he wanted the guitar to go to a collector, not a dealer, and without a whole load of publicity.

Negotiations were unsurprisingly protracted and carried on through 2005. Eventually, Gary was contacted to say a buyer had been found who would be acting through Phil Winfield, a British ex-pat who ran a dealership called Maverick Music in North Carolina. So, as far as Gary was aware, Winfield was an intermediary for an anonymous collector. Gary was paid £300,000 for the guitar (or around $500,000 based on the exchange rate at the time) the evidence for which is a copy of the sales receipt dated March 6, 2006 posted on Maverick Music's website.

Gary was then very upset to learn that rather than the guitar going quietly to this mystery collector, it was on show at a guitar festival in Dallas apparently with a price tag on it, far in excess of what he was paid. Having originally opted to keep his own counsel on this, Gary went public by speaking to *Guitar & Bass* in an article published in November 2006.

'I'm shocked and quite traumatised by the whole episode … I had the guitar for almost 35 years and it was a big wrench to let it go. He (Winfield) provoked my remarks by parading it everywhere and not sticking to his agreement, as I understood it. There was an American radio interview where I said I was very disappointed with the way it all turned out, because I was. They weren't particularly derogatory comments, but even if they were, what gives him the right to say that I had breached the contract?'

The article continued: 'Although Moore claims that a lot was taken on trust, he also says he possesses written documentation, signed by Winfield, stating that the guitar was to be purchased on behalf of a third party, and which "states clearly" that Winfield would not sell the guitar either on his website or as an individual. After the interview, a copy of a document containing this information is shown to *Guitar & Bass*.

'Following on from this, Rick Zsigmund (the west London dealer) went on to confirm his involvement in the sale and the chronology of events. He too was under the impression that it was going to a third party, stating "Phil didn't intimate to me that he was the end user." And how much did the guitar really sell for? "Knowing Gary, whatever figure he told you will be the truth, if he has told you a figure," says Zsigmund.

'When asked to answer Gary Moore's claim that he didn't receive close to a million dollars for the guitar, Winfield first of all tries to clear up any potential dollar/sterling misunderstanding. When it's established that both he and Gary Moore possess the same bill of sale, in sterling, *Guitar & Bass* asks whether the figure stated, or its sterling equivalent, appear on the bill of sale.

'"There is going to be a different figure," admits Winfield, "because I got first class air travel, first class hotels, car hire, going out for meals, attorneys, accountants … that guitar cost me substantially more than the bill of sale is going to say.

'"That's down to me if I want to spend that kind of money. But at the end of the day, when I come to recoup the money on the guitar—if and when I sell it—I can't just ignore the fact that I've paid this money out. So yeah, he may say there's a difference, but on my books and as far as my accountants are concerned that guitar has a cost attached to it."

'A request to learn the figure actually stated on the bill of sale is turned down. "You can publish Gary's bill of sale if he's going to let you. I can see that Gary is miffed about the sale …"

'But what of Gary Moore's assertion that the guitar was to go to a third party and that Winfield was only acting as an intermediary, and the signed document to that effect? "That was the case, and it changed," Winfield calmly explains. "At the time I signed that document, it was true. I've got evidence that on the day of the transaction Maverick did not buy the guitar. I can show the funds coming in from a non-Maverick source."

'He refuses to name the "very influential, well known, and well-financed" individual, but states that the third party "probably" only became involved in the latter half of the negotiations around December 2005. Winfield doubts the statements put forward by both Gary Moore and Rick Zsigmund that the deal would have been off if it had been known at any point that he was going to be the "end user" rather than an intermediary.

'"I don't know what Gary was told, but I didn't know that he wouldn't sell it to me," says Winfield. "This deal took a long time to develop and when it first came to my attention I was interested personally." According to Winfield, the third-party collector decided he wanted to sell the guitar because of all the negative publicity that surrounded the sale. In early July 2006, the guitar was sold to Maverick Music. "The third party made $50,000 profit."'

This was the story as reported in *Guitar & Bass* in 2006. Nobody was publicly talking money then, but the receipt shows what Gary was paid in March 2006, so nowhere near one million dollars.

During the negotiations between Gary, Rick Zsigmund and Phil Winfield, there may have been some collector in the background who pulled out. But nobody was ever named nor is there any evidence that this or any other mysterious buyer had the guitar after the sale in March 2006 and then went on to sell it because of 'adverse publicity'.

The only other person involved who was not named at the time was another Brit, a jeweller named Melvyn Franks. Winfield never acted 'on behalf' of Franks and admitted this in an email to the author: he and Franks were in effect business partners. It appears that the 'non-Maverick Music' source for the cash was not Franks, but his attorney wife Rebecca. Further evidence that Winfield and Franks were partners is suggested by the travel insurance documents on the Maverick Music website naming both parties.

Inevitably, in the 'you watch my back, while I stab yours' world of vintage guitar sales, especially in the ultra-litigious United States, Winfield and Franks ended up facing each other in a North Carolina district court in a dispute over ownership. Franks still had the guitar in 2012 when it was allegedly spirited out of the country and sent to the UK to avoid its seizure over an unpaid bank loan. It was given over to another guitar dealer, Phil Harris, who put the guitar on display, as Franks now wanted to sell it. Harris and Franks were also at loggerheads over unpaid debts and eventually the guitar was sold to Kirk Hammett in 2014—who took Gary at his word, 'If you want to get my sound, you need my guitar'—via yet another British dealer, Richard Henry.

And how much did Hammett pay for it? Well about the same as Gary sold it for back in 2006. Ultimately, whatever ludicrous price might have been hung on it, the guitar was only worth what somebody was prepared to pay for it. Meanwhile, although aggrieved at the whole messy business, Gary did make enough from the deal to quell his pressing financial worries and get him back on track.

Before the Phil Lynott Memorial Concert in August 2005, Gary had just one public outing, playing once again with Jack Bruce and Gary Husband at another memorial concert, this one in honour of the great British saxophonist Dick Heckstall-Smith. The enforced layoff gave Gary time for his hand to begin the healing process; he seemed back to his ferocious best in Dublin, all his fears about a career cut short now allayed.

In an interview with *Blues In Britain* magazine, Gary explained how he developed the mixture of blues covers and original material including two reprises from *Still Got The Blues* on his 2006 release *Old New Ballads Blues*:

'I had some songs of my own that I wanted to record and a couple of others that had been hanging around for a while, which can sometimes be a good thing because you can build up a nice collection of songs. I hadn't done this kind of record for a while, there hadn't been a place for these songs. So, all of a sudden, I had four or five things that were quite strong that I was ready to use.

'There were a couple of songs that I wanted to re-record. I hadn't been happy with the original versions. One of those was "All Your Love" … the version I did [before] I felt was too fast and it wasn't really respectful enough of what the song was about. It's a very sensuous, passionate song … It's got a magic about it that song. I really felt I had failed to capture the feeling of the song … I always wanted to have another shot at it. I slowed it down. I got a lot more intensity into it. The guitar sounds a lot more raw than on the original version I did … .What happened [with] *Midnight Blues* [on that album] was I used the demo because we hadn't the time to re-do the song. I always felt that just the sound of it wasn't very good and I felt that I could do a better version … We added some horns to it in the middle eight section to give it a slightly different flavour, and hopefully a better guitar solo. I think we've got a much stronger version this time.

'I always try and do at least one Willie Dixon song because he's my favourite blues songwriter. I did two on the last album, I just love his work so much. I did a song this time called "You Know My Love", which [like] "All Your Love" was recorded by Otis Rush. I love it. It's one of those songs that has a great passion to it … I also like the form of the song because it's not a twelve bar. It's not an obvious blues structure … there's a really nice shape to the whole song. It's a minor song. I've always loved minor songs going back to the time when I first heard Peter Green. He always used to do a blues in A minor. I love that spooky sound you get from those kind of things.

'I did an Elmore James song called "Done Somebody Wrong".' Gary explained that he had first heard it done by The Allman Brothers when he was on tour with Skid Row but didn't get to hear the original until later: 'I thought it was a great song, great lyric, great sentiment in the song. It was a chance to play some bottleneck which I don't do very often, but obviously, you do an Elmore James song, you've got to play bottleneck guitar.

'I'm very happy with the album. A lot of people say it's the best thing I've done in years and I hope it is. It's a very fresh sounding record. It was nice to work with people like Don Airey who played on *Still Got The Blues* and have the horn section back again.'

Don and Gary hadn't worked together since the end of the *Still Got The Blues* tour and didn't see each other until Don appeared in the dressing room on the Scars tour: 'It was nice to see him again. We had about twenty minutes together and as I left, Darrin, who was a friend, came up to me and said, "Are you back in the band?"' It is likely that Gary wanted to revisit those blues songs from 1990 with Don arranging the horns and generally helping to recreate that vibe from Gary's most commercially successful period. The other members of the band were Darrin and Jonathan Noyce on bass.

Gary went on, 'I co-produced with Ian Taylor … I hadn't worked with him for about seven or eight years, so it was really nice to have him on board again. It just made the whole thing fresh because we hadn't worked together for a while. There was a really nice atmosphere. We did the whole thing in eighteen days which is pretty quick for me. We recorded all the tracks in five days and mixed the whole album in six days and did a few overdubs with the horn section. There's a lot of live stuff on there. Tracks like "Gonna Rain Today" … we did that with just a couple of takes completely live with the vocal live. There's a lot of very spontaneous stuff going on there. I really enjoyed making it.'

The album proved that Gary was back to his dazzling best with a virtuoso display across the whole album, diamond-hard playing with a crystal-clear tone—from greasy slide playing through to that signature 'spooky' yet sweet Peter Green sound. But it was the solo on 'You Know My Love' that leaves the listener slack-jawed. In the same way as the sheer musicality of Colosseum II made Bernie Marsden laugh as he stood in the control booth (and was slung out for his troubles), you have to laugh at how Gary combined passion and power with such untrammelled technical ability. But when asked about the solo by *Guitar Techniques* magazine, Gary was self-deprecating about the song left off the previous album: 'It was the first one we did on the first day, when everybody comes in and there's lots of enthusiasm there. We just banged it down in a few takes, and you know me, I said, "I'll just get the other guys right and replace the solo later." But I grew to really like it; it's not perfect, but I really like the feel of it. Also, if I don't get a solo in the first couple of takes, I'll end up going round the world doing take after take until I get it.'

The album was also notable for another finest moment—the heartbreaking 'Flesh & Blood'. If we take Gary at his word, that songs that sound autobiographical usually are, then who is the subject of this song? There is no evidence to turn to other than the lyrics, but they do seem to point to Gary's daughter Saoirse and the immense emotional barriers they were trying to overcome between them. The feel of the song is not unlike 'Tears In Heaven'—and while the circumstance of each song is very different, they do both speak of loss.

I wish I could get through to you
Seems like you don't want me to
But still I try

I know when you're not feeling strong
When things for you are going wrong
But still I try

I remember the first time
That I looked into your eyes
I remember the first day
Of your life

You're my flesh and blood
I knew it from the very first moment
You're my flesh and blood
I knew it from the very first moment

I see the sadness in your eyes
I wish that I could paint your eyes
A brighter blue

You build these walls around yourself
Protecting you so that no-one else
Can get to you

You're my flesh and blood
I knew it from the very first moment
You're my flesh and blood
I knew it from the very first moment

Gary intended to take the studio band out on the road, but Jon and Don had other commitments, so Gary decided to recall Pete Rees and Vic Martin and renew his playing acquaintance with his friend, Brian Downey. Brian says he asked Gary what he was doing next after the Phil Lynott concert: 'He said he had a tour coming up and invited me to play. I had no second thoughts—straight in there and I was with him for the next couple of years.'

For the first five dates of the tour, Gary was asked to join the bill of what was touted as the last ever tour by B.B. King. For Gary, 'that made it even more special. I'll have Brian Downey with me on drums and it was actually Brian who turned me on to a lot of music, including B.B. King, when I was younger. He's a great blues drummer. I was going to take the horns out, with Don Airey as MD, but something else came up and he couldn't do it. And also, you don't want to look like you're competing with B.B.'s horns—that wouldn't go down too well.' Gary was being quite diplomatic here, because B.B.'s 'people' wouldn't let Gary join the legend onstage –even though one of the dates fell on April 4, Gary's birthday—and at Wembley Arena, one of the country's most prestigious venues. Towards the end of the year, Gary had two very contrasting blues encounters.

While new hot-shot blues guitarists appear on a regular basis, very rarely can you say that the music is being developed, taken to new places. Enter guitarist, banjo player, harpist and singer Otis Mark Taylor, born in Chicago in 1948.

His blues influences were acoustic rather than electric—Mississippi John Hurt was key here—but he had a brief spell playing with the incendiary Tommy Bolin in the late 60s. Other blues projects followed before he completely walked away from music and into a successful career as an antiques dealer and pro cycle coach. He returned in 1995, winning a W.C. Handy Award for Best New Artist Debut (plus three other nominations) for his album *White African* about the experience of African Americans.

By the time he first met Gary in 2007, he had picked up a clutch of W.C. Handy and *Downbeat* awards and a shower of praise from the music critics of major US publications like the *New York Times* and *Washington Post*. They lauded his stark, almost trance-like blues drones combined with chunks of white country music or psychedelic rock, or all three—driving songs of social conscience and injustice.

'I was touring in England,' says Otis, 'and playing down in Brighton and these two guys walked in and they were really rough looking. And right at the end, one of them walked up to me when everybody had gone and said, "I'm a blues guitar player." "Oh, that's nice," I said. Because I'd stopped playing for nineteen years,

I had no idea who he was. But I'm nice to all the fans. He said, "Where are you staying?" "Oh, just down the street"—I thought he wanted to rob me or something, I didn't know. "You really blew my mind," said Gary. "Every time I thought you should do something, you did it. Here's my phone number." And he just slipped out the emergency door. The owner runs up and says, "Oh, oh, that's Gary Moore." He was so excited. Next day I phoned him up and said, "Hey, I hear you're fuckin' famous. Wanna play on my record?" And we became friends after that.'

Gary made two guest appearances with Otis, recording for *Definition Of A Circle* (2007) and a later album *Pentatonic Wars And Love Songs* (2009). 'He never charged me for playing on my records and that was pretty heavy. Even my daughter [singer Cassie Taylor] didn't play on my records for free!' Otis sent Gary the tapes so he could go into a studio and overlay guitar: 'He knew my music; he didn't try to dominate. If I was playing on one of my gigs, he would sit there and watch me for the whole gig, getting himself psyched up—and I would taunt him—"Come on out here!" I think I reminded him of a lot of things, like his relationship with Phil and the older blues guys. I think I fitted into a certain psychological pocket maybe.' Gary returned the favour by taking Otis and his band out on tour: 'He was the cornerstone of my career. I learned to be the leader of a band. I'd never toured at that high level before, tour buses, trucks, sound guys. I learned about the production side and he paid his guys really well. He was very gracious. He wasn't James Brown!

'We went to Scotland [in 2007] and we had a choice of going back to London on the tour bus or flying back. Me, Pete [Rees] and Vic [Martin] decide to fly back. We're at the airport and I go, "Okay, catch you guys later." Pete says, "Where are you going? You're sticking with us. You're not roamin' round the airport." It was beautiful, man; they knew to protect the show. I'll never forget that. "No, no, no, you're in a foreign country. We're watching over you"—because I was part of the show. I would open for Gary, play acoustically and we had a whole thing we'd do—an encore song—so I was very much part of the show. I gave up the chance to play for Barack Obama on the presidential campaign, so I could do the last date of the tour in Brighton.'

Gary taught Otis how to complain about hotel rooms—the complaint would not be directed at the hotel, but through the tour manager because Gary was too shy to do that with a stranger. So, Gary was stunned when 'I got him to buy this banjo and got the guy to knock £15 off. Gary went, "How do you do that?" "It's what I do Gary. I'm not going to let you pay retail."'

There was another 'older blues guy' who played a critical role in Gary's musical education who had three blues guitar icons in his band in quick succession—Eric Clapton, Peter Green and Mick Taylor—and who now boasted the talents of a big man with the feather-light touch, Buddy Whittington.

On October 24, 2006, the day after Gary played with Otis at the Komedia in Brighton, he bought a ticket to see John Mayall at the Brighton Dome. 'John said to me, "Come and say hello to the band." And they all said, "You gonna get up and play tonight Gary?" I had to ring the babysitter up and get her to send a guitar over in a taxi! So, I got up and played and it was great. Mick Taylor was playing as well and I really enjoyed it. Then for another date we rang up to ask if it was okay to come to the gig. And they said, "Yeah! We've got your amp ready and everything."'

Buddy Whittington was John's guitarist and Gary loved playing with him in the Bluesbreakers and later when Buddy toured in his own right: 'He's really original,' said Gary, 'and even though he comes from Texas and plays a Strat—well, those Lentz guitars that are like mini-Strats—he doesn't sound like Stevie Ray. He just stands there with a little 18-watt Dr Z amp and puts those country bends in there and just walks across the strings. John tried to get a little duel thing going between us. He'd play a line and I'd harmonise with it and it sounded like The Allman Brothers. We played really sweet together and you don't often get that. I tell you what, if he lived over here, I'd play with him all the time.'

And that's an important point to note about Gary by this time. For over twenty-five years, he'd been on major tours, often headlining in front of thousands of people. Now, he was just as happy playing gigs as somebody's guest, whether a proper auditorium like the Brighton Dome or just a local pub gig up the road, both for the sheer love of playing as often as he possibly could. There was absolutely no pressure on him, just plug in and play.

Gary gave a specific example of this when he sat in with Nine Below Zero—most appropriate, because he was at Hook End recording his next album in January 2007 when the power failed and they had no electricity. Former Rory Gallagher and NBZ's harpist Mark Feltham was due to play on the album, turned up but they couldn't do anything. As Gary told *Guitar & Bass*, 'Amazingly [Mark] was playing just up the road in a pub called the Crooked Billet … so it wasn't a wasted journey. I said, "I'm not fuckin' sitting here all night in the dark with the candles freezing my arse off—I'll come and watch your gig." So, I got up there, they asked me to play and I did half a set with them. It was so small that every time the waitress passed, I had to lift my guitar up to let her go by. I love doing things like when I get the chance.'

Once they were up and running again, Gary and Ian Taylor recorded a straightforward, down the line blues album playing both to Gary's considerable strengths and to some of his recent encounters with Otis and John Mayall. The UK radio station Planet Rock asked if he might consider hosting six blues shows on which he could chose and introduce all the songs embellished with some in-studio guitar work.

'[For the new album], we decided were going to play as live as possible, so most of the solos and even some of the vocals are live because I wanted to get as much of the natural vibe as I could. Another decision I made was that I wasn't going to use any pedals. I had this thing in my head: guitar, amp, me and the songs and that was it. It's earthy and direct.'

He decided to call the album *Close As You Get*: 'You can take the title … in two ways. It's quite a personal record, so it's as close as you're going to get to the person you're seeing. But it's also about blues snobbery. That's what was really behind it—this thing about people playing the blues who aren't necessarily the "right colour" or from the right place. This is like turning round to them and saying, "Well, this is as close as you're going to get." You can take it that way as well.'

The opening track, 'If The Devil Made Whiskey', was one of five self-penned songs on the album: 'I woke up one morning and I had this riff in my head and we just went into the studio and did the whole track live. I used an old Telecaster guitar and tuned it down, like an open E-chord tuned down to D, and then used bottleneck on it to give it a very earthy feel. I was hitting the pickup on the intro to give it that kind of raw sound in between the notes. You can hear this clank of the bottom E string hitting the pickup.'

For a while on the subsequent tour, the song also opened the set, much to Vic Martin's dismay: 'I didn't find any room to put keyboards on it and when we commenced touring, Gary decided it would be good opener for the show. This meant that I would join the rest of the band onstage for the second song … and be denied that euphoria of going onstage with the band … Mercifully, after the first few gigs, the song was dropped.'

Gary's track record showed how much he enjoyed doing cover versions, but always making them his own—and he invariably avoided the most obvious choices. For this album—and as part of his trawl through the classic blues catalogue for the radio show—he went for Sonny Boy Williamson's 'Eyesight To

The Blind' and Chuck Berry's 'Thirty Days', played more in the style of Johnny Winter and on tour delivered at breakneck speed. The influence of the *Beano* album was never far away, and having guested with John Mayall, Gary included 'Have You Heard', which could stretch to over ten minutes onstage. Interestingly, he told one interviewer that despite the whole vibe of a live studio album, the one solo he did overdub was the one on 'Have You Heard', 'because I was playing too many Clapton licks from the original version. It was kind of ingrained. I had to change guitars after the band left and you hear a little bit of the spill of the original in there'.

Lisa Sharken, the sharp-eared interviewer from *Ultimate Guitar*, heard a tremolo bar sound at the end of 'Hard Times', which didn't equate with any of Gary's main guitars, but is a good example of Gary's attention to the minutiae of song construction: 'Yes you're right. That's a Burns Artist guitar from the 60s with a tiny body … it's got the original Burns pickups and it was in really good condition … you can hear the noise of the springs kind of catching at the end … it's got a personality. It's important sometimes to have things like that. It just gives the song a little bit of character.'

In that same interview, he was asked about his favourite track or solo and chose the solo on 'Trouble At Home', which gave him the chance to reiterate his feelings about how his blues guitar playing had matured over the years: 'It's the first time I've ever been able to nail what I do live and leave those big spaces in the phrasing … I think it comes across as really expressive. As a guitarist I've had to learn to leave some spaces. Guitarists have this thing where they're scared to leave a hole because they think they'll fall down in it … Actually, the bigger [the] holes you leave the better.' He told the story about Albert King encouraging him to 'play every other lick': 'Those four little words meant the whole world. It took me a long time to really take it in. But he was absolutely right. If you leave that space, if you've got a good tone and you play expressively and you can make people feel from your guitar, they won't be able to wait for the next note. It creates that tension … I grew up listening to Peter Green and he was amazing when he would leave that space. You would just go, "Come on and play the next note, man!"'

Gary was also drawn to the great blues/soul ballad singers on this album—his Otis Redding-influenced 'I Had A Dream' with a plaintive country-sounding Telecaster and Jimmy Witherspoon's version of 'Evening'. He had originally thought of doing Nina Simone's 'I Put A Spell On You', but as he told *All Out Guitar*, 'We did a couple of takes and I said, "What the fuck are we doing this for? Everyone's done this." Brian Downey said, "Look, I'll show where this song comes from." We got on the internet and found the Jimmy Witherspoon version that Brian used to do in a band called Sugar Shack when I was only sixteen, in Dublin. I remembered the song as soon as I heard it and I really wanted to do it. It's such a beautiful song and quite obscure, so not many people know it. It was much better to do something like that and much more interesting. We were able to put our own stamp on it because the Jimmy Witherspoon one has a flute and T Bone Walker is playing guitar I think. It's a bit jazzier in a way. This one is a bit spookier and quite melancholy. The lyrics are quite down, someone feeling sorry for himself, you know, very fated.'

Gary wasn't afraid to step out in front of a concert crowd and play acoustic guitar, but he had never committed one to record, until now with Son House's 'Sundown'. Gary's take on the blues was never historical or political; he came at it from a purely emotional standpoint, as the best medium for him as a guitar player, to express his feelings. But he did rediscover Son House through his blues show research. Concerning his first time round with Son House, Gary told Neville Marten about the rediscovery of Son House by young white blues fans, which led to the recording of the album *Father Of The Delta Blues*. 'And the funny thing was I'd got this vinyl record for Christmas and I'd started to collect records and I walked into this little shop and they had two blues albums, Skip James with "I'm So Glad" on it and the Son House album … I took it home and it was just wonderful. Some of the blues lyrics are like poetry.'

Speaking to Brian Holland for *All Out Guitar*, he talked about rediscovering the song to play on the album: 'It took me a while to get it because I've never done an acoustic blues in my life on an album, you know. It was quite a challenge. I ended up doing it just sitting on a couch at the back of the control room and it wasn't right, so we all went down the pub one night and had a few drinks—only out of respect to Son House, of course. That's probably how he used to do it. I got myself in the right frame of mind and we did it in one take … it came out well, so it gives you a bit of confidence in that direction.'

The band with Pete, Vic and Brian toured extensively through 2007 with dates spread out from March right through to November, taking in the UK, Scandinavia and Germany, Ukraine and Russia together with less trodden paths such as Serbia and Bulgaria. The year ended, though, on a very different note—and one of Gary's many career high spots: Gary Moore plays Jimi Hendrix.

The songs of Jimi Hendrix had been part of Gary's repertoire since his earliest playing days. More recently, those songs had crept back in—*A Different Beat* and the Fender fiftieth anniversary concert. But an opportunity arose to go the full nine yards with the launch of the DVD of *Monterey Pop*. Gary put together a trio with Darrin and bassist Dave Bronze for the film showing and concert at the London Hippodrome on October 25, where Gary also played with Billy Cox and Mitch Mitchell.

As we have seen time and again, Gary could play just about anything thrown at him—and, as ridiculous as this might sound, certainly as good if not better than the original. Darrin heard this first-hand 'in rehearsals because we just jammed around sometimes; if you played him any fucking guitarist, he could play any of his songs back—Beatles riffs, he could do Jimi songs, Sex Pistols, Rage Against The Machine. He even sussed out System of a Down and some of the Metallica ones.' Vic Martin has another example: 'Jan Akkerman was backstage with Gary in the dressing room and they sat there with Gary playing "Sylvia" better than Akkerman. He just knew everything.'

It is hard to imagine any other guitarist on the planet better equipped to stand in front of an audience and be filmed for posterity playing the music of the most influential rock guitarist of all time—and sharing the stage with Jimi's sidemen. The pressure doesn't get more intense: Gary certainly felt it as they toiled away in rehearsals, really doing their homework. While Gary possessed a very sensitive, nervous and humble disposition, deep down he must have known just how good he was otherwise he would never have had the supreme confidence to put himself on the line like this. At one level, it should not have been surprising that the evening was a complete triumph for Gary. Even so, it was still one hell of an achievement and remains a lasting testament not only to Gary's immense technical ability, but the degree to which he could harness that ability to drive the heart and soul of his emotions through six metal strings.

Two-thousand-and-seven ended well for Gary: a great showcase concert, the traumas of the accident with his hand now just a bad dream, strong albums added to the catalogue, touring as little or as often as he wanted to, solid backing in his professional and personal life. But inside twelve months, the landscape of Gary's personal life would yet again get bent out of shape.

14

TROUBLE AIN'T FAR BEHIND

—

They toured from April through to July and then went into Sphere with Gary producing *Bad For You Baby*, which signalled a return to the raunchier style last heard on *Power Of The Blues*. 'The album is a lot more aggressive than the last one because it was on the back of a tour and I've tried to inject my live style of playing inside the songs. When you've finished touring, your playing is usually at its peak. There's still a lot of energy and it's a really good time to record. We took a month off and then went to the studio where we cut eleven backing tracks in five days. Then I had ten more dates and being able to play a lot of the material that was on the album live really helped. Doing those gigs was great. It gave me a lot of confidence with the vocals when we went back in and it was also a boost to know that people seemed to like the new material.'

Reviewing the album for allmusic.com, Hal Horowitz wrote, 'Another year, another Gary Moore blues-rock album nearly interchangeable with the last. That's no problem for fans or even newcomers, because despite the surface similarities between releases, Moore never seems to be going through the motions for the sake of further bulking up his already substantial catalogue. His tough guitar lines remain biting yet classy, and his underappreciated voice is strong and convincing on originals and covers that nail all of the blues-rock bases without sounding rote. While there are no surprises here, *Bad For You Baby* is far from a disappointment. Moore continues a string of rugged, post-hard rock, power blues that he has carved his niche in since 1990's *Still Got The Blues*. He applies his throaty vocals and feral guitar to a pair of Muddy Waters tunes to impressive effect. No one will mistake his versions of Waters's "Walking Through The Park" or "Someday Baby" for the classic Chess era nuggets they are. Yet Moore's rocked up attack hits the mark for being relatively faithful to their melodies even as he wields his power blues sledgehammer. Moore boogies through J.B. Lenoir's "Mojo Boogie" like he invented the style, and even if his husky vocals will never be mistaken for Lenoir's reedy, high-pitched singing, he tears into the tune with enough energy to shake up anything in the Johnny Winter songbook. Guitar shredders will thrill to the hot fret acrobatics of the double-time "Down The Line", and those who thought Led Zeppelin's first album was their finest hour should chow down on the hard rocking Jimmy Page-isms of "Umbrella Man". Moore writes one for the ladies on the sweet ballad "Holding On", which won't win any awards for lyrical complexity but boasts a lovely melody and Otis Taylor's daughter, Cassie, on backing vocals. Cassie returns with her dad (plucking nearly inaudible banjo) for the swamped up "Preacher Man Blues" that features some surprisingly effective harp from Moore, the only time he plays it on this disc. Al Kooper's slow, yearning "I Love You More Than You'll Ever Know" from the New Yorker's Blood, Sweat & Tears stint is given an extended, nearly eleven-minute treatment that's as compelling as BS&T's. Those hoping for Moore to expand his horizons will need to wait a little longer, but for existing followers and especially those new to his gutsy approach, *Bad For You Baby* more than fills the bill.'

The end of the first part of the tour finished at a bikers' convention in Faro, Portugal, after which Gary and Jo decided to stay on for a holiday. By now, they were man and wife. After years of being pestered, Jo had finally agreed to marry Gary in November 2006. There was no best man, but Graham and Dick Meredith were the two witnesses. Dick had recently joined Gary's team as tour manager around May/June and quickly became both an integral part of the setup and close to Gary: 'The very first show I was scheduled to do with Gary I had to cancel. My wife was expecting our second boy and everything was late. So, I had to go down to Music Bank and tell Gary that I couldn't do the show, but that I had a more than adequate replacement. I got the famous brow coming down, but as soon as he heard it was about family and children, I could have done anything.

'I remember once in Denmark, Gary roasting the promoter, something wasn't right in the dressing room and he gave it to him with both barrels. This was very early on and I thought, *Oh no*—and then he turned round, looked at me and winked—and then he walked off. That summed it up. At that point, I knew I had his trust and I knew where he was coming from. I loved the honour of being at his wedding; that was a special day and seeing Jo so happy.'

Family was everything to Gary: Otis Taylor says that much of their talk was about family and it was always a focus for conversation with Darren Main, Chris Tsangarides and most of those in Gary's immediate circle. But on that holiday beach in Portugal in July 2008, Jo could sense that something was wrong.

Gary would often drink at the end of a tour as part of the winding down process, 'but this was different,' says Jo. 'He started drinking to the point where I was saying, "What's wrong with you?" In the end, I just cut the holiday short and we went home.' Jo doesn't think there was anybody in the picture at that point, at least no direct evidence, but Gary was clearly getting into a more distant and dark state of mind.

Eventually, in October, it happened. Gary's German promoter and friend George Hofmann says he blames himself: 'This girl was at every gig in the front row. Gary was due to appear on the *Schmidt & Pocher* TV show in Cologne.

After the show, we came out of the studio, walked back to the bus, a crowd outside wanting autographs and we were on our way to a Chinese restaurant. Gary said, "Get some girl to join us," and I pointed out this lady. Although she had been coming to gigs, they had not met until that night, so I consider it my fault.' The girl in question was a tall blonde in her early thirties named Petra Nioduschewski.

As usual on tour, Gary would phone home, but as Jo sussed straight away, this was a different Gary: 'I know it was Halloween because I had a load of kids dressed up and we were about to go up to the Booth Museum for their Halloween night. He phoned and then I said I had to go and he said he was fine with that, he didn't want to stay on the phone, which was weird, not like him at all. I thought, *What's wrong? Who's in the room with him?* He got home about ten days later and I just said to him, "What the fuck are you up to?"

'He tried to say it [the affair] was over, that he wanted us to stay together. But he was such an idiot: his phone was in my name. I said, "You're telling me one thing and your phone bills are telling me something different. Why are there so many calls to Germany when I'm not in the house?" Then he was saying, "Oh, I've got to get her a new car, otherwise she'll go to the papers." But it was all an excuse, really.'

Gary moved out of the family home and rented a house around the corner, ostensibly to get his head together and come back. But, says Jo, 'as soon as he moved out, there were planes coming into Gatwick from Germany and I knew this because I was getting all his credit card bills. So not smart, really.'

Jo was due to celebrate her fortieth birthday with a big party just before Christmas 2008, which she cancelled. Meanwhile, Gary put together a band for a very different party. Pete and Vic teamed up with Steve Dixon, a drummer friend of Pete's from the London circuit. 'I first met Gary while on a gig in Worthing with Buddy Whittington,' says Steve. 'Gary lived nearby and came by to jam. He was very complimentary about my playing and left with a handshake. Three weeks later I received a call from him out of the blue asking if I was busy over the Christmas period.'

To the outside world, it seems odd that major rock stars, playing to vast crowds in huge arenas, surrounded by an entourage of flunkies ready to fulfil their every whim, would be bothered to play for private parties. But a gig's a gig and some artists command fees running into the millions for one evening just to stroke the vanity of some obscenely rich businessman or politician who wants to impress his kids and business associates. Gary wasn't quite in that top drawer, but he was now a familiar face on the Russian concert scene. He was paid a reputed £250,000 plus accommodation for the whole band and crew at the Ritz Carlton Hotel in Moscow to perform at a pre-New Year's Eve party deep in the bowels of the Kremlin, attended by (then) Prime Minister Vladimir Putin, Russian President Dmitri Medvedev and forty of their friends.

Graham Lilley remembers 'huge tables, full silver service, stage at one end with a video wall that moved across the stage. There was an orchestra and opera singers, mariachi band, a Russian pop duo and Gary (who did just four or five songs) and the entertainment switched from one end to the other.' When he played 'The Blues Is Alright', Gary got the Big Men dancing.

Dick Meredith recalls one potentially tricky moment: 'The people who were close to the people wanted to see the set list and they said, "The people would like to hear 'Still Got The Blues' first." I dreaded telling Gary that; he just looked at me and I was waiting for a "Fuck off," but instead he said, "He's playing me so much money, I'll play it backwards if he wants." My abiding memory is seeing President Medvedev playing air guitar. Because it was between Xmas and New Year, Gary paid the crew double.'

They also played another private birthday party for the Mayor of Moscow who had the Kremlin Theatre decked out with a backdrop of Tower Bridge and other iconic London features and then, later in 2010, another one for some wealthy Russian in a luxury five-star hotel in Cap Ferrat, southern France. Luxury it might have been, but they still had to lug all the gear up flights of stairs. Gary's agent Prue went down there and had to get her expenses cleared when she was charged £110 for a modest salad and a glass of wine.

The band—still with Steve Dixon on drums—toured extensively in 2009, spread over the longest time between March right through to December, although with weeks off in between. Gary had told Kerry that he actually wanted to be out on the road, which wasn't like Gary at all and was indicative of how bad things were at home. He ended up buying a house in Brighton for him and Petra to live in—almost equidistant between Jo's house with Lily and Kerry's with Jack and Gus. Jo would come home to find him sitting on the stairs or helping himself to something to eat from the fridge. She told to make up his mind about where he wanted to be, although coming into 2010, her attitude was hardening about Gary coming back at all. Other times, he would be round at Kerry's. 'He would tell me that Petra was looking after him, but in all honesty, she wasn't, and they were eating out or getting takeaways every night. I had massive concerns about his health and I'd say to Jack I was worried. Gary was really bloated and very depressed, the lowest I'd ever seen him.'

Gary was wracked with guilt, but apparently just couldn't help himself. It really was all or nothing with Gary, whether it was music, drinking or relationships. As reprehensible as it might be, Gary couldn't just have one-night stands in faraway places. Darren Main, who had to get Gary up in the mornings on tour can testify that—despite offers and opportunities—this was not his style. He had to throw himself 100 percent into some over-romanticised, doomed relationship that never made him happy. Kerry says Petra told Gary that her boyfriend had kicked her out, which is why she came to live in Brighton, 'so there was never a sense that this was some deep and meaningful relationship—not at all'.

It was getting increasingly difficult for his family to contact Gary; his phone would be switched off or Petra would answer. Some thought she was trying to position herself between Gary and family, others thought Gary was just using her as a shield because he was so ashamed about what he had done. Jack Moore's view of Petra, though, is unambiguous: 'She just drained him, cut off all his family ties. He was in a really dark place and she didn't seem to want to look after him. I didn't have any concerns about his health until he moved out. He was perfectly capable of looking after himself, but he needed that extra thing and he didn't get it with Petra. She monopolised the whole situation, made it hard to contact dad, very selfish—and I don't think he liked that at all. I think she used to make him turn the phone off and strange things like that. He always seemed preoccupied. He somehow wanted both of them, but he actually said to me, "I'm not sure about Petra moving to Brighton."' Lily says that she herself changed quite a bit: 'I'd always been a huge daddy's girl. I suddenly saw in a different light what he could be like. I went the opposite way and became really clingy with my mum, a bit anxious all the time.'

There were clear signs that, in his distress, he was letting himself go. Previously a fit and strong man—walking, going to the gym or swimming fifty lengths without thinking about it—videos and photos in 2010 show he was putting on a lot of weight. As Kerry says, his diet was in freefall; at one point, Gary was a vegetarian—there were concert riders to that effect in his contracts. Darren tells a little anecdote about the bacon breakfast: 'I went downstairs at the hotel we were in to sort out Gary's breakfast. I told them what I wanted—juice, cereal, fruit, toast, eggs, tea, but no meat. I was walking up to the room with this big tureen and I thought I'd just check what was underneath. I put it down, lifted the lid and there was a mountain of bacon there! I wrapped it in a serviette and left it on top of the drinks machine outside. I went in, "Here's your breakfast, Gary." "Oh, thanks." I went back outside and dumped the bacon in a bin. Later he said, "Really liked that breakfast. Full of lovely flavours." I thought, *How ironic is that? Shall I tell him?* But I didn't.'

Gary's drug days were long gone, and he was virulently anti-smoking, frowning on anybody in the team who smoked, enforcing a backstage smoking ban and even trying to insist on smoke-free venues. As far as alcohol was concerned, there was a quote from F. Scott Fitzgerald who said he was 'drinking intermittently but generously', and that was Gary—what would be called these days 'a binge drinker'.

At times in his life, the drinking could be a problem. But then again, many people interviewed for this book say they hardly saw him drink at all. He rarely drank on the road except at the end of the tour and Jo said they would both have a couple of healthy weeks if they thought they had been drinking a bit too much. Pete Rees says, 'he'd check to see if we'd been drinking before a gig. In the end, I was hardly drinking at all, so he probably did me a favour there. You really had to concentrate on what you were doing, so you couldn't go on half-cut.'

But Gary would certainly drink when he was miserable and unhappy and when he had to fly. The combination of the two could be pretty toxic and hard to handle. Dick Meredith calls it 'the Chablis Club', the weapon needed to sedate Gary enough to get him on a plane. And woe betide anybody who thought they could keep up with Gary once he got going—because like in most aspects of his life, once he started he couldn't stop. 'I remember on one flight,' says Dick, 'some poor fella thought he'd stick with Gary on the drinking. He was suddenly Gary's best friend. By the time we got off the plane, the poor guy was slumped in the corner having urinated himself. He was just an utter mess.'

At the best of times, Gary was never one for surprises. What you really didn't want to do is put him in front of a load of journalists as he steps off a plane rather the worse for wear, which is precisely happened once in November 2009 in Budapest. As Dick explains, 'most of those East European promoters would ambush you off the plane to go and do a press conference. They've all got such bad reputations for selling tickets where the artist doesn't turn up because they were never signed. So it is in their interests, the minute the artist touches down in the country—boom—get him on TV, so they sell their tickets in a day.' Gary was completely unprepared and the car crash interview that followed can be seen on YouTube.

But all that was par for the course; with Petra, nobody has any explanation as to what was going on this time round. Jo thought she was simply being traded in for 'this year's model' and banal as it might sound, there may be an element of truth about this because the physicality of some of the music on *Bad For You Baby* heralded another shift in direction. Gary was planning to revive his Celtic rock. The way Gary's mind seemed to work, the idea that brand-new music should be accompanied by a brand-new life is not that far-fetched. Gary was very image conscience and if he had visions of stalking the corridors of the rock palaces once more, maybe he thought he needed the archetypal blond trophy girlfriend to go with it. Lily says that Gary would actually ask her advice about getting back with Jo: 'We talked about it a lot. But he would never admit he was getting older; maybe it freaked him out a bit.' Lily hints too at the possibility of a mid-life crisis.

During the first part of 2010, there were further trips to Russia, Japan and South Korea. Their flight from London to Moscow was the last one out before Icelandic volcano ash shut down European air space—and they flew from Moscow to Tokyo on the first flight allowed out. They got off the plane and the first thing Gary saw was a media gaggle waiting patiently. Dick had visions of another Budapest stitch-up, 'so I'm on the phone to the promoter and he went, "No, no, it's because of the volcano—this is the first flight that's made it back to Japan." So, Gary was fuming and then when I told him it wasn't for us; he said, "What do you mean it's not for us?" Hilarious.'

Dick was the latest in a long line of musicians and crew to be taken aback by Gary's pin-sharp hearing: 'During a soundcheck on the tour, Gary turns to Vic and says, "Your Hammond's out of tune." And he was right because he had perfect pitch. We finished the soundcheck and couldn't figure out what was wrong. The Hammond was running on generators which weren't kicking out exactly the right frequency of power. It was a tiny, tiny difference and nobody else could hear it—except Gary. Another time, we were out shopping and there was a church with a bell-ringing concert going on. They had a flyer telling you what they were ringing and what the notes were. It became a game. We would ask Gary what the note was and he was right every single time.'

Once the first part of the tour was over in April, Gary made a sudden announcement that he was breaking up the band: 'Gary told us he was doing the Celtic rock thing,' says Pete. 'He was very tearful, saying how much he would miss us. He just wanted to do something different, like he wanted to with Scars. But he did say that after that, he would be in touch with us to do another blues album and I'm sure he would have.'

The decision did make sense both musically and financially. Those type of rebel-rousing, breast-beating songs were always great crowd-pleasers. Promoters were just as keen: you could sell more seats playing rock than blues, especially in some of the more exotic and lucrative territories or even in established areas like Germany. Gary had said in an interview that he had seen Muse play and realised that rock was a young man's game whereas the blues greats went on for ever without dimming their credibility. The Celtic rock idea was different; being Irish gave Gary license to continue ploughing this furrow.

There was a negative aspect to this decision; he had become embroiled in alleged plagiarism cases over 'Still Got The Blues'. Both cases were brought in Germany. The first one arose shortly after the song was released, brought by a porn movie director who claimed that Gary pinched the riff from the score of one his films. This suit was quickly swatted into touch. The second was more serious and centred around a song called 'Nordrach' by the band Jud's Gallery. The litigation was protracted and expensive, with witnesses and experts called. At the end, the judge said he could find no evidence that Gary had deliberately plagiarised the song, which wasn't even available on record at the time Gary was alleged to have heard it. But the riff was similar enough to mean there was a case to answer. It was settled confidentially out of court, but did serve to deplete the coffers, which needed replenishing. Added to the costs of the case, cash flow was reduced as royalties had been held in escrow pending the outcome.

However, Gary had been planning this move for some time. He had tried out the new Celtic rock tracks he would play back in 2005 with Jon Noyce in the run-up to the Phil Lynott concert. Subsequently, Jon got the call as early as March 2010, when Gary still had his blues band on the road.

Rehearsals for the swerve in direction began in May. But doubts were raised in Jon's mind—and in the minds of others—as to whether Gary was really fit enough to take a very demanding rock show out on the road: 'When Darrin and I turned up for the first rehearsal at John Henry's, Gary was sitting down. I was taken aback, he looked like he'd swallowed a football. Even back the previous November when I saw him at Shepherd's Bush, he just wasn't as sharp to talk to—he'd always been lucid and direct. As time went on, it became clear that he wasn't taking best care of himself. Even Darrin had to get into shape for this very athletic set.'

Gary had to keep 'Parisienne Walkways' and 'Still Got The Blues', but dumped the whole blues set (except 'Walking By Myself') for songs culled from *Wild Frontier* and *After The War*. Although the material was very familiar for Gary, he had to push himself through a strenuous relearning process in a very short space of time. The playing was physically hard, the vocals were pitched higher in the keys of the original songs whereas he had become used to singing blues songs that were much better suited for his vocal range. Jon says, 'he spent a lot of time working on "The Boys Are Back In Town". He said he'd been working a lot on that—he was really quite worried about those machine-gun lyrics.' Much to Gary's delight, Jon and Darrin had come into the rehearsals well prepared so they had a fast turn-around for the rehearsals. Jon observes: 'Gary wanted to do something, the money was going to be good and it was all systems go. There was some serious money on the table to go back to Japan—and even America was being talked about.'

Another Japan trip made sense; having gone there with a blues set in 2010, you could go back in 2011 with a rock band, play the same venues and earn big money all over again. But at the start, there were some niggling doubts as to whether Gary could perform up to his usual high standard and the first few gigs were, in Jon's words, 'a bit hit and miss'.

They played a Swedish rock festival in June in front of 40,000 people, and Neil Carter, who had re-joined the band on keyboards, says that Gary just stood there: 'He didn't put on a show, it was a bit of an out of body experience.' Nor was Montreux on July 6 any better; Jon and Darrin both recollect that Gary made some big mistakes—a whole section was missed out of the first song—and was drunk onstage as he was for the High Voltage Festival in London on July 24. Jon says, 'Gary was frustrated because the set had been cut to fifty minutes and we had a walk-on tape that was about four or five minutes long, so we lost a tune. Dick had to go on and drag him offstage.' His musicians were just shocked—they had never seen Gary in this state before, a musician who took such pride in his performance.

They had a tour coming up October taking them all over Russia; nobody in the crew was much looking forward to it. Because of the huge distances involved between gigs, they would have to fly everywhere—and fly every day—and in a Yak 42 plane, which Neil reckons 'looked like it was going to drop out of the sky at any moment'. They knew Gary was going to be in a permanent state of anxiety, therefore drinking too much, and that was going to make life difficult. Jon says that once the trip was underway, 'a few times I had to comfort him, reassure him; he was terrified'. And if that wasn't bad enough, Gary suddenly announced on the eve of the trip that Petra was coming too.

Gary had two families: the one in Brighton, and the one on the road—and those guys were finding the situation very hard to handle. They all loved Jo and thought she was the best thing for Gary. Petra? Not so much. Gary was damaging not one family but two and it was around this time that Darren, Graham (and Dick) had the only serious cross words they ever had with him.

For Darren, it was especially heart-breaking to see what was going on after all the years of fun and good times on the road. 'Once we got out to Russia, things were getting overlooked because Dick, for example, couldn't get to Gary as he was used to, so the smooth running of the operation was compromised. It wasn't until he had a few drinks that Gary could tell me what was going on in his life. You could see the turmoil that was going on—the nights got later and I wasn't drinking so I could see the pain, and it was painful to see. Both families lost the man they knew; he became someone else and he couldn't convince anybody that he was the same Gary. There were still nice times, but when it wasn't nice, it was pretty horrible. I could see a man fighting against himself.'

It was the worst time for Petra to be around anyway because Gary was fighting hard to bed in with his new and far more strenuous live routine and cope with all the travelling. Gary didn't even seem that happy with Petra; according to the crew, he and Petra often had very public arguments. There was one private argument where Darren says they fought over a soft toy that Gary had bought for Lily, with Petra claiming the Lily didn't need any more toys or was too old for it. After they left the hotel room, Darren did his usual room check in case anything had been left behind and found it on the floor.

Darren tried to convince Petra to go home and at one point she agreed, until, as Darren puts it, 'I got called to the room.' However unpleasant and disruptive the situation, Gary was the boss and could have fired anybody on the spot. If any crew member seriously didn't like it, he knew where the door was. It never came to that, but it was a close-run thing.

While all that was going on, Graham Lilley, also acting as production manager (everybody multi-tasked in this lean outfit), had to deal with all sorts of nonsense to get the band onstage in Russia: 'You could get uneven stages that sloped from front to back, the equipment was not good: "Don't worry, a new desk is coming." "Okay, where is it?" "About 60 km away." "Well, we're on in twenty minutes." It was just painful. They just lied to you, to your face, five times a day: "Where's this?" "Where's that?" "When are we going to the airport?" "Well, you're not going to the airport, you're going to this restaurant." "Why?" You find out that the promoter had sold the show into a local promoter in this town, who's got a mate who owns this restaurant. In Vladivostok, the doors to the hotel rooms all looked like they'd been kicked in and the place was cockroach infested. We got upgraded to a better class of cockroach.'

There was never any delay getting to the shows, though: 'We were in these cars,' says Darrin Mooney, 'and I don't know what they had in front, but everyone was getting out the way. I think these things are organised by people you don't fuck about with. We had the Moscow Hell's Angels looking after us.'

But despite all this, the show improved, to the extent that Darrin says 'it was the most enjoyable set I've done with Gary. I felt really lucky. I'd done the Hendrix thing, gone away [back to Primal Scream], come back and the last set was brilliant. It was the best tour; they were big gigs, just us, no support and the crowds loved it.' Those in the front row would have known they'd been to a Gary Moore concert. 'We did try to get Gary to turn down,' says Dick, 'like in France where it's the law and in Russia where they have this mistaken belief that the front row is where the best seats are because it is all status—even though the sound isn't the best. So, the front row is where all the dignitaries sit—and that's where you get absolutely battered by Gary's sound on stage.'

Jon reckons that the drinking to get Gary onstage over the summer was getting out of control but agrees with Darrin that 'once we were on the road in Russia, he settled down and the playing settled down. That gave us a chance to really come together as a group and really play and the gigs were consistently good.'

For the band, who were relatively protected from much of the offstage trouble, it was a good tour. But it was a subdued crew that arrived back in the UK at the end of November. Gary's usual round of thanks to everybody was noticeably absent and they all went their separate ways.

Although there isn't any evidence that Gary had a whole new batch of songs ready, he did start rehearsals in January 2011, intending to lead up to recording sessions. Based on the shows from summer 2010 onwards, Gary was making it plain he was back to playing rock. George Hofmann says he had already pencilled in a new round of German dates, offers of festival appearances were coming in, there was more talk of America, South America and, according to Dick, 'a massive offer from Australia was on the table'.

Gary went into rehearsals from January 17–20 with Jon Noyce and a new drummer, Rob Green, with Neil Carter scheduled to join later. Rob was the drummer with Toploader and, as it happened, the partner of Gary's ex-wife Kerry. Rob and Gary had first met some years before when Rob came round to pick up Jack and Gus, 'so obviously I was a bit nervous. But as soon as we saw each other, we started talking about music, about drummers, nothing about relationships or anything like that. It was never awkward. It went on for years like that. I went to see him play and listened to some of the drummers, thinking, *I could do that.* Then one day he asked me to put up a television screen at his house. And he was complaining that Darrin Mooney couldn't commit to him because Primal Scream were going out again. And I said, "Well Gary, I'm always here," and we joked about that and then he said, "Do you want to come to a rehearsal?" "Absolutely! Why not?" I knew all the material anyway. I used to do a couple of Gary Moore songs in my old pub covers band in the 80s. Initially, he said to just learn these three tracks and then we went down to Music Bank to do them. He didn't know I knew the whole set backwards.'

The return to playing Celtic rock rekindled all Gary's memories of Phil. 'He talked about Phil a lot,' says Jon, 'like every day, he'd talk about Phil. He'd talk about him like a brother. Even during that last rehearsal, same thing.'

Gary wanted to spend some time with Lily and take her away over the February school half-term holiday for a few days, after which he planned to start recording the new album. But Lily didn't want to go and sleep in the same room with Gary and Petra and wasn't happy about being in a room by herself. So, the whole point of going away at all was lost. Gary and Petra drove alone to Gatwick; the driver later said Gary seemed very subdued. They arrived in Malaga on Saturday February 5 to drive to Estepona where they were booked into the five-star Kempinski Hotel.

Darren Main hadn't seen Gary since coming back from Russia. Normally, they would have met over Christmas when Gary would go back to Weston-Super-Mare to see his mother and siblings and where Darren lived with his family. They would go out together, catch up and have a meal. Gary would often take this opportunity to play with his brother Cliff, also an accomplished guitarist, at a local gig.

But Gary didn't go home over Christmas 2010 and so just on a whim, on Friday 4, Darren decided to call Gary up. 'He answered straight away, which was pretty unusual. We were on the phone for an hour and a half. He sounded really happy and positive, so refreshed and enthused. He was really pleased that Rob and Jon were so prepared for the rehearsals and was keen to get back and record. He said he'd bought three new guitars and we laughed about that because I said, "Like you need them. And who's going to have to carry them around on the road?" He said that when he got back, I should come over for a few days. It was a lovely, lovely conversation. We spoke about everything, but he didn't mention Petra once.'

On Sunday February 6, Darren took a mobile phone call around seven in the morning: 'It was Petra telling me that Gary had died at four o'clock in the morning. I asked her what had happened. She said she thought he had choked on sick. He was quiet and she couldn't hear him breathing. She said he hadn't been drinking since Russia.'

There was no more information at that point. Darren then asked Petra if she had called any of the family—she said no—so Darren said he would do all that was immediately necessary. 'I also asked her if she was okay, did she want me to call anybody for her? She said no, but I did tell her to call her family or whoever she might want to talk to.'

Darren knew he had to act fast because he didn't want the family finding out through some news flash. 'I phoned Jo but got the home answer machine and the mobile voicemail but asked her to phone me asap.' Darren had been so concerned about Gary's health in recent months that not long before Gary died, says Jon Noyce, 'Darren said to me, "I don't want to be the one phoning Jo."' Yet, tragically, this is precisely where he found himself.

Darren then phoned Gary's brother Cliff. 'We arranged I would pick him up and go and see their mum and sisters. Then I called Graham, Dick, Jo again. I phoned Petra again to try and get more information. She said she had called the security guard when she couldn't wake him, tried CPR too, beating him on the chest.

'After picking up Cliff, we went to Mrs Moore's home to be greeted by Gary's sister Maggie. Everyone was in complete shock. Winnie asked me to go to her, she put her hands on my face and drawing me to her within a few inches of her face said, "You know what you must do. Please bring my boy home."'

Eventually, Darren got through to Jo who naturally had many questions that couldn't yet be answered. The imperative was to make all the necessary arrangements to bring Gary home. Darren then made a string of calls to Brian Downey, Cass Lewis, Otis Taylor, Jack Bruce, Pete Rees, Vic Martin, Kerry, Steve Dixon, Chris Tsangarides, Darrin, Jon, Neil and Andy Crookston. Nobody could believe what had happened.

Graham had just got back from walking the dog 'when the phone rang and it was Darren. Then the phones just went … Petra left a voicemail message while I was talking to Darren; Jo was asking me to tell her it wasn't true; Don Airey was in tears. I couldn't put the phone down. We were all just playing it by ear at that point and didn't really know what was going on.'

Dick got the call around 8.30. 'I was pretty much going through a mental breakdown because my own marriage was in a hole. I could see it was Darren, I was in bed, but didn't want to talk. But the minute I hit the "refuse call" button, I knew something was wrong and I called him straight back. "What is it?" "It's Gary. He's gone." When the shock died down, I called Prue and then Simon Moran, his promoter because he was massively supportive of Gary.'

Gary's team began to get organised. It was agreed that Dick would stay in the UK to coordinate proceedings with the British consulate while Graham, Darren and Cliff would fly out to Spain on Monday. The story hit the wires by about six on Sunday evening by which time all the right people knew what had happened. Graham put a statement on the website and then shut it down.

Darren and Cliff flew out of Bristol on a 6am flight, Graham on the 11:15 from Heathrow. They met up at the Malaga hotel they were booked into, but couldn't go straight to Estepona, because they needed to meet with the local funeral director. Gary was in a Chapel of Rest in town. They had to start the repatriation process, which needed the presence of next of kin—Cliff—to answer all the necessary questions. Graham and Darren went into see Gary first; Cliff couldn't quite do it straight away, but then he went in and Graham left so the 'the Weston boys' could say their goodbyes.

Petra didn't want to visit Gary because, according to Darren, she said, 'I've already seen him dead.' A week after Gary died, the *Daily Mail* ran a story headlined 'Heartbreak of blond beauty who was Thin Lizzy guitarist Gary Moore's last love'. In it, the paper claimed because Petra was by herself at the hotel that 'by all appearances, his [Gary's] family has shunned her'. But appearances can be deceptive. Once they were out there, Graham and Darren (who says he felt quite sorry for Petra having found herself in this awful situation) did all they could to include Petra in what was going on, keep her informed and make sure she wasn't alone by offering her (more than once) accommodation in their hotel. But Darren says she refused all offers of help.

Then they all drove to Estepona and the hotel where Darren had the task of going to the fourth-floor room with a sea view and gathering Gary's personal effects and choosing a set of clothes for Gary to come home in. The *Mail* article shows Darren leaving the hotel, captioning him as 'Gary Moore's family', probably meaning Cliff, but close to the truth. To all intents and purposes, Darren was family.

Darren offered to escort Petra on the flight out, which she originally agreed to but then phoned him later, 'shouting at me, saying that she didn't need us any more, that she had made her own plans, that we couldn't be making arrangements for her. But the company still booked and paid for her flight. Then she arrived an hour late at the airport and just created a whole load of ill feeling with the check-in staff at the gate, which I helped to diffuse. We then told her that some plans had been put in place for the arrival in the UK because the family wanted to avoid the paparazzi. But she had obviously made up her mind to do it her way and when we arrived, took off at the speed of sound.'

There had been a preliminary inquest in Spain suggesting that Gary had suffered a massive heart attack. But there were unsubstantiated rumours that Gary had died, John Bonham style, of an alcohol overdose. The proper inquest opened in Brighton on 18 February held before the Coroner, Veronica Hamilton-Deeley. Petra refused to attend but gave a telephone statement to the Coroner's Officer, Penny Bailey. The court witness testimonies were given by Graham and Darren, Dr Mark Howard, a consultant pathologist who had conducted the UK post-mortem, and Dr Andrew Smith, a toxicologist from Royal Sussex Country Hospital, who had carried out the necessary toxicology tests. Jo and Kerry were also present, designated as Properly Interested Persons who could ask questions of the Coroner and the witnesses.

Given the rumours, Jo and Kerry were keen to get to the bottom of exactly how much Gary had to drink before he died. Those close to Gary knew he needed a drink before and during a flight. In her statement, Petra said Gary drank two glasses of wine in the airport lounge and had the same again on the plane. This was confirmed by one of the cabin crew, who didn't know the exact amount but said it wouldn't have been more than that otherwise she would have noticed because it was an early flight that lasted less than two hours. In any event, Petra said she asked him to stop drinking and he did.

After arriving at the hotel, they had a bite to eat—registered on the bar bill at 16.37 as a coca cola, bottle of champagne, club sandwich and a burger—then went for a walk.

They didn't bring in any duty-free alcohol nor was the hotel room mini bar touched. They went to the room to watch TV, but as there was nothing on, they came back to the bar at 18.41 for another sandwich and some more champagne, and another bill timed at 20.28 with a total of five brandies included plus a shot of a local liqueur courtesy of the barman. As Petra was not present, nobody was able to substantiate exactly how much of two bottles of champagne Gary had drunk.

From her statement to the Coroner's Officer, Petra says they went back up to the room at 9 (although the time she told others did vary between then and 11), where Gary lay on top of the bed and went to sleep. At some point, he woke up sneezing—which Darren confirmed in court was a sure sign that Gary had been drinking brandy. Then, about 4am, Petra woke up and said she was concerned because she saw something coming out of his mouth. She couldn't say whether Gary had actually been sick, he wasn't awake, so she turned him on his side and he seemed okay for about an hour. When Petra later couldn't get a response, she said she tried resuscitation and called for the hotel security guard. The guard said Gary was cold, suggesting that he had died even before Petra turned him over.

Giving evidence, Dr Smith, the toxicologist, said there was an immediate problem in undertaking proper tests because Gary's body had been embalmed as part of the repatriation requirement and so the fluid used would compromise test results. This meant that Dr Smith could only do extrapolations of any drug or alcohol findings—they could not be totally accurate. One thing was certain: there were no drugs, prescription or otherwise, in Gary's body.

Regarding alcohol, the level was well above the driving limit, which was hardly a shock given that wine, champagne, brandy and an unknown liqueur had been consumed in a 24-hour period. But the degree to which the alcohol content was enough to be fatal could not be determined clinically because the doctor could only test urine (protected in the bladder), not blood, because of the embalming fluid. So, while he was quite sure of his findings, an element of doubt remained as to whether the alcohol levels were as high as he calculated. Ultimately, though, precision around the levels were not that relevant to the outcome.

It was the pathologist, Dr Howard, who was able to shed light on what happened and it wasn't straightforward. Gary did not die simply from acute alcohol poisoning, nor did he have a heart attack. It was an unfortunate combination of factors conspiring to deal the fatal blow. Ironically, the fact that he *hadn't* been drinking in recent months made him more vulnerable.

Dr Howard found that Gary had a serious undiagnosed heart condition that had been building up for years. He also found that Gary had an enlarged liver, which was less serious, but still played its part. In a nutshell, alcohol can act as a poison on both the heart and liver. In the case of the heart, it affects the cells that help coordinate the pumping of blood round the system. With the liver, there are enzymes that deal with toxins like alcohol. In Gary's case, his liver had got used to *not* having to deal with much alcohol at all, so there weren't enough enzymes to suddenly disperse a raised level of alcohol intake. By itself, this was probably not fatal—but it was enough to tip Gary over the edge. In effect, and assuming the health problems continued to be undiagnosed, it was a disaster waiting to happen.

In hindsight, there was testimony from the inquest and from interviews given for this book that for some while Gary had not seemed to be his usual sharp and focused self. He was making mistakes onstage, repeating himself verbally and showing unusual signs of tiredness. Both Jon Noyce and Graham noted that he was taking quite a lot of breaks during rehearsals, they weren't using the fully booked time and he was tending to doze off in the car. Of course, he was a man approaching sixty, trying to get back to a punishing rock show performance and schedule, so it wasn't surprising that it was taking its toll. Even so, Gary was exhibiting all the symptoms of somebody whose heart was not getting sufficient oxygen to everywhere it needed to be—in other words, somebody with a heart condition. But he rarely went to see a doctor: it was established at the inquest that he hadn't seen his main GP, Dr Whiteson, since 2007 or his local GP, Dr Petzold, since 2009. Jo says she was desperately trying to get Gary to see Dr Whiteson, even after she had split from Gary, because she could see something was very wrong.

As far as what happened when Gary and Petra went to bed, the fact that Gary had consumed some fatty food, i.e., the burger and maybe the cheese sandwich too, would have delayed absorption of alcohol in the bloodstream. He might have appeared a bit tipsy, but by no means falling-down drunk. The effects of the alcohol would have come on slowly over time as he slipped into unconsciousness. The pathologist reckoned that once that happened, Gary was never fully conscious again and his vital organs slowly packed up: first his breathing, then his heart.

At the inquest, a key question for Kerry and Jo was, 'Could anything have been done to save Gary?' There were certainly some discrepancies in Petra's account, most notably, she said that when she went to the bathroom to get a flannel to clean up whatever was coming out of Gary's mouth, she came back to find him not only sneezing, but on the floor. The pathologist said Gary could easily have still been unconscious at that point, but he must have been alive otherwise he couldn't sneeze. And if he was the floor, how did he get back into bed? Did he get back himself or did she help him? If not, did Petra leave him on the floor? Because she would not have had the strength to lift him herself. The Coroner didn't notice this, but even if she had, the only person who could have answered this and other questions was not there. (Petra declined to be interviewed for the book).

In the light of the evidence at his disposal, Dr Howard concluded that even though Gary was probably in a coma, if he had been taken to hospital immediately, he could have been monitored. So, if Gary had stopped breathing or had a heart attack, medical staff would have been on hand. But Petra could not have been expected to know the severity of what was taking place and there was no guarantee that the outcome would have been any different if he had been taken to hospital.

The Coroner accepted Dr Howard's analysis and recorded a verdict of death by natural causes 'accelerated by an episode of acute toxicity of alcohol'.

The funeral took place on February 22 at St Margaret's Church in Rottingdean, near Brighton. It was a small and dignified affair; there were about a hundred people there—all Gary's family and close associates (except Bobby Moore who couldn't travel from Belfast because he was too ill). Guests included Jack Bruce and his wife Margrit, Jon Hiseman and Barbara Thompson, Andy Pyle, Graham Walker, Vic Martin, Neil Carter, Darrin Mooney, Jon Noyce and Stewart Young. Bob Daisley and Don Airey sent flowers. Rory Gallagher's brother Donal was also invited. Poor Rory passed away in 1995 at only forty-seven from complications following the liver transplant required after years of heavy drinking.

At one point, Chris Tsangarides turned to Jon Hiseman and said, looking around the church, 'Do you realise that at one time or another, Gary has argued or fallen out with everybody here? And yet here we all are.' There were renditions of 'While My Guitar Gently Weeps' and 'Danny Boy'. Saoirse wrote her dad a very long letter, which was placed in the casket 'and which said everything. I saw him a lot at the funeral home and spent a lot of time with him.'

Lily was the last member of Gary's family and friends to speak to him on the day before he died. She had called him, failed to get through and he later rang back sounding slightly disoriented and confused, probably because he'd not long got off the plane—and kept repeating to Lily that he 'loved her lots'. Her last words to him were, 'Bye dad. Love you lots.' Aged just twelve years old, she wrote these words for him:

> My dad, a man of extremes and rather colourful shirts
> My dad, a childlike boy with his humour
> My dad, a loved guitar player, partner, father, uncle, son and an inspiration
> for many.
> I feel proud to belong to his name.
> He is the only person I have ever known to be so
> Dependent and childlike, immature, but then he can also be the deepest, most
> creative and loving.

*Now we will all have to face a new battle—but I know we will remember
him the way he was,*
A dad, a family man, a star.
*Whatever he was, he will be remembered for ever—he was the kind of person
you could never forget.*
He had his way, that when he hugged you, you would feel instantly feel better.
*He used to tell me all these stories about how the moon was made of
cheese and how the stars were made of sugar and the clouds were made of
marshmallows.*
And there was Mirror Land and Silly Billy stories.
All these things I will miss dearly
But he would not have been who he was, if it wasn't for every single one of us
And we would not have been who we are if it wasn't for him.

Gary Moore was just fifty-eight years old when he died.

THE SOUND
& THE FURY

Apart from a 1980s swerve towards the 'in vogue' guitars favoured by the big hair bands, of which Charvel was probably the most notable example, and brief flirtations with other models, Gary was a traditionalist, favouring the Holy Trinity of Fender/Gibson/Marshall. And with the exception of the Peter Green Les Paul, there was nothing particularly unique or special about the guitars he chose; they were largely stock models. He was more likely to experiment in the studio, switching between guitars for certain songs or maybe choosing to play a guitar he would never have used onstage. He was a 'gear head': he loved nothing better than to make a beeline for the nearest music store when he was out on the road.

Because Gary bought, collected and discarded so much equipment over his long career, it would be impossible to log every item that he used in every situation. But there are many Gary Moore fans who retain a keen interest in this area and so what follows is a reasonably comprehensive overview of Gary's guitars, amplifiers and effects. Gary was always very open about his equipment and was happy to talk at length to knowledgeable journalists about his preferences at any given time—and so most of this section is in Gary's own words. But he was also forthright and erudite about the art of playing itself. So, in no particular order, here are a collection of quotes from down the years:

'When I started playing, there were not many guitarists around to teach me anything, so I didn't have any formal training. I found that helped a lot—for one thing, I never learned that there was any such thing as a left-handed guitar. I'm left-handed, but I play right-handed, which is an advantage, because I use my stronger hand for fretting. I think I'm lucky I didn't know about that, because left-handed guitars can be such a hassle. I mean, you can't get one of those (indicating his Les Paul) that's left-handed.' *GUITAR*, APRIL 1974

'I'm in a very transitional period at the moment, actually. I'm about half-way through to the point of playing how I want to play. Also, for the first time in my life, I don't think I'm consciously copying anybody. I used to really rip off early Clapton, Beck and Hendrix, I'd take lot of their licks and use them indiscriminately. I still have traces of these people in my playing, naturally enough, but there's also something else there. Now, guitarists come up to me and say, "It's great, now when we hear you play it sounds like you and no one else." In fact, when people hear me for the very first time they don't know who to compare me to. It must be working.' **SOUNDS, MAY 1, 1976**

'People ask me "how do you play"—and I don't know how I play. I don't think in terms of keys and chords when I'm playing; I'm at that stage now where I just know that neck and something else takes over when I play. Like if I was playing and you were trying to hold a conversation with me I just wouldn't hear a word you were saying—it's hard to describe. I get up there on stage and the whole world just ceases to exist apart from the music.' *BEAT INSTRUMENTAL*, **JANUARY 1979**

'Not many people can put on one of my guitars and control it. If you take your hands off the whole thing, it just goes crazy. You've got to know the instrument and how to control it. I remember a guy picking it up and saying, "how the hell do you play that?" I suppose it comes from learning on shitty guitars. I always like to tweak the action up during a tour, just to make it fight back a bit.

'Everybody says I shouldn't play so loud! But volume's part of my sound, there's no getting away from it. All that stuff about using overdrivers and turning it down is rubbish. If you want the tone of the instrument, you have to play it at a proper volume.' *GUITARIST* TRIBUTE ARTICLE, **APRIL 2011**

'If I can inspire people to play well and to take the right direction then I'm winning. If I only inspire people to play as fast as they can, if they only pick up on that aspect of my playing, then I'm not really doing anything for them. It's something I feel very strongly about.' *GUITARIST*, **NOVEMBER 1985**

'You have to relax and go with it and not get into your big ego trip thinking, *Aren't I wonderful, I pulled that lick off*. Because while you're thinking it, you're fucking up the next one. You've always got to bring the best out of yourself. It's yourself who sets the standards and if you don't satisfy yourself, then basically you might as well pack it in.' *KERRANG!*, **MAY 1985**

'I'm not as studied, technically, as you might think. My technique has really evolved naturally over the years from watching other guitarists and trying to develop my own style. I just do what works for each particular style; if I'm doing a very moody piece I'll use picking and try and keep it under control, but sometimes it's a case of just hitting everything in sight! If you're getting up to a really exciting pitch on stage you can't be that methodical about it. I do a lot of hammer on/ pull off playing as well without picking so much. I can play either way really.' **GUITARIST, JANUARY 1985**

'Well, it's something I'm labelled with, but if you listen to the albums they don't sound like the typical so-called "guitar hero" albums. All my stuff really revolves around the songs, and the guitar plays a part within those songs. You don't hear me do 10-minute guitar solos on an album—I do a couple of solo spots on stage which are about three minutes long, but I try really to contain the guitar within the framework of the song. The songs are much more important to me; they're things that I really feel for. The whole "guitar hero" thing is so dated, anyway. I mean, it's expected of me to go out on stage and show off a lot of the time, whether I feel like it or not—and sometimes I just want to go up there and play the songs—but if I don't do it people are gonna go away disappointed.' **SOUNDS, SEPTEMBER 28, 1985**

'I like to think a musician can gain subtlety and control while keeping the speed in reserve. As you get older, it becomes more interesting to create something on a melodic level than just emphasise speed the whole time. It becomes a lot less important and you can mature as a musician. Speed alone becomes meaningless.' **INTERNATIONAL MUSICIAN, OCTOBER 1982**

'When I hear music it makes me feel very intense, so when I play it I have to approach it the same way. I'm not impressed with doing things in half-measures, it's just the way I am. If I do something I really tend to do it to the extreme and playing is part of that. I feel you have to give it two hundred per cent … all the time—play every gig as if that's it. When you're playing rock you've got to put a lot into it, otherwise you're not going to get it across. It's a natural thing, and if people told me to relax I couldn't anyway.' **GUITARIST, MARCH 1989**

'There's nothing between you and the guitar … especially if you don't use a pick … you can actually just be so direct with the guitar and it can come straight from you, through the strings, into the wood, into the amp and you've got that great kind of direct expression … that's the way I feel about guitar … it's such a responsive instrument to the human touch … you can play it very gently and it'll respond accordingly. It just seems that it'll cry or scream, it'll shout or laugh or whatever … It's a very magical instrument for me anyway.' *20TH CENTURY GUITAR,* **NOVEMBER 9, 2004**

'You talk to any guitarist and he wants to be somebody else. I remember a long conversation I had with Neal Schon of Journey when we toured with them … Neal really rates Eddie Van Halen and Eddie wants to be Allan Holdsworth.' *INTERNATIONAL MUSICIAN,* **FEBRUARY 1989**

'I've heard people play my solos from a transcription and, to be honest, they haven't been that close. And your ears should be able to tell you that it doesn't sound the same. I like to play between the cracks, both timing-wise and between the notes, and that makes them almost impossible to transcribe. You try playing along with Eric; he never played with the beat. And Albert King: try to play those things in tune and you just sound like whitey boy trying to be clever, trying to play the blues. And those guys don't play it that way. Eric Bell once said to me, "We play it too right, and they don't play that way; they just play it raw and it's beautiful."' *GUITARIST,* **2004**

'I grew up on melody. And even when I was doing the heavy rock there was always melody there. I don't like unmelodic guitar playing; it's pointless and very empty and too much of that music was made at one time—people practising in public. I grew up listening to The Beatles and Hank Marvin. All the bands back then were really melodic … A great solo in the context of a poor song means nothing, but a great song with a great solo, now you're talking.' *GUITARIST,* **OCTOBER 1999**

'It was great to learn over the years from all the different styles and musicians. No matter how good or bad they were technically, there isn't a single guitarist I haven't learnt something from. That's what I've been doing all this time—searching and learning.' *GUITAR BUYER TRIBUTE ARTICLE,* **MARCH 2011**

'Another thing I've developing lately is the element of surprise; when I'm playing really low on the neck, sometimes I'll suddenly put a really high thing in, which just screams out for a second. I think it gives it more depth than if you play in the same area on the neck all the time. This is a technical thing, obviously—I used to play triplets a lot and do the easiest thing, just go up the neck a couple of frets, always staying within the same range. I think my playing really lacked depth when I did that, and it's gained a lot more dimension from working all over the neck. I've learned to use it to my advantage.' *GUITARIST*, **NOVEMBER 1985**

'I don't know what it is but as soon as I put the guitar on—whether I'm sitting in a room or up on stage—something happens and I've no control over it. I think that's why I don't have a big ego trip about my playing, because I feel it's not in my hands once I strap that guitar on. When I haven't got that guitar on I'm the same as everybody else, but when I have it on … I'm not. I've noticed the same with other players … you could be having a conversation with them, then there's a certain thing that happens when you hand them a guitar—like Jeff Beck—they suddenly growl and something happens. You're lucky if you have something like that. The first time I picked up a guitar I felt that way; it felt very natural and I just felt that's what I should be doing.' *GUITARIST*, **MARCH 1989**

'I know I'm quite successful, but I certainly haven't reached my best yet. However successful you are, you can't afford to go around thinking, *Oh great, I can sit back now—I can't get better than this*, because there's always room for improvement, you can never stop developing. … There's too much importance attached [to guitar solos]. [They] are important to the people who play them, and to other guitarists, but at the end of the day, they've got to feel good in the context of the song. You can over-analyse them. I've done it myself, time and time again. My problem is, if I don't get it down first time, I'm prone to over-analysing. But if it feels good and there are a couple of little mistakes in it, I'll probably leave it.' *GUITARIST*, **MARCH 1992**

'My guitars all have good pedigrees and all my guitars I like and use. It's strange about the sounds and effects I get. People ask me about them and I don't know what I'm doing half the time. All the way through my musical career I've been refining—chucking out old ideas or putting them in the right perspective. I often hear things I've done on record that I've completely forgotten about … As I become older, it become more interesting to create something on a melodic level than just emphasising speed all the time. It becomes a lot less important. The most effective things are the simplest, like one note sustained. Everybody gets off on that.' **INTERVIEW WITH CHRIS WELCH, 1991**

'I'll still play what I feel at the time, good or bad, but I'm not going to be flash or play what other people might want. If you do that you're just being a product; you become like a circus act. That's never been what it's about for me. And in the long run, if it's adulation and respect you're after, you'll get much more of that by being sincere and letting the music stand on its own.' *GUITARIST*, JUNE 1997

THE EARLY YEARS

Gary's first guitar, around the age of ten, was a large cello-bodied acoustic, almost too big for him to handle. In one interview from 1994, Gary said the acoustic was bought from Jackie Milligan, a showband guitarist friend of his father's. Gary recalled his mates hiding in the alleyway behind his house watching him trying to learn how to play. His first electric guitar was a Rosetti Lucky Seven, a single-cutaway hollow-bodied guitar built for Rosetti in the Netherlands by Egmond. From there, he progressed to his first serious guitar, a white Fender Telecaster with a maple neck: 'There were three Telecasters coming into Belfast and two were spoken for and I got the last one.' At some point before he left Belfast, he owned a Vox AC30 as he often told the story about him and Rory Gallagher wiring their Vox amps together to boost the power. With Platform Three, he had the luxury of a Marshall, hired on his behalf.

Once he moved to Dublin and joined Skid Row, he had acquired a red Gibson Les Paul with black covered P-90 pickups, a gold Tune-O-Matic bridge and a trapeze tail piece. He also owned an early 70s Fender Stratocaster sunburst with a black pick guard and the Gibson SG that he would later sell to pay for Peter Green's 1959 Les Paul Standard. For amplifiers, in Skid Row, Gary used Orange heads and cabinets, and also a Hiwatt amp with WEM 4x12 cabinets.

For his first solo album *Grinding Stone* (1973), Gary used the PG Les Paul, his main guitar during this period. Together with Marshall amps, this was pretty much his setup right through the rest of the 70s, taking in Thin Lizzy and Colosseum II. However, he also drove the Les Paul through a Fender Twin Reverb to emulate the fat distorted sound achieved by Bill Connors on Return To Forever's *Hymn*

Of The Seventh Galaxy album. But interviewed in 1974, just at the start of his first stint with Thin Lizzy, Gary suggested he had owned a wider range of guitars than documented: 'I've had three Strats, a 335, about three different Les Pauls, a Les Paul TV, two SGs, a Firebird,' although he was at pains to point out that he usually had these guitars one after the other rather than as a collection, a concept he could not get his head round at the time.

'Eric Clapton is reputed to have about 200 guitars. He's got about nineteen Les Pauls, he's got the very first Flying V ever made, serial number 1 on it, you know? That to me is just ridiculous. I remember seeing him play with Cream and he had four or five Les Pauls with him, all different colours. But though he broke three strings during the night, he carried on playing the same guitar. I couldn't believe it; he had all these spare guitars, for what?' Suffice to say, Gary's attitude to collecting changed over the years.

In the same interview, Gary talked about his new musical effect: 'I've got an Echoplex now and I've got into this thing of walking off stage at the end of the set and leaving the tape playing. The first time I did it, some guy started booing and accused me of miming all night! … The thing about the Echoplex is that one revolution of the tape lasts about two minutes, everything you play is recorded for two minutes. So, I can walk off stage and leave this playing. The first time I used it, even the band didn't know what was happening … they heard the guitar and thought I was still on stage with them. I was standing behind the amps laughing.' Gary says he came back onstage and started talking to Phil with the guitar still playing away.

One departure from his standard setup was his late 50s (possibly 1960) single-cutaway Gibson Melody Maker used on stage with Thin Lizzy. He told *Beat Instrumental* in January 1979, '[it's got] a DiMarzio PAF on it and a set of Grovers I bought in the States for £75. The Melody Maker is … I just can't believe it … the beautiful thing about that guitar is … I had a vision for that guitar … fuck, that sounds stupid! I had a sound in my head that I wanted to hear … I got Andy our guitar roadie to stick the DiMarzio in and the sound came out the way I wanted it. I just did a solo with it last night and the sound is just so fuckin' dirty … it's got a real edge to it and the harmonics and the top on it are great. I've got it set up with a higher action than the Les Paul and fitted with lighter strings as well, so it's a real bendy job … The strings on the Les Paul are 10, 13, 17, 30, 42 and a 52 so that's got a real heavy bottom end to it. The Melody Maker ends with a 42.'

He went on to describe a Strat that he was having completely rebuilt after the neck snapped off during a row with an unnamed girlfriend: 'I'm having DiMarzio's put on it. I also have the real heavy modified tremolo unit with a heavier bracket.' He was particularly taken with the DiMarzio pickups as being superior to the stock pickups fitted to new Gibsons and Fenders: 'I can go straight into a Marshall, crank it up and get the most beautiful sound without any pedals or anything.'

On the subject of pedals, Gary was still using the Echoplex, because it was very simple to use, but 'I use a Coloursound Overdrive, especially for the Strat because I find it really beefs it up … I also use an MXR Phase 100 and a Coloursound wah-wah, but as soon as we stop playing "Johnny The Fox" that'll be out the window.'

Would he consider using a guitar synthesiser? Gary says he saw one—the Hagström Patch 2000—at the 1978 Frankfurt Trade Fair and thought it might work fine for his speedy kind of style, 'because it works on the frets, you can play it one-handed. I think it scans the frets at 200 times a minute so there is no way I'm going to be ahead of it.' He noted several drawbacks, though: you couldn't play chords on it or bend notes and you would need a very high-quality amp to handle the instrument. But you could play it as a regular guitar and just flick a switch to bring in the synth section. 'I played it through an Oberon Expander Module and it sounded beautiful.' That said, he admitted it might work for a couple of numbers, but he wouldn't want to play it all night. He made a general comment on the ubiquitous presence of Japanese manufacturers at the fair, which led to a question about Oriental guitars.

'Yeah—I like the Yamaha … the Yamaha is like what a Gibson should be now. They're just made so well, the tones, the neck, everything, they're great. I mean Santana was a real Gibson freak and he's using the Yamaha … I've tried the one Midge from The Rich Kids has got—it's got real good sustain on it, real nice heavy body—pretty much like a Les Paul in a way.'

The conversation ended with Gary's admission about the problem he had coming to grips with the Fender Strat, never feeling that he had conquered it enough to say, 'I'm a Strat player', despite having played one for years. His aim was to try and personalise the sound using the Strat that he was having rebuilt: 'The first thing I want to get is a thicker sound, but yet have the facility of the tremolo arm. Eddie Van Halen's done it because he uses one old PAF humbucker—that's all he uses and it's not a real Strat anyway. It's a Schlason or something … It's the heaviest Strat body I have ever picked up, he's got that pickup, one volume control, no tone control and that's it—and he gets such a great sound, such a big sound … mind you, the eight Marshalls may have something to do with it!'

THE 1980s

1981 While he was recording and performing with Greg Lake, a guitar dealer turned up with a selection of guitars including a 1961 Fiesta Red Fender Strat (possibly over-sprayed from a salmon pink colour, as happened in the 1960s by UK distributors aiming to achieve the 'Hank Marvin effect'). Gary tried it acoustically first, before Greg arrived, and knew straight away it was a good one, without having to plug it in. But he had to stand there, hoping against hope that Greg would turn it down, which he did because it wasn't in pristine condition. As Graham Lilley recalls, a much-relieved Gary 'nearly bit the guy's arm off for it'. Gary had it re-fretted (possibly using Dunlop 6150 fret wire) and it became a favoured guitar for many years to come. The original owner was supposed to be the guitarist with Tommy Steele, while the new owner had it stolen at one time, as he told *Guitarist* in January 1985: 'I've got about 20 guitars at the moment—not a huge collection. I don't really collect guitars. I just buy one if I really fancy it but don't go round pawn shops in Cleveland and stuff like that. I go for new guitars; on the whole of the American tour, I used a white Strat, which I bought in a shop in LA for $600 off the rack. It's a '62 reissue.

'What happened was that my salmon pink one was stolen just before the tour, some guy in the customs here tried to nick it and then it turned up again because he found out whose guitar it was, and it turned up in Houston via Interpol. I got it back halfway through the tour but by this time I'd got the white one and got used to it and I don't like changing guitars halfway through a tour.'

1982 With a record deal under his belt and his star on the rise, Gary became a regular face in the guitar press with many front cover features over the years. He gave this general thought about his relationship to guitars to *International Musician* in October 1982:

'All my guitars I like and use. I'm not the kind of person who goes out and buys a green guitar with yellow spots with a free do-it-yourself blow job kit. I really like guitars I can use. The same goes for endorsements. If anyone gives me something I'll use it. It's unfair to mislead kids by putting your name on a product to endorse it even though you think it's a piece of shit. A lot of people do that, and I think it's wrong.'

Gary gave this insight into his use of different guitar tones for the track 'Don't Take Me For A Loser' on *Corridors Of Power*:

'The solo's got kind of a strange sound because the guitar was split in two and one side went through a Maestro octave divider and then directly to the mixing desk, and the other side went through a little monitor on a 2-track tape recorder. We routed the guitar through that and turned it up until it distorted, and then we put a mike on it. So, we had a dirty guitar sound coming through this tiny speaker, and this kind of very clean open sound with an octave divider on it.' An Octavier was used on 'End Of The World' to create bass notes underneath the arpeggios on the guitar solo.

Asked how he gets feedback and sustain in the studio, Gary replied: 'I just drive the shit out of my amp with the Strat and the distortion. You know, it's like I've got three gain stages, I suppose, because it's going through the Roland digital stuff, which has extra gain on it. So, I drive that as hard as I can. Of course, there's so much gain that I can't take my hands off the guitar without it screaming.'

For stage shows, Gary began using three volume pedals to control the sound of the other musicians: 'I've got four stacks behind me, but the top cabinets have bass, keyboards, and Neil Carter's guitar. Then I have three Boss FV-100 volume pedals on the floor in front of me so that I can balance them out as I'm playing, without having to yell at the monitor guy. I've had too many years of doing that.' In his interview, he also refers to the 1962 reissue Strat with the rosewood fingerboard he bought in the States to replace the pink Strat he thought had gone forever.

Interviewed by *International Musician* just after the Reading Festival in August, Gary referred to his rack-mounted Roland Chorus echo, which also included the reverb, a Boss overdriver on his Strat—and introduced two new guitars into interviews, citing one effect, 'a green thing' on his Ibanez, and pointing out that 'one of my Charvels has got a Floyd Rose tremolo system'. At the time, he was quite taken with his custom-built Charvel guitars: 'They're really lovely. All kinds of custom designs. He [Grover Jackson rather than Wayne Charvel] does a great job and keeps coming back to the job until you are perfectly satisfied.'

The Charvels did have their limitations though for Gary. Talking to Tony Bacon for *Music UK* around 1982/83, Gary observed: 'I use the Charvels from time to time, but I've made up my mind that what I want to do now is buy another old Strat and just take that on the road as a spare for the pink Strat. 'Cos I've been using the Charvels as spares for the Strat, which is really wrong. I have my equipment set up for the Strat, tone wise and you plug in a Charvel and it's a lot more powerful. They've got all kinds of shit on them; DiMarzios, Seymour Duncans … So, you have to run over and switch all your tones around and mess it all up—you haven't got time to do that really so you end up with a bad sounding guitar. I'd rather have another Strat and plug it straight in.'

Mashing up the interviews for *International Musician* and *Music UK*, Gary revealed other guitars in his collection. One was a Takamine, for studio work: 'They're like an Ovation setup, electric acoustic, but they've got bass, treble and volume controls up on the neck joint … and the jack socket is where the strap is … I used them on "Always Gonna Love You" … then I have a Gibson ES5 which I bought from Greg Lake. It's a blond 1955 Jazz type semi-acoustic three-pickup model. Beautiful. Not a scratch on it … .It's a real nice guitar for playing around with at home—taking it on stage would be ridiculous. It's just one of those guitars you hang on to. It's got three of those black P90s, three volume controls, one master tone control, no switches. I've also got a Gretsch Tennessean, which I hate. It was one of those impulse buys that I don't normally go in for.

'And I've got a 1955 Les Paul Junior, which used to belong to Steve Jones of the Sex Pistols … it looks like crazy paving on the front of it. He kind of left it in my flat once, just chucked it against the wall. It was there for six months and he never bothered to come back. So, I said I'd buy it off him.'

By the time of the *Music UK* interview, Gary had changed the stage amp setup from *Corridors Of Power* and had extended his range of effects. The guitar 'is now split to two Marshalls, one's dry and the other's got effect on it. But it's not split in stereo. What happens is I go from the guitar through an Overdriver into the first amp via a splitter box and out of the splitter box also comes a lead which goes back through all the effects pedals and echoes into the second amp. But the second amp is on all the time, so even when the effects aren't on, I've still got dry signal coming through the second as well as the first amp.

'So, you don't get that thing of having your echo split stereo where when you switch it on, all of a sudden another 100-watt Marshall comes in and knocks your head off! It's just a more balanced thing. I used to do it the other way, but I could never get along with the stereo effect. So, I've got the full 200 watts on all the time and when the effects come on, it's only on one side, so that for out-front, the guy can mix the effects as he wants. For instance, if I put too much echo on and it's a very ambient kind of hall, he can back off on that, but I can still hear it on stage. So, it's a more sensible set up really.

'I'm using quite a lot of effects at the moment, believe it or not. I don't normally go in for a lot of effects. I've been experimenting with a few more on this tour because I just fancied some different sounds, but I wouldn't bet my life that

I'll be continuing to do it. They can be a bit of a problem. I'm using a flanger, an octave splitter and a chorus pedal—they're all Boss pedals. The chorus I only have because the Chorus/Echo isn't very satisfactory to me—the only thing I use on the Chorus/Echo is the repeat effect itself and sometimes the reverb.'

'The flanger, chorus and octave splitter are external things. I've also got a volume pedal, which I use for violin effects … [but] I don't use them much. I think I use the flanger once all night and the chorus about twice. If you use them all the time … it sounds like shit and you also disguise everything you do.' Gary can be seen demonstrating various BOSS FX pedals on BBC2's *Rock School* programme (on YouTube).

1984 For *Victims Of The Future*, Gary's main studio guitar was the Les Paul Junior, although the Strat can be heard on a number of tracks including 'Murder In The Skies' and 'Devil In Her Heart'. Speaking to *Guitar World* that year, Gary explained how he constructed the solo on 'Shapes Of Things': 'Sometimes I work the solos out but not in terms of scales. I work them out in terms of what fits the song. In that song, I started out playing it right across the whole solo section in one go and then decided to split it into three sections. There is the high singing guitar in the first section and then the fast staccato picking over the breaks. And then there was the slide section after that … You get three different feels the way I did it.' Gary's string array was cited as Dean Markley strings: .010; .013; .017; .030; .042; and .052.

In November 1985, *International Musician* asked Gary about little tricks he might use onstage. Gary was naturally cagey about this, but did reveal that, 'I can make my guitar sound like it's coming through a wah-wah without actually using one. It's done by scratching in a certain way and I did a bit on the "Shapes Of Things" solo live. But I haven't seen anyone else do it, so I'm not telling you how it's done. I turn my back when I do it on stage. The other thing I do is when I do the triplets on the bottom string and run the palm of my hand up the fretboard. You get this kind of harmonic descending thing, like water down the drain.'

Speaking to *Music UK* in September 1984, he said, 'I think I must be the best endorsee Fender have got and yet when we inquired at the factory about one of their vintage reissues, they didn't want to know and then after we played LA and the press said we'd blown Rush off the stage, Fender sent us one. Strange, isn't it?'

Interviewed just before the four-date Irish tour at the end of 1984, Gary revealed more about his Takamine acoustics: 'They're really excellent guitars. I've got this black 12-string model and there's only two of them in the world, one built for Greg Lake and the other for me. Then I've got another one which is a 6-string semi-jazz model with the electronics and EQ built in.'

His stage rack was the Roland SDE-3000 programmable digital delay: 'You have two banks of four programmes and it's altered by a series of foot switches which shunt through programmes 1–4 and then you switch to Bank B and go through those programmes 1–4.' The whole thing was all pre-set, but Gary edited the programmes to suit his needs: 'I've got some very long delays, a couple of ADTs and a couple of flangers and choruses … it's a very practical unit for someone like me who doesn't want to be tap dancing all night.'

Gary said he had also been experimenting with a Dimension D, a chorus type of effect that didn't alter the pitch of the note, 'or give you that terrible warbling which you get from using very severe chorus—it just fattens the sound out and gives it more depth'.

This interview may have been the first mention by Gary of trying out Hamer guitars: 'I've got a Hamer Explorer which they built for me recently … out of a beautiful piece of maple. It's the closest you can have to a tasteful Explorer shape guitar. It sounds really fantastic, so I've been playing that quite a lot and also I've been playing an Ibanez Roadstar, which they built for me … It's a RS110BK with all black hardware, very smart!'

1985 Through the recording of *Run For Cover* and the subsequent tour, the Hamer had become a firm favourite in Gary's arsenal. Talking to *Guitarist* in November, he enthused: 'Hamer send me guitars which I really love and I play them because they're the best guitars I've come across in a long time. They want me to do an endorsement deal with them, but I figure the best thing I can do for them is to play their guitars. If one night I fancy a change, I don't want to feel that someone has an eye on me and will report that I didn't fulfil my contract. I'd rather just play them when I feel like it. I used the Hamers a lot on the album; I used the white one on "Out In The Fields", another one on "All Messed Up" and "Nothing To Lose" and the blue V on a couple of things. Every guitar they've sent me has been really great. I don't know what anyone else thinks, but they're great for me. Steve Stevens of Billy Idol's band uses Hamers almost exclusively, and he gets a great sound. They have a very even sound—not like some makes which are muddy at the bottom end and screechy at the top. That's important if you want to use the whole range of the guitar, as I do.'

In Gary's collection were several Hamer Chapparal solid-body guitars; Gary also possessed an Explorer, a Flying V, a Phantom A5 and an 'unofficial' Gary Moore Special. The Charvel still featured as a stage guitar, but heavily customised by Keith Page, Gary's guitar tech at the time: 'It's actually made up of other Charvels I had before! [i.e., two Charvel Strat head-style San Dimas guitars] It's a Strat-shaped body which used to have a chrome scratch plate on it and two pickups. [Keith Page] chopped it up, put on a new scratch plate a [single] EMG humbucker, they're very good and don't make too much noise. It's still got the Floyd Rose tremolo on it and we put the neck on last week.'

It looks like Keith Page built two guitars: the white coloured body with matching headstock and a single-piece maple neck with chrome hardware and then a red coloured version with a rosewood finger-board and chrome hardware.

Gary rarely if ever used the Charvel in the studio and in April 1987, he explained why to *International Musician*: 'It's a funny thing, the Charvels are never as good in the studio as they are on stage. It's the weirdest thing—they cut through great live, but somehow in the studio they never seem to have any depth to them. It could be down to the acoustics, I suppose, but it also could be that you need that bit more top on stage in order to get things to come across. I like quite a bright sound anyway, because of the way I play. If I use too mushy a sound I find the notes seem to run into each other when I'm playing fast stuff and don't come across very clearly.'

Back in 1985, because of the nature of the show, with Gary jumping up on a platform, he was forced into using a radio link instead of a lead. He was against the idea of a link in principle because even though it freed his movement across the stage, 'I haven't been able to get the tone that I want out of the guitar. It always does something funny to my sound, compress it or something … I want to hear all the notes and everything and up to now I have found that radio links have clouded the sound. You can always get into graphics and things, but you're creating more problems for yourself on stage. If you use a twenty-seven-band graphic, there are so many variations that you can mess around with each night … I like to stay away from graphics and stick to the normal tone controls.'

For the *Run For Cover* tour, Gary was using a new effects rack made by Quark: 'I've only been using it for three shows … but I'm pretty pleased with it inasmuch as I can control everything from one source … Basically what Quark do is modulise your pedals—so that the pedals I used before like Tube Screamer, I've got two of those on the rack now and I just control them from the pedal board.

The only problem is that I can't move the knobs when I'm on stage, where I'm used to being able to bend down and adjust them if I want to. Now I'm having to try and get it right at the start of the set.

'I've got two Roland 555 tape echoes—in fact there's two of everything as a back-up. There is a Roland SDE-3000 digital delay with eight programmes on it, a Dimension D and a Yamaha Digital Reverb with four pre-sets—the R1000. I use it on "Empty Rooms" and "Parisienne Walkways", only for the softer stuff, otherwise it gets very messy when you're playing big power chords. It's a drag because in the rehearsal room when you play the heavier stuff the reverb makes it sound huge, but in a hall, it just gets lost.

'I've seen the new Yamaha Reverb and there's a new Roland, each of which have lots of pre-sets and are MIDI-controlled, but they're not really practical for a guitarist on stage because you a) don't need that many and b) you don't really need MIDI yet—until they start making amps that use MIDI … In a set you don't need more than eight delays, surely! I stand there sometimes watching all the pre-sets go by! That's why I stand there looking at the side of the stage … they haven't built LEDs into the pedal board and you can't go backwards.'

Asked about his amp setup, Gary confirmed he was still loyal to Marshall, which couldn't be beaten onstage, but did say he'd been using Dean Markley and Gallien-Krueger amps in rehearsal and on *Run For Cover*. The Krueger amps were small, and almost looked like practice amps, but pumped out 50 watts a channel and driving them through Marshall cabinets brought them to life. Gary was impressed: 'They were just brilliant … very even, uniform sounds, you could put the two amps up, two cabinets and stick mikes in front of them and you'd get virtually the same sound in the control room … it's hard to find an amp you can trust like that.' Gary said he used the first Dean Markley amp he was sent, on 'Out Of My System', one of the demo tracks recorded with producer Beau Hill, 'it just sang sweetly. A lovely amp.'

But when it came to the live shows, it just had to be Marshall: 'It's a sound you don't just hear, you feel it! A very physical sound. The other amps for all the tonal variation you can get from them, all the warmth and all the versatility, they just don't project it on stage.

'My amps are fifteen feet behind me and they're hidden by the metallic staging—in that situation, the amps have got to push the sound out. The only other way is putting your guitar through wedges and side-fills and we're trying to leave all that out at the moment. We just have vocals, bass drum and snare through the monitors to keep it really clean. Once you start putting the guitar in there it goes crazy, you're deafening the rest of the band, and invariably you'll put the fader up and it'll come out the wrong side and get into all sorts of problems.'

1987 By the time Gary came to start recording *Wild Frontier* in 1986, he was trying out Paul Reed Smith guitars. As he told *Bass* in April, 'they're really great because they sort of combine the old and the new in so much as the tremolo stays in tune, but it's not a normal locking trem. It looks like a Strat one but it's got these locking machines instead of a gadget across the neck. You don't have to have a degree in Engineering to put the strings on or have to carry a toolbox around with you like you do with the Floyd Rose. They've also got a six-position switch that can give you all these great tones, from Strat sounds all the way across to humbucking sounds which makes for a very versatile guitar. Beautifully made too; they're hand built from Curly Maple and come in all these different colours, but they've all got this tiger stripe running through, which is really tasteful. They're dead easy to play—you've got 24 frets and you can bend right up to a high G. I'd like to take them out on the road now and see what happens with them.'

In the same interview, Gary also explained his home studio setup on which he wrote *Wild Frontier*. He used 'a little 8-track setup in my front room. There's a Fostex 80 with the 450 mixer, the Yamaha RX11 and the Gallien-Krueger amplifier heads. I don't use any speakers with those. I DI them straight into the desk—you get a really good guitar sound that way, better than I get in the studios a lot of the time. I've tried a lot of effects—I had the Korg SDD-1000 Digital Delay and a Midiverb which I thought was brilliant. I'd like to move up to a 16-track purely because I'm basically very lazy. I'm not into bouncing things down; I prefer just to get everything down on separate tracks really quickly so that I can play it all back and then start to refine things. It'd also be nice to be able to have stereo guitars, stereo keyboards and maybe some double-tracked vocals to create the illusion of a really big sound, in order to see whether it's worth carrying on with that particular song or arrangement.'

1989 As Gary's main rock era was drawing to a close, *International Musician* published a diagram of his full live rig, which, written out, included:

5 stacks of Marshall cabs on each side of the drum kit, on a central riser.
Looking at the stacks, from left of the stage to the drum riser, bottom row:

1. Bass cab, on a separate volume pedal driven by a Marshall JCM 800 1959 100-watt amp.

2. Gary 4x12 driven by a Marshall JMP 1959 100-watt amp

3. Gary 4x12 driven by a Marshall JMP 1959 100-watt amp

4. Gary 4x12 driven by a Marshall JMP 1959 100-watt amp

5. Dummy cab

Top row, left to right:

1. Dummy cab

2. Gary 4x12 driven by a Marshall JMP 1987 50-watt amp (there was a choice of 2 different 1987 amps: small box and larger box)

3. Dummy cab

4. Dummy cab

5. Dummy cab

Recessed in the steps of the drum riser/platform were 2 x TOA three-way keyboard cabinets, on a separate volume pedal.

Roland SRE555

Alesis Midiverb

Roland SDE-3000 digital delay

Roland Dimension D

Ibanez ST-9 super tube screamer

Ibanez TS -10 tube screamer

Boss DM-3 delay

BOSS Dimension C pedal (possibly)

The electric guitars were listed as:

Charvel White

Jackson Soloist x 2

Gibson Les Paul Standard 1959 ex Peter Green

Heritage H-150CM x 2. Brown sunburst on stage, a Cherry sunburst in the dressing room.

The Heritage guitar company was established in the old Gibson factory in Kalamazoo, Michigan in 1985, by three ex-Gibson employees who didn't want to uproot their families and move to the other Gibson plant in Nashville.

During the recording sessions for the *After The War* album, the UK distributor of Heritage guitars sent Gary a cherry sunburst H-150CM Les Paul-style guitar to try out. And then sent a brown sunburst H-150CM, factory fitted with PJ Marx humbuckers, and an engraved truss rod cover with Gary's name on it, with the idea that it might be a Signature Gary Moore guitar. The bridge pickup was swapped out for an EMG 81, and the guitar was then featured on the cover of the *After The War* album and used onstage during the tour to support that album. The same guitar was also used on the *Still Got The Blues* tour in 1990 but doesn't feature on the album of the same name. After using and getting on well with the brown sunburst model, Gary agreed for a very limited run of 75 guitars only, in an amber sunburst colour. The signature guitar was to reflect the brown sunburst Gary had been using while on tour, with a pair of EMG 81s, his name on the headstock, instead of the truss rod cover and a standard Schaller tailpiece, not the version with the fine tuners on it, which had been factory fitted to his brown one, and since replaced during the tour.

With the huge demand for the Heritage Gary Moore guitars, Heritage asked to do another batch of the model. But as the original model had been announced as a strictly limited edition in one colour, Gary wasn't keen to go back on that announcement. Then, the idea was to do the guitar again, but in another colour, to mark it out it from the previous batch. Again, this run was limited to 75 guitars only, worldwide, and this time in an almond sunburst.

THE 1990s

Gary entered the blues period now and this saw a change of approach to playing and reintroduced him to the Fender Telecaster—Albert Collins's guitar. But maybe the influence of Roy Buchanan was greater when it came to slide guitar work, more obviously a feature of blues playing than heavy rock. In fact, Gary had already recorded 'The Messiah Will Come Again' using a Roy Buchanan signature Telecaster by Fritz Brothers, borrowed from George Harrison on the *After The War* album. Gary told *Guitar & Bass* in 1992 that the guitar was 'horrible to play, it's a 60s one and it's an old bastard, but it's got an amazing sound'. But in 2007, he still had the 'old bastard', as he told *Guitar Buyer* in November: 'I've had the '63 Tele for years. I used it on "Moving On", which was the first track on the *Still Got The Blues* album. It was tuned to open A, and I did all the slide stuff on it. It's always had a really good sound, but the intonation's not incredible and it's quite hard to play. It's got a later neck on it, that someone put on before I bought it, but it's got character and it really works. You can get some very mournful sounds out of it as well as a hard, in-your-face sound. It's a real old battle-axe.'

1990 For the recording of *Still Got The Blues*, Gary used his (other) '59 Les Paul Standard, a Marshall Guv'nor pedal, a fresh out the factory Marshall JTM45 reissue and a Marshall 1960B 4x12 with Electrovoice 12M speakers instead of the regular Celestions. During this early 1990s blues period, Gary also experimented with Soldano SLO-100 amps, adding the Soldano HR50s for the 1992 *After Hours* tour, in addition to the SLO100s. But they were replaced as reissue classic model Marshalls came onstream around the time of the BBM project.

1992 The whole saga of the Peter Green guitar was chewed over in many interviews given by Gary and came out in dribs and drabs. The essence of the story of how Gary obtained the guitar and its subsequent history has been covered earlier. And much has been written about how that special 'out-of-phase' sound was achieved.

However, readers of *Guitar* magazine that year were treated to some more of the back story in an interview that included a section on Gary's Les Paul collection.

'I remember once the police stopped me and took me to the station then searched my guitar case for drugs. When I got back the handle disappeared, so from them on I had to walk around with the case cradled in my arms.'

In the same interview, Gary suggested that Peter deliberately turned the bass pickup backwards to get the sound on 'Need Your Love So Bad', which doesn't precisely chime with other accounts, but certainly some helpful people tried to fix it: 'Once Neil Murray took it home to clean it,' Gary recalled, 'and the next day he said, "Oh, by the way, the bass pickup was the wrong way round so I've changed it." Aaaahh! Then about two years ago, I took the guitar to a shop to be re-fretted and exactly the same thing happened—so I burnt down the shop. Well, not quite, but I felt like it.'

Interviewed for this book, Neil Murray recalls: 'For years people thought that the neck pickup was reversed and that's what created the unique sound. But that had virtually no impact on the sound at all. This guitar was filthy. So, Gary asked me to look after it—I took it home and cleaned it, unscrewed the pickups, got all the filth out, but I couldn't put the pickup back the wrong way. So, from then on it was round the right way. They discovered later on one of the coils in that pickup went and [Peter] had it rewound by the guitar repairer—and what happened was either the coil was out of phase with the other coil or the magnet was reversed. So, if you heard the pickup on its own, it sounded alright. The minute you combined it with the other pickup, suddenly you get this "out of phase-ness" that you only get by having one of the coils on that pickup mis-repaired.'

Later, in May 2003, Gary told *Vintage Guitar*: 'When I got that guitar, my place didn't have a lock on the door, so I used to sleep with it under my bed and I'd even take it to the movies. Even the case was interesting because Peter told me that Eric Clapton gave it to him after the Les Paul had been stolen, so I think I've got the case from the guitar on the *Blues Breakers* album and I've got the guitar that was on *Hard Road*. Scary!' The case went missing from his garage in Henley sometime in 1989/90.

Another story often told was the one where the guitar almost suffered terminal injuries: 'I was in a bad car crash and the guitar was in the boot of the car. It was a very strange experience. I had a dream one night that somebody stole the guitar … I was leaving for the studio to do some demos and this guy picked me up in a car and just as I was leaving I said, "I want to bring the Les Paul with me today because I had this terrible dream." And he said, "Oh, you're getting really paranoid!" So, we put it in the boot of his car and we were driving to the studio when we stopped at the lights at the Chiswick Flyover and this great big fucking truck just came behind us just as we were about to pull away from the lights and BOOF!—straight into the back of us. I opened the boot and although the guitar was in a flight case, its neck was completely broken.

'I used the Peter Green Les Paul on "Since I Met You Baby" and "Jumpin' At Shadows" … I used another slightly newer '59 Les Paul on most of *Still Got The Blues*. I bought it during the *After The War* album, but I didn't play it for a year 'cause I stupidly decided I didn't like it. When it came to doing the blues album, I got it out of the case and found it was just what I was looking for. The two Les Pauls look similar and their serial numbers are very close, but they're totally different in sound and feel. The Peter Green is much stiffer and harder to play whereas the other has a faster neck which is easier to get around and a harder sound which cuts through better live. The newer '59 sings with that Les Paul sustain and the finish is slightly worn where I pick the strings.

'I just bought a '58 Standard which is on the sleeve of [*After Hours*]. It's got a lot more red in the sunburst finish—the two '59s are very faded. I haven't recorded with it yet, so don't expect me to tell you exactly how it sounds—I've had it partly re-fretted and I'm still getting used it.

'I also have a '57 Goldtop with PAF humbuckers from just before they replaced the Goldtop with the Standard model—but it's basically the same model. I used it for a couple of bits on the new album, but not nearly as much as the two '59s, which are my favourites.'

1995 Interviewed by Neville Marten for *Guitarist* about the *Blues For Greeny* album, Gary described his very stripped back studio setup: 'A little Fender Vibroverb reissue, a Matchless DC-30 Amp amplifier and cabinet and a 60s Fender Bassman. A lot of the time we were going through a 4 x12 Marshall cabinet, fitted with Celestion "Greenback" 25-watt speakers, sometimes wired to just a 2x12 configuration at 8 ohms.'

Gary described how he approached accessing the Peter Green sound for *Blues For Greeny*: 'The key elements in recreating Peter's sound are basically that guitar and the touch, really. You can't recreate his sound to the point where it's the same—you can only approximate it—but luckily I've got the guitar. I mean everyone knows that one of the pickups is turned round the wrong way. But I've played other guitars where people have done that and it doesn't sound anything like it! There's still something else about that particular guitar. It has a characteristic sound so there's that and there's the point of not overdriving it too much, obviously. Peter always had a clean sound and I think it's down to the playing; after that, it's down to the touch and the sensitivity of the player and the phrasing and the space you leave. It's all those things.'

1997 Talking to Neville Marten for the June issue of *Guitarist* about *Dark Days In Paradise*, Gary emphasised that rather than this being yet another guitar-led album, the amount of guitar used was judged against the needs of the song, using a Telecaster on 'Afraid of Tomorrow', for the solo on 'Where Did We Go Wrong?' and the slide solo on 'One Good Reason'. For that special tone on 'Like Angels', he came up with using a thin screwdriver on a Strat but switched for the big solo to a 1960 Gibson 355: 'I got it about 18 months ago and the six-way Varitone switch isn't wired in, so it's like a 335, really.' The amps used on the album were familiar Marshalls and Fenders, but Gary says he used the 15-watt all-tube Trace Elliott Velocette for the rhythm guitar on 'One Fine Day'.

1999 For the October issue of *Guitarist*, Gary and Graham Lilley explained about the range of guitars heard on *A Different Beat*. Gary explained about the signature Les Paul with no binding and a large neck, which was 'a bit like an old Junior. It's not wired out of phase like the Peter Green Les Paul, but the front pickup has been turned round.' Graham explained about the Fernandes stock Les Paul, 'with a Floyd Rose and the single-coil Sustainer pickup at the front—there's a dummy cover on there just to fill the space. Some of the long sustainy notes on the album are this and another one we have without the Floyd Rose.' Graham also cited the 'pink' Strat as featured on the album.

Gary: 'The first note you hear on the album is [the] Jerry Jones baritone guitar, based on the old Danelectros.' Gary goes to mention the Vigier Surfreter, saying that he first heard about it in the magazine: 'I used this for the first solo you hear on the record … "Go On Home", and it sounds like a proper slide guitar solo, but it's played on this one. It's fretless with a metal fingerboard and so it's great for doing slide impersonations.'

Finally, Graham name checks the Ted McCarty Archtop PRS: 'This guitar is definitely on the record; it's doing the big tracked-up rhythm things on "Worry No More". It's probably not something we'd use live—it's too pretty for one thing. Gary didn't really like the first PRSs he played, they didn't sound right for him. But this Archtop sounds and plays great.'

In the main body of the article, Gary restated his love of the 355 and said that he was trying out the Fender Prosonic: 'that's a lovely amp, but it's just not loud enough for stage. I've even tried four of them together! I use it on half power—30 watts—because it's much sweeter, but it's just not loud enough. I love the reverb on it, though; it's got that really spooky haunting reverb that I love. I've also used the new Cornford 50-watt head on a couple of tracks. It's great; it's like a miniature Soldano, very contained, warm and sweet. So, I'm definitely going for a more traditional authentic type of sound; like I've removed one gain stage.'

THE 2000s

2001 With all of the 'new music' experiments at an end, it was *Back To The Blues* for Gary and this interview from the August edition of *Guitar World* where apart from the odd appearance of a Les Paul, Gary was sticking to his 355: 'For the straight blues sounds, I played that direct into an early 70s Fender Dual Showman. I also used a Marshall DSL 100-watt which was the prototype … In a few places, I used a Marshall Guv'nor pedal, a Line 6 distortion, a CryBaby wah-wah and an Ibanez chorus pedal, but mostly it was straightforward tones.'

2004 Through the Scars period, there were no significant changes in equipment, other than a number of new Gibson Explorers and a Mesa Boogie Rectifier amp, used on the track 'Rectify' and a number of new Fuzz pedals, etc., which, says

Graham, 'almost ended in a kind of "pedal wars" between Gary and Cass on the FX front!!' Gary's main guitar during that time was the salmon pink/fiesta red Strat for that power trio rock sound. His return to the blues in 2004 saw a return to Gibsons. Interviewed once again by Neville Marten for the summer issue of *Guitarist*, Gary detailed his guitars and tones for the album *Power Of The Blues*:

'It's funny how we guitarists go through phases—like, "I'll never play one of those again"—and I went totally against the Fender sound for this album. It was after the Monsters of Rock thing and after doing "Rectify" on the Scars album, using the Explorer. I started pulling out that guitar and really liking it. Then, of course, I used all Gibson for the Monsters of Rock tour—the white Explorer and the Les Paul. It's more me, I think.

'I remember when Eric stopped playing Gibsons and picked up the Stratocaster, I was devastated, and I think people prefer me when I play a Gibson. The Les Paul is what people associate with me. A Strat makes you play a certain way and that's the good thing about it. A Strat makes you very clean and articulate, whereas the Gibson is a lot sleazier. I'm a sloppy player anyway and the Gibson is very fluid, so it's suits me more. But a Strat is a great guitar; get a good one of each and you don't need anything else.

'My white Explorer got broken (chip in the neck, which was repaired) and I was really upset about it, because I really liked that guitar. But I used an Explorer on "I Can't Quit You Baby"—I've got a wine red one now. I played my '62–63 Les Paul SG Standard on "Evil" and a little swamp ash Explorer for open-A slide in "Tell Me Woman". And of course, it's the Peter Green Les Paul on the last track— the big ballad. It's the "Out Of Reach" sound and I think I've finally nailed it on that track; it's been such a sound to strive for and in fact I put it through a Fender Vibroverb reissue, backed the amp off and whacked the reverb right up; the treble pickup, one mike on the amp and that's it. Peter didn't really revisit that sound because he discovered the out-of-phase sound. To get that I usually have both volume controls up full, but sometimes it's better to knock one back a bit—I'm always fiddling with the controls anyway.

'On the road, I'm thinking of a Marshall head and a 4x12 cab into that open-backed combo's speakers, so I get the tightness of the 4x12 and the openness of the combo cabinet. I even thought of taking half a 4x12 back off. Marshall do a little 18-watt combo that sounds brilliant—four of those'd be good!' ('After recording much of *Power Of The Blues* with a battered 2x12 Marshall combo,' says Graham.)

2007 That year's album *Close As You Get* saw Gary continuing down the blues highway and saw the return of the Telecaster. Interviewed by *All Out Guitar*, Gary said, 'I used a Telecaster on three songs actually. On the opening track, "If The Devil Made Whiskey" with the bottleneck. It's in open E tuning dropped down to D. "Thirty Days", the old Chuck Berry song, is a Telecaster as well. [The third Telecaster track was "I Had a Dream"] … I haven't really used it since the *Still Got The Blues* album … it's a great old guitar, a real old battle-axe. You know, one of those, you can throw down the street, pick it up and it's still in tune.'

For 'Trouble At Home', Gary used the Fender '63 Vibroverb reissue from the early 1990s, 'the little brown one with the two ten-inch speakers … I bought two at the same time. It's a great little amp. It's 40 watts with volume, bass treble and reverb. That's all you need. Just whack up the reverb and whack up the volume to where it's just on the edge of breaking up. That's a Les Paul on there on both pickups.' Gary bought an Ozark Resonator especially for the song 'Sundown'.

Apart from the Fender, Gary explained his gear setup for some of the other tracks: 'I used a mid-60s Vox AC30 on "Thirty Days" and on the opening track, "If The Devil Made Whiskey", I used an Orange Tiny Terror. It's a 15-watt and it looks like a little toy. I haven't even got the wood around it. It's in a while metal casing with a handle and it comes in a gig bag. It switches from 15 watts down to seven … I used it with a little Marshall 2/12 hand wired cabinet on "Eyesight To The Blind". I used my DSL Marshall 100 or 50 on "Have You Heard", "Checkin' Up On My Baby" and stuff like that.'

Gary's preferred main live amp remained the DSL Marshall, which he had been using since being sent the prototype ten years earlier: 'They've got new ones out now, but I still prefer the DSL … I've got to get some more before they stop making them. They're such a great amp. They've got a good normal channel, a lead channel as well, which I rarely use to be honest. I kind of use the normal channel and a pedal for gain. It had a good spring reverb on it, so when I want to go into that slow minor blues, I just whack up the reverb and it's all there … I use a 100-watt one of those onstage with four Celestion Vintage 30s, one top and one bottom. I started onstage using a '59 reissue, which is the old 4-input Marshall, the standard one. I've got it next to the other one onstage now. I switch between them. I never use both amps at once or anything like that.'

As far as pedals were concerned, Gary didn't use any on *Close As You Get*: 'I kind of made that a rule before I went in. I just wanted to see what I could do with a guitar and the amp. Onstage I use T-Rex pedals. At the moment, I'm using a

T-Rex Moller Overdrive, Mudhoney Overdrive and the blue one (T-Rex Alberta). I also use the Room-Mate reverb and the Replica Delay. So, I use, like, five of their pedals … They sound real big and very warm … The Moller Overdrive has two foot switches on it, a boost and a distortion … the clean boost [and the distortion are] great. If you whack them both in together you get almost into a Hendrix sort of territory.'

For the Hendrix tribute gig in 2007, after extensive research and purchase of all the current Roger Mayer pedals, Gary didn't use any of them. He went with a Boss TU2 Tuner/Mute, Dunlop Hendrix Wah, MXR GT-OD overdrive, Electro Harmonix graphic fuzz, Boss RT20 delay, Ibanez CS-9 Chorus and TC Electronic Nova Reverb (two different settings), 2 x Marshall 1959HW amps with 2 x Marshall 1960b cabs fitted with Celestion vintage 30 speakers.

2009 Early in the year, the guitar press published some of the last interviews they would conduct with Gary as he was promoting what turned out to be his final studio album, *Bad For You Baby*.

Gary talked *Guitarist* through the album track by track. For the title track, 'I used the Tele—it's a '63 with a different neck—through a Roger Mayer Stone Fuzz which gives it a sort of Hendrix vibe.' Gary used the same guitar for 'Down The Line', then for 'Umbrella Man', 'that's the Goldtop with the dark back with the 50-watt Marshall JCM800. There's quite a big sound on that guitar which worked out quite well—I just walked into a shop and bought it.' For 'Holding On', Gary used a 1963 335, bought from Horslips guitarist Johnny Fean. 'Walkin' Thru The Park' again featured the Telecaster, a guitar he certainly seemed to have a love/hate relationship with. He always loved the sound, but it was a guitar that would bite back: 'You've got to fight back with it, that helps your phrasing because you can't rush off on that guitar.' Gary used the Goldtop again on 'I Love You More Than You'll Ever Know', 'with my cheap Midiverb II. I love my Midiverb II because I always think cheap things work better with guitar—I've used it for years.'

For 'Mojo Boogie', it was the turn of the red Gibson BFG through a Fender Dual Showman. Speaking in more detail about the BFG to *Guitar & Bass*, he said, 'I've always liked that fiery slide thing that Johnny Winter does, and for that track I used a Gibson BFG, the cheap Les Paul they put out with a Burstbucker and a P90. It's a great guitar because when you pick it up it sounds just like old Les Pauls … hollowed and stripped down. They didn't even put a plastic cover on the toggle switch, so you can easily rip your hands apart. But it's a very raw sounding guitar, and I use it onstage as well. With a little bit of reverb, it cuts through everything and works really well with a big Marshall amp … although two Marshalls are even better!'

Sticking with a Les Paul on 'Someday Baby', 'Ashley Pangbourne put this together when he was in the Hamburg Custom Shop. It's got to be mid-90s, one of the earliest '59 reissues. It turned up with an out-of-phase set of sorts, but they weren't as good as these. These are the Bare Knuckles PG Blues pickups. When I go for the out-of-phase sound I always have the tone controls up full. I wouldn't use it on too many tracks, but it sounds great through the Fender amp. It's a real old-fashioned sound.' Gary went on to use the 335 on 'Did You Ever Feel Lonely'; a Gibson Firebird on 'Preacher Man Blues'; and finally, the Goldtop again on 'Trouble Ain't Far Behind'.

Gary's live setup for the final 2010 tour was Boss TU2 Tuner, Luxury Drive, Ibanez Reissue 808 Tubescreamer, Digitech Bad Monkey, T-Rex Mudhoney II, T-Rex The Twister, Boss RV-5, Electro Harmonix Holy Grail Nano, Fender '63 Reverb, Line 6 Delay, Radial Tonebone Switcher/splitter, 2 x Marshall SLP59 Amps and Marshall 1960BX cabs fitted with Celestion Vintage 30 speakers.

AND FINALLY …

'It's no good owning the best equipment that money can buy, practising scales and technique eight hours a day and learning transcriptions from the pages of magazines like *Guitar Techniques* if you don't use your ears. Any musician will tell you they're your most important musical tools. People ask me for my amp settings, my pedal setup or what pickup my guitar was on for this solo or that solo and I'm happy to tell them. But that in itself won't make you sound like me. I pick the strings a certain way, fret the notes a certain way, use certain fingers and not others; even stand a certain distance from my amp for this song or that. So, there's a lot more to it than just the transcription. But can you tell the sound of a Strat from a Les Paul on record, or distinguish what pickup or pickups are being used? Can you hear which string a solo starts on, or picture where on the neck a guitarist is playing? Well, that's how I learned and I'm sure it's how Eric, Jimi, Peter and Stevie Ray learned, too. Ears … you'll find one on each side of your head. Use them!' *GUITAR TECHNIQUES, SUMMER 2002*

TRIBUTES

'He was perhaps closer to *Guitarist*'s raison d'être than any other artist: a pure natural, guitars and music ran through him to the core.' **MICK TAYLOR, *GUITARIST* EDITOR**

'Gary was one of the finest blues/rock players to ever pick up the guitar. All of us at Marshall are truly honoured and flattered that he chose to record and perform so much of his wonderful passion-filled music using our amplifiers.' **JIM MARSHALL**

'Gary Moore was an unbelievable guitarist—one of the best I've ever heard. He was also a lovely man.' **OZZY OSBOURNE**

'He was my friend. I feel really angry he's not here and it still upsets me when I think about it. And the guitar world has lightened profoundly—kind of just gigantically since his passing too.' **GARY HUSBAND**

'He introduced himself to me a long time ago and I got an incredible feeling for the guy that he was a genuine good man and a great player. And when he died I thought, *This was so sad*. And … well, it wasn't ignored, but it wasn't given a great deal of significance, so I just wanted to say thank you by doing this and I wanted his family to know as much as anybody in the public that I cared. And I thought a good way to do it would be to take it away from his version and show that song itself is strong enough to be adaptable, so I did it in a jazzy, clubby kind of way.' **ERIC CLAPTON ON 'STILL GOT THE BLUES (FOR YOU)', HIS TRIBUTE TO GARY AT THE ROYAL ALBERT HALL, MAY 24, 2011**

'He was a ferocious player and has no fear of his instrument. It was wonderful, sad, sublime, angry, tense, fist-biting, tears, belly laughs—the complete A–Z. But I'm glad that Gary and I got to mend our relationship.' **GLENN HUGHES**

'Gary Moore is definitely in my list of top five guitar influences, right up there with Jimi Hendrix, Eddie Van Halen, Stevie Ray Vaughan and Michael Schenker.

His influence is strong to the point that the opening lick of the guitar solo of "Master Of Puppets" is a variation of a lick that Gary Moore played a lot. He just blew me away from the first time I heard him.' **KIRK HAMMETT**

'What a wonderful player he was … his recordings will testify forever. But live … he was a demon. I know because we toured with Thin Lizzy all around the States … Gary was awesome every night and the nicest guy you could imagine.' **BRIAN MAY**

'The most powerful, genuine authentic blues rock guitarist of his day. Nobody better in my opinion and maybe my all-round favourite to play with because we had real communication going—those same kind of Celtic roots.' **JACK BRUCE**

'His brilliance as a musician will last forever in his recorded work and in the hearts of his fans. It has been a privilege to have known and worked alongside him.' **NEIL CARTER**

'Gary is the finest musician I have ever played with and I think he is one of the great guitar heroes of all time. Gary has been a big part of my musical journey and I will never forget that and miss him dearly.' **DARRIN MOONEY**

'I have love and respect for Gary as a musician and as a person, he was one of the greatest.' **BOB DAISLEY**

'Touring and recording with Gary was a highlight of my career. I will not forget his generosity and all that he did for me.' **OTIS TAYLOR**

'He was a huge guitar influence. I probably ripped off Gary Moore more than any other guitar player.' **VIVIAN CAMPBELL**

'He was one of my premier influences in guitar playing … Gary opened the door for me and a lot of other blues rock guitarists. He was a legend, a musical titan and a very nice man … He also said he enjoyed my work and congratulated me on the success I was having. He was a class act and a true original.' **JOE BONAMASSA**

'One of the greatest British rock & roll guitarists. There will never another Gary Moore.' **SLASH**

'One of the greatest blues players of all time. Van Morrison, Rory Gallagher and Gary Moore—the glorious trinity of the Irish blues men. His playing was exceptional and beautiful. We won't see his like again.' **BOB GELDOF**

'In my humble opinion, he was one of the greatest blues players of our time. And a tremendous all-round musician generally. Great voice, killer licks and tone and he really could play any kind of music.' **PAT SIMMONS, DOOBIE BROTHERS**

'Gary was a friend and a truly great man. I respect that he played the game his way—no time for bullshit. He was focused and passionate about music and was one of the best.' **PAUL RODGERS**

'He was truly one of the great guitarists, had a huge talent and was a musical force beyond par.' **ROGER GLOVER**

'It's always sad to hear of the death of a fellow musician, but especially so when it's a guitarist of the calibre of Gary Moore. A great sound, fabulous vibrato and an exceptional singer.' **STEVE HACKETT**

'The world lost a giant. Gary Moore. I was a fan for sure. Amazing touch and chops … phew … fire! He was such a nice guy and a monster player.' **STEVE LUKATHER**

'My memories of Gary will be of someone who was dedicated to playing the guitar as well as he possibly could and with total focus, energy and intense commitment. I don't think I ever heard him play a wrong note … he was a very funny, down-to-earth guy. His passing is a giant loss to music.' **NEIL MURRAY**

'I will always thank him for the opportunity he gave me to play with him. He really was a brilliant musician. And I always felt like he helped take me to another level as a drummer and musician. It was an experience and an education I will never forget and take with me everywhere I go.' **ERIC SINGER**

'Whether it was hard rock, heavy metal, delicate folk or heavy blues, no one on Earth possessed quite the same touch as the inimitable Gary Moore. He was one of the most soulful, emotional, incredible players on the planet.' **GEORGE PACHECO,** *CAPE COD ROCK MUSIC EXAMINER*

'He had incredible enthusiasm for music, great energy, very dedicated musician. He was a good laugh as well; a lot of people said he was kind of grumpy, but I never saw him that way ... His enthusiasm for the instrument was remarkable. He had a feel for it. It can sort of get that way. It's just you and the guitar against the world, really. That was what it was like in the early days for myself and Gary and he won through.' **ERIC BELL**

'He was genius player ... his contribution to the Irish rock canon was immense.' **NIALL STOKES, *HOT PRESS* EDITOR**

'Gary Moore was truly a giant of contemporary guitarists. We feel honoured to have worked with him, released his amazing music and indeed to have called him a friend ... He leaves a gap that simply cannot be filled.' **LINDSAY BROWN, EAGLE ROCK**

'He was an amazing musician, self-effacing, highly intelligent and possessing a rapier wit. ... When the hits started coming, there were astounding virtuoso performances. During the 1990 *Still Got The Blues* tour, if you looked out into the audience whilst Gary was soloing, you'd see blokes so moved by what they were hearing, they'd propose to their girlfriends.' **DON AIREY**

'He was equal or better than any guitarist you could name.' **BRIAN DOWNEY**

'He had a stunning sense of harmony; he was secretly a jazzer but would never admit this. He was very much like Jeff Beck, both searching, leaving bands, gaining reputations, but never sure where they wanted to be. We played a charity gig, Vibes From The Vine, and when it came to getting Gary up, I said, "Will you please welcome a good friend of ours, the finest guitarist in his price bracket—Gary Moore!"' **MO FOSTER**

'I've played behind lots of musicians over the years, but nothing like playing behind Gary—the expertise obviously, but the power, the presence was frightening, just scary how good he was.' **ROB GREEN**

'I was so, so pleased that it was Gary I worked for over that length of time. He was the boss, but he was always fair and everybody was given the chance to do their job. There is so much I miss, the trips to guitar shops, long journeys in cars where we discussed everything about our families, other musicians. Socially, he was a quiet man. So many people wanted to know him and he found it hard to chat freely. But once he knew and trusted you, he was such a sweet, gentle and caring man. We were in Spain once and he saw this homeless man on the street. He gave him all the money in his wallet. It must have been around £300.' **DARREN MAIN**

'In August 2010, we played the Pinkpop Classic Festival in Holland. Billy Duffy from The Cult and us were all watching The Fun Lovin' Criminals and Billy said, "Oh, I'd love to meet Gary Moore." So, I put them together and immediately Gary took him under his wing. He was wonderful with other musicians—great or small and upcoming—unless they had massive egos—then he'd have nothing to do with them.' **DICK MEREDITH**

'He made us all better musicians. I've never seen anyone sweat like that on stage—and it was different every night, never formulaic and he gave it everything. Some nights were just mesmerising.' **VIC MARTIN**

'I was in the same room as Gary on many occasions; he was a very mild-mannered chap once you knew him, very intelligent and could speak on many subjects, not just music. But he had absolute confidence and infallibility in his playing, so you could be talking very quietly with him—but put a guitar in his hands and it was like the metamorphosis of the Incredible Hulk—he became Gary the Beast. He clearly went to another place, drawing on a deep well that only he had access to.' **NEVILLE MARTEN**

'You know what popped into my head when I heard that he had died? Him coming round to my house and pounding on my door, shouting, "Hey man, you have to try this Wilkinson Sword razor!! See you later, mate." I try and keep a little distance between me and the artist, but Gary would invite me over for dinner with Kerry and our wives would go shopping together. He was a very special person in my life.' **JEFF GLIXMAN**

'I think I had as good a relationship with him as anybody in my position could have. He was extremely professional, dedicated and hard-working and extremely aware of his God-given talent. And he could play anybody off—and I mean anybody.' **STEVE BARNETT**

'An incredibly gentle soul underneath that exterior. I only have fond memories of him being a good guy.' **RICHARD GRIFFITHS**

'I find it hard to come to terms with him not being here. When I think of him, I don't think of him as being dead. We did become very close and lived through the guitar. That was our family in a way.' **GREG LAKE**

'I think I am a better person and a better player for having met Gary Moore.' **SCOTT GORHAM**

'I can recall one time when I was backstage in the catering area—we would always have good food on the road—and Gary and I were chatting about the gig. There were three cooks, five or six crew, a tour manager, a promoter, theatre staff, security, Gary's personal staff, three musicians, all there and all relying on Gary for their employment. In just over an hour, he was to go on stage to play to over 5,000 people for two and half hours. He was in good humour. With this amount of responsibility, you could have forgiven him for being moody more often, but this was not so. I enjoyed my short time with Gary, he will be sadly missed.' **STEVE DIXON**

'Gary Moore knew … music, this life-sustaining calm in the centre of things and could reach out and capture it. He had the sublime ability to bring it down to earth to decode it, lay it out in *a priori* sequences for us lesser mortals to hear, understand, appreciate and marvel at.' **TIM BOOTH, DR STRANGELY STRANGE**

'I've never been flavour of the month. But sometimes you write a song and, for whatever reason, no one knows, it just gets picked up on. Either it touches something, evokes something for people's past or just makes them feel something. I've seen people in the audience crying or kissing each other when you play a certain song. And it's pretty amazing to think that something you've done can have that effect on people. When some guy comes up to you in the street and says, "Your song 'Empty Rooms' me and my wife fell in love to that and we'd just like to thank you for it." That's some complete stranger on the other side of the world and it really means more than all the fame and all the money put together.' **GARY MOORE TO GUITARIST, OCTOBER 1999**

ON THE ROAD

TOURING BANDS AND SELECTED GUEST APPEARANCES

The exact period of each band is now lost in the mists, but the chronology is roughly as follows:

1964–67

THE BEAT BOYS *1964–65* • Gary (guitar and vocals), Bill Downey (guitar and vocals), Robert Thompson (bass and vocals), Robert Wilkinson (drums).

THE BARONS *1965–66* • Gary (guitar), Pete McClelland (vocals), Bill Downey (guitar), Barney Crothers (bass), Brian Smith (drums). Sam Cook (bass) and Brian Scott (keyboards) were also briefly in the band too.

THE SUBURBANS/LIFE *1966–67* • Reggie Carson (vocals), Billy Hunter (bass), Graham Drennan (guitar), Robert Apps (drums). Gary sat in with The Suburbans for some numbers and then took Hunter and Apps to form Life, with Gary on vocals.

PLATFORM THREE *1967–68* • Gary (guitar and vocals), Colin Martin (bass), Dave Finlay (drums).

1968–73

THE METHOD *1968* • Gary (guitar and vocals), Nigel Smith (bass), Wilgar Campbell (drums).

SKID ROW *1968–71*
SR1 • Phil Lynott (vocals), Gary (guitar), Brush Shiels (bass), Noel Bridgeman (drums). Robbie Brennan deputised on drums after Noel went to play for a while in Germany.

SR2 • Gary (guitar), Brush Shiels (bass and vocals),

Noel Bridgeman (drums). During this period, there were guest appearances with Dr Strangely Strange, Granny's Intentions, Peter Green and, according to one account, with a band called Spinning Wheel, which included Rick Wakeman and later Colosseum II vocalist Mike Starrs.

THE GARY MOORE BAND *1972–73*
GMB1 • Gary (guitar and vocals), Chuck Carpenter (guitar), Sam Cook (bass), Pearse Kelly (drums).

GMB2 • Gary (guitar and vocals), Phil Donnelly (guitar), Frank Boylan (bass), Jan Schelhaas (keyboards), Pearse Kelly (drums).

GMB3 • Gary (guitar and vocals), John Curtis (bass), Pearse Kelly (drums). During this period, there were some gigs with Steve York (bass), Graham Bell (vocals) and Pearse Kelly (drums), and guest appearances with Thin Lizzy when they played the Marquee.

1974–79

THIN LIZZY *Jan–May 1974* • Gary (guitar), Phil Lynott (bass and vocals), Brian Downey (drums).

COLOSSEUM II *May 1975–Aug 1976* • Gary (guitar and vocals), Jon Hiseman (drums), Neil Murray (bass), Mike Starrs (vocals), Don Airey (keyboards). During the year it took to get the band off the ground, Hiseman took Gary to Germany to guest with the United Jazz and Rock Ensemble.

COLOSSEUM II *Aug 1976–Jan 1977* • Gary (guitar and vocals), Jon Hiseman (drums), John Mole (bass), Don Airey (keyboards).

THIN LIZZY *Jan–Mar 1977* • Gary (guitar), Phil Lynott (bass and vocals), Scott Gorham (guitar), Brian Downey (drums).

COLOSSEUM II *Mar 1977–Jul 1978* • Gary (guitar and vocals), Jon Hiseman (drums), John Mole (bass), Don Airey (keyboards). The band played a live version of *Variations* with added musicians Barbara Thompson (sax, flute) and Rod Argent (keyboards).

THIN LIZZY *Jul 1978–Jul 1979* • Gary (guitar), Phil Lynott (bass and vocals), Scott Gorham (guitar), Mark Nauseef (drums August–October 1978), Brian Downey (drums).

Early 1978 • Phil Lynott put together The Greedy Bastards (aka The Greedies) with Gary, Scott Gorham, Brian Downey, plus, variously Chris Spedding (guitar), Steve Jones (guitar), Jimmy Bain (bass), Paul Cook (drums), Bob Geldof (vocals), Johnny Fingers (piano). They played one London gig in July 1978 and three more in December.

Jan 1979 • Gary put a band together for an appearance on The Old Grey Whistle Test to promote *Back On The Streets* (1978). The band comprised Gary, Don Airey, Cozy Powell, Scott Gorham and Phil Lynott.

1979–82

RED ALERT/MOORE *Jul–Aug 1979* • Gary (guitar), Glenn Hughes (bass and vocals), Mark Nauseef (drums).

G-FORCE *Aug 1979–c. Aug 1980* • Gary (guitar and vocals), Tony Newton (bass), Willie Dee (vocals), Mark Nauseef (drums).

GARY MOORE & FRIENDS *Nov–Dec 1980* • Gary (guitar and vocals), Andy Pyle (bass), Kenny Driscoll, (vocals), Don Airey (keyboards), Tommy Aldridge (drums). Short-lived line-up that recorded one live album; Gary then replaced Pyle with Jimmy

Bain, and Driscoll with Charlie Huhn, to record *Dirty Fingers* in January/February 1981.

GREG LAKE BAND *1981–82* • Gary (guitar and vocals), Greg Lake (guitar and vocals), Tristram Margetts (bass), Tommy Eyre (keyboards), Ted McKenna (drums).

1982–95

GARY MOORE

GM1 *Aug 1982* • Gary (guitar, vocals), Charlie Huhn (guitar, vocals), Neil Murray (bass), Tommy Eyre (keyboards), Ian Paice (drums).

GM2 *Nov 1982–Feb 1983* • as GM1, except John Sloman (keyboards, vocals) replaced Charlie Huhn.

GM3 *Mar 1982–Jul 1983* • as GM1, but no second vocalist—Gary did all the vocals.

Mar 1983 • Gary was a guest at the farewell Thin Lizzy concert at London's Hammersmith Odeon.

GM4 *Jan–Mar 1984* • Gary (guitar, vocals), Craig Gruber (bass), Neil Carter (guitar, keyboards, vocals), Ian Paice (drums).

GM5 *May–Jul 1984* • as GM4, except Bobby Chouinard replaced Ian Paice.

GM6 *Aug–Sep 1984* • as GM5, except Paul Thompson replaced Bobby Chouinard.

GM7 *Dec 1984* • Gary (guitar, vocals), Neil Carter (keyboards, guitar, vocals), Bob Daisley (bass), Paul Thompson (drums).

GM8 *Sep 1985–Aug 1986* • Gary (guitar, vocals), Bob Daisley (bass), Neil Carter (guitar, keyboards, vocals), Gary Ferguson (drums). Phil Lynott guested on three dates on the 1985 UK tour.

GM9 *Mar–Sep 1987* • as GM8, except Eric Singer replaced Gary Ferguson.

GM10 *Mar–May 1989* • as GM9, except Eric Singer left to be replaced originally by Cozy Powell and then eventually Chris Slade.

GARY MOORE & THE MIDNIGHT BLUES BAND
GMMBB1 *Apr–Sep 1990* • Gary (guitar, vocals), Andy Pyle (bass), Don Airey (keyboards), Graham Walker (drums), the Midnight Horns (Frank Mead alto and tenor sax, harmonica; Nick Payn baritone sax; Nick Pentelow tenor sax; Martin Drower trumpet). Albert Collins was special guest on several dates.

GMMBB2 *Mar–Nov 1992* • as the first MBB line-up, but with the addition of back-up vocalists Candy MacKenzie and Carol Thompson.

Apr 1992 • Gary was a guest performer at George Harrison's Royal Albert Hall concert in aid of the Natural Law Party.

GMMBB3 *Jul 1993* • just a few dates with Gary, Pyle, Eyre and Walker.

Aug–Nov 1993 • Gary played one date in Germany with Jack Bruce and Gary Husband, which led to Gary being invited to play at Jack's fiftieth birthday celebration event in Cologne, and from there came BBM.

BBM *May–Jul 1994* • Gary (guitar, vocals), Jack Bruce (bass, vocals), Ginger Baker (drums), Tommy Eyre (keyboards).

GMMBB4 *Apr–Aug 1995* • same line-up as MBB3, but with Nick Pentelow and Nick Payne added.

1997–2003

GM11 *Jun–Oct 1997* • Gary (guitar, vocals), Guy Pratt (bass, vocals), Magnus Fiennes (keyboards), Gary Husband (drums).

Jul 1998 • three more dates for Gary with Jack Bruce and Gary Husband.

GM12 *Jul–Aug 1999* • Gary (guitar, vocals), Pete Rees (bass), Vic Martin (keyboards), Gary Husband (drums).

GM13 *Oct–Dec 1999* • as GM12, except Darrin Mooney replaced Gary Husband.

GM14 *Mar–Jun 2000* • as GM13, except Graham Walker replaced Darrin Mooney.

GM15 *Feb–Sep 2001* • as GM13.

SCARS *Feb 2002–Jul 2003* • Gary (guitar, vocals), Cass Lewis (bass), Darrin Mooney (drums).

Oct 2003 • Gary was part of an all-star line-up led by Roger Daltrey who played a charity gig at Ronnie Scott's Club. Named The RD Crusaders, the band included Zoot Money and Greg Lake. They played another gig in October 2004 joined by Gary Brooker and Russ Ballard.

2004–10

GM16 *Jun–Jul 2004* • Gary (guitar, vocals), Bob Daisley (bass), Darrin Mooney (drums).

Sep 2004 • Gary took part in Fender's fiftieth anniversary charity concert at Wembley Arena, London. The astonishing line-up of guitarists can be appreciated on the *Strat Pack Live In Concert* DVD.

Jun 2005 • Gary teamed up with Jack Bruce and Gary Husband for the Dick Heckstall-Smith Memorial Concert at London's Astoria.

GM17 *Mar 2006–Nov 2007* • Gary (guitar, vocals), Pete Rees (bass), Vic Martin (keyboards), Brian Downey (drums).

Aug 2006 • Gary appeared at the Vibes from the Vines Festival charity gig (and again in 2009) organised by Mo Foster.

Oct–Nov 2006 • Gary guested with Paul Rodgers at the Royal Albert Hall. In the same month, he appeared with Otis Taylor in Brighton and London, and similarly with John Mayall & The Bluesbreakers in Brighton, and then again in November at the Shepherd's Bush Empire, London.

Jan 2007 • Gary lined up with Paul Weller, Joe Walsh, Jon Lord, Stevie Winwood and others to pay tribute to Jim Capaldi.

Sep 2007 • Gary took part in the Sunflower Jam organised by Jackie Paice in aid of complementary therapy cancer treatment. Others taking part included Ian Paice, Roger Glover, Jon Lord and Status Quo.

GM18 *Mar 2008* • as GM17, except Sam Kelly replaced Brian Downey.

GM19 *Apr–Nov 2008* • as GM17.

Sep 2008 • Gary flew to Dublin to take part in a tribute concert to the great Irish guitarist Jimmy Faulkner. Brian Downey, Brush Shiels and Noel Bridgeman were among many top Irish musicians who appeared.

GM20 *Dec 2008–Apr 2010* • as GM17, except Steve Dixon replaced Brian Downey.

GM 21 *Apr–Oct 2010* • Gary (guitar, vocals), Jon Noyce (bass), Neil Carter (guitar, keyboards, vocals), Darrin Mooney (drums). This was the last band Gary took on the road. In February 2011, he went into a rehearsal studio with Jon Noyce and drummer Rob Green. Neil Carter was scheduled to join later, but sadly we will never know who would have been in the touring band for the potential 2011 gigs.

DISCOGRAPHY

STUDIO ALBUMS

GRINDING STONE
CBS Records 65527, May 1973
Grinding Stone • Time To Heal • Sail Across The Mountain • The Energy Dance • Spirit • Boogie My Way Back Home
Personnel Gary Moore (guitars, vocals), Pearse Kelly (drums), John Curtis (bass), Philip Donnelly (rhythm guitar), Jan Schelhaas (keyboards), Frank Boylan (bass)

BACK ON THE STREETS
MCA Records MCF 2853, September 1978
Back On The Streets • Don't Believe A Word • Fanatical
Fascists • Flight Of The Snow Moose • Hurricane • Song For Donna • What Would You Rather Bee Or A Wasp • Parisienne Walkways
Bonus tracks *Spanish Guitar (Phil's vocal) • Spanish Guitar (Instrumental) • Spanish Guitar (Gary's vocal) • Parisienne Walkways (Gary's vocal) • Don't Believe A Word (Gary's vocal) • Track Nine*
Personnel Gary Moore (guitars, vocals, bass, mandolin, accordion, string synth), Phil Lynott (bass, vocals, double bass, acoustic guitar), Brian Downey (drums),

John Mole (bass), Don Airey (keyboards), Simon Philips (drums)

DIRTY FINGERS
Jet Records JETLP 241, July 1983 (Japan) / June 1984 (Europe)
Hiroshima • Dirty Fingers • Bad News • Don't Let Me Be Misunderstood • Run To Your Mama • Nuclear Attack • Kidnapped • Really Gonna Rock • Lonely Nights • Rest In Peace
Personnel Gary Moore (guitars, vocals), Tommy Aldridge (drums), Jimmy Bain (bass), Don Airey (keyboards), Charlie Huhn (vocal)

CORRIDORS OF POWER
**Virgin Records V 2245,
September 1982**
Don't Take Me For A Loser • Always Gonna Love You • Wishing Well • Gonna Break My Heart Again • Falling In Love With You • End Of The World • Rockin' Every Night • Cold Hearted • I Can't Wait Until Tomorrow
Bonus tracks *Love Can Make A Fool Of You • Falling In Love With You (Remix) • Falling In Love With You (Remix instrumental)*
Personnel Gary Moore (guitars, vocals), Ian Paice (drums), Neil Murray (bass), Tommy Eyre (keyboards), Jack Bruce (vocal), Bobby Chouinard (drums), Mo Foster (bass), John Sloman (backing vocal), Don Airey (keyboards)

VICTIMS OF THE FUTURE
**10 Records DIX 2,
December 1983**
Victims Of The Future • Teenage Idol • Shapes Of Things • Empty Rooms • Murder In The Skies • All I Want • Hold On To Love • Law Of The Jungle
Bonus tracks *Devil In Her Heart • Blinder • Empty Rooms (1984 remix) • Teenage Idol (different version)*
Personnel Gary Moore (guitars, vocals, bass), Ian Paice (drums), Neil Carter (keyboards, backing vocals), Neil Murray (bass), Noddy Holder (backing vocal), Bobby Chouinard (drums), Bob Daisley (bass), Mo Foster (bass)

RUN FOR COVER
**10 Records DIX 16,
September 1985**
Run For Cover • Reach For The Sky • Military Man • Empty Rooms • Out In The Fields • Nothing To Lose • Once In A Lifetime • All Messed Up • Listen To Your Heartbeat
Bonus tracks *Once In A Lifetime • Still In Love With You • Murder In The Skies (live) • Stop Messin' Around (live)*
Personnel Gary Moore (guitars, vocals), Bob Daisley (bass), Neil Carter (keyboards, backing vocals), Don Airey (keyboards), Andy Richards (keyboards), Gary Ferguson (drums), Charlie Morgan (drums), Paul Thompson (drums), James Barton (sampled drums), Glenn Hughes (bass, vocals), Phil Lynott (bass, vocals)

WILD FRONTIER
10 Records DIX 56, March 1987
Over The Hills And Far Away • Wild Frontier • Take A Little Time • The Loner • Friday On My Mind • Strangers In The Darkness • Thunder Rising • Johnny Boy
Bonus tracks *Wild Frontier (12-inch version) • Over The Hills And Far Away (12-inch version) • Crying In The Shadows • The Loner (Extended mix) • Friday On My Mind (12-inch version) • Out In The Fields (live)*
Personnel Gary Moore (guitars, vocals), Bob Daisley (bass), Neil Carter (keyboards, backing vocals), Roland Kerridge (drum programming/electronic kit)

AFTER THE WAR
**Virgin Records V 2575,
January 1989**
Dunluce (Part 1) • After The War • Speak For Yourself • Livin' On Dreams • Led Clones • The Messiah Will Come Along • Running From The Storm • This Thing Called Love • Ready For Love • Blood of Emeralds • Dunluce (Part 2)
Bonus tracks *Emerald • Over The Hills And Far Away (live) • Military Man (live) • Wild Frontier (live)*
Personnel Gary Moore (guitars, vocals), Bob Daisley (bass), Neil Carter (keyboards, backing vocals), Cozy Powell (drums), Ozzy Osbourne (vocals), Chris Thompson (vocals), Don Airey (keyboards), Laurence Cottle (bass), Charlie Morgan (drums), Simon Phillips (drums), Brian Downey (drums), Chris Thompson (backing vocals), Andrew Eldritch (backing vocals), Sam Brown (backing vocals), Miriam Stockley (backing vocals)

STILL GOT THE BLUES
**Virgin Records V 2612,
March 1990**
Moving On • Oh, Pretty Woman • Walking By Myself • Still Got The Blues (For You) • Texas Strut • Too Tired • King Of The Blues • As The Years Go Passing By • Midnight Blues
Bonus tracks *All Your Love • Stop Messin' Around • That Kind Of Woman • The Stumble • Left Me With The Blues • Further On Up The Road • Mean Cruel Woman • The Sky Is Crying*
Personnel Gary Moore (guitars,

vocals), Andy Pyle (bass), Bob Daisley (bass), Brian Downey (drums), Graham Walker (drums), Don Airey (keyboards), Mick Weaver (piano), Nicky Hopkins (piano), Martin Drover (trumpet), Raul d'Oliveira (trumpet), Frank Mead (tenor saxophone), Nick Pentelow (tenor saxophone), Nick Payn (baritone saxophone), Albert Collins (guitar), George Harrison (guitar, vocals), Albert King (guitar)

AFTER HOURS
Virgin Records V 2684,
March 1992
Cold Day In Hell • Don't You Lie To Me • Story Of The Blues • Since I Met You Baby • Separate Ways • Only Fool In Town • Key To Love • Jumpin' At Shadows • The Blues Is Alright • The Hurt Inside • Nothing's The Same
Bonus tracks Once In A Blue Mood • All Time Low • Don't Start Me Talkin' • Woke Up This Morning • Movin' On Down The Road
Personnel Gary Moore (guitars, bass, vocals), Will Lee (bass), Bob Daisley (bass), Johnny B. Gaydon (bass), Graham Walker (drums), Anton Fig (drums), Tommy Eyre (keyboards), Martin Drover (trumpet), Frank Mead (tenor saxophone), Nick Pentelow (tenor saxophone), Nick Payn (baritone saxophone), Andrew Love (tenor saxophone), Wayne Jackson (trumpet, trombone), Carol Kenyon (backing vocals), Linda Taylor (backing vocals), Richard Morgan (oboe), B.B. King (guitar, vocals), Albert Collins (guitar)

BLUES FOR GREENY
Virgin Records V 2784,
May 1995
If You Be My Baby • Long Grey Mare • Merry Go Round • I Loved Another Woman • Need Your Love So Bad • The Same Way • The Supernatural • Driftin' • Showbiz Blues • Love That Burns • Looking For Somebody
Bonus tracks The World Keeps On Turnin' (acoustic version) • The Same Way (acoustic version) • Stop Messin' Around (acoustic version)
Personnel Gary Moore (guitars, vocals), Tommy Eyre (keyboards), Andy Pyle (bass), Graham Walker (drums), Nick Payn (baritone saxophone), Nick Pentelow (tenor saxophone)

DARK DAYS IN PARADISE
Virgin Records CDV 2826,
June 1997
One Good Reason • Cold Wind Blows • I Have Found My Love In You • One Fine Day • Like Angels • What Are We Here For? • Always There For You • Afraid Of Tomorrow • Where Did We Go Wrong? • Business as Usual • Dark Days In Paradise (hidden track)
Bonus tracks Burning in Our Hearts • There Must Be A Way
Personnel Gary Moore (guitars, vocals), Guy Pratt (bass), Gary Husband (drums), Magnus Fiennes (keyboards, programming), Phil Nicholas (keyboards, programming), Dee Lewis (backing vocals), Chyna Gordon (backing vocals)

A DIFFERENT BEAT
Raw Power RAW CD 142,
September 1999
Go On Home • Lost In Your Love • Worry No More • Fire • Surrender • House Full Of Blues • Bring My Baby Back • Can't Help Myself • Fatboy • We Want Love • Can't Help Myself (E-Z Rollers Remix)
Personnel Gary Moore (guitars, bass, vocals, keyboards), Gary Husband (drums), Roger King (keyboards, programming), Phil Nicholls (programming)

BACK TO THE BLUES
Sanctuary Records SANCD072,
March 2001
Enough Of The Blues • You Upset Me Baby • Cold Black Night • Stormy Monday • Ain't Got You • Picture Of The Moon • Looking Back • The Prophet • How Many Lies • Drowning In Tears
Personnel Gary Moore (guitars, vocals), Pete Rees (bass), Vic Martin (keyboards), Darrin Mooney (drums), Martin Drover (trumpet), Frank Mead (tenor saxophone), Nick Payn (baritone saxophone), Nick Pentelow (tenor saxophone)

POWER OF THE BLUES
Sanctuary Records SANCD267,
June 2004
Power Of The Blues • There's A Hole • Tell Me Woman • I Can't Quit You Baby • That's Why I Play The Blues • Evil • Getaway Blues • Memory Pain • Can't Find My Baby • Torn Inside
Personnel Gary Moore (guitars, vocals), Bob Daisley (bass), Darrin Mooney (drums), Jim Watson (keyboards)

OLD NEW BALLADS BLUES
Eagle Records EAGCD314,
May 2006
Done Somebody Wrong • You
Know My Love • Midnight Blues
(2006) • Ain't Nobody • Gonna
Rain Today • All Your Love
(2006) • Flesh & Blood • Cut It
Out • No Reason to Cry • I'll Play
The Blues For You
Personnel Gary Moore (guitars,
vocals), Jonathan Noyce (bass),
Don Airey (keyboards), Darrin
Mooney (drums)

CLOSE AS YOU GET
Eagle Records EAGCD346,
May 2007
If The Devil Made Whiskey •
Trouble At Home • Thirty Days •
Hard Times • Have You Heard •
Eyesight To The Blind • Evenin' •
Nowhere Fast • Checkin' Up On
My Baby • I Had A Dream •
Sundown
Personnel Gary Moore (guitars,
vocals), Pete Rees (bass), Vic
Martin (keyboards), Brian
Downey (drums), Mark Feltham
(harmonica)

BAD FOR YOU BABY
Eagle Records EAGCD379,
September 2008
Bad For You Baby • Down The
Line • Umbrella Man • Holding
On • Walkin' Thru The Park • I
Love You More Than You'll Ever
Know • Mojo Boogie • Someday
Baby • Did You Ever Feel
Lonely? • Preacher Man Blues •
Trouble Ain't Far Behind
Bonus track Picture On The Wall
Personnel Gary Moore (guitars,
vocals, harmonica), Pete Rees
(bass), Vic Martin (keyboards),
Sam Kelly (drums), Otis Taylor
(banjo), Cassie Taylor (backing
vocals)

LIVE ALBUMS

LIVE AT THE MARQUEE
Jet Records JET LP 245, 1983
(Japan) / June 1984 (Europe)
Back On The Streets • Run To Your
Mama • Dancin' • She's Got
You • Parisienne Walkways •
You • Nuclear Attack • Dallas
Warhead
Personnel Gary Moore (guitars,
vocals), Don Airey (keyboards),
Kenny Driscoll (vocals), Andy Pyle
(bass), Tommy Aldridge (drums).
Recorded in London, November
1980.

**ROCKIN' EVERY NIGHT—LIVE
IN JAPAN**
10 Records XID 1, June 1986
May 1983 (Japan) / June
1986 (Europe)
Rockin' Every Night • Wishing
Well • I Can't Wait Until
Tomorrow • Nuclear Attack •

White Knuckles • Rockin' And
Rollin' • Back On The Streets •
Sunset
Personnel Gary Moore (guitars,
vocals), Don Airey (keyboards),
Neil Murray (bass), John Sloman
(vocals, keyboards), Ian Paice
(drums). Recorded in Tokyo,
January 1983.

WE WANT MOORE!
10 Records GMDL 1, October
1984
Murder In The Skies • Shapes Of
Things • Victims Of The Future •
Cold Hearted • End Of The
World • Back On The Streets • So
Far Away • Empty Rooms • Don't
Take Me For A Loser • Rockin'
And Rollin'
Personnel Gary Moore (guitars,
vocals), Neil Carter (keyboards,
guitar, vocals), Craig Gruber

(bass), Ian Paice (drums), Bobby
Chouinard (drums), Jimmy Nail
(vocals). Recorded in London,
Glasgow, Detroit and Tokyo in
February–June 1984.

BLUES ALIVE
Virgin Records V 2716, May
1993
Cold Day In Hell • Walking By
Myself • Story Of The Blues • Oh,
Pretty Woman • Separate
Ways • Too Tired • Still Got The
Blues (For You) • Since I Met You
Baby • The Sky Is Crying • Further
On Up The Road • King Of The
Blues • Parisienne Walkways •
Jumpin' At Shadows
Personnel Gary Moore (guitars,
vocals), Tommy Eyre (keyboards),
Andy Pyle (bass), Graham Walker
(drums), Candy MacKenzie
(backing vocal), Carol Thompson

(backing vocal), Frank Mead (alto saxophone, harmonica), Nick Payn (baritone saxophone), Nick Pentelow (tenor saxophone), Martin Drover (trumpet), Albert Collins (guitar). Recorded in Los Angeles, Paris and London in May–October 1992.

LIVE AT MONSTERS OF ROCK
Sanctuary Records SANCD215,
September 2003
Shapes Of Things • Wishing Well • Rectify • Guitar Intro • Stand Up • Just Can't Let You Go • Walking By Myself • Don't Believe A Word • Out In The

Fields • Parisienne Walkways
Personnel Gary Moore (guitars, vocals), Cass Lewis (bass, vocals), Darrin Mooney (drums). Recorded in Glasgow, May 2003.

POSTHUMOUS LIVE ALBUMS

LIVE AT MONTREUX 2010
Eagle Records EAGCD434,
September 2011
Over The Hills And Far Away • Military Man • Days Of Heroes • Where Are You Now? • So Far Away / Empty Rooms • Oh Wild One • Blood Of Emeralds • Out In The Fields • Walking By Myself • Johnny Boy • Parisienne Walkways
Personnel Gary Moore (guitars, vocals), Neil Carter (keyboards, guitar, vocals), Jonathan Noyce (bass), Darrin Mooney (drums). Recorded in Montreux, Switzerland, July 2010.

BLUES FOR JIMI
Eagle Records EAGCD491,
September 2012
Purple Haze • Manic Depression • Foxy Lady • The Wind Cries Mary • I Don't Live Today • My Angel • Angel • Fire • Red House • Stone Free • Hey Joe • Voodoo Chile (Slight Return)

Personnel Gary Moore (guitars, vocals), Dave Bronze (bass), Darrin Mooney (drums), Mitch Mitchell (drums), Billy Cox (bass) Recorded in London, October 2007.

LIVE AT BUSH HALL 2007
Eagle Records EAGCD535,
September 2014
If The Devil Made Whisky • Thirty Days • Trouble At Home • Hard Times • Eyesight To The Blind • I Had A Dream • Too Tired • Gary's Blues • Don't Believe A Word • Still Got The Blues (For You) • Walking By Myself • The Blues Is Alright • Sundown
Personnel Gary Moore (guitars, vocals), Pete Rees (bass), Vic Martin (keyboards), Brian Downey (drums). Recorded in London, May 2007.

LIVE FROM LONDON 2009
Provogue PRD 760552,
January 2020
Pretty Woman • Bad For You

Baby • Down The Line • I Met You Baby • Still Got The Blues • Have You Heard • All Your Love • The Mojo (Boogie) • I Love You More Than You'll Ever Know • Too Tired • Walking By Myself • The Blues Is Alright • Parisienne Walkways
Personnel Gary Moore (guitars, vocals), Pete Rees (bass), Vic Martin (keyboards), Steve Dixon (drums). Recorded in London, December 2009.

HOW BLUE CAN YOU GET
Provogue PRD76462, April 2021
I'm Tore Down • Steppin' Out • In My Dreams • How Blue Can You Get • Looking At Your Picture • Love Can Make A Fool Of You • Done Somebody Wrong • Living With The Blues
Personnel Gary Moore (guitars, vocals), Pete Rees (bass), Vic Martin (keyboards), Darrin Mooney & Graham Walker (drums)

SINGLES

BACK ON THE STREETS
MCA Records MCA 386,
September 1978 (UK)
Back On The Streets • Track Nine

PARISIENNE WALKWAYS
MCA Records MCA 419,
April 1979 (UK)
Parisienne Walkways • Fanatical
Fascists

SPANISH GUITAR
MCA Records MCA 534,
October 1979 (UK)
Spanish Guitar • Spanish Guitar
(instrumental version)

NUCLEAR ATTACK
Jet Records JET 12016,
September 1981 (UK)
Nuclear Attack • Don't Let Me Be
Misunderstood • Run to Your
Mama

ALWAYS GONNA LOVE YOU
Virgin Records VS 528,
September 1982 (UK)
Always Gonna Love You • Cold
Hearted

FALLING IN LOVE WITH YOU
Virgin Records VS 564,
February 1983 (UK)
Falling in Love With You (single
edit) • Falling in Love With You
(instrumental)

PARISIENNE WALKWAY
Jet Records / CBS Records
07SP 717, September 1983
(Japan)
Parisienne Walkways (live

November 5 or 6, 1980) • She's
Got You (live November 5 or 6,
1980)

**DON'T LET ME BE
MISUNDERSTOOD**
Jet Records JET 7043,
June 1984 (UK)
Don't Let Me Be Misunderstood •
She's Got You (live November 5
or 6, 1980)

EMPTY ROOMS
10 Records TEN 25,
August 1984 (UK)
Empty Rooms (single edit) •
Nuclear Attack (live January 24
1983)

HOLD ON TO LOVE
10 Records TEN 13,
January 1984 (UK)
Hold On to Love (single edit) •
Devil in Her Heart

SHAPES OF THINGS
10 Records TEN 19, March
1984 (UK)
Shapes Of Things (new version) •
Blinder

EMPTY ROOMS
10 Records TEN 58,
July 1985 (UK)
Empty Rooms (summer 1985
version) • Out Of My System

LISTEN TO YOUR HEARTBEAT
10 Records 107 840-100,
1985 (Germany)
Listen To Your Heartbeat • Out Of
My System

OUT IN THE FIELDS
10 Records TEN 49,
May 1985 (UK)
Out In The Fields • Military Man

RUN FOR COVER
Virgin Records VS 650,
1985 (South Africa)
Run For Cover • Parisienne
Walkways (live December 18,
1984)

CRYING IN THE SHADOWS
10 Records / Toshiba EMI
07VA-1052, October 1986
(Japan)
Crying In The Shadows • Once In
A Lifetime

PARISIENNE WALKWAYS
10 Records 108 226, 1986
(Sweden)
Parisienne Walkways (live
December 18, 1984) • Once In A
Lifetime • Victims Of The Future

**OVER THE HILLS AND FAR
AWAY**
10 Records TEN 134,
December 1986 (UK)
Over The Hills And Far Away
(single version) • Crying In The
Shadows

FRIDAY ON MY MIND
10 Records TEN 164,
May 1987 (UK)
Friday On My Mind (single
version) • Reach For The Sky (live
September 28, 1985)

WILD FRONTIER
10 Records TEN 159,
February 1987 (UK)
Wild Frontier • Run For Cover
(live September 28, 1985)

TAKE A LITTLE TIME
10 Records TEND 190,
November 1987 (UK)
Take A Little Time • Out In The
Fields • All Messed Up (live April
25, 1987) • Thunder Rising (live
April 25, 1987)

THE LONER
10 Records TEN 178,
August 1987 (UK)
The Loner (single edit) • Johnny
Boy

AFTER THE WAR
GMS 1, January 1989 (UK)
After The War • This Thing
Called Love

LIVIN' ON DREAMS
Virgin Records VS 1219,
October 1989
Livin' On Dreams (remix) • The
Messiah Will Come Again

LED CLONES
Virgin Records America
7-99211, July 1989
Led Clones (edit version) •
Speak For Yourself

READY FOR LOVE
Virgin Records GMS 2,
February 1989
Ready For Love (edit version) •
Wild Frontier (live April 25, 1987)

OH, PRETTY WOMAN
Virgin Records VSC 1233,
March 1990
Oh, Pretty Woman • King Of The
Blues (non-album version)

TOO TIRED
Virgin Records VS 1306,
November 1990
Too Tired • Texas Strut

WALKING BY MYSELF
Virgin Records VS 1281,
August 1990
Walking By Myself • Still Got The
Blues (For You) (live June 5, 1990)

STILL GOT THE BLUES (FOR
YOU)
Virgin Records VS 1267,
April 1990
Still Got The Blues (For You) (single
edit) • Left Me With The Blues

COLD DAY IN HELL
Virgin Records VSC 1393,
February 1992
Cold Day In Hell • All Time Low

SEPARATE WAYS
Virgin Records VS 1437,
October 1992
Separate Ways (single edit) •
Only Fool In Town

SINCE I MET YOU BABY
Virgin Records VS 1423,
July 1992
Since I Met You Baby • The Hurt
Inside

STORY OF THE BLUES
Virgin Records VS 1412,
April 1992
Story Of The Blues (single edit) •
Movin' Down The Road

PARISIENNE WALKWAYS '93
Virgin Records VS 1456,
April 1993
Parisienne Walkways (edit '93,
live October 5, 1992) • Still Got
The Blues (For You) (live
November 11, 1992)
Bonus tracks *Since I Met You*
Baby (live November 11, 1992) •
Key To Love (live November 11,
1992)

STILL GOT THE BLUES
Virgin France 921482,
May 1993
Still Got The Blues (For You) (fade
out, live November 11, 1992 •
The Thrill Is Gone (live November
11, 1992) • King Of The Blues
(live June 13, 1992)

ONE DAY
Virgin Records 8927152,
October 1994
One Day • Story Of The Blues
(The Dry Mix) • Empty Rooms •
The Loner • Parisienne Walkways
(edit '93, live) • Falling In Love
With You

NEED YOUR LOVE SO BAD
Virgin Records VS 1546,
June 1995
Need Your Love So Bad (single
edit) • The Same Way (acoustic
version) • World Keeps On
Turning (acoustic version) • Stop
Messin' Around (acoustic version)

ONE GOOD REASON
Virgin Records VSCDT 1632,
May 1997
One Good Reason • Burning In
Our Hearts • There Must Be A
Way • Beasts Of Burden

I HAVE FOUND MY LOVE IN YOU
Virgin Records VSCDT 1640,
June 1997
I Have Found My Love In You
(single edit) • All The Way From
Africa • My Foolish Pride • One
Good Reason • Burning In Our
Hearts • There Must Be A Way •
Beasts Of Burden

ALWAYS THERE FOR YOU
Virgin Records VSCDT 1674,
November 1997
Always There For You (new
version) • Rhythm Of Our Lives
(Stretch mix) • Rhythm Of Our
Lives (Gary's mix)

PICTURE OF THE MOON
Sanctuary Records SANX4072,
May 2001
Picture Of The Moon (single
edit) • Cold Black Night (live at
VH-1 Studio) • Stormy Monday
(live at VH-1 Studio)

PROMO ONLY SINGLES
End Of The World (1982) •
Military Man (1985) • Reach For
The Sky (1986) • Wild Frontier
Live (1987) • Moving On
(1990) • Midnight Blues
(1990) • Only Fool In Town
(1992) • Walking By Myself Live
(1993) • Empty Rooms (1994) • I
Loved Another Woman (1995) •
The New Single (1997) • Enough
Of The Blues (2001) • Parisienne
Walkways Live (2014)

COMPILATIONS

Only a selection of many different
releases and versions.

WHITE KNUCKLES
Raw Power, 1985

ANTHOLOGY
Raw Power, 1986

PARISIENNE WALKWAYS
MCA Records, 1987

THE COLLECTION
Castle Communications, 1990

THE EARLY YEARS
Epic, 1991 (USA)

BALLADS & BLUES 1982–1994
Virgin Records, 1994

OUT IN THE FIELDS—THE VERY BEST OF
Virgin Records, 1998

THE BEST OF THE BLUES
Virgin Records, 2002

HAVE SOME MOORE—THE BEST OF
EMI Finland, 2002 (Finland only)

PARISIENNE WALKWAYS—THE BLUES COLLECTION
EMI, 2003

BACK ON THE STREETS—THE ROCK COLLECTION
EMI, 2003

THE PLATINUM COLLECTION
Virgin Records / EMI, 2006

HAVE SOME MOORE 2—THE BEST OF
EMI Finland, 2008 (Finland only)

GARY MOORE MEMORIAL COLLECTION
Universal, 2011 (Japan only)

PARISIENNE WALKWAYS—JET TO THE BEST
Victor, 2013 (Japan only)

BLUES AND BEYOND
BMG, November 2017

PARISIENNE WALKWAYS: THE COLLECTION
BMG, January 2020

STUDIO ALBUMS WITH BANDS

WITH SKID ROW
SKID ROW: SKID
CBS Records S 63965,
October 1970
Mad Dog Woman • Virgo's
Daughter • Heading Home
Again • An Awful Lot Of
Woman • Unco-Up Showband
Blues • For Those Who Do • After
I'm Gone • The Man Who Never
Was • Felicity
Personnel Gary Moore (guitars,
vocals), Brush Shiels (bass,
vocals), Noel Bridgeman (drums).
Re-recorded version from 1970.

SKID ROW aka DUBLIN GAS
COMY. COOKER & METER
FACTORY
CBS Records 63965,
March 1983
Sandie's Gone • The Man Who
Never Was • Heading Home
Again • Felicity • Unco-Op
Showband Blues • Morning Star
Avenue • Oi'll Tell You Later •
Virgo's Daughter • New Faces
Old Places
Personnel Gary Moore (guitars,
vocals), Brush Shiels (bass,
vocals), Noel Bridgeman (drums).
Original recording from 1970.

34 HOURS
CBS Records 64411,
September 1971
Night Of The Warm Witch • First
Thing In The Morning • Mar • Go,
I'm Never Gonna Let You •
Lonesome Still • The Love Story
Personnel Gary Moore (guitars,
vocals), Brush Shiels (bass, vocals,
guitar), Noel Bridgeman (drums,

accordion), Paul Scully (bass)

GARY MOORE / BRUSH
SHIELS / NOEL BRIDGEMAN
Castle Communications ESSLP
025, July 1990
Benedict's Cherry Wine •
Saturday Morning Man • Crystal
Ball • Mr. De-Luxe • Girl Called
Winter • Morning Star Avenue •
Silver Bird
Personnel Gary Moore (guitars,
vocals), Brush Shiels (bass,
vocals), Noel Bridgeman (drums).
Recorded in late 1971 but
released in 1990.

WITH COLOSSEUM II
STRANGE NEW FLESH
Bronze Records ILPS 9356,
April 1976
Dark Side Of The Moog • Down
To You • Gemini And Leo • Secret
Places • On Second Thoughts •
Winds
Personnel Gary Moore (guitars,
vocals), Jon Hiseman (drums), Don
Airey (keyboards), Neil Murray
(bass), Mike Starrs (vocals)

ELECTRIC SAVAGE
MCA Records MCF-2800,
June 1977
Put It This Way • All Skin And
Bone • Rivers • The Scorch •
Lament • Desperado • Am I •
Intergalactic Strut
Personnel Gary Moore (guitars,
vocals), Jon Hiseman (drums),
Don Airey (keyboards), John
Mole (bass)

WAR DANCE
MCA Records MCF 2817
November 1977
War Dance • Major Keys • Put It
That Way • Castles • Fighting
Talk • The Inquisition • Star
Maiden • Mysterioso • Quasar •
Last Exit
Personnel Gary Moore (guitars,
vocals), Jon Hiseman (drums),
Don Airey (keyboards), John Mole
(bass)

WITH THIN LIZZY
BLACK ROSE—A ROCK
LEGEND
Vertigo/Phonogram 9102 032,
April 1979
Do Anything You Want To •
Toughest Street In Town • S &
M • Waiting For An Alibi •
Sarah • Got To Give It Up • Get
Out Of Here • With Love • Róisín
Dubh (Black Rose) A Rock Legend
Personnel Gary Moore (guitars,
vocals), Phil Lynott (bass, vocals),
Scott Gorham (guitar), Brian
Downey (drums)

WITH G-FORCE
G-FORCE
Jet Records JETLP 229,
May 1980
You • White Knuckles • Rockin'
And Rollin' • She's Got You • I
Look At You • Because Of Your
Love • You Kissed Me Sweetly •
Hot Gossip • The Woman's In
Love • Dancin'
Personnel Gary Moore (guitars,
vocals), Willie Dee (vocals), Tony
Newton (bass), Mark Nauseef
(drums)

WITH BBM
AROUND THE NEXT DREAM
Virgin Records V 2745,
May 1994
Waiting In The Wings • City Of
Gold • Where In The World •
Can't Fool The Blues • High Cost
Of Loving • Glory Days • Why
Does Love Have To Go Wrong? •
Naked Flame • I Wonder Why
(Are You So Mean To Me?) •
Wrong Side Of Town
Bonus tracks Danger Zone • The

World Keeps On Turnin' • Sitting
On Top The World (live) • I
Wonder Why (Are You So Mean
To Me?) (live)
Personnel Gary Moore (guitars,
vocals), Jack Bruce (bass, vocals),
Ginger Baker (drums), Tommy
Eyre (keyboards), Arran Ahmun
(drums), Morris Murphy (trumpet)

WITH SCARS
SCARS
Sanctuary Records SANCD120,

September 2002
When The Sun Goes Down •
Rectify • Wasn't Born In
Chicago • Stand Up • Just Can't
Let You Go • My Baby (She's So
Good To Me) • World Of
Confusion • Ball And Chain •
World Keep Turnin' Round •
Who Knows (What Tomorrow
May Bring)?
Personnel Gary Moore (guitars,
vocals), Cass Lewis (bass), Darrin
Mooney (drums)

SESSION WORK & GUEST APPEARANCES

THE JACOBITES
'Like Now' Pye Records
7N.17852, October 1969

GRANNY'S INTENTIONS
Honest Injun Decca/Deram
DML 1060, March 1970

DR STRANGELY STRANGE
Heavy Petting Vertigo 6360
009 August 1970
Alternative Medicine Ace
Records / Big Beat Records
CDWIKD 177, October 1997

CLIFF BENNETT'S REBELLION
'Amos Moses' CBS Records CBS
S 7231, April 1971

JONATHAN KELLY
**Wait Till They Change The
Backdrop** RCA/Victor SF 8353,
May 1973

THIN LIZZY
Nightlife Vertigo 6360 116 1974
Life/Live Vertigo VERD 6, 812
882-1, 1983

EDDIE HOWELL
**The Eddie Howell Gramophone
Record** Warner Bros. Records K
56154, October 1975

JACK LANCASTER
Peter And The Wolf RSO
2479-167, November 1975
Skinningrove Bay Acrobat
Records 1 C 064-64056, 1978

GARY BOYLE
Electric Glide Gull Records GULP
1028, November 1978

ANDREW LLOYD WEBBER
Variations MCA Records MCF
2824, 1978

ROD ARGENT
Moving Home MCA Records
MCF 2854, March 1979

COZY POWELL
Over The Top Ariola ARL 5038,
October 1979
Tilt Polydor POLD 5047, June
1981

Octopuss Polydor POLD5093,
February 1983

PHILIP LYNOTT
Solo In Soho Vertigo/
Phonogram 9102 038, April
1980

GREG LAKE
Greg Lake Chrysalis Records
CHR 1357, September 1981
Manoeuvres Chrysalis Records
CHR 1392, July 1983
**Live On The King Biscuit Flower
Hour** Pinnacle KBFH018, 1995

KAROL KRISTIAN
'Love City' Hobo HOS 013, 1981

JOHNNY DUHAN
Johnny Duhan Philips 6373019,
1982

KEITH EMERSON
The Christmas Album Emerson
Records KEITH LP1, November
1988

CHRIS THOMPSON
Out Of The Night Ultra Phone
6.25484, March 1983

THE BEACH BOYS
The Beach Boys Caribou
Records/Brother Records CRB
26378, 1985

MINAKO HONDA
Cancel Toshiba-EMI WTP-90433,
September 1986

**FRANKIE GOES TO
HOLLYWOOD**
'Warriors' (Attack mix) 12
ZTAK 25, November 1986

MO FOSTER
Bel Assis MMC Records/EMI
LPMMC 1013, August 1988
Southern Reunion Relativity
Records 88561-1050-2, July
1991

DON AIREY
*Royal Philharmonic Orchestra
& Friends* Arrested RCA RCALP
8001, February 1983
*K2 Tales Of Triumph And
Tragedy* MCA Records 255
981-1, November 1988
Keyed Up Mascot Label Group
MTR 7408 2, 2014

VICKI BROWN
Lady Of Time BMG Ariola
Benelux/RCA PL 74276, 1989
About Love And Life Polydor
847 266-2 December, 1990

TRAVELING WILBURYS
Vol. 3 Wilbury Records PL 74522,
October 1990 (UK) / November
1990 (US)

JIM CAPALDI
Living On The Outside SPV SPV
085-72512 CD, October 2001
Poor Boy Blue SPV SPV
085-70412 CD, November 2004
*Dear Mr Fantasy: A
Celebration For Jim Capaldi*
Eagle Records EDGCD364,
August 2007

MICK JAGGER
'Don't Tear Me Up' Atlantic
A7368CD, 1993

JIMMY NAIL
Growing Up In Public East
West/Warner Music UK
4509-90144-1, August 1992

JACK BRUCE
Cities Of The Heart CMP Records
CMP CD 1004, March 1994
The Cream Of Cream Rittor
Music 1998 video release
Shadows In The Air Sanctuary
Records SANCD084, July 2001

ALBERT COLLINS
Collins Mix The Best Of Virgin
Records / Pointblank VPBCD 17,
October 1993

PAUL RODGERS
*Muddy Water Blues A Tribute
To Muddy Waters* Victory Music
828 414-2, April 1993

SNOWY WHITE
Highway To The Sun Bellaphon
290.07.205, May 1994

VARIOUS
*Evita (The Complete Motion
Picture Music Soundtrack)*
Warner Bros Records 9362-
46346-2, 1996

GARY HUSBAND
*Interplay And Improvisation
On The Drums* Rittor Music,
1998 (video release)

JOHN MAYALL
Along For The Ride Eagle
Records EAGCD150, April 2001

VARIOUS
*From Clarksdale To Heaven:
Remembering John Lee
Hooker* Eagle Records
EAGCD228, GAS 0000228
EAG, 2002

TRILOK GURTU
Broken Rhythms Cream Records
JMS 18734-2, March 2004

VARIOUS
*The Strat Pack Live in Concert
Red House* Eagle Vision
EREDV464AP, 2004

ONE WORLD PROJECT
Grief Never Grows Old One
World Records OWR1, 2005

OTIS TAYLOR
Definition Of A Circle Telarc
CD-83659, February 2007
*Pentatonic Wars And Love
Songs* Telarc CD-83690, June
2009
Clovis People Vol. 3 Telarc
TEL-31849-02, May 2010

SERGEI VORONOV
Irony Moroz Records OM 09359
CD, June 2009

GIPSY AND THE WOLF
Perfect Rose digital-only
six-track EP, May 2010

VIDEO RELEASES

EMERALD AISLES—LIVE IN IRELAND
VHS/LaserDisc, June 1985
Out In The Fields (promo video) • Empty Rooms • Rockin' Every Night • Wishing Well • Victims Of The Future • Murder In The Skies • Shapes Of Things • Parisienne Walkways • Rockin' And Rollin' • Nuclear Attack • End Of The World • Back On The Streets

THE VIDEO SINGLES
VHS, August 1987
Out In The Fields • Empty Rooms • Over The Hills And Far Away • Wild Frontier • Friday On My Mind • The Loner

WILD FRONTIER TOUR—LIVE AT ISSTADION STOCKHOLM
VHS, November 1987
Over The Hills And Far Away • Thunder Rising • Wild Frontier • Military Man • Empty Rooms • All Messed Up • Out In The Fields • Rockin' Every Night • The Loner

AN EVENING OF THE BLUES WITH GARY MOORE & THE MIDNIGHT BLUES BAND
VHS/LaserDisc, November 1991
Oh, Pretty Woman • Walking By Myself • All Your Love • Still Got The Blues (For You) • Too Tired • Further On Up The Road • Texas Strut • Moving On • Midnight Blues • King Of The Blues • Stormy Monday • Caledonia
Bonus content interview and behind-the-scenes footage

LIVE BLUES
VHS/LaserDisc, May 1993
Cold Day In Hell • Walking By Myself • Story Of The Blues • Oh, Pretty Woman • Separate Ways • Too Tired • Still Got The Blues (For You) • Since I Met You Baby • The Thrill Is Gone • The Sky Is Crying • Further On Up The Road • King Of The Blues • Jumpin' At Shadows • Stop Messin' Around

BALLADS & BLUES 1982–1994
VHS/LaserDisc/DVD, November 1994
Always Gonna Love You • Still Got The Blues (For You) • Empty Rooms • Parisienne Walkways (live) • Separate Ways • Story Of The Blues • Midnight Blues (live) • Jumpin' At Shadows (live) • The Loner • Still Got The Blues (For You) (live)

BLUES FOR GREENY LIVE
VHS, April 1996
World Keep On Turning • I Loved Another Woman • Merry Go Round • If You Be My Baby • Long Grey Mare • Need Your Love So Bad • You Don't Love Me • Driftin' • The Same Way • Since I Met You Baby • Love That Burns • Stop Messin' Around • Showbiz Blues • Dust My Broom • Jumpin' At Shadows
Bonus content interview and soundcheck footage

LIVE AT MONSTERS OF ROCK
DVD/VHS, October 2003
Shapes Of Things • Wishing

Well • Rectify • Guitar Intro • Stand Up • Just Can't Let You Go • Walking By Myself • Don't Believe A Word • Out In The Fields • Parisienne Walkways
Bonus content interview and soundcheck footage

LIVE AT MONTREUX 1990
DVD, November 2004
Oh, Pretty Woman • Walking By Myself • The Stumble • All Your Love • Midnight Blues • You Don't Love Me • Still Got The Blues (For You) • Texas Strut • Moving On • Too Tired • Cold, Cold Feeling • Further On Up The Road • King Of The Blues • Stop Messin' Around • The Blues Is Alright • The Messiah Will Come Again
Bonus content feature from 1997: *Out In The Fields • Over The Hills And Far Away • Parisienne Walkways*

ONE NIGHT IN DUBLIN—A TRIBUTE TO PHIL LYNOTT
DVD/Blu-ray, March 2006
Walking By Myself • Jailbreak • Don't Believe A Word • Emerald • Still In Love With You • Black Rose • Cowboy Song • The Boys Are Back In Town • Whiskey In The Jar • Old Town (excerpt) • Parisienne Walkways
Bonus content interview and soundcheck footage

DEFINITIVE MONTREUX COLLECTION
DVD, October 2007
1990 *Midnight Blues • Texas Strut • Moving On • Cold, Cold*

Feeling • Stop Messin' Around • The Blues Is Alright • The Messiah Will Come Again **1995** If You Be My Baby • Long Grey Mare • Merry-Go-Round • The Stumble • You Don't Love Me • Key To Love • All Your Love • Still Got The Blues(For You) • Since I Met Your Baby •

The Sky Is Crying • Jumpin' At Shadows **1997** One Fine Day • Cold Wind Blows • I Have Found My Love In You • Always There For You • Business As Usual • Out In The Fields **1999** Oh, Pretty Woman • Need Your Love So Bad • Tore Down • I

Loved Another Woman • Too Tired • Further On Up The Road • Parisienne Walkways **2001** You Upset Me Baby • Cold Black Night • Stormy Monday • Walking By Myself • How Many Lies • Fire • Enough Of The Blues • The Prophet

POSTHUMOUS VIDEO RELEASES

LIVE AT MONTREUX 2010 DVD/Blu-ray, September 2011 Over The Hills And Far Away • Thunder Rising • Military Man • Days Of Heroes • Where Are You Now? • So Far Away • Empty Rooms • Oh Wild One • Blood Of Emeralds • Out In The Fields • Still Got The Blues (For You) •

Walking By Myself • Johnny Boy • Parisienne Walkways **Bonus content** feature from 1997: One Good Reason • Oh, Pretty Woman • Still Got The Blues (For You) • Walking By Myself

BLUES FOR JIMI DVD/Blu-ray, September 2012 Purple Haze • Manic Depression • Foxey Lady • The Wind Cries Mary • I Don't Live Today • My Angel • Angel • Fire • Red House • Stone Free • Hey Joe • Voodoo Child (Slight Return)

PROMO VIDEOS

GARY MOORE
Parisienne Walkways (1979) • Always Gonna Love You (1982) • Shapes Of Things (1984) • Empty Rooms (1984) • Out In The Fields (1985) • Over The Hills And Far Away (1986) • Wild Frontier (1987) • The Loner (1987) • Friday On My Mind (1987) • After The War (1989) • Ready For Love (1989) • Still Got The Blues (For You) (1990) • Oh, Pretty Woman (1990) • Too Tired (1990) • Walking By Myself

(1990) • Cold Day In Hell (1992) • Separate Ways (1992) • Story Of The Blues (1992) • Since I Met You Baby (1992) • Parisienne Walkways '93 (1993) • Need Your Love So Bad (1995) • One Good Reason (1997) • I Have Found My Love In You (1997) • Always There For You (1997)

THIN LIZZY
The Rocker (1974) • With Love (1979) • Waiting For An Alibi

(1979) • Do Anything You Want To (1979) • Sarah (1979, Gary does not appear in the video)

G-FORCE
Hot Gossip (1980)

TRAVELING WILBURYS
She's My Baby (1990, Gary does not appear in the video)

BBM
Where In The World (1994)

INDEX

LYRIC PERMISSIONS

'I Can't Wait Until Tomorrow'
Words and music by Gary Moore
Lyrics reproduced by kind permission of BMG Rights Management (UK) Ltd
© 1982, BMG Rights Management (UK) Ltd

'Dark Days in Paradise'
'I Have Found My Love In You'
Words and music by Gary Moore
Lyrics reproduced with kind permission of Bonuswise Ltd
© 1997 Bonuswise Ltd, administered by BMG Rights Management (UK) Ltd

'Rivers' (Electric Savage)
'Hot Gossip' (G Force)
'Flesh And Blood' (Old New Ballads Blues)
Words and music by Gary Moore
Lyrics reproduced courtesy of Maxwood © 1977, 1980 and 2006, respectively

PHOTOGRAPHS

Unless otherwise noted, all photographs used in this book are © Orionstar Ltd. All efforts have been made to contact copyright holders, but if you feel there has been a mistaken attribution, please contact the publishers.

ALSO AVAILABLE FROM JAWBONE PRESS

I Am Morbid: Ten Lessons Learned From Extreme Metal, Outlaw Country, And The Power Of Self-Determination David Vincent with Joel McIver

Zeppelin Over Dayton: Guided By Voices Album By Album Jeff Gomez

What Makes The Monkey Dance: The Life And Music Of Chuck Prophet And Green On Red Stevie Simkin

So Much For The 30 Year Plan: Therapy? The Authorised Biography Simon Young

She Bop: The Definitive History Of Women In Popular Music Lucy O'Brien

Relax Baby Be Cool: The Artistry And Audacity Of Serge Gainsbourg Jeremy Allen

Seeing Sideways: A Memoir Of Music And Motherhood Kristin Hersh

Two Steps Forward, One Step Back: My Life In The Music Business Miles A. Copeland III

It Ain't Retro: Daptone Records & The 21st-Century Soul Revolution Jessica Lipsky

Renegade Snares: The Resistance & Resilience Of Drum & Bass Ben Murphy and Carl Loben

Southern Man: Music And Mayhem In The American South Alan Walden with S.E. Feinberg

Frank & Co: Conversations With Frank Zappa 1977–1993 Co de Kloet

All I Ever Wanted: A Rock 'n' Roll Memoir Kathy Valentine

Here They Come With Their Make-Up On: Suede, Coming Up . . . And More Adventures Beyond The Wild Frontiers Jane Savidge

My Bloody Roots: From Sepultua To Soulfly And Beyond: The Autobiography Max Cavalera with Joel McIver

This Band Has No Past: How Cheap Trick Became Cheap Trick Brian J. Kramp